SOMETHING ABOUT THE AUTHOR®

Something about
the Author *was named
an* "**Outstanding
Reference Source,**"
*the highest honor given
by the American
Library Association
Reference and Adult
Services Division.*

ISSN 0276-816X

SOMETHING ABOUT THE AUTHOR®

**Facts and Pictures about Authors
and Illustrators of Books for Young People**

volume 156

THOMSON

GALE

Detroit • New York • San Francisco • San Diego • New Haven, Conn. • Waterville, Maine • London • Munich

Something About the Author, Volume 156

Project Editor
Maikue Vang

Editorial
Katy Balcer, Sara Constantakis, Michelle Kazensky, Julie Keppen, Joshua Kondek, Lisa Kumar, Tracey Matthews, Mary Ruby, Lemma Shomali

Permissions
Lori Hines, Ron Montgomery, Shalice Shah-Caldwell

Imaging and Multimedia
Leitha Etheridge-Simms, Lezlie Light, Mike Logusz

Composition and Electronic Capture
Carolyn Roney

Manufacturing
Drew Kalasky

Product Manager
Chris Nasso

LIBRARY OF CONGRESS CATALOG CARD NUMBER 62-52046

ISBN 0-7876-8780-4
ISSN 0276-816X

Printed in the United States of America
10 9 8 7 6 5 4 3 2 1

Contents

Authors in Forthcoming Volumes

Below are some of the authors and illustrators that will be featured in upcoming volumes of *SATA*. These include new entries on the swiftly rising stars of the field, as well as completely revised and updated entries (indicated with *) on some of the most notable and best-loved creators of books for children.

*Aliki Brandenberg ❚ Versatile and varied author-illustrator Aliki has tallied over one hundred and twenty titles since she began writing and illustrating children's books over forty years ago. Considered a staple author of books for preschool to middle-grade readers, her nonfiction resume contains a number of popular titles about dinosaurs, fossils, and others on basic concepts of the sciences. Recently she has penned well-received titles on the arts, two being *William Shakespeare and the Globe* and *Ah, Music!*. The newest Aliki title, *A Play's the Thing*, continues the theme.

*Charles de Lint ❚ Dutch-born Canadian author Charles de Lint, winner of the 2000 World Fantasy Award, brings forth his craft through novel, novella, and short-story, like many writers of fantasy fiction. De Lint, however, has set himself apart from the crowd using a self-described "organic" style to convey more contemporary-feeling fantasy worlds, melding the world of magic with modern landscapes. In de Lint's 2003 novel *Spirits in the Wires*, the digital world provides an actual setting for its characters; cyberspace is used as a fantasy realm.

Frances O'Roark Dowell ❚ Dowell burst onto the scene of young adult literature in 2000 with her first novel, *Dovey Coe*, which won the Edgar Allen Poe Award for Best Juvenile Novel and the William Allen White Award. Dowell quickly followed this historical novel with two set in the present, *Where I'd Like to Be* and *The Secret Language of Girls*. A former co-publisher of Dream/Girl magazine, Dowell is often praised for her ability to create realistic characters to whom readers can easily relate.

E.R. Frank ❚ E. R. Frank has written four novels for young adults. Many of her books' topics and themes share ties with the content of her career as a social worker and psychologist, addressing difficult and sometimes controversial issues. In *Life Is Funny*, *America*, *Friction*, and *Wave*, Frank brings her experience and expertise in the area of teen problems to bear in novels about young New Yorkers at risk and dealing with trauma.

*Kathryn Lasky ❚ A prolific writer, Lasky is the creator of contemporary and historical fiction, informational books, and picture books that incorporate both fictional and nonfiction elements. Praised for exploring topics not often covered in books for the young and explaining them in an accessible manner, Lasky has also contributed titles to the popular "Royal Diaries," "Dear America" and "My America" series, in which she introduces historical figures such as Elizabeth I and Marie Antoinette, or transmits knowledge of past eras through the diaries of fictional characters.

*Julius Lester ❚ Julius Lester has been a noted name in literature for young people since the publication of *To Be a Slave* in 1969, a work that used the very words of those who had been enslaved to tell of their lives and experiences. Lester has continued to produce books that reflect his interests in African-American history, folklore, and politics. Lester has also written novels for adult and young adult readers, drawing on literature and history in titles like *Othello* and *Pharaoh's Daughter*. A 2005 title for young children is *Let's Talk about Race*.

*Han Nolan ❚ The 1997 winner of the National Book Award for her young adult novel, *Dancing on the Edge*, Han Nolan speaks directly to teenage readers in a voice at once empathic and down-home humorous. The author of six published novels, Nolan has captured a wide and loyal readership with her themes of tolerance and understanding, and addresses such issues as neo-Nazis and religious zealotry. Critics have praised Nolan for ability to portray her characters in a realistic and truthful fashion, as seen with Nolan's most recent publication *When We Were Saints*.

*Ifeoma Onyefulu ❚ Nigerian author, Ifeoma Onyefulu, bridges the gap between Westren culture and African village life through her picture books for young readers. In such works as *Saying Goodbye* and *Here Comes Our Bride!* Onyefulu reveals to her audience the universality of many cultural customs, including courtship, marriage and death. All of Onyefulu's picture books feature photographs taken by the author, giving readers a colorful and real-life glimpse into the African way of life.

Christopher Paolini ❚ Author Christopher Paolini garnered worldwide attention with the publication of his fantasy-fiction novel, *Eragon*, the beginning volume of the "Inheritance" trilogy. Penned while Paolini was still in his teens, *Eragon* grabbed the attention of critics for its maturity, sweeping storytelling and overall inventiveness. *Eragon* quickly climbed the bestseller charts after the revised edition was released by Alfred E. Knopf in 2003 and the novel was also adapted as an audiobook. The film version of *Eragon* is scheduled for production in 2005.

Ntozake Shange ❚ African-American poet and dramatist, Ntozake Shange, is best known for her play, *For Colored Girls Who Have Considered Suicide/When the Rainbow is Enuf*, a "chorepoem" that infuses the elements of poetry, music, dance and drama. In the same fashion, Shange's works for children blends components of storytelling and poetry and delves on such mature issues as racism and cultural history. Shange's most recent picture book, *Ellington Was Not a Street* artfully combines Shange's poetry with the illustrations of Kadir Nelson and pays tribute to famous African-American artists and leaders.

Introduction

Something about the Author (*SATA*) is an ongoing reference series that examines the lives and works of authors and illustrators of books for children. *SATA* includes not only well-known writers and artists but also less prominent individuals whose works are just coming to be recognized. This series is often the only readily available information source on emerging authors and illustrators. You'll find *SATA* informative and entertaining, whether you are a student, a librarian, an English teacher, a parent, or simply an adult who enjoys children's literature.

What's Inside *SATA*

SATA provides detailed information about authors and illustrators who span the full time range of children's literature, from early figures like John Newbery and L. Frank Baum to contemporary figures like Judy Blume and Richard Peck. Authors in the series represent primarily English-speaking countries, particularly the United States, Canada, and the United Kingdom. Also included, however, are authors from around the world whose works are available in English translation. The writings represented in *SATA* include those created intentionally for children and young adults as well as those written for a general audience and known to interest younger readers. These writings cover the entire spectrum of children's literature, including picture books, humor, folk and fairy tales, animal stories, mystery and adventure, science fiction and fantasy, historical fiction, poetry and nonsense verse, drama, biography, and nonfiction. Obituaries are also included in *SATA* and are intended not only as death notices but also as concise overviews of people's lives and work. Additionally, each edition features newly revised and updated entries for a selection of *SATA* listees who remain of interest to today's readers and who have been active enough to require extensive revisions of their earlier biographies.

Autobiography Feature

Beginning with Volume 103, *SATA* features two or more specially commissioned autobiographical essays in each volume. These unique essays, averaging about ten thousand words in length and illustrated with an abundance of personal photos, present an entertaining and informative first-person perspective on the lives and careers of prominent authors and illustrators profiled in *SATA*.

Two Convenient Indexes

In response to suggestions from librarians, *SATA* indexes no longer appear in every volume but are included in alternate (odd-numbered) volumes of the series, beginning with Volume 57.

SATA continues to include two indexes that cumulate with each alternate volume: the Illustrations Index, arranged by the name of the illustrator, gives the number of the volume and page where the illustrator's work appears in the current volume as well as all preceding volumes in the series; the Author Index gives the number of the volume in which a person's biographical sketch, autobiographical essay, or obituary appears in the current volume as well as all preceding volumes in the series.

These indexes also include references to authors and illustrators who appear in *Gale's Yesterday's Authors of Books for Children, Children's Literature Review,* and *Something about the Author Autobiography Series.*

Easy-to-Use Entry Format

Whether you're already familiar with the *SATA* series or just getting acquainted, you will want to be aware of the kind of information that an entry provides. In every *SATA* entry the editors attempt to give as complete a picture of the person's life and work as possible. A typical entry in *SATA* includes the following clearly labeled information sections:

PERSONAL: date and place of birth and death, parents' names and occupations, name of spouse, date of marriage, names of children, educational institutions attended, degrees received, religious and political affiliations, hobbies and other interests.

ADDRESSES: complete home, office, electronic mail, and agent addresses, whenever available.

CAREER: name of employer, position, and dates for each career post; art exhibitions; military service; memberships and offices held in professional and civic organizations.

MEMBER: professional, civic, and other association memberships and any official posts held.

AWARDS, HONORS: literary and professional awards received.

WRITINGS: title-by-title chronological bibliography of books written and/or illustrated, listed by genre when known; lists of other notable publications, such as plays, screenplays, and periodical contributions.

ADAPTATIONS: a list of films, television programs, plays, CD-ROMs, recordings, and other media presentations that have been adapted from the author's work.

WORK IN PROGRESS: description of projects in progress.

SIDELIGHTS: a biographical portrait of the author or illustrator's development, either directly from the biographee—and often written specifically for the *SATA* entry—or gathered from diaries, letters, interviews, or other published sources.

BIOGRAPHICAL AND CRITICAL SOURCES: cites sources quoted in "Sidelights" along with references for further reading.

EXTENSIVE ILLUSTRATIONS: photographs, movie stills, book illustrations, and other interesting visual materials supplement the text.

How a *SATA* Entry Is Compiled

A *SATA* entry progresses through a series of steps. If the biographee is living, the *SATA* editors try to secure information directly from him or her through a questionnaire. From the information that the biographee supplies, the editors prepare an entry, filling in any essential missing details with research and/or telephone interviews. If possible, the author or illustrator is sent a copy of the entry to check for accuracy and completeness.

If the biographee is deceased or cannot be reached by questionnaire, the *SATA* editors examine a wide variety of published sources to gather information for an entry. Biographical and bibliographic sources are consulted, as are book reviews, feature articles, published interviews, and material sometimes obtained from the biographee's family, publishers, agent, or other associates.

Entries that have not been verified by the biographees or their representatives are marked with an asterisk (*).

Contact the Editor

We encourage our readers to examine the entire *SATA* series. Please write and tell us if we can make *SATA* even more helpful to you. Give your comments and suggestions to the editor:

Editor
Something about the Author
Thomson Gale
27500 Drake Rd.
Farmington Hills MI 48331-3535

Toll-free: 800-877-GALE
Fax: 248-699-8054

Something about the Author Product Advisory Board

The editors of *Something about the Author* are dedicated to maintaining a high standard of excellence by publishing comprehensive, accurate, and highly readable entries on a wide array of writers for children and young adults. In addition to the quality of the content, the editors take pride in the graphic design of the series, which is intended to be orderly yet inviting, allowing readers to utilize the pages of *SATA* easily and with efficiency. Despite the longevity of the *SATA* print series, and the success of its format, we are mindful that the vitality of a literary reference product is dependent on its ability to serve its users over time. As literature, and attitudes about literature, constantly evolve, so do the reference needs of students, teachers, scholars, journalists, researchers, and book club members. To be certain that we continue to keep pace with the expectations of our customers, the editors of *SATA* listen carefully to their comments regarding the value, utility, and quality of the series. Librarians, who have firsthand knowledge of the needs of library users, are a valuable resource for us. The *Something about the Author* Product Advisory Board, made up of school, public, and academic librarians, is a forum to promote focused feedback about *SATA* on a regular basis. The nine-member advisory board includes the following individuals, whom the editors wish to thank for sharing their expertise:

Eva M. Davis
Youth Department Manager,
Ann Arbor District Library,
Ann Arbor, Michigan

Joan B. Eisenberg
Lower School Librarian,
Milton Academy,
Milton, Massachusetts

Francisca Goldsmith
Teen Services Librarian,
Berkeley Public Library,
Berkeley, California

Susan Dove Lempke
Children's Services Supervisor,
Niles Public Library District,
Niles, Illinois

Robyn Lupa
Head of Children's Services,
Jefferson County Public Library,
Lakewood, Colorado

Victor L. Schill
Assistant Branch Librarian/Children's Librarian,
Harris County Public Library/Fairbanks Branch,
Houston, Texas

Caryn Sipos
Community Librarian,
Three Creeks Community Library,
Vancouver, Washington

Steven Weiner
Director,
Maynard Public Library,
Maynard, Massachusetts

Acknowledgments

Grateful acknowledgment is made to the following publishers, authors, and artists whose works appear in this volume.

ABBEY, MARILYN LORRAINE ▮ Targete, Jean Pierre, illustrator. From a cover of *Thieves' World Turning Points,* edited by Lynn Abbey. A Tom Doherty Associates Book, 2002. Reprinted by permission of St. Martins Press, LLC.

ATTEMA, MARTHA ▮ McCallum, Stephen, illustrator. From an illustration in *Daughter of Light,* by Martha Attema. Orca Book Publishers, 2001. Reproduced by permission.

BAKER, JEANNIE ▮ Baker, Jeannie, photograph. Reproduced by permission.

BALLIETT, BLUE ▮ Helquist, Brett, illustrator. From an illustration in *Chasing Vermeer,* by Blue Balliett. Scholastic Press, 2004. Illustrations copyright © 2004 by Brett Helquist. Reprinted by permission of Scholastic Inc.

BARRETT, TRACY ▮ From a cover of *Anna of Byzantium,* by Tracy Barrett. Delacorte Press, 1999. Jacket illustration © 1999 by David Bowers. Used by permission of Random House Children's Books, a division of Random House, Inc./ Barrett, Tracy, photograph by David Crenshaw. Reproduced by permission.

CARLSTROM, NANCY WHITE ▮ Degen, Bruce, illustrator. From an illustration in *Climb the Family Tree, Jesse Bear!,* by Nancy White Carlstrom. Simon & Schuster Books for Young Readers, 2004. Illustrations copyright © 2004 by Bruce Degen. All rights reserved. Reproduced by permission of Simon & Schuster Books for Young Readers, an imprint of Simon & Schuster Children's Publishing division./ Carlstrom, Nancy White, photograph. Reproduced by permission.

CHICESTER CLARK, EMMA ▮ Chicester Clark, Emma, illustrator. From an illustration in her *Mimi's Book of Counting.* Charlesbridge, 2003. Text and illustrations copyright © 2002 by Emma Chichester Clark. Reproduced by permission./ Chichester Clark, Emma, illustrator. From an illustration in her *Up in Heaven.* Doubleday, 2003. Copyright © 2003 by Emma Chichester Clark. Used by permission of Random House Children's Books, a division of Random House, Inc., and by Andersen Press Ltd.

CUYLER, MARGERY ▮ Schindler, S.D., illustrator. From an illustration in *Skeleton Hiccups,* by Margery Cuyler. Simon & Schuster, 2002. Illustrations copyright © 2002 by S. D. Schindler. Reproduced by permission of Margaret K. McElderry Books, an imprint of Simon & Schuster Children's Publishing./ Tucker, Ezra, illustrator. From an illustration in *Big Friends,* by Margery Cuyler. Walker & Company, 2004. Illustrations copyright © 2004 by Ezra Tucker. All rights reserved. Reproduced by permission.

DELACRE, LULU ▮ Delacre, Lulu, illustrator. From an illustration in her *Golden Tales.* Scholastic, 1996. Illustration copyright © 1996 by Lulu Delacre. Reprinted by permission of Scholastic Inc.

DOYLE, BRIAN ▮ Fuller, Tim, photographer. From a jacket cover of *Boy O' Boy,* Brian Doyle. Groundwood Books, 2003. Cover photograph copyright © 2003 by Tim Fuller. Reproduced by permission of Groundwood Books Ltd./ Fuller, Tim, photographer. From a jacket of *Easy Avenue,* by Brian Doyle. Groundwood Books, 1988. Reproduced by permission of Groundwood Books Ltd./ Fuller, Tim, photographer. From a jacket of *Uncle Ronald,* by Brian Doyle. Groundwood Books, 1996. Jacket illustration copyright © 1996 by Ludmilla Temertey. Reproduced by permission of Groundwood Books Ltd./ Fuller, Tom, photographer. From a cover of *Mary Ann Alice,* by Brian Doyle. Groundwood Books, 2001. Reproduced by permission of Groundwood Books Ltd.

EARLS, NICK ▮ G.K. & Vikki Hart/Getty Images and Roger Wright/Getty Images, photographers. From a cover of *48 Shades of Brown,* by Nick Earls. Houghton Mifflin, 1999. Reproduced by permission.

FLEISCHMAN, PAUL ▮ Ibatoulline, Bagram, illustrator. From an illustration in *The Animal Hedge,* by Paul Fleischman. Illustrations copyright © 2003 by Bagram Ibatoulline. Text copyright © 1983, 2003 Paul Fleischman. Calligraphy by Judythe Sieek. Reproduced by permission of the publisher Candlewick Press, Inc., Cambridge, MA./ Fleischman, Paul, photograph by David Toerge/Black Star. Reproduced by permission.

GEORGE, KRISTINE O'CONNELL ▮ Otani, June, illustrator. From an illustration in *Little Dog and Duncan,* by Kristine O'Connell George. Clarion Books, 2002. Illustrations copyright © 2002 by June Otani. All rights reserved. Reproduced by permission of Houghton Mifflin Company./ Tilley, Debbie, illustrator. From a jacket cover of *Swimming Upstream: Middle School Poems,* by Kristine O'Connell George. Clarion Books, 2002. Illustration copyright © 2002 by Debbie Tilley. All rights reserved. Reproduced by permission of Houghton Mifflin Company.

GLEITZMAN, MORRIS ▮ Clement, Rod, illustrator. From a jacket cover of *Toad Rage,* by Morris Gleitzman. Random House, 1999. Copyright © 1999 by Creative Input Pty, Ltd. Illustrations copyright © 1999 by Rod Clement. All rights reserved. Reproduced by permission of Random House Children's Books, a division of Random House, Inc./ Gleitzman, Morris, photograph by Martin Slater. Reproduced by permission of Morris Gleitzman.

GOING, K(ELLY) L. ▮ Hundley, Sterling, photographer. From a jacket cover of *Fat Kid Rules World,* by Kelly Going. G.P. Putnam's Sons, 2003. Jacket art © 2003 by Sterling Hundley. All rights reserved. Used by permission of Grosset & Dunlap, a division of Penguin Young Readers Group, a member of the Penguin Group (USA) Inc., 345 Hudson Street, New York, NY 10014.

GORDON, AMY ▮ Cordell, Matthew, illustrator. From a jacket cover of *The Gorillas of Grill Park,* by Amy Gordon. Holiday House, 2003. Illustrations copyright © 2003 by Matthew Cordell. All rights reserved. Reproduced by permission of Holiday House, Inc./ Tauss, Marc, illustrator. From a jacket cover of *The Secret Life of a Boarding School Brat,* by Amy Gordon. Holiday House, 2004. Reproduced by permission of Holiday House, Inc.

HAMPTON, WILBORN ∎ Booher, Andrea/FEMA News Photo, photographer. Flag raised over the ruins of the World Trade Center, from a photograph in *September 11, 2001: Attack on New York City,* written by Wilborn Hampton. Candlewick Press, 2003.

HATHORN, ELIZABETH ∎ All photographs courtesy of the Libby Hathorn. .

HERRICK, STEVEN ∎ Herrick, Steven, photograph by Mark Gio. Reproduced by permission of Steven Herrick.

IBBOTSON, EVA ∎ Hawkes, Kevin, illustrator. From a cover of *Journey to the River Sea,* by Eva Ibbotson. Puffin Books, 2001. Illustrations copyright © 2001 by Kevin Hawkes. Reproduced by permission of Dutton Children's Books, a division of Penguin Young Readers Group, a member of the Penguin Group (USA) Inc., 345 Hudson St., New York, NY 10014. All rights reserved./ Hawkes, Kevin, illustrator. From an illustration in *Island of the Aunts,* by Eva Ibbotson. Puffin Books, 1999. Illustrations copyright © Kevin Hawkes, 2000. Reproduced by permission of Dutton Children's Books, a division of Penguin Young Readers Group, a member of Penguin Group (USA) Inc., 345 Hudson St., New York, NY 10014. All rights reserved./ Ibbotson, Eva, photograph. Reproduced by permission.

JUBY, SUSAN ∎ Huang, Howard, photographer. From a cover of *Alice, I Think,* by Susan Juby. HarperTempest, 2003. Cover art © 2004 by Howard Huang. Used by permission of HarperCollins Publishers.

KACZMAN, JAMES ∎ Kaczman, James, illustrator. From an illustration in *A Bird and His Worm,* by James Kaczman. Houghton Mifflin Company 2002. Reproduced by permission of Houghton Mifflin Company.

KATZ, SUSAN ∎ Alley, R.W., illustrator. From an illustration in *Mrs. Brown on Exhibit: And Other Museum Poems,* by Susan Katz. Simon & Schuster Books for Young Readers, 2002. Illustrations copyright © 2002 by R. W. Alley. All rights reserved. Reproduced with the permission of Simon & Schuster Books for Young Readers, and imprint of Simon & Schuster Children's Publishing division./ Katz, Susan, photograph. Photo courtesy of Susan Katz.

KIMMELMAN, LESLIE (GRODINSKY) ∎ Cote, Nancy, illustrator. From an illustration in *Happy 4th of July, Jenny Sweeney!,* by Leslie Kimmelman. Albert Whitman & Company, 2003. Illustrations copyright © 2003 by Nancy Cote. All rights reserved. Reproduced by permission.

KOESTLER-GRACK, RACHEL A. ∎ Barton, Clara, photograph. From *The Story of Clara Barton,* by Rachel Koestler-Grack. Chelsea Clubhouse 1973. © Corbis.

LAFAYE, A(LEXANDRIA R.T.) ∎ Sheban, Chris, illustrator. From a jacket of *Dad, in Spirit,* by A. LaFaye. Simon & Schuster Books for Young Readers, 2001. Jacket illustrations copyright © 2001 by Chris Sheban. Reproduced by permission of the illustrator./ Chapman-Crane, Jeff, illustrator. From a cover of *Edith Shay,* by A. LaFaye. Aladdin Paperbacks, 2001. Cover illustration copyright © 2000 by Jeff Chapman-Crane. Reproduced by permission of the illustrator./ Chapman-Crane, Jeff, illustrator. From a cover of *Nissa's Place,* by A. LaFaye. Aladdin Paperbacks, 2001. Cover illustration copyright © 2000 by Jeff Chapman-Crane. Reproduced by permission of Aladdin Paperbacks, an imprint of Simon & Schuster Macmillan./ Ascensios, Natalie, illustrator. From a jacket of *The Year of the Sawdust Man,* by A. LaFaye. Simon & Schuster Books for Young Readers, 1998. Jacket illustration ©

1998 by Natalie Ascensios. Reproduced by permission of the illustrator./ LaFaye, Alexandria R. T., photograph by Charles Edward Taylor III. Reproduced by permission of A. LaFaye.

LOW, ALICE ∎ Brandenberg, Aliki, illustration. From an illustration in *Mommy's Briefcase,* by Alice Low. Scholastic Inc., 1995. Illustrations copyright © 1995 by Aliki Brandenberg. Reprinted by permission of Scholastic Inc.

MACDONALD, AMY ∎ All photographs courtesy of Amy MacDonald.

MACKLER, CAROLYN ∎ From a cover of *Love And Other Four-Letter Words,* by Carolyn Mackler. Laurel-Leaf, 2002. Copyright © 2000 by Carolyn Mackler. Reproduced by permission of Dell Publishing, a division of Random House, Inc./ Mackler, Carolyn, photograph.

MARSTON, ELSA ∎ Frerck, Robert, illustrator. From a cover of *The Byzantine Empire,* by Elsa Marston. Benchmark Books, 2003. Reproduced by permission./ From an illustration in *The Phoenicians,* by Elsa Marston. Benchmark Books, 2002. Reproduced by permission./ Marston, Elsa, author photograph.

MCFADDEN, KEVIN CHRISTOPHER ∎ Rostant, Larry, photographer. From a jacket cover of *Alosha,* by Christopher Pike. Tor, 2004. Reprinted by permission of St. Martins Press, LLC./ Taglienti, Maria and Chip Forelli, photographers. From a jacket cover of *The Blind Mirror,* by Christopher Pike. Tor, 2003. Reprinted by permission of St. Martins Press, LLC.

MCMENEMY, SARAH ∎ McMenemy, Sarah, illustrator. From an illustration in her *Waggle.* Candlewick Press, 2003. Copyright © 2003 Sara McMenemy. Reproduced by permission of the publisher Candlewick Press, Inc., Cambridge, MA., on behalf of Walker Books Ltd., London.

OLDER, JULES ∎ Severance, Lyn, illustrator. From a cover of *Ice Cream,* by Jules Older. Charlesbridge, 2002. Text copyright © 2002 by Jules Older. Illustrations copyright © 2002 by Lyn Severance. All rights reserved. Used with permission of Charlesbridge Publishing, Inc./ Severance, Lyn, illustrator. From a cover of *Pig,* by Jules Older. Charlesbridge, 2004. Text copyright © 2004 by Jules Older. Illustrations copyright © 2004 by Lyn Severance. All rights reserved. Used with permission by Charlesbridge Publishing, Inc.

PECK, ROBERT NEWTON ∎ Hess, Richard, illustrator. From a cover of *A Day No Pigs Would Die,* by Robert Newton Peck. Random House Sprinter Books, 1994. Cover illustration © 1972 by Richard Hess. Used by permission of Alfred A. Knopf, an imprint of Random House Children's Books, a division of Random House, Inc./ Peck, Robert Newton, photograph. Reproduced by permission.

RAND, GLORIA ∎ Rand, Ted, illustrator. From an illustration in *Home for Spooky,* by Gloria Rand. Henry Holt and Company, 1998. Illustrations copyright © 1998 by Ted Rand. All rights reserved. Reprinted by permission of Henry Holt and Company, LLC./ Alley, R. W., illustrator. From an illustration in *Little Flower,* by Gloria Rand. Henry Holt and Company, 2002. Illustrations copyright © 2002 by R. W. Alley. Reprinted by permission of Henry Holt and Company, LLC.

SHOUP, BARBARA ∎ From a jacket cover of *Vermeer's Daughter,* by Barbara Shoup. Emmis Books / Guild Press, 1979. Photograph © 1979 The Metropolitan Museum of Art. Reproduced by permission.

SHREEVE, ELIZABETH ∎ Shreeve, Elizabeth, photograph. Photo by Craig Kollo. Courtesy of Elizabeth Shreeve.

SMITH, SHERRI L ∎ Frost, Michael, photographer. From a cover of *Lucy the Giant,* by Sherri L. Smith. Laurel-Leaf Books, 2002. Reproduced by permission of Dell Publishing, a division of Random House, Inc.

sOmeTHING
ABOUT THE
AUTHOR

ABBEY, Lynn
  See ABBEY, Marilyn Lorraine

*   *   *

ABBEY, Marilyn Lorraine 1948-
  (Lynn Abbey)

Personal

Born September 18, 1948, in Peekskill, NY; daughter of Ronald Lionel (an insurance manager) and Doris Lorraine (a homemaker; maiden name, De Wees) Abbey; married Ralph Dressler, July 14, 1969 (divorced October 31, 1972); married Robert Asprin (a writer), August 28, 1982 (divorced, 1993). *Education:* University of Rochester, A.B., 1969; New York University, M.A., 1971. *Hobbies and other interests:* "History (particularly eleventh century and the Normans), embroidery."

Addresses

Home—FL. *Agent*—Spectrum Literary Agency, 432 Park Ave. S., Suite 1205, New York, NY 10016. *E-mail*—labbey@iag.net.

Career

Metropolitan Life Insurance Company, New York, NY, actuarial assistant, 1969-76; Citizens Hanover Insurance, Howell, MI, systems analyst, 1976-80; commu- nity resources teacher at public schools in Ann Arbor, MI, 1980-82; American Automobile Association, Dearborn, MI, systems analyst, 1982-84. Writer.

Member

Science Fiction Writers of America.

Writings

FANTASY NOVELS; UNDER NAME LYNN ABBEY

The Guardians, Ace Books (New York, NY), 1982.
(With C. J. Cherry and Janet Morris) *The Soul of the City,* Ace Books (New York, NY), 1986.
(With Robert Asprin) *Catwoman,* Warner (New York, NY), 1992, published as *Catwoman: Tiger Hunt,* Millennium (London, England), 1992.
Siege of Shadows, Ace Books (New York, NY), 1996.
Aquitania, TSR (Lake Geneva, WI), 1997.
The Simbul's Gift, TSR (Lake Geneva, WI), 1997.
Planeswalker, TSR (Lake Geneva, WI), 1998.
Jerlayne, Penguin USA (New York, NY), 1999.
The Nether Scroll: Lost Empires, Wizards Publishing, 2000.

"RIFKIND SAGA"; UNDER NAME LYNN ABBEY

Daughter of the Bright Moon, Ace Books (New York, NY), 1979.
The Black Flame, Ace Books (New York, NY), 1980.

1

"UNICORN AND DRAGON" SERIES; UNDER NAME LYNN ABBEY

Unicorn & Dragon, Avon (New York, NY), 1987.
Conquest, Avon (New York, NY), 1988, published as *The Green Man,* Hodder Headline (London, England), 1989.

"ULTIMA SAGA"; UNDER NAME LYNN ABBEY

The Forge of Virtue, Warner (New York, NY), 1991.
The Temper of Wisdom, Warner (New York, NY), 1992.

"WALENSOR SAGA"; UNDER NAME LYNN ABBEY

The Wooden Sword, Ace Books (New York, NY), 1991.
Beneath the Web, Ace Books (New York, NY), 1994.

"DARK SUN" TRILOGY; UNDER NAME LYNN ABBEY

The Brazen Gambit, TSR (Lake Geneva, WI), 1994.
Cinnabar Shadows, TSR (Lake Geneva, WI), 1995.
The Rise and Fall of a Dragonking, TSR (Lake Geneva, WI), 1996.

"EMMA MERRIGAN" SERIES; UNDER NAME LYNN ABBEY

Out of Time, Ace Books (New York, NY), 2000.
Behind Time, Ace Books (New York, NY), 2001.
Taking Time, Ace Books (New York, NY), 2004.
Down Time, Ace Books (New York, NY), forthcoming.

"THIEVES' WORLD" SERIES; UNDER NAME LYNN ABBEY

(Editor with Robert Asprin) *The Face of Chaos* (also see below), Ace Books (New York, NY), 1983.
(Editor with Robert Asprin) *Wings of Omen* (also see below), Ace Books (New York, NY), 1984.
(Editor with Robert Asprin) *Cross-Currents* (omnibus; includes *Storm Season, The Face of Chaos,* and *Wings of Omen*), Doubleday (New York, NY), 1984.
(Editor with Robert Asprin) *The Dead of Winter* (also see below), Ace Books (New York, NY), 1985.
(Editor with Robert Asprin) *Soul of the City* (also see below), Ace Books (New York, NY), 1986.
(Editor with Robert Asprin) *Blood Ties* (also see below), Ace Books (New York, NY), 1986.
(Editor with Robert Asprin) *The Shattered Sphere* (omnibus; includes *The Dead of Winter, Soul of the City,* and *Blood Ties*), Doubleday (New York, NY), 1986.
(Editor with Robert Asprin) *Aftermath* (also see below), Ace Books (New York, NY), 1987.
(Editor with Robert Asprin) *Uneasy Alliances* (also see below), Ace Books (New York, NY), 1988.
(Editor with Robert Asprin) *Stealer's Sky* (also see below), Ace Books (New York, NY), 1989.
(Editor with Robert Asprin) *The Price of Victory* (omnibus; includes *Aftermath, Uneasy Alliances,* and *Stealer's Sky*), Doubleday (New York, NY), 1990.

(Editor) *Turning Points,* Tor (New York, NY), 2002.
Sanctuary: An Epic Novel of Thieves' World, Tor (New York, NY), 2002.
(Editor with Robert Asprin) *First Blood* (anthology), Tor (New York, NY), 2003.
(Editor) *Enemies of Fortune,* Tor (New York, NY), 2004.

Also adaptor of "Thieves' World" as a graphic-novel series, Starblaze Graphics (Norfolk, VA), 1985-87, and Donning Co. (Norfolk, VA), beginning 1986.

"ELFQUEST" SERIES; EDITOR WITH ROBERT ASPRIN AND RICHARD PINI; UNDER NAME LYNN ABBEY

The Blood of Ten Chiefs, Tor (New York, NY), 1986.
Wolfsong: The Blood of Ten Chiefs, Tor (New York, NY), 1988.

Adaptations

"Thieves' World" was licensed as a board game and a fantasy role-playing game.

Sidelights

Writing under the name Lynn Abbey, Marilyn Lorraine Abbey is noted for her creation and co-editorship of the long-running "Thieves' World" fiction anthology series, as well as for her many fantasy novels. According to *St. James Guide to Fantasy Writers* essayist Mary Corran, "Abbey's talent is unmistakable . . . , most particularly in the creation of cheerless terrains peopled by sinister creatures of every type. She has constructed her own type of fantasy, where the endings are not always happy nor the heroes and heroines noble or fulfilled by their quests. . . .. Abbey possesses the ability to create dark nightmares, where motives for valour are more complex than simple virtue. Her characters reflect the worlds they inhabit, filled with unsettling, malign emotions. The dismal settings may occasionally irritate; but they are very well drawn, and filled with a rare depth of detail which is formidably imagined."

Abbey came to her career as a fiction writer after working for several years as a systems programmer for New York and Midwest-basted insurance companies. Always interested in science fiction, she was eventually inspired to write her first sci-fi story while recovering from an automobile accident in 1977. Since her first book, *Daughter of the Bright Moon* was published in 1979, she has gone on to write numerous other fantasy novels set in widely varying worlds. Both *Daughter of the Bright Moon* and its sequel, *The Black Flame,* focus on Rifkind, a warrior, priestess, healer, and witch who, while also finding love with Domnhall, ultimately loses him to her ultimate destiny: battling evil in a hostile world of deserts and dangerous swamps. Abbey's "Ultima Saga," which includes *The Forge of Virtue* and *The Temper of Wisdom,* is set in a more conventional, near-medieval world.

Abbey's complex, detailed settings are a key ingredient in her work. As Corran noted, "whether the plot involves a quest, or a conflict of good versus evil, each world displays dirt and squalor and constant perils, both human and magical. These settings are designed to repel, not appeal to, the senses, and the major characters are similarly contrived to lack attractive or sympathetic qualities." In *The Wooden Sword,* for example, Abbey casts as protagonist a shepherdess named Berika, who avoids marriage to a deformed and mentally stunted man by running away with a mysterious stranger, who is ultimately killed. Although avoiding an ill-fated marriage, Berika ultimately is drawn into a tangle of political rivalries and revenge, and it is questionable whether her lot has improved by story's end.

The "Emma Merrigan" series is something of a change of pace for Abbey in that the setting is not as gritty as those featured in much of the author's fiction. A forty-something librarian, Merrigan is introduced in the 2000 novel *Out of Time,* when she discovers that she has inherited magical powers from a mother she has not seen in years. In *Behind Time,* Merrigan is called upon to rescue her mother from the underworld, battling demons at every turn, and when Mom is recovered and attempts to help Emma master her time-travel abilities—in *Taking Time*—she turns out to look and act like a twenty-year-old. In a review of *Taking Time, Kliatt* contributor Lesley Farmer wrote that Abbey's fantasy world in the "Emma Merrigan" books is "believable and fun," her characters "generally well developed," and her plot full of "interesting twists to sustain the reader's interest." Praising *Behind Time* as "compact and literate," Roland Green noted in a *Booklist* review that Abbey has created a "carefully and intelligently worked out system" of magic that "skillfully curb[s] . . . the bloating tendency of most fantasy fiction." Together with former husband and fellow novelist Robert Asprin, Abbey created a unique body of work within the fantasy-sci-fi genre with their shared-world concept known as "Thieves' World." The series, which began in the late 1970s, assembles fiction by a number of well known writers, each story based on characters and plots centered in the imaginary town of Sanctuary, founded by runaway slaves and described by a *Kirkus Reviews* writer as a "lawless, cynical, pun-filled, sometimes satiric and always-atmospheric pseudo-medieval fantasy realm." As Abbey once explained the "shared-world" concept: "Certain settings and characters were provided by us at the beginning of the project; each author is responsible for developing new characters. These settings and characters are 'shared' to the extent that, while retaining the author's individual style and outlook in a particular story, each volume of the series presents unified themes and advances along a single, predetermined chronology."

With the success of "Thieves' World," other publishers began to experiment with the shared-world concept, and similar projects have been published that collect not only science-fiction and fantasy, but also horror and

Notable writers pen eleven tales of adventure and villiany in the lawless city of Sanctuary in a collection of fantasy fiction edited by Abbey. (Cover illustration by Jean Pierre Targete.)

mystery short fiction. Although Abbey's own series went into a hiatus after 1990, it was restarted in 2002 with *Turning Points,* which contains stories by Abbey, Jody Lynn Nye, Jeff Grubb, Andrew Offutt, and Diana L. Paxton, among others. *Enemies of Fortune* further extends the popular series, and features characters that a *Kirkus Reviews* contributor described as "magical malcontents, scheming underlings, and charming criminal lowlifes" within its thirteen interrelated stories. Offutt, Nye, and Grub are joined by C. J. Cherryh, Jane Fancher, and other respected writers in the fantasy genre, their stories interwoven by Abbey "so deftly that the book reads like a novel," according to *Booklist* contributor Frieda Murray. The "Thieves' World" books have also inspired a series of role-playing games, and have been the basis for a graphic-novel series. In addition, Abbey has authored an entire novel based on the series. Appropriately titled *Sanctuary,* the book features many of the characters that series fans have come to know. Containing much of the history of the town of Sanctuary, the novel provides a refresher course for those out of touch with the two-decade-old series; according to Greene in *Booklist,* "coming from Abbey's capable pen," this well-crafted introduction for Thieves' World neophytes "is good news for all heroic fantasy fans."

Biographical and Critical Sources

BOOKS

St. James Guide to Fantasy Writers, St. James Press (Detroit, MI), 1996.

PERIODICALS

Booklist, August, 1994, p. 2029; June 1, 2001, Roland Green, review of *Behind Time,* p. 1855; April 15, 2002, Roland Green, review of *Sanctuary,* p. 1386; November 15, 2002, Roland Green, review of *Thieves' World: Turning Points,* p. 584; November 15, 2004, Frieda Murray, review of *Thieves' World: Enemies of Fortune,* p. 571.
Kirkus Reviews, October 1, 2002, review of *Thieves' World: Turning Points,* p. 1433; July, 2004, Lesley Farmer, review of *Taking Time,* p. 26.
Library Journal, June 15, 2002, Jackie Cassada, review of *Sanctuary,* p. 99l; November 15, 2002, Jackie Cassada, review of *Thieves World: Turning Points,* p. 106; November 15, 2004, Jackie Cassada, review of *Thieves' World: Enemies of Fortune,* p. 54.
Publishers Weekly, August 16, 1991, review of *The Wooden Sword,* p. 55.

ONLINE

Lynn Abbey Web site, http://www.lynnabbey.com/ (January 5, 2004).*

*   *   *

ATTEMA, Martha 1949-

Personal

Born December 22, 1949, in Menaldum, Netherlands; immigrated to Canada, 1981; daughter of Wilke (a farmer) and Romkje (a homemaker; maiden name, Noordenbos) Hoogterp; married Albert Attema, 1971; children: Romkje, Rikst (daughters), Sjoerd (son). *Education:* Attended teacher's college in the Netherlands, 1966-70; Laurentian University, B.A., 1986, B.Ed., 1989. *Hobbies and other interests:* Sewing clothes, crafts.

Addresses

Home—376 Voyer Rd., Corbeil, Ontario, Canada P0H 1K0. *E-mail*—martatte@vianet.on.ca.

Career

Kindergarten teacher in Giekerk, Netherlands, 1969-73; teacher of kindergarten in North Bay, Ontario, beginning 1987; Vincent Massey Public School, North Bay, first grade language arts teacher, beginning c. 1997.

Member

Canadian Society of Children's Authors, Illustrators, and Publishers, Writers' Union of Canada, North Bay Children's Writers Group, North Bay Writers Club.

Awards, Honors

Blue Heron Award for young adults, and Geoffrey Bilson Award for Historical Fiction shortlist, Canadian Children's Book Centre, both 1996, both for *A Time to Choose.*

Writings

FOR CHILDREN

The Unhappy Pinetree: A Little Book for Winter Nights (picture book), privately printed, 1992.
A Time to Choose (young adult historical novel), Orca Book Publishers (Victoria, British Columbia, Canada), 1995.
A Light in the Dunes (young adult novel), Orca Book Publishers (Custer, WA), 1997.
Daughter of Light (juvenile novel), illustrated by Stephen McCallum, Orca Book Publishers (Victoria, British Columbia, Canada), 2001.
When the War Is Over (young adult novel), Orca Book Publishers (Victoria, British Columbia, Canada), 2002.
Hero (juvenile novel), illustrated by Stephen McCallum, Orca Book Publishers (Victoria, British Columbia, Canada), 2003.

Attema's work has been translated into Italian.

OTHER

Contributor of poetry and short fiction to books, including *"To Be One with the Waves": A Canadian Poetry Association Anthology,* edited by Jennifer Footman, Broken Jaw Press (Fredericton, New Brunswick, Canada), 1995, and *Fryslan door de ogen van vrouwen* (title means "Short Stories and Poems by Immigrant Writers"), Bornmeer (Leeuwarden, Netherlands), 2000, and to periodicals.

Sidelights

Canadian-based writer Martha Attema is the author of several historical novels for children and teen readers that draw on her interest in the history of the Netherlands, where she was born and lived for over three decades. In books such as *Daughter of Light* and *Hero* she makes Nazi-occupied Holland come to life for elementary-school readers, while more mature concerns surrounding teens living during wartime are addressed in books such as *When the War Is Over.*

"Writing has always been part of my life," the Dutch-born Attema once told *Something about the Author* (*SATA*). "In my teenage years I wrote poetry to sort out the world and my personal problems and to find an outlet. During those years I began to envy my grandfather, who was a published playwright and poet. When I became a teacher and later a mother, I wrote stories, poems, and puppet plays for my students and for my own children. My writing was all in the Frisian language. Friesland is one of the northern provinces in the Netherlands. The Frisians are a proud and stubborn people who have their own language."

Even after Attema and her family immigrated to Canada in 1981, she continued to write in Frisian. "I felt myself between languages," she recalled. "I didn't get enough exposure to the Frisian language, and I wasn't proficient enough in English to feel comfortable writing stories and poems in this language. A creative writing course at the local college inspired me. The instructor and my other classmates gave me hope and encouraged me to market my stories." Finding something to write about was never a problem for Attema, whose motivation has always been "to share some of my Frisian background and culture with young people here." "The Frisian language is a rich language, full of sagas, legends, and folktales," Attema also explained to *SATA*. Her young-adult novel *A Light in the Dunes* draws on just such a legend, one that comes from an island off the coast of Friesland. In her novel Attema weaves the legend into the story of a fourteen year old who, while dismayed to discover she has been named after a local witch whose ghost is said to haunt a local bird sanctuary, is even more upset when she finds herself kidnaped by a band of drug dealers. "I owed our youngest daughter this story," Attema admitted, noting that Rikst Attema was also named after the Frisian witch.

Designed for readers in the mid-elementary grades, *Daughter of Light* and *Hero* both focus on children caught up in the drama of wartime. In *Daughter of Light* nine-year-old Ria watches as her town is occupied by German soldiers and her friend Rachel, along with the rest of the area's Jews, are sent to Poland or Germany. While adults live in fear and dare not stand up to the occupation forces, when the heat and electricity are cut off, Ria bravely petitions the town government for help in a novel that *Booklist* reviewer Carolyn Phelan praised as an "exciting story" that "realistically dramatiz[es] . . . the hardships and dangers of the times," while Alison Grant noted in *School Library Journal* that Attema's young protagonist "asks a timeless question of why some are singled out for hate and discrimination and often death." Like *Daughter of Light, Hero* focuses on a child during wartime, in this case eight-year-old Jan, who is sent from Amsterdam to live

on a horse farm and finds that his quick thinking may be all that stands in the way of the German army confiscating the horses Jan quickly comes to love.

Attema's young-adult novel *A Time to Choose* is based on facts and stories she collected from survivors of World War II. "I am pleased that I was able to preserve some of the stories from a generation of people who will not be here much longer to tell their own stories," she noted in *SATA,* adding: "I am glad to be able to tell young people not to forget this war or any other war, that in every war the conflicts are not just between the good and bad guys, that war is much more complex and conflicts occur within families and among friends." Her novel *When the War Is Over* also focuses on the human side of World War II as it focuses on sixteen-year-old Janke Visser. Reacting to the German occupation of her small Frisian town, despite her mother's objections Janke decides to follow the example of her father and brother and join the resistance, where she becomes a bicycle courier. As her job expands from transporting letters and papers to guiding and hiding war refugees,

During World War II in Holland young Ria, whose father is in hiding, valiantly plots to help her pregnant mother find a safe and comfortable place to give birth. (From Daughter of Light, *written by Martha Attema and illustrated by Stephen McCallum.)*

Janke finds herself in increasing danger of discovery. Meanwhile, her task is also complicated by a growing romantic attachment to a young German soldier named Helmut. Ultimately, Helmut's disillusion over German militarism unites the pair, who plan their escape to Canada. In *Resource Links* reviewer Patrick Romaine noted that *When the War Is Over* gives readers "a good insight into life in the occupied Netherlands and the work, the tactics of, and dangers to the resistance during World War II."

"In my future writing I hope to preserve more history, folk tales, and legends by giving these tales and facts new life in young adult novels and picture books," Attema explained to *SATA*. "Besides writing, I enjoy research and reading. I collect folk tales and legends from Friesland and I love to read about the history of the area where I grew up. As a teacher of grade one, I'm exposed to many excellent picture books. By sharing these picture books as well as my own stories and poems, I hope to foster a love for reading and writing in my students.

"I never dreamed that I would actually become a published author. I always thought the language would be a major handicap and a drawback. Now that I have become an author, I encourage young people never to give up their dreams, but to be determined and try hard to fulfill them."

Biographical and Critical Sources

PERIODICALS

Booklist, February 1, 2002, Carolyn Phelan, review of *Daughter of Light,* p. 938.
Quill and Quire, January, 1996, p. 369.
Resource Links, October, 1997, review of *Light in the Dunes,* p. 35; June, 2001, Evette Signarowski, review of *Daughter of Light,* p. 8; February, 2003, Patrick Romaine, review of *When the War Is Over,* p. 36; February, 2004, Stephanie Olson, review of *Hero,* p. 8.
School Library Journal, December, 2001, Alison Grant, review of *Daughter of Light,* p. 88.

ONLINE

Martha Attema Web site, http://www.marthaattema.com/ (January 5, 2005).*

*   *   *

AVERY, Lorraine
See OLDER, Jules

*   *   *

AVI
See WORTIS, Edward (Irving)

B

BAKER, Jeannie 1950-

Personal
Born November 2, 1950, in England; daughter of Bernard Victor (a welder) and Barbara Joan (a tracer; maiden name, Weir) Baker. *Education:* Attended Croydon College of Art, 1967-69; Brighton College of Art, B.S. (with honors), 1979. *Politics:* "Left."

Addresses
Home and office—42 Cross St., Double Bay, Sydney, New South Wales 2028, Australia.

Career
Freelance collage artist, filmmaker, and illustrator, 1972–. *Exhibitions:* Exhibitor at group shows, including Royal Academy Summer Exhibition, 1974, 1975; Portal Gallery, London, 1975; Crafts Council of Australia Gallery, Sydney, 1977-79; Hogarth Gallery, Sydney, 1978; Robin Gibson Gallery, Sydney, 1979; and Interiors State Gallery of New South Wales, Sydney, 1981. Exhibitor at one-woman shows at Brettenham House, Waterloo Bridge, London, 1975; Gallery One, Hobart, Australia, 1977; Bonython Gallery, Adelaide, Australia, 1980; Crafts Council of Australia Gallery, Sydney, 1980; Newcastle Regional Art Gallery, New South Wales, 1980. Work represented in permanent collections of Australian National Gallery; State Gallery of Queensland, and Droomkeen Museum of Children's Literature, Riddall, Victoria, Australia.

Awards, Honors
Visual arts grants, Australia Council, 1977-78, 1978-79; commended picture book of the year, Children's Book Council of Australia (CBCA), 1985, for *Home in the Sky; Boston Globe* Picture Book honor, CBCA Picture Book honour, Earthworm Award from Reading Magic Award, and Picture Book award from Young Australian Best Book, all 1988, and International Board on Books

Jeannie Baker

for Young People illustration/Australia category award, and primary category award from KOALA, both 1990, all for *Where the Forest Meets the Sea;* CBCA Picture Book award, and Young Australian Best Book designation, both 1992, both for *Window.*

Writings

SELF-ILLUSTRATED; FOR CHILDREN

Grandfather, Dutton (New York, NY), 1977, revised edition, 1980.

Grandmother, Dutton (New York, NY), 1978, revised edition, 1980.

Millicent, Dutton (New York, NY), 1980.

One Hungry Spider, Deutsch (London, England), 1982.

Home in the Sky, Greenwillow (New York, NY), 1984.

Where the Forest Meets the Sea, Greenwillow (New York, NY), 1987.

Window, Greenwillow (New York, NY), 1991.

The Story of Rosy Dock, Greenwillow (New York, NY), 1995.

The Hidden Forest, Greenwillow (New York, NY), 2000.

Home, Greenwillow (New York, NY), 2004.

Belonging, Walker Books (Sydney, Australia), 2004.

ILLUSTRATOR

Elaine Moss, *Polar* (picture book), Deutsch (London, England), 1975, Dutton (New York, NY), 1979.

Also contributor of illustrations to periodicals, including *New Scientist, Nova, Observer,* and London *Times.*

Adaptations

The Story of Rosy Dock was adapted as a short film.

Sidelights

Australian-based artist and illustrator Jeannie Baker has gained international attention through a unique style she calls "relief collage." As she once told *Something about the Author* (SATA), this method of illustration "is very painstaking and detailed. I use such natural materials as stone, veneer, paint peeled from old doors and window-sills, and plaster from old walls. I collect grass and leaves. For hair on my characters I use real hair. If they are to wear woolen jumpers, I knit them myself." Baker explained that when her relief collages are "photographed for reproduction, shadows will be cast, often in strange places, giving the reproduction a slightly three-dimensional effect."

Baker is best known for creating books with ecological themes, such as *Where the Forest Meets the Sea* and *Window,* and she has received praise for her ability to present powerful messages about the environment with conviction as well as subtlety. *Horn Book* critic Mary M. Burns called Baker's picture book *Where the Forest Meets the Sea* an "uncanny and unforgettable experience" that "represents a truly notable achievement in the picture-book genre, breaking new ground, adding new dimensions."

Born in England, where she graduated from art school in 1979, Baker began her illustration career with *Polar,* a story written by Elaine Moss about a tobogganing teddy. She then began to write and illustrate her own picture books. In her first solo work, *Grandfather,* Baker portrays a girl sitting on her grandfather's lap. The girl's hair looks real, and the textures of her sweater and skirt and her grandfather's tweed cap stand out. In the companion volume, *Grandmother,* Baker presents a girl visiting the home of her grandmother, a place described by a *Bulletin of the Center for Children's Books* reviewer as "cozy [and] cluttered." As Baker explained, "eccentrics (especially old people)" fascinate her, and she is inspired by "wild overgrown places and houses and textures—the crumbling erosion of decay."

Home in the Sky reflects its creator's love of the wild places and textures that can be found in an urban setting as it follows a white homing pigeon in its flight over Manhattan. Kristi Thomas Beavin remarked in *School Library Journal* that Baker's "busy city-scape" creates "a visually pleasing and intriguing jumble." *Horn Book* contributor Gertrude Herman wrote that Baker's collage illustrations create vivid images of the bustling city, and her "textured surfaces, stretched tightly, pulsate with imagery and resonate with life." A *Junior Bookshelf* critic called *Home in the Sky* the work of a "poet of the city streets."

In *Where the Forest Meets the Sea* a boy tells how he travels on a boat named *Time Machine* through a reef with his father to get to an ancient rain forest, and Baker brings this story to life using paper, clay, paint, leaves, and other natural materials. According to Ilene Cooper in a *Booklist* review, the collages "are masterworks of both technical skill and artistic endeavor." *School Library Journal* critic Judith Gloyer also enjoyed the illustrations, calling Baker's book a "visual treat" that "moves from beautiful sandy beaches inland along a creek into the densely tangled primordial forest." During his boat trip through the reef the boy imagines the dinosaurs, animals, and even aboriginal children he might have seen in those long-ago times, and he wonders about the forest's future. These imaginings are brought to life in Baker's illustrations, and the author also includes a note and map on the Daintree Wilderness, in North Queensland, Australia, in which the story is set.

Like *Where the Forest Meets the Sea,* the wordless picture book *Window* carries a message about the environment. The book focuses on one man and a window over the course of twenty years. When the man is just a baby in his mother's arms, the view outside is relatively pristine Australian bush, but as he grows older an urban world replaces the natural one. "Development becomes suburb, then city, complete with billboards, high-rises, noise pollution, litter, and overpopulation," related Susan Scheps in a review for *School Library Journal.* As a critic for *Kirkus Reviews* pointed out, the boy begins to litter and trap "creatures," and his toys begin to include "plastic dinosaurs" and "rockets." Finally, when the man has his own house in the country, he shows his infant child the view out another window where the countryside is already being prepared for development. Ann A. Flowers praised the work in *Horn Book,* asserting that it effectively "presents an artistically unique examination of a pressing world-wide problem."

Development is not the only threat to the environment, as Baker shows in her picture book *The Story of Rosy Dock.* Rosy dock is a plant with attractive red seedpods, and when Europeans settled in Australia, they included the plant along with those they brought from the old country. In only a century, rosy dock had spread throughout the desert outback region, where the cycle of droughts and floods did not kill it. Now it threatens to choke out native plants and disrupt the ecosystem of the region. Using actual plant materials in her collage illustrations, Baker's work on *The Story of Rosy Dock* was described by *Booklist* contributor Kay Weisman as "particularly effective." On her Web site Baker explained how she is able to incorporate plant material in her artwork: "I bathe the vegetation in a mixture of special chemicals for about a week. These chemicals preserve the vegetation and remove all the juices in the vegetation, which would in time destroy it. Then I finely spray the vegetation with paint to give it a permanent colour, before sticking onto my collages."

Baker moves under water in *The Hidden Forest,* as Ben, her young protagonist, submerges to go in search of a lost fishing trap and discovers an amazing new world. Focusing on the kelp forests that grow off the coast of Tasmania, Baker's collages include clay, seaweed, sand, sponges, and other materials, all of which combine to form "vibrantly colorful and amazingly detailed collages," according to *School Library Journal* contributor Marian Drabkin. In *Horn Book,* a reviewer noted that the book's "overt conservation message . . . will resonate with readers" of *The Hidden Forest* and praised Baker for including a brief explanation about kelp forests and their endangerment.

As she wrote in the author's note in *Window,* Baker hopes to help children understand how people change the environment. She once told *SATA:* "I am inspired by my surroundings, and I feel the occasional need for personal new adventures into my surroundings to nurture my creative growth."

Biographical and Critical Sources

BOOKS

Baker, Jeannie, *Where the Forest Meets the Sea,* Greenwillow (New York, NY), 1987.

PERIODICALS

Booklist, June 15, 1988, Ilene Cooper, review of *Where the Forest Meets the Sea,* p. 1733; April 2, 2995, Kay Weisman, review of *The Story of Rosy Dock,* p. 1394; September 1, 2000, Susan Dove Lempke, review of *The Hidden Forest,* p. 112.
Bulletin of the Center for Children's Books, May, 1979, review of *Grandmother;* January, 1983, review of *One Hungry Spider.*

Entertainment Weekly, June 18, 1993, Leonard S. Marcus, review of *Home in the Sky,* p. 70.
Horn Book, March, 1985, Gertrude Herman, "A Picture Is Worth Several Hundred Words," p. 211; July-August, 1988, Mary M., Burns, review of *Where the Forest Meets the Sea,* pp. 475-476; May, 1991, Ann A. Flowers, review of *Window,* pp. 312-313; July, 2000, review of *The Hidden Forest,* p. 431.
Junior Bookshelf, February, 1985, review of *Home in the Sky,* p. 10; October, 1988, review of *One Hungry Spider,* p. 227.
Kirkus Reviews, March 1, 1991, review of *Window,* p. 315.
Los Angeles Times Book Review, August 25, 1991, p. 9.
New York Times Book Review, December 30, 1984, p. 19.
Publishers Weekly, May 11, 1990, review of *Polar,* p. 258; April 5, 1991, review of *Window,* p. 143; April 17, 1995, review of *The Story of Rosy Dock,* p. 59.
School Library Journal, January, 1985, Kristi Thomas Beavin, review of *Home in the Sky,* pp. 62-63; June-July, 1988, Judith Gloyer, review of *Where the Forest Meets the Sea,* p. 83; March, 1991, Susan Scheps, review of *Window,* p. 166; May, 1995, p. 98; May, 2000, Marian Drabkin, review of *The Hidden Forest,* p. 130.
Vogue Living, June, 1980.

ONLINE

Jeannie Baker Web site, http://www.jeanniebaker.com/ (December 2, 2004).*

*   *   *

BALLIETT, Blue 1955-

Personal

Born 1955; daughter of Whitney Balliett (a journalist) and Elizabeth Platt; children: two. *Education:* Attended Brown University.

Addresses

Agent—Amanda Lewis, Doe Coover Agency, P.O. Box 668, Winchester, MA 01890.

Career

University of Chicago Laboratory School, Chicago, IL, third-grade teacher, c. 1980-2002; freelance writer.

Writings

The Ghosts of Nantucket: Twenty-three True Accounts, Down East Books (Camden, ME), 1984.
Nantucket Hauntings, Down East Books, 1990.
Chasing Vermeer, illustrated by Brett Helquist, Scholastic Press (New York, NY), 2003.

Work in Progress

A second novel for children featuring the characters from *Chasing Vermeer,* due in spring, 2006.

Young Petra Andalee and Calder Pillay attempt to solve the mystery of a stolen painting by Vermeer, which is confounding FBI agents with an ever-growing list of suspects. (From Chasing Vermeer, *written by Blue Balliett and illustrated by Brett Helquist.)*

Sidelights

Blue Balliett is the author of *Chasing Vermeer,* a children's mystery novel about two sixth-graders who attempt to solve the mystery of a missing painting. Friends and fellow middle-school students Petra Andalee and Calder Pillay share a common interest in unexplained phenomena. Therefore, when it appears that some of seventeenth-century Dutch artist Johannes Vermeer's paintings may have actually been painted by someone else, the pair is quickly united in their search for the answer. The plot thickens when one of Vermeer's famous paintings mysteriously disappears while being transported from the National Gallery to Chicago's Art Institute, leaving the budding sleuths following a trail of clues that leads to their very own Chicago neighborhood.

Reviewer Marie Orlando, reviewing *Chasing Vermeer* in *School Library Journal,* praised Balliett's debut children's book, noting that "Puzzles, codes, letters, number and wordplay, a bit of danger, a vivid sense of

place, and a wealth of quirky characters" help make the book an "exciting, fast-paced story that's sure to be relished by mystery lovers." A *Publishers Weekly* contributor also enjoyed the book, stating that the author's "ingeniously plotted and lightly delivered first novel . . . also touches on the nature of coincidence, truth, art and similarly meaty topics."

Balliett spent five years writing *Chasing Vermeer,* and she drew much of her inspiration from her ten-year-long career teaching third graders, as well as from her own lifelong love of fine art. She was also inspired by her love of codes, enigmas, and the patterns found in life, all of which, Balliett contends, young people almost instinctively grasp. As she explained to a *Publishers Weekly* interviewer, children "have an ability to see connections and to put the world together in so much more of an elastic and fluid way than adults." Scattered throughout the text, along with the puzzles, wordplay, and other mind benders, are enough misleading clues to keep readers interested, added Orlando, comparing *Chasing Vermeer* to novels by popular juvenile fiction writers Ellen Raskin and E. L. Konigsburg.

Biographical and Critical Sources

PERIODICALS

Atlantic Monthly, September, 1984, Phoebe-Lou Adams, review of *The Ghosts of Nantucket,* p. 128.
Booklist, April 1, 2004, Ilene Cooper, review of *Chasing Vermeer,* p. 1365; May 1, 2004, Ilene Cooper, review of *Chasing Vermeer,* p. 1496.
Horn Book, July-August, 2004, Peter D. Sieruta, review of *Chasing Vermeer,* p. 446.
Kirkus Reviews, May 15, 2004, review of *Chasing Vermeer,* p. 487.
Publishers Weekly, June 14, 2004, review of *Chasing Vermeer,* p. 63; June 28, 2004, "Flying Starts," p. 19.
School Library Journal, July, 2004, Marie Orlando, review of *Chasing Vermeer,* p. 98.

ONLINE

BookPage.com, http://www.bookpage.com/ (January 5, 2005), Linda M. Castellitto, "Mystery at the Museum" (interview with Balliett).

*   *   *

BARRETT, Tracy 1955-

Personal

Born March 1, 1955, in Cleveland, OH; daughter of Richard Sears (a psychologist) and Shirley Irene (a teacher and literacy volunteer; maiden name, Peters) Barrett;

Tracy Barrett

married Gregory Giles (a telephone interconnect owner), November, 1983; children: Laura, Patrick. *Education:* Attended Intercollegiate Center for Classical Studies, Rome, Italy, 1974-75; Brown University, A.B. (classics; magna cum laude; with honors), 1976; University of California, Berkeley, M.A. (Italian), 1979, Ph.D. (medieval Italian), 1988. *Politics:* Democrat. *Hobbies and other interests:* Knitting, traveling to Italy with her family.

Addresses

Home—P.O. Box 120061, Nashville, TN 37212. *E-mail*—tracytbarrett@yahoo.com.

Career

Vanderbilt University, Nashville, TN, senior lecturer in Italian and director of Italian language program, 1984—, affiliated with women's studies, humanities, and comparative literature programs. Presenter at numerous conferences.

Member

Society of Children's Book Writers and Illustrators (regional advisor to Mid-South region, beginning 1999), Authors Guild.

Awards, Honors

National Endowment for the Humanities summer study grant; American Library Association Best Book for Young Adults designation, National Council for the Social Studies Notable Trade Book Designation, and Arizona State University English Education Honor List designation, all 2000, all for *Anna of Byzantium;* New York Public Library Best Book for the Teenage designation, and Bank Street College Children's Book Committee's Best Children's Books of the Year listee, both 2004, both for *Cold in Summer.*

Writings

JUVENILE NONFICTION EXCEPT AS NOTED

Nat Turner and the Slave Revolt, Millbrook Press (Brookfield, CT), 1993.
Harpers Ferry: The Story of John Brown's Raid, Millbrook Press (Brookfield, CT), 1993.
Growing up in Colonial America, Millbrook Press (Brookfield, CT), 1995.
Virginia, Marshall Cavendish Corporation, 1997, 2nd edition, Benchmark Books (New York, NY), 2004.
Tennessee, Marshall Cavendish Corporation, 1997.
Kidding around Nashville: What to Do, Where to Go, and How to Have Fun in Nashville, John Muir Publications, 1998.
Anna of Byzantium (fiction), Delacorte (New York, NY), 1999.
Kentucky, Benchmark Books (New York, NY), 1999.
The Trail of Tears: An American Tragedy, Perfection Learning (Logan, IA), 2000.
Cold in Summer, Henry Holt (New York, NY), 2003.
(With Jennifer T. Roberts) *The Ancient Greek World,* Oxford University Press (New York, NY), 2004.
(With Terry Kleeman) *The Ancient Chinese World,* Oxford University Press (New York, NY), 2004.
On Etruscan Time (fiction), Henry Holt (New York, NY), 2005.

Also author of five children's stories for the educational series "Reading Works," 1975. Contributor to periodicals, including *Appleseeds.*

Barrett's work has been translated into Dutch, Japanese, French, and Italian.

OTHER

(Translator and author of introduction) *Cecco, as I Am and Was: The Poems of Cecco Angiolieri,* International Pocket Library, 1994.

Editorial assistant, *Romance Philology,* 1978-79, and *Kidney International,* 1984.

Work in Progress

A middle-grade mystery series set in the Middle Ages; a young-adult historical novel set in the Viking era; research on medieval women's writings about women.

Sidelights

A senior lecturer in Italian literature and civilization at Nashville's Vanderbilt University, Tracy Barrett has balanced her academic writing with a mix of fact and fiction geared for younger readers. Beginning her second career as a children's book author by penning nonfiction based on American history, Barrett expanded into fiction with the 1999 novel *Anna of Byzantium*. That book, which was highly praised by critics, has sparked further fiction, although Barrett has also continued to dedicate much of her writing to sharing her interest and enthusiasm for history with children. Reviewing *The Ancient Greek World*, a book Barrett coauthored with Jennifer T. Roberts, *School Library Journal* reviewer Cynthia M. Sturgis praised the text as "lively" and added that the coauthors' "infusion of humor" makes the book "a palatable, solid resource" for middle-grade students.

"I grew up in a town where many authors lived," Barrett recalled to *Something about the Author (SATA)*, "and thought of writers as just ordinary neighbors. The wonderful Jean Fritz was one of these authors. She gave me an original illustration from her book that is still my favorite, *The Cabin Faced West*. And since I liked writing I thought it might be a good job to have someday.

"But when I grew older I got discouraged about writing, because every time I read a wonderful book I would think, 'Oh, I could never write that. Why even try?' And I was right. I could never write *Charlotte's Web* or *Mrs. Mike,* two of my favorite books. It took until I was grown up to realize that this was okay—I didn't need to write those books. Someone else had already done it! But there were other books that no one but I could write. So I started writing again. My first book wasn't published until I was almost forty, and I regret that I wasted all that time being discouraged."

Barrett's first book *Nat Turner and the Slave Revolt,* published as part of the "Gateway Civil Rights" series, tells the story of the African-American slave and preacher who came to believe that God wanted him to free the slaves. Based on his visions, Turner led a group of slaves in a bloody revolt that took the lives of over 260 people. The book begins with Turner's court conviction in 1831, traces his upbringing and education, and concludes with the famous revolt. In a review for *Booklist*, Janice Del Negro praised Barrett's objectivity, stating that she "attempts to place the event in its historical context in a concise, noninflammatory text."

Harpers Ferry: The Story of John Brown's Raid, published as part of the "Spotlight on American History" series, profiles another revolt from American history. John Brown, an abolitionist inspired by his extreme religious zeal to organize a small civilian force and make war on the United States in the hopes of ending slavery, took weapons during a raid on the U.S. arsenal at Harpers Ferry, West Virginia, in 1859. Reviewing *Harpers Ferry* and several other books in the series for *School Library Journal*, George Gleason noted that the volumes "cover their subjects well and occasionally include unusual tidbits of information."Barrett has also contributed to the "Celebrate the States" series from Benchmark Press with *Virginia, Tennessee,* and *Kentucky.* Each book features information on the geography, history, economy, and way of life of the state under examination. Of special interest, according to Denise E. Agosto in *School Library Journal,* is a section called "state survey," in which famous people and popular tourist sites are discussed. Describing the books as "well-written," Agosto concluded that they "will be useful for reports." In *Growing up in Colonial America,* Barrett covers aspects of the lives of the children of the European settlers in the American colonies, carefully differentiating between her subject and the lives of Native American children and the children of slaves. In the first part of the book, the author details food, clothing, chores, education, and recreation among colonial children in the Plymouth and Chesapeake settlements. In the second part, common child-rearing practices of the day are recounted. Elaine Fort Weischedel in *School Library Journal* observed that similar books on children in the colonial era do not address the care of infants as Barrett does. The section containing chapters on housing, attire, and recreation will be "of keenest interest to modern readers," added Susan Dove Lempke in *Booklist,* noting that the volume serves as "a good choice for reports or pleasure reading."

Barrett's first novel, *Anna of Byzantium,* centers on the real-life twelfth-century princess Anna Commena. In a first-person narrative, Barrett details the claustrophobic circumstances of seventeen-year-old Anna, who has been exiled to a convent for plotting to overthrow her brother. From there, Barrett uses flashbacks to detail Anna's earlier life as the chosen successor for her father the king, her education and upbringing, and her cruel fall from favor following the birth of a brother. The novel then traces Anna's transformation from beloved child to pawn in her grandmother's power schemes to outcast and eventually to scholar. "Barrett uses an effective first-person narrative to draw readers into Anna's story," remarked Ilene Cooper in *Booklist,* going on to praise Barrett's use of detail in making Anna's world real to modern readers. Reviewers highlighted the fact that the crucial Byzantium empire is rarely treated in juvenile novels. And though Barrett's treatment of Anna's brother in particular contradicts the historical record, *Anna of Byzantium* succeeds as "a plausible character study of a brilliant and tempestuous young woman," according to Shirley Wilton in *School Library Journal.*

A more modern protagonist is the focus of Barrett's *Cold in Summer,* which takes place in a small town in Tennessee. Seventh-grader Ariadne hates the fact that she has left her friends and school in Florida to move to her new town, a move caused by her mother's job teaching at a local college. Soon she meets a new friend

Seventeen-year-old Anna, the exceedingly smart and power-hungry daughter of the Emperor of Byzantium, narrates her tale from exile after attempting to kill her brother in order to claim the throne. (Cover illustration by David Bowers.)

named May, who becomes her new confidante, only May's behavior, her clothes, and her startling comings and goings cause Ariadne some concern. During a social studies class, she learns about a local girl named May Butler who disappeared a century earlier, and suddenly finds her time taken up with solving the mystery of her reclusive new friend. Praising Barrett's portrayal of the "mutual concern" between the two girls, *School Library Journal* reviewer Alison Ching dubbed *Cold in Summer* a "light, easy read," while a *Kirkus Reviews* critic as a "genuine ghost story . . . that will draw readers eerily in."

Barrett once told *SATA:* "I started writing for children in 1992 when I began feeling that my teaching was getting repetitive and I needed to branch out into different areas. As a child, I had always said I would be a writer when I grew up, but this ambition got lost in the shuffle of graduate school, marriage, and family. Perhaps because of my academic background, I am more drawn to nonfiction than to fiction when writing for children. I enjoy researching complicated and sometimes confusing events and organizing them into coherent and exciting narratives." She also shared her thoughts on writing

nonfiction for children, noting that authors "must pay scrupulous attention to accuracy and must present a balanced view. Children are interested in the truth and are willing to think about quite 'adult' issues if they are presented in a way accessible to them. This does not mean talking down to children; it means keeping in mind their more limited exposure to ideas and helping them learn how to formulate their own ideas and opinions."

Biographical and Critical Sources

PERIODICALS

Booklist, August, 1993, Janice Del Negro, review of *Nat Turner and the Slave Revolt,* pp. 2051-2052; December 15, 1995, Susan Dove Lempke, review of *Growing up in Colonial America,* p. 700; April 1, 1999, Ilene Cooper, review of *Anna of Byzantium,* p. 1425; April 1, 2003, Carolyn Phelan, review of *Cold in Summer,* p. 1395.

Bulletin of the Center for Children's Books, April, 1993, Betsy Hearne, review of *Nat Turner and the Slave Revolt,* p. 240.

Horn Book, May-June, 2003, Betty Carter, review of *Cold in Summer,* p. 338.

Kirkus Reviews, May 1, 2003, review of *Cold in Summer,* p. 674.

Publishers Weekly, June 28, 1999, review of *Anna of Byzantium,* p. 80; May 5, 2003, review of *Cold in Summer,* p. 221.

School Library Journal, January, 1994, George Gleason, review of *Harpers Ferry: The Story of John Brown's Raid,* p. 118; December, 1995, Elaine Fort Weischedel, review of *Growing up in Colonial America,* p. 112; June, 1997, Denise E. Agosto, review of *Virginia,* p.130; July, 1999, Shirley Wilton, review of *Anna of Byzantium,* p. 92; July, 2003, Alison Ching, review of *Cold in Summer,* p. 123; August, 2004, Cynthia M. Sturgis, review of *The Ancient Greek World,* p. 142.

ONLINE

Tracy Barrett Web site, http://www.tracybarrett.com/ (January 16, 2005).

*　　　*　　　*

BARTRAM, Simon

Personal

Male. *Education:* Birmingham Polytechnic (illustration; first class), 1990.

Addresses

Home—Newcastle upon Tyne, England. *Agent*—c/o Author Mail, Dutton's Children's Books, Dutton, Penguin Putnam, 375 Hudson St., New York, NY 10014.

Career

Illustrator and author of children's books. Freelance graphic artist.

Awards, Honors

Mother Goose Award runner up, 1999, for *Pinocchio;* Kate Greenaway Medal shortlist, 2002, for *Man on the Moon: A Day in the Life of Bob.*

Writings

SELF-ILLUSTRATED

Man on the Moon: A Day in the Life of Bob, Candlewick Press (Cambridge, MA), 2002.

ILLUSTRATOR

Carlo Collodi, *Pinocchio,* translated and adapted by Jane Fior, Dorling Kindersley (New York, NY), 1999.
Wolfgang Somary, *Night and the Candlemaker,* Barefoot Books (Bristol, England), 2000.
Tim Preston, *Pumpkin Moon,* Dutton Children's Books (New York, NY), 2001.
Marcus Sedgwick, *A Winter's Tale,* Templar Publishing (Dorking, England), 2003, published as *A Christmas Wish,* Dutton Children's Books (New York, NY), 2003.

Contributor of illustrations to periodicals, including *ES* and London *Independent on Sunday.*

Work in Progress

Dougal, the Deep Sea-Diver, a sequel to *Man on the Moon.*

Biographical and Critical Sources

PERIODICALS

Publishers Weekly, September 23, 2002, review of *Man on the Moon: A Day in the Life of Bob,* p. 72; September 22, 2003, review of *A Christmas Wish,* p. 71.
School Library Journal, January, 2001, Miriam Lang Budin, review of *Night and the Candlemaker,* p. 108; October, 2002, John Peters, review of *Man on the Moon: A Day in the Life of Bob,* p. 98.*

*   *   *

BLISS, Harry 1964-

Personal

Born March 9, 1964, in NY; married; children. *Education:* Attended Pennsylvania Academy of the Fine Arts; University of the Arts, B.F.A. (illustration); Syracuse University, M.A.

Addresses

Home—Northern VT. *Agent*—c/o Author Mail, Joanna Cotler Books/HarperCollins Children's, 1350 Avenue of the Americas, New York, NY 10019.

Career

Cartoonist and illustrator. *New Yorker,* New York, NY, cartoonist and cover artist.

Member

Society of Illustrators.

Awards, Honors

Award of Excellence from *Print,* Society of Illustrators, National Society of News Design, and Art Directors Club of New York.

Illustrator

Sharon Creech, *A Fine, Fine School,* Joanna Cotler Books (New York, NY), 2001.
William Steig, *Which Would You Rather Be?,* Joanna Cotler Books (New York, NY), 2002.
Alison McGhee, *Countdown to Kindergarten,* Harcourt (San Diego, CA), 2002.
Marc Gellman, *And God Cried, Too: A Kid's Book of Healing and Hope,* HarperTrophy (New York, NY), 2002.
Doreen Cronin, *Diary of a Worm,* Joanna Cotler Books (New York, NY), 2003.
Alison McGhee, *Mrs. Watson Wants Your Teeth,* Harcourt (Orlando, FL), 2004.
Robie H. Harris, *Don't Forget to Come Back!,* Candlewick Press (Cambridge, MA), 2004.
Doreen Cronin, *Diary of A Spider,* Joanna Cotler Books (New York, NY), 2005.

Contributor of cartoons to periodicals, including *New Yorker, Playboy, Archaeology,* and *Nickelodeon.* Illustrator of book covers.

Sidelights

Well known to adults as a regular cartoonist for the *New Yorker* magazine, Harry Bliss has also illustrated numerous children's books, among them Doreen Cronin's *Diary of a Worm,* Marc Gellman's *And God Cried, Too: A Kid's Book of Healing and Hope,* Alison McGhee's *Countdown to Kindergarten,* and *Which Would You Rather Be?,* by award-winning children's author William Steig. A *Publishers Weekly* reviewer commented that the "droll watercolor illustrations" Bliss contributed to *Diary of a Worm* "are a marvel" because the artist "gives each worm an individual character with a few deft lines." Michael Cart, writing in *Booklist,* enjoyed Bliss's illustrations for Steig's *Which Would You Rather Be?,* a picture book in which a rabbit-eared magician asks his young audience which of various animals they would be happiest as. "Bliss's pictures . . . invest Steig's simple words with wit and a sense of story," Cart noted, adding that "Steig's words and Bliss's pictures make a winning choice."

An award-winning graphic artist, Bliss began illustrating children's books after working for several years as a popular cartoonist for the *New Yorker* as well as for other magazines. He began his career as a freelance artist for magazines while he was still in college earning his undergraduate degree in illustration. Continuing to work for magazines as well as designing book jackets for New York City publishers, he came to the attention of the art editor of the *New Yorker* in 1997. His first cover appeared on the magazine's January 5, 1998 issue, and he began creating black-and-white cartoons for the magazine soon after. His first book-illustration project, Sharon Creech's *A Fine, Fine School,* was an instant success, marking what a *Publishers Weekly* contributor dubbed an "impressive debut" for the cartoonist. While his growing family has inspired Bliss to continue working as a picture-book illustrator, he has yet to disappoint fans of his *New Yorker* cartoons.

Biographical and Critical Sources

PERIODICALS

Booklist, August, 2002, Michael Cart, review of *Which Would You Rather Be?,* p. 1977; October 1, 2002, Stephanie Zvirin, review of *And God Cried, Too: A Kid's Book of Healing and Hope,* p. 341.

Childhood Education, winter, 2001, review of *A Fine, Fine School,* p. 110.

Kirkus Reviews, July 1, 2002, review of *Countdown to Kindergarten,* p. 959.

Publishers Weekly, July 23, 2001, review of *A Fine, Fine School,* p. 75; May 20, 2002, review of *Which Would You Rather Be?,* p. 64; July 8, 2002, review of *Countdown to Kindergarten,* p. 48; July 21, 2003, review of *Diary of a Worm,* p. 194.

School Library Journal, June, 2002, Carol L. MacKay, review of *Which Would You Rather Be?,* p. 110; September, 2002, Mary Elam, review of *Countdown to Kindergarten,* p. 201; December, 2002, Linda Beck, review of *And God Cried, Too,* p. 160.

ONLINE

Harry Bliss Cartoon Collection Web site, http://www.harry bliss.com/ (January 5, 2005).*

C

CARLSTROM, Nancy White 1948-

Personal

Born August 4, 1948, in Washington, PA; daughter of William J. (a steel mill worker) and Eva (Lawrence) White; married David R. Carlstrom, September 7, 1974; children: Jesse David, Joshua White. *Education:* Wheaton College, B.A., 1970; studied at Harvard Extension and Radcliffe College, 1974-76. *Religion:* Christian. *Hobbies and other interests:* Reading, swimming, walking our dog.

Addresses

Home—Seattle, WA. *Agent*—Elizabeth Harding, Curtis Brown Ltd, 10 Astor Pl., New York, NY 10003.

Career

Writer, 1983–. A. Leo Weil Elementary School, Pittsburgh, PA, teacher, 1970-72; Plum Cove Elementary School, Gloucester, MA, teacher, 1972-74; Secret Garden Children's Bookshop, Seattle, WA, owner and manager, 1977-83. Worked with children in West Africa and the West Indies; worked at school for children with Down's syndrome in Merida, Yucatan, Mexico.

Member

Society of Children's Book Writers and Illustrators.

Awards, Honors

Editor's Choice, *Booklist,* 1986, and Children's Choice designation, International Reading Association/ Children's Book Council (IRA/CBC), 1987, both for *Jesse Bear, What Will You Wear?;* American Booksellers Pick of the List, and Notable Book designation, National Council of Teachers of English (NCTE), both 1987, both for *Wild Wild Sunflower Child Anna;* Best Book of 1990, *Parents'* magazine, for *Where Does the Night Hide?;* IRA/CBC Children's Choice, and Parents' Choice designation, *Booklist,* both 1991, both for *Blow Me a Kiss, Miss Lilly;* NCTE Notable Book designation, 1991, for *Goodbye Geese.*

Nancy White Carlstrom

Writings

FOR CHILDREN

Jesse Bear, What Will You Wear?, illustrated by Bruce Degen, Macmillan (New York, NY), 1986.

The Moon Came, Too, illustrated by Stella Ormai, Macmillan (New York, NY), 1987.

Wild Wild Sunflower Child Anna, illustrated by Jerry Pinkney, Macmillan (New York, NY), 1987.

Better Not Get Wet, Jesse Bear, illustrated by Bruce Degen, Macmillan (New York, NY), 1988.

Where Does the Night Hide?, illustrated by Thomas B. Allen and Laura Allen, Macmillan (New York, NY), 1988.

Graham Cracker Animals 1-2-3, illustrated by John Sandford, Macmillan (New York, NY), 1989.

Blow Me a Kiss, Miss Lilly, illustrated by Amy Schwartz, Harper (New York, NY), 1990.

Heather Hiding, illustrated by Dennis Nolan, Macmillan (New York, NY), 1990.

It's about Time, Jesse Bear, and Other Rhymes, illustrated by Bruce Degen, Macmillan (New York, NY), 1990.

I'm Not Moving, Mama!, illustrated by Thor Wickstrom, Macmillan (New York, NY), 1990.

Grandpappy, illustrated by Laurel Molk, Little, Brown (Boston, MA), 1990.

No Nap for Benjamin Badger, illustrated by Dennis Nolan, Macmillan (New York, NY), 1990.

Light: Stories of a Small Kindness, illustrated by Lisa Desimini, Little, Brown (Boston, MA), 1990.

Moose in the Garden, illustrated by Lisa Desimini, Harper (New York, NY), 1990.

Goodbye Geese, illustrated by Ed Young, Philomel (New York, NY), 1991.

Who Gets the Sun out of Bed?, illustrated by David McPhail, Little, Brown (Boston, MA), 1992.

Northern Lullaby, illustrated by Leo and Diane Dillon, Philomel (New York, NY), 1992.

Kiss Your Sister, Rose Marie!, illustrated by Thor Wickstrom, Macmillan (New York, NY), 1992.

How Do You Say It Today, Jesse Bear?, illustrated by Bruce Degen, Macmillan (New York, NY), 1992.

Baby-O, illustrated by Sucie Stevenson, Little, Brown (Boston, MA), 1992.

The Snow Speaks, illustrated by Jane Dyer, Little, Brown (Boston, MA), 1993.

What Does the Rain Play?, illustrated by Henri Sorensen, Macmillan (New York, NY), 1993.

Swim the Silver Sea, Joshie Otter, illustrated by Ken Kuori, Philomel (New York, NY), 1993.

Rise and Shine, illustrated by Dominic Catalano, HarperCollins (New York, NY), 1993.

How Does the Wind Walk?, illustrated by Deborah K. Ray, Macmillan (New York, NY), 1993.

Fish and Flamingo, illustrated by Lisa Desimini, Little, Brown (Boston, MA), 1993.

Wishing at Dawn in Summer, illustrated by Diane Wolfolk Allison, Little, Brown (Boston, MA), 1993.

Does God Know How to Tie Shoes?, illustrated by Lori McElrath-Eslick, Eerdmans (Grand Rapids, MI), 1993.

What Would You Do If You Lived at the Zoo?, illustrated by Lizi Boyd, Little, Brown (Boston, MA), 1994.

Jesse Bear's Yum-Yum Crumble, Aladdin Books (New York, NY), 1994.

Jesse Bear's Wiggle-Jiggle Jump-Up, Aladdin Books (New York, NY), 1994.

Jesse Bear's Tum Tum Tickle, Aladdin Books (New York, NY), 1994.

Jesse Bear's Tra-La Tub, Aladdin Books (New York, NY), 1994.

Happy Birthday, Jesse Bear!, illustrated by Bruce Degen, Macmillan (New York, NY), 1994.

Barney Is Best, illustrated by James G. Hale, HarperCollins (New York, NY), 1994.

Who Said Boo?: Halloween Poems for the Very Young, illustrated by R. W. Alley, Simon & Schuster (New York, NY), 1995.

I Am Christmas, illustrated by Lori McElrath-Eslick, Eerdmans (Grand Rapids, MI), 1995.

Let's Count It out, Jesse Bear, illustrated by Bruce Degen, Simon & Schuster (New York, NY), 1996.

Ten Christmas Sheep, illustrated by Cynthia Fisher, Eerdmans (Grand Rapids, MI), 1996.

Raven and River, illustrated by Jon Van Zyle, Little, Brown (Boston, MA), 1997.

I Love You, Papa, in All Kinds of Weather, illustrated by Bruce Degen, Little Simon (New York, NY), 1997.

I Love You, Mama, Any Time of Year, illustrated by Bruce Degen, Little Simon (New York, NY), 1997.

Hooray for Me, Hooray for You, Hooray for Blue: Jesse Bear's Colors, illustrated by Bruce Degen, Little Simon (New York, NY), 1997.

Bizz Buzz Chug-a-Chug: Jesse Bear's Sounds, illustrated by Bruce Degen, Little Simon (New York, NY), 1997.

Guess Who's Coming, Jesse Bear, illustrated by Bruce Degen, Simon & Schuster (New York, NY), 1998.

Midnight Dance of the Snowshoe Hare: Poems of Alaska, illustrated by Ken Kuori, Philomel (New York, NY), 1998.

What a Scare, Jesse Bear!, illustrated by Bruce Degen, Simon & Schuster (New York, NY), 1999.

Thanksgiving Day at Our House: Thanksgiving Poems for the Very Young, illustrated by R. W. Alley, Simon & Schuster (New York, NY), 1999.

Where Is Christmas, Jesse Bear?, illustrated by Bruce Degen, Simon & Schuster (New York, NY), 2000.

The Way to Wyatt's House, illustrated by Mary Morgan, Walker & Co. (New York, NY), 2000.

What Does the Sky Say?, illustrated by Tim Ladwig, Eerdmans (Grand Rapids, MI), 2001.

Glory, illustrated by Debra Reid Jenkins, Eerdmans (Grand Rapids, MI), 2001.

Before You Were Born, illustrated by Linda Saport, Eerdmans (Grand Rapids, MI), 2002.

Giggle-Wiggle Wake-up!, illustrated by Melissa Sweet, Knopf (New York, NY), 2003.

Climb the Family Tree, Jesse Bear!, illustrated by Bruce Degen, Simon & Schuster (New York, NY), 2004.

Sidelights

Nancy White Carlstrom is the author of the popular "Jesse Bear" series, which is illustrated by Bruce Degen and features such titles as *Where Is Christmas, Jesse Bear?* and *Jesse Bear, What Will You Wear?* Known for her tight lines of verse filled with vivid description and evocation of the everyday, Carlstrom presents hopeful and humorous picture and board books for very young readers, books with simple vocabulary and subjects ranging from counting and colors to more sophisticated topics like inter-generational and multicultural relationships.

Carlstrom's concerns with society and nature are a reflection of her own upbringing and world view. Growing up without television, she learned early on to create her own fantasies and to entertain herself. Carlstrom decided to become a writer of children's books at an early age; she worked in the children's department of her local library during her high school years, and "that's where my dream of writing children's books was born," as she once told *Something about the Author* (*SATA*). After earning a B.A. in education from Wheaton College, she taught primary school in Pittsburgh while working summers with children in the West Indies and in West Africa. She also studied art and children's literature, then moved with her husband to the Yucatan where she worked at a school for children with Down's syndrome. Upon their return to the United States, the couple moved to Seattle, where Carlstrom became proprietor of The Secret Garden, a children's bookstore, and promoted quality children's books via book fairs and public presentations.

In 1981 Carlstrom participated in a two-week writer's workshop led by children's book author Jane Yolen. During that workshop she wrote the poem that would eventually become the text of *Wild Wild Sunflower Child Anna*. While several years passed before this text found a publisher, in the meantime, Carlstrom wrote *Jesse Bear, What Will You Wear?* "My husband and I often called our son Jesse Bear," Carlstrom recalled to *SATA*, "and the book . . . began as a little song I sang while dressing him. I finished the picture book text for Jesse's first birthday." The book progresses through the day as little Jesse dresses and then messes and must dress again. Liza Bliss, writing in *School Library Journal*, noted in particular that "the rhymes, besides having a charming lilt to them, are clean and catchy and beg to be recited." A *Bulletin of the Center for Children's Books* reviewer drew attention to Carlstrom's lyrics, as well, and determined that, "without crossing the line into sentimentality, this offers a happy, humorous soundfest that will associate reading aloud with a sense of play." Lines like Jesse's reply to his mother—"I'll wear the sun / On my legs that run / Sun on the run in the morning"—tempt one "to sing Carlstrom's words aloud," commented a *Kirkus Reviews* critic, who praised the author for her "rich imagination."Carlstrom has gone on to create many more books for children, a large number of which continue the further adventures of Jesse Bear. *Better Not Get Wet, Jesse Bear* is a "winsome picture book," according to a *Publishers Weekly* reviewer, with "lilting, strongly rhymed text"; Ellen Fader wrote in *Horn Book* that "the book never loses its claim to the sensibility of young children, who will be won over by Jesse Bear's delight in water play and his final triumphant splash." Clocks and the times of the day are at the heart of Carlstrom's third "Jesse Bear" title, *It's about Time, Jesse Bear, and Other Rhymes*, a book that "children are sure to enjoy," according to Patricia Pearl in *School Library Journal*. *How Do You Say It Today, Jesse Bear?* celebrates the holidays of the year, from Independence Day to Halloween and

Young Jesse Bear attends a family reunion in a title from Carlstrom's series about preschool experiences through the eyes of the little engaging bruin. (*From* Climb the Family Tree, Jesse Bear!, *illustrated by Bruce Degen.*)

Christmas. Carolyn Phelan of *Booklist* commented on this work: "A good way to learn about the months and holidays, or read it just for fun."

The sixth volume in the series, *Let's Count It out, Jesse Bear,* finds the playful bear "in a high-impact counting game," according to a *Publishers Weekly* reviewer. The rhyme for number two in this counting book is indicative of the humor and joy of the whole: "Jumping high, / Landing loud. / New shoes dancing, / New shoes proud." *Where Is Christmas, Jesse Bear?* proves that "There's no hibernating for this little bear," as *Booklist* reviewer Shelley Townsend-Hudson noted. Praising Carlstrom's "child-centered focus," Townsend-Hudson dubbed the 2000 picture book "infectiously jubilant," while in *School Library Journal* Marian Drabkin noted that *Where Is Christmas, Jesse Bear?* calls forth the "sights . . . that traditionally shout Christmas." The "Jesse Bear" series has prompted spin-off board books and a stuffed bear, as well as a loyal following among readers.

Carlstrom has also written many books outside of the "Jesse Bear" series. The first text she wrote, *Wild Wild Sunflower Child Anna,* about a child's exploration and discovery of the natural world around her, found a publisher in 1987 and is, according to Carlstrom, "still my favorite book of all I have written." Denise M. Wilms of *Booklist* maintained that "audiences young and old will find [Anna's] pleasure in the day most contagious." Ellen Fader, writing in *Horn Book,* concluded that "an exceptional treat awaits the parent and child who lose themselves in this book." Carlstrom further celebrates the lives of preschoolers in books such as *Heather Hiding,* the tale of a hide-and-seek game, *Graham Cracker Animals 1-2-3,* and *Blow Me a Kiss, Miss Lilly,* which deals with the death of a loved one. *Light: Stories of a Small Kindness* draws somewhat on Carlstrom's time spent in Mexico in that the gathered tales all have Hispanic settings and all deal with small but significant gestures of affection. "Tender, thought-provoking, moving are just a few of the words to describe these seven short stories," commented Ilene Cooper in a *Booklist* review.

Much the same format is employed in *Baby-O,* in which the rhythms of the West Indies are celebrated in a rhyming cumulative story of a family on its way to market to sell their produce. "Sing it, chant it, clap it, or stamp it," Jane Marino declared in a *School Library Journal* review. "Just don't miss it." Carlstrom has dealt with topics as various as the relationship between a young boy and his grandfather in *Grandpappy,* unlikely friendships in *Fish and Flamingo,* a child's fears of a trip to the hospital in *Barney Is Best,* and the possibilities that life holds at the start of a brand new week in *Giggle-Wiggle Wake-up!,* the last in which Carlstrom's "infectiously singsong text dances in readers' ears," according to a *Publishers Weekly* reviewer.

A move to Alaska in 1987 provided the author with new settings and themes for her writing—"freely wandering moose, northern lights, and extreme seasonal changes to name a few," she told *SATA.* Books such as *Moose in the Garden, The Snow Speaks, Northern Lullaby,* and *Goodbye Geese* have all been inspired by the wilderness and wildlife of the far north. "A first-rate choice for toddlers" is how *School Library Journal* contributor Ellen Fader described *Moose in the Garden,* which tells of a moose invading a garden and—to the delight of the young boy of the family—eating all the vegetables the boy does not like. The northern winter is lovingly examined in *Goodbye Geese* through the question and answer exchange between a father and his curious child: "Papa, is winter coming? / Yes, and when the winter comes, she'll touch every living thing." *Booklist* reviewer Carolyn Phelan found *Goodbye Geese* to be "an effective mood book for story hour . . . a vivid introduction to personification." In *Northern Lullaby* Carlstrom also personifies the natural elements such as the moon and stars, along with wild creatures to conjure up a vision of the vastness of the far north. "The end effect," commented *Bulletin of the Center for Children's Books* reviewer Betsy Hearne, "is both simple and sophisticated." A *Kirkus Reviews* critic noted the book's "gently cadenced verse," and a *Publishers Weekly* reviewer praised *Northern Lullaby* as a "stunning, seamlessly executed work." Wintertime in Alaska also inspired Carlstrom's *The Snow Speaks,* in which two children experience the first snowfall of the season.

Booklist reviewer Carolyn Phelan noted that Carlstrom used "lyrical language to turn down-to-earth experiences into something more," and Jane Marino in *School Library Journal* thought that it was "a book to be enjoyed all winter, long after the decorations have been packed away."

Natural phenomena form the core of many of Carlstrom's books. In *Where Does the Night Hide?, Who Gets the Sun out of Bed?, What Does the Rain Play?,* and *How Does the Wind Walk?* she uses question-and-answer rhymes and riddles to look at nature. With *Who Gets the Sun out of Bed?* the author reverses the good-night story, relating instead a tale about waking up. *School Library Journal* contributor Ruth K. MacDonald found this work to be "an altogether successful story about the coming of the day," noting that "the persistent gentle patterns of questions and answers leads up to a climax that is warm but not boisterous—a fitting, final ending to a story that . . . functions as an appropriate bedtime tale." The sounds of rain take center stage in *What Does the Rain Play?,* which focuses on a little boy who loves the various noises rain makes, even at night. Emily Melton in *Booklist* noted that "the gently calming writing and softly lulling rhythms of the rain sounds make this book a perfect bedtime choice." In *How Does the Wind Walk?* another little boy looks at the different moods of the wind in different seasons, the book employing a question-and-answer format. A critic in *Kirkus Reviews* noted that Carlstrom's text includes "lots of alliteration and some subtle internal rhymes" to produce "wonderfully evocative effects."

Harkening back to her own childhood enjoyment of the Bible and her strong Christian tradition, Carlstrom has also created several faith-based books for young readers. She encourages a child's questions about God in *Does God Know How to Tie Shoes?,* and has also authored several nativity tales, including *I Am Christmas* and *Ten Christmas Sheep.* Her picture book *Glory,* which *Booklist* reviewer Ilene Cooper included in her Top-Ten list of best religious books for young readers in 2001, contains a prayer that recounts how all the creatures on Earth are connected to God in one way or another. Praising the colorful illustrations provided by Debra Reid Jenkins, *School Library Journal* reviewer Gay Lynn van Vleck wrote that Carlstrom's book reinforces "how good it feels to be alive," and will serve as a special treat for young animal lovers. Carlstrom also draws from Psalm 139 in her book *Before You Were Born,* which describes how life changes with the birth of a new child. Dubbing the book a "beautiful portrayal of the transformation of a couple into a family," a *Kirkus Reviews* critic added that the text of *Before You Were Born* contains "effulgent imagery" that reassuringly shows that parents hold children to be central to their lives.

Carlstrom practices the craft of writing with care and intelligence. "A picture book, like a poem, is what I call a bare bones kind of writing," she once explained to

SATA. "Usually I start with many more words than I need or want. I keep cutting away until I am down to the bare bones of what I want to say. It is then up to the illustrator to create pictures that will enlarge and enhance the text. . .. Often a title of a story will come first. I write it down and tend to think about it for a long time before actually sitting down to work on it. Sometimes I just get a few pieces of the story and they have to simmer on the back burner, like a good pot of soup. When the time is right, the writing of the story comes easily." In *Books That Invite Talk, Wonder, and Play,* she also noted that she often sings her words to get the correct rhythm. "Language is a musical experience for me. Rhythm, rhyme, and cadence all become an important part of the process. I love the way a young child, just learning the language, rolls a word around on her tongue and, if she likes the sound of it, may chant it over and over."

All of Carlstrom's books share the common denominator of humor and hope. "No matter how bad things get, in this world or in my life," Carlstrom commented in a *Speaking of Poets* interview, "I do believe in joy and hope because I believe there's someone greater than myself in charge. It is my own religious faith that affects both the way I live my life and the way I write." "I can't always explain exactly why my poems come out the way they do," she later added, "but there is a joy that I have that I do want to express. And for me, writing is my way of celebrating."

Biographical and Critical Sources

BOOKS

Books That Invite Talk, Wonder, and Play, edited by Amy A. McClure and Janice V. Kristo, NCTE, 1996, pp. 236-238.

Carlstrom, Nancy White, *Goodbye Geese,* Philomel (New York, NY), 1991.

Carlstrom, Nancy White, *Jesse Bear, What Will You Wear?,* Macmillan (New York, NY), 1986.

Carlstrom, Nancy White, *Let's Count It out, Jesse Bear,* Simon & Schuster (New York, NY), 1996.

Speaking of Poets, Volume 2, edited by Jeffrey S. Copeland and Vicky L. Copeland, NCTE, 1994, pp. 194-202.

PERIODICALS

Booklist, October 1, 1987, Denise M. Wilms, review of *Wild Wild Sunflower Child Anna,* p. 257; December 1, 1989, pp. 740-741; March 15, 1990, p. 1443; December 15, 1990, Ilene Cooper, review of *Light: Stories of a Small Kindness,* p. 855, 860; November 1, 1991, p. 530; November 15, 1991, Carolyn Phelan, review of *Goodbye Geese,* p. 628; September 15, 1992, Carolyn Phelan, review of *The Snow Speaks* and *How Do You Say It Today, Jesse Bear?,* p. 154; March 15, 1993, p. 1358; April 1, 1993, Emily Melton, review of *What Does the Rain Play?,* p. 1436; December 1, 1993, p. 692; November 1, 1994, p. 505; September 1, 1995, p. 54; February 15, 1998, Lauren Peterson, review of *Guess Who's Coming, Jesse Bear;* September, 2000, Lauren Peterson, review of *The Way to Wyatt's House,* p. 121; November 15, 2000, Shelley Townsend-Hudson, review of *Where Is Christmas, Jesse Bear?,* p. 646; July, 2001, Denise Wilms, review of *What Does the Sky Say?,* p. 2017; October 1, 2002, Ilene Cooper, review of *Glory,* p. 344.

Bulletin of the Center for Children's Books, May, 1986, review of *Jesse Bear, What Will You Wear?,* p. 162; May, 1990, p. 210; October, 1992, Betsy Hearne, review of *Northern Lullaby,* p. 40; October, 1996, p. 51.

Horn Book, November-December, 1987, Ellen Fader, review of *Wild Wild Sunflower Child Anna,* pp. 721-722; May-June, 1988, Ellen Fader, review of *Better Not Get Wet, Jesse Bear,* pp. 338-339; May-June, 1990, p. 319.

Kirkus Reviews, February 15, 1986, review of *Jesse Bear, What Will You Wear?,* p. 300; October 15, 1992, review of *Northern Lullaby,* p. 1307; April 1, 1993, p.453; April 15, 1993, p. 525; September 1, 1993, review of *How Does the Wind Walk?,* p. 1141; October 15, 1994, p. 1406; October, 1995, p. 1424; December 15, 2001, review of *Before You Were Born,* p. 1755; October 1, 2003, review of *Giggle-Wiggle Wake-up!,* p. 1221.

New York Times Book Review, July 20, 1986, p. 24; December 20, 1992, p. 19; April 18, 1993, p. 25; September 19, 1993, p. 36.

Publishers Weekly, February 27, 1987, p. 162; March 11, 1988, review of *Better Not Get Wet, Jesse Bear,* p. 102; October 19, 1992, review of *Northern Lullaby,* p.75; March 22, 1993, p. 78; April 12, 1993, p. 62; May 17, 1993, p. 77; July 5, 1993, p. 72; April 25, 1994, p.76; October 3, 1994, p. 67; June 17, 1996, review of *Let's Count It out, Jesse Bear,* p. 63; November 15, 1999, review of *I'm Not Moving Mama!,* p. 69; February 14, 2000, review of *Happy Birthday, Jesse Bear!,* p. 203; September 25, 2000, review of *The Way to Wyatt's House,* p. 115; November 24, 2003, review of *Giggle-Wiggle Wake-up!,* p. 62.

Quill & Quire, October, 1992, p. 39.

School Library Journal, April, 1986, Liza Bliss, review of *Jesse Bear, What Will You Wear?,* pp. 68-69; June-July, 1987, p. 78; February, 1988, p. 58; May, 1988, p. 81; December, 1989, p. 77; April, 1990, Patricia Pearl, review of *It's about Time, Jesse Bear, and Other Rhymes,* p. 87; June, 1990, p. 97; July, 1990, p. 56; October, 1990, Ellen Fader, review of *Moose in the Garden,* p. 86; December, 1990, p. 100; December, 1991, p.80; April, 1992, Jane Marino, review of *Baby-O,* p. 89; September, 1992, Ruth K. MacDonald, review of *Who Gets the Sun out of Bed?,* p. 199; October, 1992, Jane Marino, review of *The Snow Speaks,* p. 38; May, 1993, p. 82; March, 1994, p. 190; July, 1994, p. 74; December, 1994, p. 72; September, 1995, p. 192; October, 1999, Anne Parker, review of *What a Scare, Jesse Bear;* October, 2000, Marian Drabkin, review of *Where Is Christmas, Jesse Bear?,* p. 57, and *The Way to Wyatt's House,* p. 119; December, 2001, Be Astengo, review of *What Does the Sky Say?,* p. 118; December, 2001, Gay Lynn van Vleck, review of *Glory,* p. 118; June, 2002, Martha Topol, review of *Before You Were Born,* p. 90; August, 2004, Wendy Woodfill, review of *Climb the Family Tree, Jesse Bear!*

Times Literary Supplement, April 3, 1987, p. 356.

*   *   *

Chichester CLARK, Emma 1955-

Personal

Born October 15, 1955, in London, England; daughter of Robin Chichester Clark (a company director) and Jane Helen (Goddard; present surname, Falloon); married Lucas van Praag (a management consultant). *Education:* Chelsea School of Art, B.A. (with honors), 1978; Royal College of Art, M.A. (with honors), 1983.

Addresses

Home—47 Richford St., London W12 8BU, England. *Agent*—Laura Cecil, 17 Alwyne Villas, London N1, England.

Career

Author, illustrator, and editor of children's books, 1983–. Worked in a design studio and as a freelance illustrator of newspapers, periodicals, and book jackets. Visiting lecturer at Middlesex Polytechnic and City and Guilds School of Art, 1984-86. *Exhibitions:* Exhibitor at the Thumb Gallery, England, 1984 and 1987.

Member

Chelsea Arts Club.

Awards, Honors

Mother Goose Award, 1988, for *Listen to This;* Golden Duck Award, 1999, for *Noah and the Space Ark;* Kate Greenaway Medal shortlist, 1999, for *I Love You, Blue Kangaroo!;* Kurt Maschler Award shortlist, 1999, for *Elf Hill: Tales from Hans Christian Andersen.*

Writings

SELF-ILLUSTRATED PICTURE BOOKS

Catch That Hat!, Bodley Head (London, England), 1988, Little, Brown (Boston, MA), 1990.
The Story of Horrible Hilda and Henry, Little, Brown (Boston, MA), 1988.
Myrtle, Tertle, and Gertle, Bodley Head (London, England), 1989.

The Bouncing Dinosaur, Farrar, Straus (New York, NY), 1990.
Tea with Aunt Augusta, Methuen (London, England), 1991, published as *Lunch with Aunt Augusta,* Dial (New York), 1992.
Miss Bilberry's New House, Methuen (London, England), 1993, published as *Across the Blue Mountains,* Harcourt (San Diego, CA), 1993.
Little Miss Muffet Counts to Ten, Andersen (London, England), 1997, published as *Little Miss Muffet's Count-Along Surprise,* Bantam (New York, NY), 1997.
More!, Andersen (London, England), 1998, Bantam (New York, NY), 1999.
I Love You, Blue Kangaroo!, Bantam (New York, NY), 1999.
Follow My Leader, Andersen (London, England), 1999.
Where Are You, Blue Kangaroo?, Andersen (London, England), 2000, Random House (New York, NY), 2001.
It Was You, Blue Kangaroo!, Andersen (London, England), 2001, Random House (New York, NY), 2002.
No More Kissing!, Doubleday (New York, NY), 2002.
What Shall We Do, Blue Kangaroo?, Random House (New York, NY), 2003.
Mimi's Book of Opposites, Charlesbridge (Watertown, MA), 2003.
Mimi's Book of Counting, Charlesbridge (Watertown, MA), 2003.
Follow the Leader!, Margaret K. McElderry Books (New York, NY), 2003.
Up in Heaven, Andersen (London, England), 2003, Random House (New York, NY), 2004.
Merry Christmas to You, Blue Kangaroo!, Random House (New York, NY), 2004.
No More Teasing, Andersen (London, England), 2005.

Several of Clark's books have been translated into Spanish.

ILLUSTRATOR

Laura Cecil, compiler, *Listen to This,* Greenwillow (New York, NY), 1987.
Janet Lunn, *Shadow in Hawthorn Bay,* Walker (London, England), 1988.
Laura Cecil, compiler, *Stuff and Nonsense,* Greenwillow (New York, NY), 1989.
Primrose Lockwood, *Cissy Lavender,* Little, Brown (Boston, MA), 1989.
James Reeves, *Ragged Robin: Poems from A to Z,* Little, Brown (Boston, MA), 1990.
Margaret Ryan, *Fat Witch Rides Again,* Methuen (London, England), 1990.
Laura Cecil, compiler, *Boo! Stories to Make You Jump,* Greenwillow (New York, NY), 1990.
Jane Rohmer, *Rock-a-Bye Baby,* 1990.
Roald Dahl, *James and the Giant Peach,* Unwin Hyman (London, England), 1990.
(And compiler) *I Never Saw a Purple Cow and Other Nonsense Rhymes* (anthology), Little, Brown (Boston, MA), 1990.
Pat Thomson, *Beware of the Aunts!,* Margaret K. McElderry Books (New York), 1991.

Margaret Mahy, *The Queen's Goat,* Dial (New York, NY), 1991.

Diana Wynne Jones, *Wild Robert,* Mammoth (London, England), 1991, Chivers North America, 1992.

Diana Wynne Jones, *Castle in the Air,* Mammoth (London, England), 1991.

Jenny Nimmo, *Delilah and the Dogspell,* Methuen (London, England), 1991.

Laura Cecil, compiler, *A Thousand Yards of the Sea,* Methuen (London, England), 1992, published as *A Thousand Yards of Sea,* Greenwillow (New York, NY), 1993.

D. J. Enright, *The Way of the Cat,* HarperCollins (New York, NY), 1992.

Anne Fine, *The Haunting of Pip Parker,* Walker (London, England), 1992.

Ben Frankel, *Tertius and Plinty,* Harcourt (San Diego, CA), 1992.

Geraldine McCaughrean, reteller, *The Orchard Book of Greek Myths,* Orchard (London, England), 1992, published as *Greek Myths,* Margaret K. McElderry Books (New York, NY), 1993.

Peter Dickinson, *Time and the Clockmice, et cetera,* Doubleday (London, England), 1993, Delacorte (New York, NY), 1994.

Rosemary Sutcliff, *The Princess and the Dragon Pup,* Walker (London, England), 1993, Candlewick (Cambridge, MA), 1996.

Ann Turnbull, *Too Tired,* Hamish Hamilton (London, England), 1993, Harcourt (San Diego, CA), 1994.

Laura Cecil, *The Frog Princess,* Jonathan Cape (London, England), 1994, Greenwillow (New York, NY), 1995.

Laura Cecil, compiler, *Preposterous Pets,* Hamish Hamilton (London, England), 1994, Greenwillow (New York, NY), 1995.

Charles Ashton, *Ruth and the Blue Horse,* Walker (London, England), 1994.

Kate McMullan, *Good Night, Stella,* Candlewick (Cambridge, MA), 1994.

William S. Gilbert and Arthur Sullivan, *I Have a Song to Sing, O!: An Introduction to the Songs of Gilbert and Sullivan,* selected and edited by John Langstaff, Margaret K. McElderry Books (New York, NY), 1994.

Laura Cecil, *Piper,* Jonathan Cape (London, England), 1995.

Something Rich and Strange: A Treasury of Shakespeare's Verse, compiled by Gina Pollinger, Larousse Kingfisher Chambers (New York, NY), 1995, published as *A Treasury of Shakespeare's Verse,* Kingfisher (New York, NY), 2000.

Allan Ahlberg, *Mrs. Vole the Vet,* Puffin (London, England), 1996.

(And editor with Catherine Asholt and Quentin Blake) *The Candlewick Book of First Rhymes* (anthology), Candlewick (Cambridge, MA), 1996.

Henrietta Branford, *Dimanche Diller at Sea,* Collins (London, England), 1996.

Ian Whybrow, *Miss Wire and the Three Kind Mice,* Kingfisher (London, England), 1996.

Sam McBratney, editor, *Little Red Riding Hood,* 1996.

Emma Alcock, *Sinan,* 1996.

Laura Mare, *Mehmet the Conqueror,* 1997.

Laura Cecil, *Noah and the Space Ark,* Hamish Hamilton (London, England), 1997, Lerner (New York, NY), 1998.

Geraldine McCaughrean, reteller, *The Orchard Book of Greek Gods and Goddesses,* Orchard (London, England), 1997.

Jane Falloon, reteller, *Thumbelina,* Pavilion (London, England), 1997.

The Little Book of Shakespeare, compiled by Gina Pollinger, Kingfisher (London, England), 1997.

John Yeoman, *The Glove Puppet Man,* Collins (London, England), 1997.

Adrian Mitchell, reteller, *The Adventures of Robin Hood and Marian,* Orchard (London, England), 1998.

Mathew Price, *Where's Alfie?,* Orchard (London, England), 1999.

Mathew Price, *Don't Worry, Alfie,* Orchard (London, England), 1999.

Naomi Lewis, *Elf Hill: Tales from Hans Christian Andersen,* Star Bright Books, 1999.

Mathew Price, *Patch and the Rabbits,* Orchard (London, England), 1999, Orchard (New York, NY), 2000.

Mathew Price, *Patch Finds a Friend,* Orchard (New York, NY), 2000.

Laura Cecil, compiler, *The Kingfisher Book of Toy Stories,* Kingfisher (New York, NY), 2000.

Geraldine McCaughrean, reteller, *Roman Myths,* Margaret K. McElderry Books (New York, NY), 2001.

Michael Morpurgo, *The McElderry Book of Aesop's Fables,* Margaret K. McElderry Books (New York, NY), 2005.

Contributor of illustrations to *Tom's Pirate Ship and Other Stories* and *Mostly Animal Poetry,* both Heinemann (London, England), 1997, and *Alphabet Gallery,* Mammoth (London, England), 1999. Illustrations have also appeared in newspapers and periodicals, including the London *Sunday Times, Cosmopolitan,* and *New Scientist.*

Sidelights

A popular and prolific author, illustrator, and anthologist, Emma Chichester Clark is considered one of England's most distinguished picture-book creators. Cited alongside noted illustrators Beatrix Potter, Edward Ardizzone, Tony Ross, and Quentin Blake—her former teacher—she has written and illustrated many of her own picture books while also creating accompanying artwork for numerous stories, picture books, anthologies, and retellings by other writers, including Roald Dahl, Anne Fine, Peter Dickinson, Allan Ahlberg, Rosemary Sutcliff, Sam McBratney, Diana Wynne Jones, John Yeoman, Naomi Lewis, Matthew Price, Janet Lunn, Jenny Nimmo, and Geraldine McCaughrean. In her own books, which include *Up in Heaven, The Story of Horrible Hilda and Henry,* and the award-winning *I Love You, Blue Kangaroo!,* she features child, adult, and animal characters in situations that, although usually humorous and fantastic, provide realistic portrayals of human feelings and foibles. Gwyneth Evans noted in an essay for the *St. James Guide to Children's Writers* that Chichester Clark's original stories "are reassuring, but have an underlying toughness." Their protagonists—boys and girls, older women, and anthropomorphized animals ranging from donkeys to lemurs—are not perfect: they fight, tease, overeat, and are greedy and absent minded. However, they ultimately make positive choices and; at the end of their adventures, return home, satisfied with their situation.

As an artist, Chichester Clark is praised for her distinctive, easily recognizable style, as well as for her use of color and her ability to evoke action and emotion. She often works in watercolor and pen, and her pictures range from bucolic scenes in gentle pastels to luminous, vivid paintings teeming with activity. "While her illustrations often suggest the serenity and charm of a timeless world," stated Evans, "her work has a vitality and a multicultural perspective which also makes it contemporary."

Born in London, England, Chichester Clark was brought to Ireland at the age of three and grew up in an old, white farmhouse surrounded by fields. Her family kept many pets, including dogs, roosters, mice, rabbits, and, as the artist wrote in *Ladybug*, "a very old pony who was pretty vicious." Because she lived a long way from any other children, Chichester Clark and her siblings "had to entertain ourselves, which was easy there. I used to draw a lot, houses with windows jammed into the four corners and people with no necks." She also made her own small books, "with proper spines that my mother sewed up for me." "All the way through school," she added, "it didn't ever occur to me that I would do anything other than illustrate books when I was 'grown up.'"

In 1975, Chichester Clark left Ireland to attend the Chelsea School of Art in London. After graduating with honors, she began to submit original picture books to publishers. When two of them were rejected, she suspended her quest to work in a design studio. Instead, she designed book jackets and submitted illustrations to newspapers and magazines. A few years later, she enrolled at the Royal College of Art, where she was taught by Quentin Blake and prominent author/illustrator Michael Foreman. After receiving her master's degree, again with honors, she received a phone call from an editor at London publisher Bodley Head, who had found copies of the drawings Chichester Clark had submitted several years previously. She was asked to illustrate the story anthology *Listen to This,* which began her fruitful collaboration with the book's editor, Laura Cecil.

Listen to This contains thirteen stories, including works by Rudyard Kipling, Philippa Pearce, Virginia Hamilton, Margaret Mahy, and the Brothers Grimm. Writing in the *Times Educational Supplement,* Jenny Marshall noted that Chichester Clark's colorful illustrations "have verve and wit," while Lesley Chamberlain concluded in the *Times Literary Supplement* that the artist "has brought an energetic and unsentimental streak to very varied material." In response to her work the illustrator received the Mother Goose Award in 1988, acknowledging her position as the most exciting newcomer to British children's book illustration.

Chichester Clark and Cecil have continued their collaboration on several well-received compilations, as well as original stories by Cecil. *Noah and the Space Ark,* Cecil's picture book with an environmental theme, places the Biblical character in a future in which Earth is so polluted that people and animals are in danger of extinction. Noah builds a rocket ship and takes the small animals—the larger ones have already died out—into space to find a new home. After they find a planet that resembles Earth, they disembark and vow to take better care of it than the stewards of Earth had done.

Chichester Clark serves as compiler and illustrator of *I Never Saw a Purple Cow, and Other Nonsense Rhymes,* which includes over one hundred poems by such writers as Edward Lear, Lewis Carroll, and Hilaire Belloc. Filled out by an additional selection of traditional rhymes, riddles, limericks, and ballads, the book is arranged according to animal species and behavior. A *Kirkus Review* critic dubbed Chichester Clark's witty illustrations "just right" and called *I Never Saw a Purple Cow* a "delightful compilation, handsomely presented." Writing in *School Librarian,* Joan Nellist claimed that Chichester Clark matches the rhymes and poems "with a beautiful simplicity which is sure to please young and old alike." While she has illustrated many works by others, Chichester Clark has gained much of her following for her original stories. She began her writing career with the picture book *Catch That Hat!,* published in 1988. In this work, which is written in rhyme, Rose loses her pink hat to the wind as she chases a cat. As she retrieves and then again loses her hat, Rose is aided by animals such as a cow, a rabbit, and a kangaroo, as well as by a boy. Her hat finally lands in a monkey puzzle tree that no one can climb. A cockatoo lands on the hat and makes a nest, which pleases Rose even as she sheds a tear for her lost chapeau. At the end of the story, Rose's friends give her a new hat, complete with a ribbon to tie under her chin, that is even better than the old one. *Booklist* contributor Barbara Elleman predicted that children "will enjoy the whimsy of this airy, light-as-a-breeze tale."

Called "bibliotherapy at its best" by *School Library Journal* reviewer Rosalyn Pierini, *Up in Heaven* tackles a subject that almost every child has to face at some point: the death of a beloved pet. Arthur spends much of his play time with the family dog, Daisy, but eventually the elderly Daisy starts to sit out the most rambunctious games on the sidelines. When Daisy finally passes away, she looks down from Doggy Heaven and sees how sad Arthur is, so sends the young boy a dream to let him know that she is happy and that it is okay to give his affection to a new puppy. Martha V. Parravano praised the story in *Horn Book* as "comforting and uplifting but not in the least saccharine," while in *Booklist*

Arthur mourns the loss of his dog, Daisy, until she lets him know she is romping happily in heaven in Chichester Clark's self-illustrated story of loss, grief, and comfort. (From Up in Heaven.*)*

Hazel Rochman noted that in her "joyful fantasy" Chichester Clark presents a forthright way to view the loss of a loved one; because *Up in Heaven* "never denies the child's sorrow and loss, the hopeful, loving scenes will help preschoolers move on," Rochman added.

The Story of Horrible Hilda and Henry is a cautionary tale in picture-book form about a brother and sister who like to misbehave: They trash their house, squirt their parents with a hose, have food fights, and tease each other unmercifully. Finally, the children's parents send them to the zoo. After annoying the animals, Hilda and Henry are placed in a cage with Brian, a bad-tempered lion who frightens the siblings so much that they become model children. Their parents take Brian home along with Hilda and Henry, hoping that the lion will act as insurance; however, Clark's last picture shows the children reverting back to their former disobedient ways. Writing in *Booklist,* Ilene Cooper noted that Chichester Clarks's use of "comic-book strips, full-page pictures, and two-page spreads" all work to relay her humorous story "to good effect," while a *Kirkus Reviews* critic claimed that young readers will enjoy the "gleefully exaggerated pranks here, which [Chichester] Clark illustrates with her usual zest."

Tea with Aunt Augusta—published in the United States as *Lunch with Aunt Augusta*—is one of Chichester Clark's most popular works. The story outlines what happens when Jemima, a ring-tailed lemur who is the youngest in her family, goes with her two older broth-

ers to visit their beloved Aunt Augusta. After Jemima gorges herself on the lavish variety of mixed fruits provided by Aunt Augusta, the little lemur cannot keep up with her older brothers on their way home. Lost in the dark, she is rescued by a group of friendly fruit bats, who carry her home in a leaf sling. Jemima is lectured by her parents on overeating, but they welcome her with hugs and kisses. Her brothers, on the other hand, are sent to bed without supper for abandoning their sister in the jungle. Calling Chichester Clark's illustrations "delightfully vivid, witty, and tender," *Times Educational Supplement* reviewer Andrew Davies concluded, "I've never given ring-tailed lemurs much thought before. Now I wish I owned one. In fact I wish I was one." A *Publisher Weekly* reviewer noted the book's "unique and captivating cast" and "playful artwork," while in *Booklist* Hazel Rochman concluded that, "with all its nonsense . . . this satisfying story combines the small child's fear of being lost with the dream of adventure."

With *Little Miss Muffet Counts to Ten*—published in the United States as *Little Miss Muffet's Count-Along Surprise*—Chichester Clark extends the traditional nursery rhyme in a concept book that teaches basic mathematics. Instead of frightening Miss Muffet away, the spider asks her politely to stay. The arachnid is pleased when her animal friends—including bears with chairs and puffins with muffins—arrive to give her a surprise birthday party. When two crocodiles with greedy smiles show up, things get tense; however, they are just bringing the cake. Writing in *School Librarian,* Sarah Reed termed the book a "successful combination of a counting book, traditional rhyme, repetition, a chain story, all beautifully illustrated," while *FamilyFun* reviewer Sandy MacDonald wrote that "The rhymes are tightly sprung, the imagery deliciously imaginative." A critic for *Kirkus Reviews* concluded by calling *Little Miss Muffet's Count-Along Surprise* "a wonderful variation on the nursery rhyme that for once will frighten no one away."

In *More!* little Billy stalls, demanding one more story, one more ice cream, one more game to avoid the dreaded bedtime. When his mother refuses, Billy stomps off to his room, gathers his stuffed toys and the life-size lion that lives behind the curtain, and goes off to the center of the Earth, where he gets more rides, more spins, and more lollipops than he could ever want. Billy becomes over-saturated and finally realizes that all he wants to do is to go home to bed, which he does. *School*

Librarian critic Jane Doonan raved that, with *More!*, "she succeeds in picturing the indescribable."

Shortlisted for the coveted Kate Greenaway Medal for illustration, *I Love You, Blue Kangaroo!* begins a series that includes some of Chichester Clark's most popular books. Lily loves her stuffed blue kangaroo more than any of her other toys, but when she receives new stuffed animals, Blue Kangaroo is pushed to the side. The toy eventually makes his way to the crib of Lily's baby brother, where he is welcomed joyfully. Not surprisingly, when Lily sees Blue Kangaroo in her brother's arms, she realizes that she still loves him and wants him back. Ultimately, Lily comes up with a mutually beneficial plan: she trades all of her new stuffed toys to her baby brother in exchange for her beloved Blue Kangaroo. Writing in the *Times Educational Supplement,* William Feaver stated that Chichester Clark "has perfect pitch as an author/illustrator" and hailed *Blue*

Mimi and her grandma count various things from one to ten as they share a day together in Chichester Clark's self-illustrated picture book. (From Mimi's Book of Counting.)

Kangaroo as "a winner." Stephanie Zvirin, writing in *Booklist,* praised the book's illustrations, noting that they "can open the way to parent-child discussions of selfishness and generosity." A reviewer for *School Library Journal* called *I Love You, Blue Kangaroo!* a "heartwarming story . . . wholly satisfactory."Other books featuring Blue Kangaroo include *Where Are You, Blue Kangaroo?, It Was You, Blue Kangaroo!,* and *What Shall We Do, Blue Kangaroo?,* the last which finds Lily and her favorite toy thinking about ways to pass some free time, and ultimately host a garden tea party to which all of the household toys are invited. Noting that Chichester Clark's technique of depicting the kangaroo's face close up "pulls [readers] . . . into his perspective" and presents a view of childhood from the toy's perspective, *Horn Book* contributor Christine M. Heppermann praised the author/illustrator's use of an "appealingly repetitive text and joyful spring-like colors" throughout the "Blue Kangaroo" series. Citing the "can-do message" of *What Shall We Do, Blue Kangaroo?,* Lisa Dennis added in her *School Library Journal* review that the illustrations "show a cozy, idealized domestic setting. . .—the perfect place for a preschooler to develop a bit of independence."

A pair of young monkeys are the focus of several books by Chichester Clark. In *No More Kissing!* Momo ducks the kisses of relatives, and decides that even among his own affectionate family, there's just too much smooching going on. Realizing that not only monkeys but also lion, snake, and even crocodile families engage in this off-putting practice, Momo goes to the extreme of wearing a sign pronouncing "No More Kissing" when he walks through the jungle, as a way to make his point. However, his attitude starts to change when a new baby brother enters the family, causing *School Library Journal* contributor Linda M. Kenton to note that *No More Kissing!* provides parents with "a fresh approach to introducing a new baby in a family." In the board books *Mimi's Book of Opposites* and *Mimi's Book of Counting* Momo's older cousin is introduced, presenting basic concept to toddlers with the help of several family members. Momo returns to share center stage with his cousin in the picture-book *No More Teasing!,* as Mimi becomes exasperated by Momo's constant joking and just plain pestering. Fortunately, Grandma comes to the rescue and together the two hatch a plot that the impish Momo will not forget. Although their solution involves a cape and a scary mask, Chichester Clark's art "with its happy colors and exotic locale, is not so terrifying as to curdle young readers' blood," concluded a *Kirkus Reviews* contributor.

Biographical and Critical Sources

BOOKS

St. James Guide to Children's Writers, edited by Sara and Tom Pendergast, St. James Press (Detroit, MI), 1999, pp. 230-232.

PERIODICALS

Booklist, April 15, 1989, Ilene Cooper, review of *The Story of Horrible Hilda and Henry,* p. 1464; May 15, 1990, Barbara Elleman, review of *Catch That Hat!,* pp. 1797-1798; May 1, 1992, Hazel Rochman, review of *Lunch with Aunt Augusta,* p. 1606; January 1, 1999, Stephanie Zvirin, review of *I Love You, Blue Kangaroo!,* p. 886; November 1, 2002, Hazel Rochman, review of *It Was You, Blue Kangaroo!,* p. 504; May 15, 2003, Gillian Engberg, review of *What Shall We Do, Blue Kangaroo?,* p. 1669; February 1, 2004, Hazel Rochman, review of *Up in Heaven,* p. 979.

Books for Keeps, January, 1998, p. 18.

FamilyFun, November, 1997, Sandy MacDonald, review of *Little Miss Muffet's Count-Along Surprise.*

Horn Book, March-April, 2002, Martha V. Parravano, review of *No More Kissing!,* p. 201; March-April, 2004, Martha V. Parravano, review of *Up in Heaven,* p. 169; September-October, 2003, Christine M. Heppermann, review of *What Shall We Do, Blue Kangaroo?,* p. 492.

Independent (London, England), May 14, 1998. Sally Williams, review of *More!*

Junior Bookshelf, April, 1996, p. 56.

Kirkus Reviews, April 15, 1989, review of *The Story of Horrible Hilda and Henry,* p. 622; April 15, 1991, review of *I Never Saw a Purple Cow and Other Nonsense Rhymes;* September 15, 1997, review of *Little Miss Muffet's Count-Along Surprise,* p. 1454; December 15, 2001, review of *No More Kissing!,* p. 1755; February 14, 2004, review of *Up in Heaven,* p. 175; January 1, 2005, review of *No More Teasing!,* p. 50; June 1, 2002, review of *It Was You, Blue Kangaroo!,* p. 802.

Ladybug, March, 1997, "Meet the Artist: Emma Chichester Clark," p. 39.

Magpies, September, 1998, p. 28; November, 1998, p. 26.

Publishers Weekly, January 6, 1992, review of *Lunch with Aunt Augusta,* p. 65; January 20, 2003, review of *Follow the Leader!,* p. 80.

School Librarian, August, 1987, Sarah Reed, review of *Little Miss Muffet Counts to Ten,* p. 130; May, 1991, Joan Nellist, review of *I Never Saw a Purple Cow and Other Nonsense Rhymes,* pp. 681-682; autumn, 1998, Jane Doonan, review of *More!,* p. 129.

School Library Journal, April, 1999, review of *I Love You, Blue Kangaroo!;* January, 2002, Linda M. Kenton, review of *No More Kissing!,* p. 96; May, 2003, Rosalyn Pierini, review of *Follow the Leader!,* p. 110; July, 2003, Lisa Dennis, review of *What Shall We Do, Blue Kangaroo?,* p. 88; November, 2003, Olga R. Kuharets, review of *Mimi's Book of Counting,* p. 90; March, 2004, Rosalyn Pierini, review of *Up in Heaven,* p. 155.

Times Educational Supplement, November 6, 1987, Jenny Marshall, "Storybook Worlds," p. 27; February 14, 1992, Andrew Davies, "Having a Good Time," p. 27; December 11, 1998, William Feaver, "Leap of Imagination," p. 37.

Times Literary Supplement, December 4, 1989, Lesley Chamberlain, "Igniting the Imagination," p. 1361.

ONLINE

Andersen Press Web site, http://www.andersenpress.co.uk/ (December 2, 2004).*

*   *   *

COLÓN, Raul

Personal
Male.

Addresses
Agent—c/o Author Mail, Atheneum, Simon & Schuster, 1230 Avenue of the Americas, New York, NY 10020. *E-mail*—raulcolon@aol.com.

Career
Artist and illustrator. Also works as a freelance commercial artist.

Awards, Honors
Silver Medal, and Gold Medal, Society of Illustrators.

Writings

(And illustrator) *Orson Blasts Off!,* Atheneum Books for Young Readers (New York, NY), 2004.

ILLUSTRATOR

Sharon Dennis Wyeth, *Always My Dad,* Knopf (New York, NY), 1995.
Libba Moore Gray, *My Mama Had a Dancing Heart,* Orchard Books (New York, NY), 1995.
John Archambault, *Grandmother's Garden,* Silver Press (Parsippany, NJ), 1997.
Jane Resh Thomas, *Celebration!,* Hyperion Books for Children (New York, NY), 1997.
Pat Mora, *Tomás and the Library Lady,* Knopf (New York, NY), 1997.
Bruce Balan, *Buoy, Home at Sea,* Delacorte Press (New York, NY), 1998.
Robert D. San Souci, *A Weave of Words: An Armenian Tale,* Orchard Books (New York, NY), 1998.
Robert Burleigh, *Hercules,* Silver Whistle (San Diego, CA), 1999.
Deborah Hopkinson, *A Band of Angels: A Story Inspired by the Jubilee Singers,* Atheneum Books for Young Readers (New York, NY), 1999.
Helena Clare Pittman, *The Snowman's Path,* Dial Books for Young Readers (New York, NY), 2000.
Ann Warren Turner, *Secrets from the Dollhouse,* HarperCollins (New York, NY), 2000.

Mary Calhoun, *A Shepherd's Gift,* HarperCollins (New York, NY), 2001.
Robert Burleigh, *Pandora,* Silver Whistle (San Diego, CA), 2002.
Eileen Spinelli, *Rise the Moon,* Dial Books for Young Readers (New York, NY), 2003.
Jane Yolen, *Mightier than the Sword: World Folktales for Strong Boys,* Harcourt (San Diego, CA), 2003.
Susanna Reich, *José!: The Story of José Limón,* Simon & Schuster Books for Young Readers (New York, NY), 2005.
Jonah Winter, *Roberto Clemente: Pride of the Pittsburgh Pirates,* Atheneum Books for Young Readers (New York, NY), 2005.
Karma Wilson, *How to Bake an American Pie,* Margaret K. McElderry Books (New York, NY), in press.

Illustrations have also appeared in periodicals, including *Time, New York Times,* and *Wall Street Journal.*

Sidelights
Growing up to become an artist after becoming inspired by the drawings in his favorite comic books, Raúl Colón has illustrated several children's books, including titles by such noted authors as Jane Yolen, Robert D. San Souci, and Robert Burleigh. In 2004 Colón made his authorial debut with *Orson Blasts Off!,* the story of a young boy who learns to use his imagination. After his computer malfunctions, Orson is first angry, then becomes bored. However, when a toy jack-in-the-box on his bed-side table suddenly comes to life, Orson embarks on an exciting adventure . . . all by using his own creativity. "Imagination takes flight in Colón's familiar but pleasantly illustrated dream story," stated a *Publishers Weekly* reviewer, while Ilene Cooper noted in *Booklist* that although the author is "best known for his gleaming scratchboard-style illustrations," in *Orson Blasts Off!* "he shows he can craft a good story as well." "A flight not only into imaginary realms but also into the delicious world of language awaits readers in this fanciful journey," added *School Library Journal* contributor Marianne Saccardi, praising *Orson Blasts Off!* for its "expansive" watercolor and pencil illustrations.

Biographical and Critical Sources

PERIODICALS

Booklist, June 1, 2002, Gillian Engberg, review of *Pandora,* p. 1711; April 1, 2003, Ed Sullivan, review of *Mightier than the Sword: World Folktales for Strong Boys,* p. 1394; February 1, 2004, Ilene Cooper, review of *Orson Blasts Off!,* p. 974.
Horn Book, May-June, 2003, Susan Dove Lempke, review of *Mightier than the Sword,* p. 362.
Kirkus Reviews, May 1, 2002, review of *Pandora,* p. 650; January 15, 2003, review of *Rise the Moon,* p. 147; April 15, 2004, review of *Mightier than the Sword,* p.614; March 1, 2004, review of *Orson Blasts Off!,* p.220.

Publishers Weekly, December 17, 2001, review of *A Band of Angels: A Story Inspired by the Jubilee Singers,* p.94; April 1, 2002, review of *Pandora,* p. 83; December 16, 2002, review of *Rise the Moon,* p. 66; March 29, 2004, review of *Orson Blasts Off!,* p. 62.

School Library Journal, May, 2002, Patricia Lothrop-Green, review of *Pandora,* p. 134; April, 2003, Rosalyn Pierini, review of *Rise the Moon,* p. 138; May, 2003, Miriam Lang Budin, review of *Mightier than the Sword,* p. 143; April, 2004, Marianne Saccardi, review of *Orson Blasts Off!,* p. 103.

ONLINE

Raul Colón Web site, http://www.raulcolon.com/ (January 5, 2005).*

*   *   *

CUYLER, Margery (Stuyvesant) 1948-
(Daisy Wallace)

Personal

Born December 31, 1948, in Princeton, NJ; daughter of Lewis Baker and Margery Pepperell (Merrill) Cuyler; married John Newman Hewson Perkins (a psychoanalyst), August 23, 1979; children Thomas, Timothy. *Education:* Sarah Lawrence College, B.A., 1970.

Addresses

Home—32 Edgehill St., Princeton, NJ 08540.

Career

Atlantic Monthly Press, Boston, MA, assistant to editor of children's books, 1970-71; Walker & Co., New York, NY, editor of children's books, 1972-74; Holiday House, New York, NY, vice president and editor-in-chief of children's books, 1974-95; Henry Holt & Co., New York, NY, vice president and associate publisher, Books for Young Readers, 1996-97; Golden Books Family Entertainment, vice president and director of trade publishing, 1997-99; Windslow Press, New York, NY, vice president and editor-in-chief, beginning 1999; Marshall Cavendish, Tarrytown, NY, currently director of trade publishing. Lecturer on children's book editing, Rutgers University, 1974, New School for Social Research, 1975, and Vassar College, 1984. Board member, Women's National Book Association and Children's Book Council, 1980-82. Library trustee and member of alumnae board, Sarah Lawrence College

Awards, Honors

Children's Choice designation, International Reading Association/Children's Book Council, for *The Trouble with Soap* and *Witch Poems;* New Jersey Institute of Technology Author's Award, 1988, for *Fat Santa.*

Writings

PICTURE BOOKS

Jewish Holidays, illustrated by Lisa C. Wesson, Holt (New York, NY), 1978.

The All-around Pumpkin Book, illustrated by Corbett Jones, Holt (New York, NY), 1980.

The All-around Christmas Book, illustrated by Corbett Jones, Holt (New York, NY), 1982.

Sir William and the Pumpkin Monster, illustrated by Marcia Winborn, Holt (New York, NY), 1984.

Freckles and Willie, illustrated by Marcia Winborn, Holt (New York, NY), 1986.

Fat Santa, illustrated by Marcia Winborn, Holt (New York, NY), 1987.

Freckles and Jane, illustrated by Leslie Holt Morrill, Holt (New York, NY), 1989.

Shadow's Baby, illustrated by Ellen Weiss, Clarion (New York, NY), 1989.

Baby Dot, illustrated by Ellen Weiss, Clarion (New York, NY), 1990.

Daisy's Crazy Thanksgiving, illustrated by Robin Kramer, Holt (New York, NY), 1990.

That's Good! That's Bad!, illustrated by David Catrow, Holt (New York, NY), 1991.

The Christmas Snowman, illustrated by Johanna Westerman, Arcade, 1992.

Buddy Bear and the Bad Guys, illustrated by Janet Stevens, Clarion, 1993.

The Biggest, Best Snowman, illustrated by Will Hillenbrand, Scholastic (New York, NY), 1998.

From Here to There, illustrated by Yu Cha Pak, Henry Holt (New York, NY), 1999.

One Hundredth-Day Worries, illustrated by Arthur Howard, Simon & Schuster (New York, NY), 2000.

Road Signs: A Harey Race with a Tortoise: An Aesop Fable Adapted, illustrated by Steve Haskamp, 2000.

Stop, Drop, and Roll: Fire Safety, illustrated by Arthur Howard, Simon & Schuster (New York, NY), 2001.

Skeleton Hiccups, illustrated by S. D. Schindler, Margaret K. McElderry Books (New York, NY), 2002.

That's Good! That's Bad! In the Grand Canyon, illustrated by David Catrow, Henry Holt (New York, NY), 2002.

Ah-choo!, illustrated by Bruce McNally, Scholastic (New York, NY), 2002.

Please Say Please!: Penguin's Guide to Manners, illustrated by Will Hillenbrand, Scholastic (New York, NY), 2004.

Big Friends, illustrated by Ezra Tucker, Walker & Co. (New York, NY), 2004.

The Bumpy Little Pumpkin, illustrated by Will Hillenbrand, Scholastic (New York, NY), 2005.

FOR YOUNG READERS

The Trouble with Soap, Dutton (New York, NY), 1982.

Weird Wolf, illustrated by Dirk Zimmer, Holt (New York, NY), 1989.

Invisible in the Third Grade, illustrated by Mirko Gabler, Holt (New York, NY), 1995.

The Battlefield Ghost, illustrated by Arthur Howard, Scholastic (New York, NY), 1999.

FOR CHILDREN; EDITOR, UNDER PSEUDONYM DAISY WALLACE

Monster Poems, illustrated by Kay Chorao, Holiday House (New York, NY), 1976.

Witch Poems, illustrated by Trina Schart Hyman, Holiday House (New York, NY), 1976.

Giant Poems, illustrated by Margot Tomes, Holiday House (New York, NY), 1978.

Ghost Poems, illustrated by Tomie De Paola, Holiday House (New York, NY), 1979.

Fairy Poems, illustrated by Trina Schart Hyman, Holiday House (New York, NY), 1980.

Adaptations

Several of Cuyler's books have been adapted as audiobooks, including *That's Good! That's Bad!* and *One Hundredth-Day Worries.*

Sidelights

Writer Margery Cuyler was already an experienced editor of children's books for the publishing firm of Holiday House when she decided to try her hand at writing. While she once admitted to *Something about the Author* (*SATA*) that her passion has been for editing children's books, she has come to love writing as well, "since it exercises my imagination in a more personal and introspective fashion." In addition to authoring a wide range of both nonfiction and fiction picture books, including *Freckles and Willie, Fat Santa, Skeleton Hiccups,* and *Daisy's Crazy Thanksgiving,* Cuyler has written several popular chapter books for more talented readers.

Born in Princeton, New Jersey, Cuyler was raised in a large family and grew up in the oldest house in town. Competing with four siblings and an equal number of cousins who had joined Cuyler's family after their own mother died, she learned early how to fend for herself, as she once told *SATA.* After graduating from high school, she attended Sarah Lawrence College, earning her bachelor's degree in 1970. From there, it was a quick move to Boston to work for Atlantic Monthly Press before Cuyler returned to New York City and found a job with Holiday House. "I'm a great supporter of the type of small institution that allows the creative spirit to flourish," the author/editor once told *SATA.* "For example, both Sarah Lawrence and Holiday House value independent thinking, and provide the kind of nourishing environment where new ideas can take seed and ripen naturally." Cuyler found Holiday House to be the perfect fit with her own career aspirations; beginning there in 1974, she served as its editor-in-chief for children's fiction for many years before expanding her career opportunities at other publishers, among them Henry Holt, Golden Books, and Winslow Press.

Cuyler's first self-penned work, 1978's *Jewish Holidays,* is a book she admits she should never have written because, not being Jewish, she was not completely familiar with her subject matter and had to rely on the generous assistance of Jewish friends to get her facts straight. Still, it was a first step that led to greater successes. Her second picture book, *The All-around Pumpkin Book,* was written in three days, and was inspired by a dream. "I woke up . . . at two in the morning and I started writing," she told interviewer Jim Roginski in *Behind the Covers: Interviews with Authors and Illustrators of Books for Children and Young Adults.* Visualizing all the illustrations in her mind, she quickly made a dummy of the book, sketched out the pictures as she imagined them, and then added the text. Following the entire life span of the typical Halloween jack-o'-lantern, from seed to garden to its ultimate destiny as either scary goblin or pumpkin pie, the book was described by Ethel L. Heins of *Horn Book* as "a compendium of fascinating and practical facts," as well as a list of nontraditional uses for the fall squash. Pumpkin hamburgers anyone? "Here's a way to stretch Halloween all around the year," commented Barbara Elleman in her *Booklist* appraisal of *The All-around Pumpkin Book.*

Cuyler's *The All-around Christmas Book* uses much the same format as *The All-around Pumpkin Book.* After presenting the story of the Nativity, Cuyler includes a discussion of folklore, crafts, recipes, games, and other information about the Christian holiday, both in its religious and secular manifestations. The wide variety of celebrations undertaken by many different cultures around the world is explored, with answers to such questions as where the tradition of decorating trees came from and an explanation of the history of advent wreaths. Praising the information presented, a *Publishers Weekly* reviewer termed the work "a treasure of holiday lore."

Although her earliest books were nonfiction, Cuyler has penned a number of entertaining picture books for preschoolers and children in the early grades. In *Shadow's Baby,* a little dog is determined to take care of the new baby in his house, but when the infant grows older and wants to play with other things, the attentive Shadow gets in the way. Fortunately, the dog's owner realizes that Shadow feels useless with nothing to care for; the introduction of a new puppy into the home provides a ready solution. Ann A. Flowers, reviewing the book for *Horn Book,* called *Shadow's Baby* "as warm and affectionate as a puppy," while a *Publishers Weekly* critic commended Cuyler's "sensitivity to the feelings of all involved" in this warmhearted story.

Although the author admits to being a cat owner, dogs and their human companions figure prominently in several of Cuyler's stories, including her tales about Freckles the dog and Willie, the teenage boy. In *Freckles and Willie,* Freckles feels forlorn when Willie starts to spend most of his time with a girl named Jane; the girl, for her part, is obviously not a person of character—she dislikes dogs and makes Willie keep Freckles away from her when she's around, which is most of the time. Ultimately, Willie realizes where his true loyalty lies, and boy and dog are once again the best of friends—"a nice lesson in relationships and loyalty," according to a *Publishers Weekly* critic. However, despite her mistake in bringing a jar of flea powder to Freckles's birthday party, Jane redeems herself in *Freckles and Jane,* as Freckles gets the stuck-up teen out of a tight situation involving a German shepherd on the loose and finally gains her affection. A *Kirkus Reviews* commentator dubbed *Freckles and Jane* "a satisfying 'here and now' story."

With *Fat Santa,* Cuyler returns to the subject of Christmas. Molly is determined to wait up for Santa's arrival; she settles into a comfortable chair and listens to Christmas carols on her headphones while she waits. Awakened out of a semi-sleep in the wee hours of the morning by a cloud of ash, Molly hears a voice coming from inside her fireplace—Santa has gotten stuck in the chimney! One experience of being stuck in the chimney is enough for the old fellow; he convinces Molly to don his red jacket and make the rest of his gift-giving rounds, which she does. Praising the book's energy, *Bulletin of the Center for Children's Books* contributor Betsy Hearne cited *Fat Santa* as "a holiday picture book that will be easy for children to listen to, look at, and like." Phillis Wilson of *Booklist* pointed out that "the open end works in this well-constructed plot," while a *Publishers Weekly* critic praised Cuyler for "amiably captur[ing]" the spirit of Christmas Eve.

Cuyler focuses on another holiday in *Daisy's Crazy Thanksgiving.* Daisy begs to be excused from her parents' busy restaurant to join her grandparents, only to discover pandemonium in a house full of eccentric relatives, a menagerie of pet animals, and an absentminded Granny who has again forgotten to turn on the oven for the turkey. "No getting around the success of the story's wacky humor," observed *Booklist* reviewer Denise Wilms, the critic going on to dub the book "offbeat and, intermittently, very funny." A more serious story is at the center of *From Here to There,* which helps young children gain perspective on their role as part of the larger world. Maria Mendoza introduces herself, at first within the context of her role in her family, then to her neighborhood, state, country, and beyond, Cuyler's concept-driven text is enhanced by "gorgeously rendered" watercolor and pastel illustrations by Yu Cha Pak, according to a *Publishers Weekly* critic. Praising *From Here to There* as a "heartfelt picture book," the *Publishers Weekly* reviewer added that, through their book, Cuyler and Pak take readers on an "enlightening journey" that serves as "both a meditation on humanity's small place in the universe and a celebration of each person's immutable individuality."

Skeleton Hiccups also contains a seasonal theme as it relates the efforts of a frustrated skeleton who cannot rid himself of the hiccups. Unfortunately, when you're

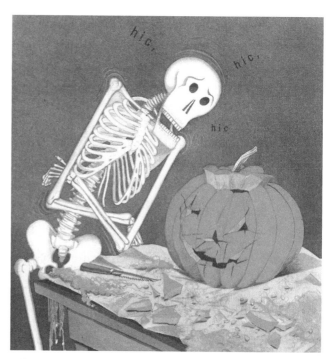

When Skeleton gets hiccups, his friend Ghost searches for a solution in Cuyler's novel Halloween tale. *(From* Skeleton Hiccups, *illustrated by S. D. Schindler.)*

a skeleton the tried-and-true remedy of getting the hiccups scared out of you doesn't work; the most frightening "boo!" of Skeleton's best friend Ghost is nothing new, and drinking water while hanging his head upside down just leaks the liquid out of his empty eye sockets. Praising the quirky artwork of S. D. Schindler, *Booklist* reviewer Jeanette Larson dubbed *Skeleton Hiccups* "a treat for children who can laugh at the slightly macabre," while in *Horn Book* Joanna Rudge Long noted that Cuyler's simple text, with its "hic, hic, hic" refrain, is "sure to have kids giggling and joining in."

That's Good! That's Bad!, Cuyler's story of a little boy traveling by balloon in a wild trip over a zoo, successfully combines sound effects, a large format, and plenty of opportunity for audience participation where "kids will enjoy the push-me-pull-me tension," according to Roger Sutton in his review for the *Bulletin of the Center for Children's Books.* In a sequel, *That's Good! That's Bad! In the Grand Canyon* the young boy joins his grandmother for a trip to the Grand Canyon, where he again encounters good and bad in a series of adventures. *School Library Journal* contributor Marian Drabkin noted that the book, with its humorous plot and sing-songey text, "begs to be read aloud" and would be a "natural for storytime."

Cuyler's first novel, *The Trouble with Soap,* was written after she attended a writer's conference in her capacity as editor. "I sat around for two weeks listening to people read their stuff," she told interviewer Roginski. "Then I started writing." *The Trouble with Soap* is based on its author's own experiences as a not-so-model child. In the novel, thirteen-year-old Lucinda Sokoloff—a/k/a

Soap—is suspended from school due to her excessive zeal in playing practical jokes. After an incident involving Saran Wrap and the toilets in the boys' lavatory cause her to be shipped off to Miss Pringle's Private School for Girls along with partner-in-crime and narrator Laurie Endersby, Soap rejects the snobbish students in favor of her own company. Laurie, on the other hand, desperately wants to be accepted by the in-crowd at her new school, and she ultimately tells a painful secret about her friend's father as a way of gaining that acceptance. A *Publishers Weekly* writer observed that the novel is completely unlike any of Cuyler's former works and "displays impressive versatility.""I wanted to write about what it is that makes twelve-and thirteen-year-old kids so sensitive to peer pressure," Cuyler explained to Roginski of her decision to write books for older readers. "Why do they care so much about what other kids think of them? They're really imprisoned by collective values—how they think, how they dress, how they look at the world. It's a very conformist way of living. It's hard to be outside the collective spirit at that age and yet my character Soap is. That fascinates me because the whole key of life is to break through the walls that parents and society build around you, to be an individual, to express yourself."

The Trouble with Soap has been followed by several more novels for young people, including *Invisible in*

A giant sets off to an island in search of a friend, only to find the inhabitant of the island has come in search of him. (From Big Friends, *written by Cuyler and illustrated by Ezra Tucker.*)

the *Third Grade, Weird Wolf,* and *The Battlefield Ghost.* In *Weird Wolf* Cuyler's protagonist again has trouble fitting in with his friends. It's not so much that nine-year-old Harry Walpole is unpopular, but he has a terribly embarrassing problem: he turns into a wolf when the moon is full. As inconvenient as this is—it gets increasingly difficult to come up with excuses for being caught running around naked outside at sunrise—Harry is fortunate that his blood lust only extends to hamburgers. A research trip to the library results in several possible cures for his problem, and one of them actually works, in a book critics praised as appropriately seductive for even the most reluctant of readers. Indeed, *Weird Wolf* is "destined for greatness in the opinion of werewolf-crazy eight year olds," noted Kathryn Pierson in a review for the *Bulletin of the Center for Children's Books.*

The Battlefield Ghost marks a bit of a departure for Cuyler, because the story mixes historical fact with fiction. Actually, the book was inspired by the author's interest in her home town of Princeton, where she lives in the same colonial-era house where she grew up. In the story, John and his sister move into what their new Princeton neighbors claim is a house haunted by the spirits of the 1777 Battle of Princeton. After a series of uncanny but not terribly frightening hauntings, the children learn that their home is haunted by a Hessian mercenary soldier who was killed while fighting for the British. When they discover that the soldier is wandering in search of his horse, John and his sister figure out how to put the spirit to rest in a novel that *Booklist* reviewer Jean Franklin praised as a "fast read" that "offers a nice blend of realism and the supernatural." A *Publishers Weekly* contributor also praised Cuyler for presenting the history of the battle in an entertaining fashion, noting that in addition to providing historical notes, *The Battlefield Ghost* ends with a "vivid, ghostly reenactment on the battlefield."

Biographical and Critical Sources

BOOKS

Behind the Covers: Interviews with Authors and Illustra-
    tors of Books for Children and Young Adults, Librar-
    ies Unlimited (Littleton, CO), 1985, pp. 51-58.
Seventh Book of Junior Authors and Illustrators, H. W.
    Wilson (Bronx, NY), 1996, pp. 73-74.

PERIODICALS

Booklist, July 15, 1980, Barbara Elleman, review of *The*
    All-around Pumpkin Book, p. 1674; November 1,
    1987, Phillis Wilson, review of *Fat Santa,* p. 474; Oc-
    tober 1, 1990, Denise Wilms, review of *Daisy's Crazy*
    Thanksgiving, p. 338; December 1, 1991, Deborah
    Abbott, review of *That's Good! That's Bad!,* pp. 702-
    703; December 15, 1998, Lauren Peterson, review of

The Biggest, Best Snowman, p. 754; June 1, 1999, Susan Dove Lempke, review of *From Here to There,* p. 1838; November 1, 1999, GraceAnne A. DeCandido, review of *The Hundredth-Day Worries,* p. 537; November 15, 1999, Jean Franklin, review of *The Battlefield Ghost,* p. 626; December 1, 2000, Michael Cart, review of *Roadsigns: A Harey Race with a Tortoise,* p. 717; September 15, 2002, John Peters, review of *Skeleton Hiccups,* p. 245.

Bulletin of the Center for Children's Books, January, 1979, Zena Sutherland, review of *Jewish Holidays,* p. 77; November, 1982, p. 45; October, 1984, p. 22; February, 1986, pp. 105-106; November, 1987, Betsy Hearne, review of *Fat Santa,* p. 46; January, 1990, Kathryn Pierson, review of *Weird Wolf,* pp. 107-108; November, 1990, p. 57; December, 1991, Roger Sutton, review of *That's Good! That's Bad!,* p. 87; April 15, 2004, Hazel Rochman, review of *Big Friends,* p. 1445.

Horn Book, October, 1980, Ethel L. Heins, review of *The All-around Pumpkin Book,* p. 534; April, 1982, pp. 162-163; January, 1990, Ann A. Flowers, review of *Shadow's Baby,* p. 50; November, 1990, p. 718; September-October, 2002, Joanna Rudge Long, review of *Skeleton Hiccups,* p. 549; May-June, 2004, Christine M. Hepperman, review of *Please Say Please!: Penguin's Guide to Manners,* p. 310.

Kirkus Reviews, November 1, 1989, review of *Freckles and Jane,* p. 602; March 15, 2002, review of *That's Good! That's Bad! In the Grand Canyon,* p. 408; April 1, 2004, review of *Skeleton Hiccups,* p. 327.

New York Times Book Review, October 26, 1980, p. 27.

Publishers Weekly, May 28, 1982, review of *The Trouble with Soap,* p. 72; September 17, 1982, review of *The All-around Christmas Book,* p. 115; April 25, 1986, review of *Freckles and Willie,* p. 78; October 13, 1989, review of *Shadow's Baby,* p. 51; October 30, 1987, review of *Fat Santa,* p. 70; November 9, 1998, review of *The Biggest, Best Snowman,* p. 75; March 15, 1999, review of *From Here to There,* p. 56; September 27, 1999, review of *The Battlefield Ghost,* p. 106; December 13, 1999, review of *One Hundredth-Day Worries,* p. 81; July 10, 2000, review of *Roadsigns,* p. 62; September 23, 2002, review of *Skeleton Hiccups,* p. 22; April 19, 2004, review of *Please Say Please!,* p. 59.

School Library Journal, January, 1979, Joan C. Feldman, review of *Jewish Holidays,* p. 41. December, 1984, p. 69; April, 1986, p. 69; April, 1990, p. 116; February, 1990, p. 72; November, 1991, p. 92; September, 2000, Louise L. Sherman, review of *Roadsigns,* p. 193; April, 2001, Teresa Bateman, review of *One Hundredth-Day Worries,* p. 74; October, 2001, Roxanne Burg, review of *Stop, Drop, and Roll: Fire Safety,* p. 113; June, 2002, Marian Drabkin, review of *That's Good! That's Bad! In the Grand Canyon,* p. 92; October, 2002, Piper L. Nyman, review of *Skeleton Hiccups,* p. 100.

ONLINE

Margery Cuyler Web site, http://www.margerycuyler.com/ (December 2, 2004).*

D

DAVENPORT, John 1960-

Personal
Born November 2, 1960, in San Francisco, CA; son of Eugene (a car salesman) and Rose (a secretary; maiden name, Kendziorski) Davenport; married Jennifer Locatelli (a preschool teacher), August 12, 1988; children: William, Andrew. *Education:* San Francisco State University, B.A., 1990; University of Connecticut, M.A., 1991, Ph.D., 1999. *Hobbies and other interests:* Archery, fishing.

Addresses
Home—46 Hilltop Drive, San Carlos, CA 94070. *E-mail*—johncdaven@aol.com.

Career
Social studies and language arts teacher at St. Raymond Elementary School, Menlo Park, CA, 1997-02, and Corte Madera Middle School, Portola Valley, CA, beginning 2002. *Military service:* U.S. Army, 1978-82.

Member
American Historical Society, Society for History Education, National Council for the Social Studies.

Writings

Saladin, Chelsea House (Philadelphia, PA), 2003.
The U.S.-Mexico Border: The Treaty of Guadalupe Hildalgo, Chelsea House (Philadelphia, PA), 2004.
The Mason-Dixon Line, Chelsea House (Philadelphia, PA), 2004.
C. S. Lewis, Chelsea House (Philadelphia, PA), 2004.
The Louisiana Territory, Chelsea House (Philadelphia, PA), 2005.

Contributor to books, including Mark Stafford, *W. E. B. Du Bois: Scholar and Activist,* Chelsea House (Philadelphia, PA), 2004; Mary Lawler, *Marcus Garvey:* *Black Nationalist Leader,* Chelsea House, 2004; and Terry Bisson, *Nat Turner: Slave Revolt Leader,* Chelsea House, 2004. Contributor to periodicals, including *Journal of History* and *Retrospection.*

Work in Progress
The Young Readers' Who, What, When, Where, How, and Why Book of the Holocaust.

Sidelights
John Davenport is a middle-school history teacher and the author of several educational books for young readers, including *Saladin, The U.S.-Mexico Border: The Treaty of Guadalupe Hildalgo,* and *The Mason-Dixon Line,* all of which focus on the history of North America. In addition, Davenport's biography *C. S. Lewis* sheds light on the life of the twentieth-century English author noted for penning the popular "Chronicles of Narnia." The author's overall goal in writing is to further educate today's youth by providing young people with a broader view of their place in the world and a sense of how they can impact the ever-forming history of tomorrow.

Davenport told *Something about the Author:* "I write in order to communicate to young people the joy and sorrow, the triumph and tragedy of human life. My hope is that my readers will come to appreciate, by examining the lives of other people at other times, the full richness of their own existence. I strive, moreover, to help my audience locate itself within the historical sweep of the larger society and culture they will someday inherit. Taken together, I work to give young people a better sense of themselves and their place in the world. This task, this challenge drives my pen through its strokes."

*   *   *

DELACRE, Lulu 1957-

Personal
Born December 20, 1957, in Hato Rey, Puerto Rico; daughter of Georges Carlos (a philosophy professor)

and Marta (a French professor; maiden name, Orzabal) Delacre; married Arturo E. Betancourt (a physician), August 2, 1980. *Education:* Attended University of Puerto Rico, 1976-77; Ecole Supérieure d'Arts Graphiques, degree (first in class), 1980. *Religion:* Roman Catholic.

Addresses

Home and office—11429 Oak Leaf Dr., Silver Springs, MD 20109. *E-mail*—luludela@erols.com.

Career

Children's book author and freelance illustrator, 1980—. Juror for Society of Illustrators Original Art Show, 1997, and National Book Award, 2003. *Exhibitions:* Artwork exhibited at Muséo de Arte de Puerto Rico, San Juan; University of Puerto Rico Art Museum, Memorial Art Gallery, Rochester, NY; Keene State College Children's Literature Gallery; Museo de Arte de Ponce, Puerto Rico; and elsewhere.

Member

Authors Guild, Children's Book Guild of Washington, DC, Society of Children's Book Writers and Illustrators.

Awards, Honors

American Bookseller Pick of the Lists designation, 1991, for *Peter Cottontail's Easter Book,* 1993, for *Vejigantes Masquerader,* and 1994 for *The Bossy Gallito; Américas* Book Award, and National Council of Teachers of English Notable Children's Book in Language Arts designation, both 1993, both for *Vejigantes Masquerader;* Notable Trade Book in the Field of Social Studies designation, Aesop Accolade listee, and New York Public Library Best Book for Reading and Sharing designation, all 1994, and Pura Belpré Honor, American Library Association, 1996, all for *The Bossy Gallito; Américas* Commended Title, 1996, for *Golden Tales: Myths, Legends, and Folktales from Latin America,* and 2000, for *Salsa Stories;* named Maryland Woman in the Arts, 1998; named Write from Maryland Author, 1999; Notable Book for a Global Society designation, and Outstanding International Books listee, both International Reading Association, and Notable Social Studies Trade Book for Young People designation, Children's Book Council, all 2000, and *Criticas* Best Books for 2002 listee, all for *Salsa Stories.*

Writings

SELF-ILLUSTRATED

A.B.C. Rhymes, Little Simon (New York, NY), 1984.
Counting Rhymes, Little Simon (New York, NY), 1984.
Kitten Rhymes, Little Simon (New York, NY), 1984.

Lullabies, Little Simon (New York, NY), 1984.
Nathan and Nicholas Alexander, Scholastic Inc. (New York, NY), 1986.
Nathan's Fishing Trip, Scholastic Inc. (New York, NY), 1988.
Good Time with Baby, Grosset & Dunlap (New York, NY), 1989.
Time for School, Nathan!, Scholastic Inc. (New York, NY), 1989.
Arroz con leche: Popular Songs and Rhymes from Latin America, translation by Elena Paz, Scholastic Inc. (New York, NY), 1989.
Las navidades: Popular Christmas Songs from Latin America, translation by Elena Paz, Scholastic (New York, NY), 1990.
Peter Cottontail's Easter Book, Scholastic Inc. (New York, NY), 1991.
Nathan's Balloon Adventure, Scholastic Inc. (New York, NY), 1991.
Vejigantes Masquerader, Scholastic Inc. (New York, NY), 1993.
Golden Tales: Myths, Legends, and Folktales from Latin America, Scholastic Inc. (New York, NY), 1996.
Salsa Stories, Scholastic Inc. (New York, NY), 2000.
Rafi and Rosi, HarperCollins (New York, NY), 2003.
Arrorró mi niño: Latino Lullabies and Gentle Games, Lee & Low Books (New York, NY), 2004.
Rafi and Rosi: Carnival!, HarperCollins (New York, NY), in press.

ILLUSTRATOR

Hannah Kimball, *Maria and Mr. Feathers,* Follett Pub. Co. (Chicago, IL), 1982.
Oretta Leigh, *Aloysius Sebastian Mozart Mouse,* Simon & Schuster (New York, NY), 1984.
Beatrix Potter, *The Tale of Peter Rabbit, and Other Stories,* J. Messner (New York, NY), 1985.
Kenneth Grahame, *The Wind in the Willows: The Open Road,* Little Simon (New York, NY), 1985.
Lucía M. González, reteller, *The Bossy Gallito,* Scholastic Inc. (New York, NY), 1994.
Lucía M. González, reteller, *Señor Cat's Romance, and Other Favorite Stories from Latin America,* Scholastic Inc. (New York, NY), 1997.
Carmen T. Bernier-Grand, *Shake It, Morena!, and Other Folklore from Puerto Rico,* Millbrook Press (Brookfield, CT), 2002.
Georgina Lázaro, *El flamboyán amarillo,* Lectorum Publications (New York, NY), 2004.

Contributor of illustrations to periodicals, including *Sesame Street, World, Your Big Backyard, Nuestra Gente,* and *Scholastic Storyworks,* as well as to textbooks for Macmillan, Houghton Mifflin, Follett Publishing Co., Scott Foresman, Addison Wesley, and Rigby Elsevier.

Sidelights

Lulu Delacre began her career as an illustrator in 1980, shortly after graduating from art school, but quickly moved into writing her own picture-book texts for young children with her 1986 work *Nathan and Nicholas Alexander*. While continuing to create artwork for authors such as Georgina Lázaro, Carmen T. Bernier-Grand, and Lucía M. González, Delacre has also explored her own Latina heritage in works such as *Golden Tales: Myths, Legends, and Folktales from Latin America, Arrorró mi niño: Latino Lullabies and Gentle Games,* and *Rafi and Rosi,* the last a picture book that depicts the day-to-day goings-on in the lives of two tree frogs in Delacre's characteristic pastel-toned colored pencil and watercolor wash. "I delight in creating books that portray my own culture with authenticity in both words and pictures," Delacre noted on her Web site. "And if painting the people and the places of Latin America true to their own beauty fosters respect; or if sharing some of their golden tales builds bridges, I want to keep on doing it."

Golden Tales: Myths, Legends, and Folktales from Latin America collects stories that the author/illustrator recalls from her childhood in Puerto Rico. Some of the stories included are taken from native cultures, while others concern the Spanish conquistadores or have even more recent origins. Delacre also includes a map showing the areas referred to in the stories, as well as a guide to the pronunciation of Spanish and native Indian terms that provides help for careful readers. Praising the book as "impressively presented," *Booklist* contributor Annie Ayers commended Delacre for assembling an anthology sure to be "welcomed by all who have . . . sought in vain for such an introductory treasury." Containing what *Booklist* reviewer Hazel Rochman described as "bright beautiful oil-wash illustrations," Delacre's *Arrorró mi niño* similarly collects fifteen lullabies, singing games, and other cradle songs that "reflect the diversity of the Latino experience."Of Argentinian ancestry, Delacre was born in Puerto Rico, and had an idyllic childhood exploring the nearby beaches with her older sister Cecilia. The two sisters often were put in the care of their grandmother, and Delacre once recalled to *Something about the Author* (*SATA*) that the woman "had set a space aside where each one of us had a big pile of drawings that we did while at her home. I liked to colour a lot and always rejoiced at the sight of the growing pile." Encouraging the girls' efforts, Delacre's grandmother never threw away any of their work, and when Delacre—who described herself as "a skinny, small, big-eared girl"—turned ten years old, her equally supportive parents enrolled her in drawing lessons.

By the time she was in high school, Delacre was certain that she wanted to become a commercial artist. After graduation she moved to Paris, France, where she studied photography, typography, design, and illustration at

Enhanced by her vibrant oil paintings, Lulu Delacre presents the culture and history of thirteen countries in her collection of writings from Latin America. (From Golden Tales, *retold and illustrated by Delacre.)*

the Ecole Supérieure d'Arts Graphiques and graduated at the top of her class. As she recalled to *SATA:* "One day, during my second year of studies in Paris, I went to see an exhibit at a small gallery near the school. It was an exhibit on the work of Maurice Sendak. When I left the gallery, very much impressed, I suddenly realized that I wanted to become a good children's book illustrator; something I am still working at." Reviewers have consistently praised Delacre's contributions to illustrated children's literature, Maeve Visser Knoth noting in a *Horn Book* review of Lucia M. González' *Señor Cat's Romance, and Other Favorite Stories from Latin America* that Delacre's "vivid, sprightly paintings" contain the "many regional details" that strengthen the book's multicultural appeal.

Now making her home in the United States, Delacre has traveled widely, visiting many schools across the country and also touring overseas. "Besides living in Puerto Rico, Argentina, Paris, and the United States," she once explained, "I have been to Egypt, Israel, Greece, Italy, Spain, Netherlands, Brazil, Mexico, Ecuador, Peru, the Dominican Republic, Thailand, and England. My mother language is Spanish, but I speak fluent French and English." "I believe childhood should be a wonderful stage in a person's life," she once told

SATA, and if my drawings add a little happiness in a child's day, I consider my life fulfilled."

Biographical and Critical Sources

PERIODICALS

Booklist, May 15, 1994, Ilene Cooper, review of *The Bossy Gallito,* p. 1680; December 15, 1996, Annie Ayers, review of *Golden Tales: Myths, Legends and Folktales from Latin America,* p. 722; February 1, 1997, Karen Morgan, review of *Señor Cat's Romance, and Other Favorite Stories from Latin America,* p. 943; May 1, 2000, Gillian Engberg, review of *Salsa Stories,* p.1665; July, 2004, Hazel Rochman, review of *Arrorró mi niño: Latino Lullabies and Gentle Games,* p. 1846.

Horn Book, September-October, 1994, Maeve Visser Knoth, review of *The Bossy Gallito: A Traditional Cuban Folk Tale,* p. 602; March-April, 1997, Maeve Visser Knoth, review of *Señor Cat's Romance, and Other Favorite Stories from Latin America,* p. 207.

Kirkus Reviews, March 15, 2002, review of *Shake It, Morena!, and Other Folklore from Puerto Rico,* p. 406.

Publishers Weekly, January 11, 1993, review of *Vejigantes Masquerader,* p. 63; January 6, 1997, review of *Señor Cat's Romance, and Other Favorite Stories from Latin America,* p. 73; March 20, 2000, review of *Salsa Stories,* p. 94.

School Library Journal, March, 2000, Ann Welton, review of *Salsa Stories,* p. 237; August, 2002, Paul M. Kienlen, review of *Salsa Stories,* p. S59.

ONLINE

Lulu Delacre Web site, http://www.luludelacre.com/ (January 5, 2005).

*   *   *

DOYLE, Brian 1935-

Personal

Born August 12, 1935, in Ottawa, Ontario, Canada; son of Hulbert (a government worker and customs broker) and Charlotte (a homemaker and poet; maiden name, Duff) Doyle; married Jacqueline Aronson (a homemaker and government worker), December 26, 1960; children: Megan, Ryan. *Education:* Carleton College, B.A., 1957; graduate study at Ottawa University.

Addresses

Home—118 Ossington Ave., Ottawa, Ontario, Canada K1S 3B8.

Career

Author, playwright, scriptwriter, educator. Worked variously as a journalist, waiter, taxi driver, driving instructor, office worker, bricklayer, and jazz singer. Teacher at Glebe Collegiate Institute (high school) and Ottawa Technical High School, Ottawa, Ontario, Canada; head of English department at Glebe Collegiate; served on Ottawa Board of Education; member of faculty, Queen's University, Kingston, Ontario. *Military service:* Canadian Naval Reserve, 1955-56.

Member

James Joyce Society of Ottawa (chairman).

Awards, Honors

Book of the Year Award, Canadian Library Association (CLA), 1983, for *Up to Low,* and 1989, for *Easy Avenue;* three-time runner-up, Governor General's Literary Award, Canada Council; Mr. Christie's Book Award, Canadian Children's Book Centre/Communications Jeunesse, 1990, for *Covered Bridge;* Vicky Metcalf Award, Canadian Authors Association, 1991, for body of work; CLA Book of the Year Award, and Mr. Christie's Book Award, both 1997, both for *Uncle Ronald;* Hans Christian Andersen Author Award shortlist, International Board on Books for Young People, 1998; National Chapter Award, Leishman Prize, Geoffrey Bilson Award nomination, Rugh Schwartz Award nomination, Governor General's Literary Award nomination, and Mr. Christie's Book Award Silver Seal, all 2001, all for *Mary Ann Alice.*

Writings

Hey, Dad!, Groundwood Books (Toronto, Ontario, Canada), 1978.

You Can Pick Me up at Peggy's Cove, Groundwood Books (Toronto, Ontario, Canada), 1978.

Up to Low (also see below), Groundwood Books (Toronto, Ontario, Canada), 1982.

Angel Square (also see below), Groundwood Books (Toronto, Ontario, Canada), 1984, Bradbury Press (New York, NY), 1986.

Easy Avenue (also see below), Groundwood Books (Toronto, Ontario, Canada), 1988.

Covered Bridge (also see below), Groundwood Books (Toronto, Ontario, Canada), 1990.

Spud Sweetgrass, Groundwood Books (Toronto, Ontario, Canada), 1992.

Spud in Winter, Groundwood Books (Toronto, Ontario, Canada), 1995.

Uncle Ronald (also see below), Groundwood Books (Toronto, Ontario, Canada), 1996.

The Low Life: Five Great Tales from up and down the River (includes *Uncle Ronald, Angel Square, Easy Avenue, Covered Bridge,* and *Up to Low*), Groundwood Books (Toronto, Ontario, Canada), 1999, Douglas & McIntyre (Berkeley, CA), 2002.

Mary Ann Alice, Groundwood Books (Toronto, Ontario, Canada), 2001, Douglas & McIntyre (Berkeley, CA), 2002.

Boy O'Boy, Douglas & McIntyre (Berkeley, CA), 2003.

Author of plays for children. Contributor of articles and short stories to newspapers and magazines, including the Toronto *Globe and Mail* and *Fiddlehead*. Doyle's works have been translated into French and published in Braille editions.

Author's works have been translated into German, French, Italian, and Scandinavian.

Adaptations

You Can Pick Me up at Peggy's Cove was made into a film directed by Don McBrearty and into a video released by Beacon Films, Inc., in 1982. CNIB released sound recordings of *You Can Pick Me up at Peggy's Cove* in 1984, *Angel Square* in 1985, *Easy Avenue* in 1994, and *Covered Bridge* in 1995; *Easy Avenue* was also released as a sound recording by the Library Services Branch, Vancouver, British Columbia, in 1994. *Meet the Author: Brian Doyle* was released as a short film in 1987. *Angel Square* was made into a film directed by Ann Wheeler and released by the National Film Board of Canada, Edmonton, Alberta, 1990.

Sidelights

Among Canada's most distinguished authors of middle-grade and young-adult novels, Brian Doyle is acclaimed as an exceptional storyteller as well as a talented writer whose works reflect both insight and sensitivity in depicting the moral dilemmas of young people. Doyle's books, which take place in both historical and contemporary periods, often draw on Doyle's own experiences while growing up in near Ottawa, Canada. His works are unique within Canadian literature due to his focus on the inner lives of his characters and themes such as the relationships between parents and children, the power of love, the acceptance of death and loss, and the need for tolerance. Doyle's novels, which include *Uncle Ronald, Mary Ann Alice, Covered Bridge,* and *You Can Pick Me up at Peggy's Cove,* depict teens coming of age as they confront personal strife and social injustice, drawing on their inner strength to come to terms with the chaos around them. Considered somewhat sophisticated, his prose has been compared to that of authors such as Charles Dickens, J. D. Salinger, Kurt Vonnegut, and Judy Blume. Noting the author's "delicious way with metaphors," *Quill and Quire* contributor Sandra Martin also praised his ability to pen "lean nostalgic tales in spare elegant prose."

Although his works contain death—including murder and suicide—as well as child and spousal abuse, drunkenness, and violent racial strife, Doyle's sense of humor is considered one of his most appealing features. He favors fast-moving plots and an intimate narrative style that is considered both spare and elegant; his works—which reflect the author's love of wordplay and the tall tale as well as his frequent use of the three-word paragraph—also include puns, songs, colloquialisms, headlines, jingles, and recipes. Writing in *Books for Young*

People, Eva Martin called Doyle "one of the most daring and experimental writers of young-adult novels. He deals with the most sensitive of issues—race, violence, anti-social activity of all sorts—with a tongue-in-cheek humor that never denigrates the human spirit." Writing in *Magpies,* Agnes Nieuwenhuizen concluded, "Perhaps Doyle's most extraordinary feat is that there is never a sense of design or message or moralising. What shines through his work is a breath of vision and tolerance and a quirky exuberance and curiosity even in the face of adversity and resistance." Many of Doyle's most popular early novels are collected in the 1999 anthology *The Low Life.*

Born in Ottawa, Doyle grew up in two "homes": his family's home in the ethnically diverse section of Ottawa where he spent the school year and a log cabin on the Gatineau River near Low, Quebec, about forty miles north of town, where he spent his summers. Doyle's memories of his parents, siblings, and neighbors as well as the landscape and atmosphere he encountered as a child greatly influenced his writing, as did his experiences raising his own two children. As Nieuwenhuizen described it in *Magpies,* "Family is at the centre of Doyle's life and work." For his part, the author credits his father, Hulbert Doyle, and his paternal grandfather for nurturing his instincts as a storyteller. As Doyle once told *Something about the Author (SATA),* "I loved sitting around listening to my father and my grandfather. Both of them were wonderful storytellers, and they didn't tell stories so much as they just talked." Doyle recalled that his grandfather was "constantly reciting verse—songs and poems, ballads mostly—about this adventure and that adventure. My father wasn't a literary person, although he was the best raconteur I ever met. If in my work there is a kind of sound, that's where it comes from, rhythms inherited from sitting around listening to my father's family exchanging their world vision." Doyle's mother, Charlotte Duff Doyle, also influenced her son's development as a writer; she was "a literary person. She was not a verbal person at all. However, she wrote well and wrote privately. She was very private, but she'd show her poetry to me." Doyle's mother wrote the poem "Sea Savour," which begins the author's second novel *You Can Pick Me up at Peggy's Cove.*

Despite fond memories of his family's storytelling tradition, Doyle grew up in a difficult home environment: his father was cruel when he drank and his mother, who cared for Doyle's mentally disabled older sister, Pamela, as well as for the rest of the family, was often overwhelmed. When he was in the eighth grade, Pamela, who had Down's syndrome, passed away; Doyle's memories of Pamela and the toll her caretaking took on his mother, has led him to include several characters with disabilities in his books. Although Doyle did not shine as a student until he reached college, he enjoyed reading comic books and childhood classics such as *Heidi* and *The Adventures of Huckleberry Finn.* When he was about ten years old, Doyle decided that he wanted to be a writer. "The first writing I did was in the snow," he recalled to *SATA*. "I wrote 'Gerald is a bastard,'" referring to a boyhood friend. When Hulbert Doyle discovered what his son had written, he took the boy inside the house, and, the author remembered, "put a piece of paper down on the table and gave me a pencil. Then he said, 'Say some more, but don't write it in the snow because he'll see it.'"

In high school at Ottawa's Glebe Collegiate Institute, Doyle began submitting short stories to magazines, some of which came back with personal rejection letters. However, writing only occupied a small part of his teen years. Doyle played football, won medals in gymnastics, and published poetry in the yearbook; he also fought, stole, and skipped school. As the author recalled in an essay for *Something about the Author Autobiography Series* (*SAAS*), "Once, on a Christmas exam in geometry, I got three out of a hundred. Three percent. Then something very peculiar happens. On the Easter exam, I got 99 out of a hundred! How can that be? It's as though I just suddenly woke up! The teacher is convinced I cheated." Later, he was nominated for head

boy, but had his name taken off the list by the vice principal, who, the author recalled, called Doyle "a show-off. And . . . a bum. And I'll never amount to anything. And my shirt is always hanging out of my pants. When he says this I realize I've been a pain for six years. But what he says about 'never amounting to anything.' That hurts."

After graduating from Glebe Collegiate, Doyle attended Carleton College in Ottawa, where he majored in journalism and met Jackie Aronson, the woman he would later marry. He read novels, plays, and poetry by prominent Canadian writers as well as by such authors as Homer, William Shakespeare, Mark Twain, James Joyce, Ernest Hemingway, J. D. Salinger, and Dylan Thomas while working dozens of jobs to pay for college. Just before graduation, he won a prize for an essay he wrote on the Gatineau River Valley; right after graduation, he became a reporter for the Toronto *Telegram*. He soon left journalism to teach high school in Ottawa; he also completed the course work for a master's degree in literature at Ottawa University, but left before writing his thesis.

While working as a teacher, Doyle continued his writing, working as a columnist for a local newspaper and publishing a short story in the literary magazine *Fiddlehead*. After he and his wife adopted two children, Megan and Ryan, and became involved in local theater, his writing took a new turn when he began writing well-received plays for his students. Doyle also became somewhat of a celebrity when one of his articles on the ineffectuality of teacher training was quoted in the Toronto *Globe and Mail*. Offered a position at his alma mater, Glebe Collegiate, Doyle became head of that school's English department and continued to write well-received student plays, including ten musicals and a satirical parody of Shakespeare's *Hamlet* before retiring from teaching in 1991.

Doyle published his first book for young readers, *Hey, Dad!*, in 1978. A story for middle graders that he wrote for his daughter Megan, *Hey, Dad!* uses the journey motif—both literal and symbolic—to represent the growing maturity of its young protagonist. In an interview with Nieuwenhuizen for *Magpies*, Doyle explained that his original intention was to "write a very personal tale about and to my ten-year-old daughter. She was not reading very much and I was hunting around for reading material but didn't much like what was around. . . . We had gone on a family trip across Canada and had both kept journals, so I strung together an episodic chronicle about our trip. I made it funny, but included stuff she had been grappling with. Stuff about time and mortality."

In *Hey, Dad!*, thirteen-year-old Megan grows beyond her childhood self-absorption and begins to question the connection between love and death during a family trip. Writing in *In Review*, Irma McDonough described the book as "a new author with a new approach to realistic

In a town near the Gatineau River in 1926, Mary Ann Alice tries to solve a mystery while her precious home is threatened by the construction of a dam in Doyle's novel. (Cover photo by Tim Fuller.)

writing for young people. Doyle has written a junior novel we have been waiting for—one that is not a trend book or a social documentary; rather, a novel that will reinforce young people's tender feelings and gently encourage them to find their own answers to the age-old questions." Doyle followed *Hey, Dad!* with *You Can Pick Me up at Peggy's Cove,* another story for middle graders that he wrote for his son Ryan. In this novel the young narrator—also named Ryan—is sent to stay in the Nova Scotia fishing town of Peggy's Cove, a popular tourist attraction, after his father deserts the family during a mid-life crisis. Thinking that his dad will return if he gets into trouble, Ryan starts stealing from tourists; however, his friendship with fisherman Eddie and Eddie's mute partner Wingding leads Ryan to self-knowledge and, eventually, to heroism. Writing in *In Review,* Mickie McClear commented that Doyle "has that rare gift of insight which enables him to breathe life into his portrayals of adolescents," while Jon C. Stott concluded in a *World of Children's Books* review that *You Can Pick Me up at Peggy's Cove* is a "sensitive and compelling story which will continue to find readers for many years to come."

Set in the town of Martindale, near Quebec's Gatineau River, during the Canadian government's 1926 Paugam dam project, *Mary Ann Alice* finds seventh-grader Mary Ann Alice McCrank watching as her community and its surrounding landscape are transformed by a huge man-made lake that leaves much of the area under water. As narrator, Mary Ann, a young poetess, describes the drowning of the landscape in what *Horn Book* contributor Martha V. Parravano called a "conversational, idiosyncratic voice"; as work on the dam changes the lives of those around her Mary Ann also learns compassion, and gains understanding about even the frustrating people in her life. Calling Mary Ann a "bluntly spoken" character, *School Library Journal* reviewer Robyn Ryan Vandenbroek praised Doyle's novel for containing a "fast-paced plot that comes alive with memorable characters." In *Resource Links* Joan Marshall wrote that Doyle's "wry, observant wit shines in every corner of this marvelous story," and added that, with her "cheeky, irreverent attitude," the central character of *Mary Ann Alice* "is like the town historian who sees all the connections."*Mary Ann Alice,* like many of Doyle's novels, relies on a young, relatively immature narrator for many of its insights. As the novelist once explained to *SATA:* "As a child, I recall sitting around listening to the adults in my life talking away. They never left me out, and they didn't explain or anything either. I think that's how I would like to treat kids that are around me, put it out there, let them figure it out." "Kids at ten know a lot," he observed. "They're very wise, although they're not slippery, not good enough liars yet. A ten-year-old boy or girl is as smart as she'll ever get or he'll ever get. So it's with that kind of belief I'm comfortable making the ten-year-old's insights as deep as I want."

Boy O'Boy reflects Doyle's interest in creating realistic young protagonists, as well as the author's willingness

Doyle's protagonist young Martin O'Boy struggles with tensions at home and unwelcome sexual advances from the church organist in the course of an Ottawa summer during World War II. (Cover photo by Tim Fuller.)

to tackle difficult subjects. The novel focuses on Martin O'Boy, who lives with his mother, alcoholic father, and mentally ill twin brother in Ottawa. With his favorite grandmother recently passed away and World War II having taken its toll on both his family and his community, Martin finds that his job singing in the church choir is one of his few pleasures. Tragically, the choir's director, Mr. George, preys on the boy's youth and innocence, until Martin and friend Billy, a fellow victim of Mr. George's sexual abuse, find a way to gain their revenge. Noting that Doyle creates a world that is "believably real," *School Library Journal* reviewer Coop Renner added that the "naive voice" of the book's observant youthful narrator "mirrors the limited understanding of the book's prospective reader." *Booklist* reviewer Todd Morning added that the narration, in present tense, incorporates "a precise, highly observant voice that always seems genuine," and the novel's "lively colloquial dialogue and period details create a rich historical portrait." Praising the optimism underlying Doyle's depiction of the young protagonist wresting with moral questions, a *Publishers Weekly* reviewer noted that, regardless of Martin's "relentlessly bleak circumstances, he manages to keep some hope alive."

With *Up to Low* Doyle produced his first young-adult novel. Set in Quebec's Gatineau Hills and based on the author's boyhood experiences at his family's cabin, *Up to Low* takes place during the early 1950s and features teenage narrator Young Tommy, a boy who has recently lost his mother. Tommy travels to the town of Low with his father and his father's alcoholic friend Frank. On the way, the group stops at many taverns, where the men tell Tommy about Mean Hughie, the meanest man in Gatineau, who has vanished into the wilderness to die of cancer. When the companions reach Low, a town filled with comic residents, Tommy is awestruck by the beauty of Mean Hughie's eighteen-year-old daughter Baby Bridget, a girl with striking green eyes whose arm was cut off accidentally by a binding machine. Bridget and Tommy embark on a journey to find Mean Hughie, and the strength of their growing love for each other provides spiritual healing for both teens. Writing in *Quill and Quire,* Joan McGrath noted that *Up to Low* "is something special among books for young adults," while Mary Ainslie Smith in *Books in Canada* praised the book as "Doyle's best novel yet." In *Angel Square* Doyle again features Tommy as narrator, but this time the setting is the multicultural Lowertown area of urban Ottawa. On his way home from school, Tommy crosses Angel Square, a place where fights between French Canadian, Irish Catholic, and Jewish kids take place daily. When anti-Semitism results in the critical injury of the father of Tommy's best friend, Sammy Rosenberg, Tommy fights back and finds the culprit by working with a network of his Jewish, Irish, and French-Canadian friends. As Nieuwenhuizen noted, the children "get together to deal with an adult situation." Writing in *Quill and Quire,* Paul Kropp called *Angel Square* "a real triumph of young adult writing," while a reviewer for the *Children's Book News* concluded: "Through Tommy's eyes we see the absurdity of racism and the hope that at least one child will understand our differences. This is Brian Doyle's best and guarantees an enjoyable yet sobering read for all." Explaining to *SATA* that *Angel Square* is "very close to what my youth was," Doyle added that the novel "was hard to relax with, because it touched on some pain." In this book he includes a portrait of his retarded sister Pamela, who shares her name with the character in the novel. "There's a little bit of her in each book," he admitted.

In *Uncle Ronald,* Doyle features a character first introduced in *Up to Low:* "Crazy Mickey," Tommy's hundred-year-old great-grandfather. Now one hundred and twelve, Mickey narrates the events of the winter he was twelve years old. The son of a drunken and abusive father, Mickey is smuggled by his mother onto a train that takes the boy from Ottawa into the Gatineau Hills, where he is to stay with his Uncle Ronald and his middle-aged aunts, the O'Malley girls. Mickey's relatives prove to be warm and welcoming, and he bonds

In Doyle's novel, peppered with historical events from turn-of-the-century Ottawa, Mickey goes to stay with his Uncle Ronald, kind and gentle and just the person Mickey needs to heal the psychological wounds left by his abusive father. (Cover illustration by Ludmilla Temertey.)

with his uncle's horse, Second-Chance Lance. Fascinated by the stories about the exploits of the locals, Mickey joins in their attempt to outsmart the government bailiffs trying to collect back taxes. Underpinning the story is Mickey's fear that his father will try to come and collect him and his newly arrived mother; when he does, the man meets a violent end when he falls under the wheels of a train while trying to steal Second-Chance Lance. Writing in *Horn Book,* Martha V. Parravano called *Uncle Ronald* a "not-to-be-missed read—for the evocation of setting, for the genuine feel of the lively local stories, and for the sheer joy of Doyle's prose." "This book is mainly remarkable for the warmth and compassion," observed Mary-Ann Stouck, adding in her *Canadian Children's Literature* review that *Uncle Ronald* "never descend[s] . . . into sentimentality." *Easy Avenue,* a novel for young adults, introduces narrator Hubbo O'Driscoll, an impoverished orphan who is left in the care of a very old, very kind distant relative known only as Mrs. Driscoll. Hubbo becomes involved with Fleurette Featherstone Fitchell, a fellow resident of the Uplands Emergency Shelter and the daughter of a Lowertown prostitute. When he enters Glebe Collegiate Institute—the high school Doyle attended and where he later taught—Hubbo becomes caught between the people from the shelter and the elite Glebe students. When he gets a job as the companion to a wealthy elderly woman and begins to receive money from a mysterious benefactor, Hubbo fabricates an identity that is acceptable to the snobbish members of an exclusive club he wishes to join, but eventually recognizes where his true loyalties are. *Easy Avenue* was praised as "a delightful mix of comedy, irony, and sentiment" by a *Maclean's* contributor, while in *Canadian Children's Literature,* Lionel Adey dubbed the novel a "sometimes grim, sometimes amusing, but never unwholesome tale."

Set in 1950 and inspired by the author's memories of his first real job, *Covered Bridge* is the second of Doyle's stories about Hubbo. Having moved to a farm in the small Quebec community of Mushrat Creek, Hubbo becomes the part-time caretaker of a wooden covered bridge that has become a memorial to the tragic romance of two lovers, Ophelia and Oscar. Ophelia, who suffered from a brain tumor, jumped from the bridge to her death; her suicide caused the local priest to ban her from being buried in consecrated ground. When the bridge is slated for demolition in the name of progress, Hubbo works to preserve it, and in the process helps to correct the moral injustice done Ophelia, whose ghost he has seen. Nieuwenhuizen called *Covered Bridge* a "hauntingly beautiful tribute to conserving and respecting old things."

Doyle's two books about John "Spud" Sweetgrass, a half-Irish, half-Ojibway teen who is nicknamed for his ability to cook the perfect French fry, are considered somewhat of a departure from his earlier works. Comic mysteries for young adults written in a staccato style, *Spud Sweetgrass* and *Spud in Winter* involve a young protagonist who is trying to come to terms with his father's death, with his boss's shady business dealings, and with a gang-style slaying he has witnessed. In the first book, Spud and his friends Connie Pan and Dink the Thinker attempt to discover who is dumping grease from Spud's french-fry stand into the Ottawa River. A critic in *Kirkus Reviews* commented that, "Replete with laughs, tears, and twists, plus a young hero to admire and a cardboard villain to hate, "*Spud Sweetgrass* "will slide down effortlessly, like all proper snacks." Connie Tyrrell Burns noted in her *School Library Journal* review that the author "paints a vivid, touching portrait of one boy's coming-of-age. . ... Doyle captures perfectly adolescent thoughts and feelings, and writes of them with humor and tenderness." In *Spud in Winter,* Spud draws on his Native Canadian heritage to find the courage to identify a mafiosi killer. Writing in *Quill and Quire,* Mary Beaty called the "Spud Sweetgrass" books "divertimenti: enjoyable, but not as memorable as Doyle's other works," but also found *Spud in Winter* as

"a definite match for the first Spud book." In her review of both volumes for the *Bulletin of the Center for Children's Books,* Deborah Stevenson noted: "What really makes these books sparkle is Doyle's writing. . ... These will offer readers some literary northern light." Writing in *Canadian Children's Literature,* Jim Gellert acknowledged that the "Spud" books blend "humour and a recognizable Canadian setting to provide a convincing, realistic context in which Doyle probes contemporary social themes and issues."

Doyle explained to *SATA* that "There is a perception that young people are worried about menstruation, divorce, masturbation, hitchhiking—subjects that just carloads of kids' books are written about. These are not the concerns of young people at all as far as I'm concerned. They are the concerns of adults who have young people. Kids' concerns are classical concerns: Am I brave? Am I a hero? Am I honest? Do I love this person? Am I afraid? Am I admired? Am I weak? Am I strong? These are their concerns, and that's what I write about."

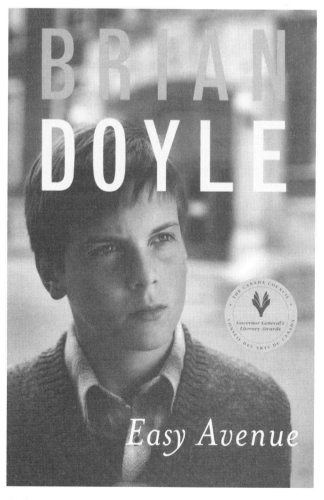

As he approaches high school in Canada during the years just following World War II, Hubbo O'Driscoll falls in love with a girl from another social class. (Cover illustration by Ludmilla Temertey.)

Biographical and Critical Sources

BOOKS

Children's Books and Their Creators, edited by Anita Silvey, Houghton Mifflin (Boston, MA), 1995, p. 210.
Children's Literature Review, Volume 22, Gale (Detroit, MI), 1991, pp. 27-34.
Something about the Author Autobiography Series, Volume 16, Gale (Detroit, MI), 1993, pp. 127-141.
Twentieth-Century Young-Adult Writers, St. James Press (Detroit, MI), 1994, pp. 189-191.

PERIODICALS

Booklist, June 1, 1996, pp. 1696-1697; April 1, 2004, Todd Morning, review of *Boy O'Boy,* p. 1360.
Books for Young People, October, 1988, Eva Martin, "'Easy Avenue' Is Vintage Doyle," pp. 12, 18.
Books in Canada, February, 1983, Mary Ainslie Smith, review of *Up to Low,* pp. 32-33.
Bulletin of the Center for Children's Books, July-August, 1996, Deborah Stevenson, review of *Spud Sweetgrass* and *Spud in Winter,* p. 67; February, 1997, p. 203.
Canadian Children's Literature, number 54, 1989, Lionel Adey, "Doyle for the Early Teens," pp. 71-72; number 64, 1991, pp. 90-91; winter, 1995, Jim Gellert, "Spud Does Ottawa—Again," p. 80; summer, 1998, Mary-Ann Stouck, review of *Uncle Ronald,* pp. 67-68.
Canadian Materials, March, 1991, p. 88.
Children's Book News (Toronto, Ontario, Canada), December, 1984, review of *Angel Square,* p. 3.
Horn Book, May-June, 1997, Martha V. Parravano, review of *Uncle Ronald,* p. 318; May-June, 2002, Martha V. Parravano, review of *Mary Ann Alice,* p. 327.

In Review, autumn, 1978, Irma McDonough, review of *Hey, Dad!,* p. 57; August, 1980, Mickie McClear, review of *You Can Pick Me up at Peggy's Cove,* p. 45.
Kirkus Reviews, March 1, 1996, review of *Spud Sweetgrass,* p. 372.
Maclean's, December 26, 1988, "Tidings of Fun," p. N6.
Magpies, November, 1994, Agnes Nieuwenhuizen, "Looking Deeply but Not Far" (interview), pp. 11-13.
Publishers Weekly, April 5, 2004, review of *Boy O'Boy,* p.63.
Quill and Quire, November, 1982, Joan McGrath, "A Clutch of Juvenile Novels with No-Nonsense Plots," p. 26; December, 1982, Ann Vanderhoof, "Prankster, Teacher, Writer: Brian Doyle Is up to Good," p. 27; November, 1984, Paul Kropp, "Growing up Is Hard to Do: Leaving the Boy Behind," p. 18; October, 1990, Sandra Martin, review of *Covered Bridge,* p. 13; March, 1995, Mary Beaty, review of *Spud in Winter,* p. 75; October, 1996, Maureen Garvie, review of *Uncle Ronald,* p. 49.
Resource Links, February, 2002, Joan Marshall, review of *Mary Ann Alice,* p. 24.
School Library Journal, September, 1996, Connie Tyrrell Burns, review of *Spud Sweetgrass,* p. 224; June, 2002, Robyn Ryan Vandenbroek, review of *Mary Ann Alice,* p. 137; February, 2004, Coop Renner, review of *Boy O'Boy,* p. 146.
World of Children's Books, Volume VI, 1981, Jon C. Stott, review of *You Can Pick Me up at Peggy's Cove,* pp. 27-33.

ONLINE

Groundwood Books Web site, http://www.groundwoodbooks.com/ (December 2, 2004), "Brian Doyle."*

E-F

EARLS, Nick 1963-

Personal

Born October 8, 1963, in Newtownards, Northern Ireland; immigrated to Australia, 1972; son of John (a management consultant) and Angela (a medical practitioner; maiden name, Sloan) Earls; married Sarah Garvey (a legal policy officer), April 13, 1991. *Education:* University of Queensland, M.B.B.S. (second-class honours), 1986. *Hobbies and other interests:* Tennis, travel.

Addresses

Home—Brisbane, Queensland, Australia. *Agent*—Curtis Brown, P.O. Box 19, Paddington, New South Wales 2021, Australia. *E-mail*—nickearls@mpx.com.au.

Career

Physician working in Brisbane, Queensland, Australia, 1987-94; freelance writer, 1988—. *Medical Observer,* Queensland, continuing medical education editor, beginning 1994. Has worked variously as a heath insurance fund senior medical officer, actor, blood collector, and record album executive producer. Mater Hospitals Trust, ambassador; Kids Who Make a Difference, patron; War Child U.K., Australian founding chair. Has appeared in television commercials promoting Brisbane.

Awards, Honors

Steele Rudd Award runner-up, 1993, for *Passion;* 3M Talking Book of the Year Award, Young People's category, 1996, and CBE/International Youth Library (Munich) Notable Book, 1997, both for *After January;* Talking Book of the Year Award shortlist, 1997, and Betty Trask Award (United Kingdom), 1998, both for *Zigzag Street;* Queensland Premier's Export Award finalist, 1999; Children's Book Council of Australia Book of the Year for Older Readers, 2000, for *Forty-eight Shades of Brown.*

Writings

FOR YOUNG ADULTS

After January (young adult novel), University of Queensland Press (St. Lucia, Queensland, Australia), 1996, published as *After Summer,* Houghton Mifflin (Boston, MA), 2005.
Forty-eight Shades of Brown, Penguin (Ringwood, Victoria, Australia), 1999, Graphia (Boston, MA), 2004.
Making Laws for Clouds, Penguin (Ringwood, Victoria, Australia), 2002.

ADULT FICTION

Passion (short stories), University of Queensland Press (St. Lucia, Australia), 1992.
Zigzag Street, Anchor (New York, NY), 1996.
Bachelor Kisses (also see below), Penguin (Ringwood, Victoria, Australia), 1998.
Headgames (short stories), Viking (Ringwood, Victoria, Australia), 1999.
Perfect Skin (also see below), Viking (Ringwood, Victoria, Australia), 2000, St. Martin's Press (New York, NY), 2001.
Solid Gold (includes *Bachelor Kisses* and *Perfect Skin*), 2001.
World of Chickens, Viking (Ringwood, Victoria, Australia), 2001, published as *Two to Go,* St. Martin's Griffin (New York, NY), 2003.
The Thompson Gunner, Viking (Ringwood, Victoria, Australia), 2004.

Contributor of short fiction to anthologies, including *Nightmares in Paradise,* University of Queensland Press, 1995.

Adaptations

After January and *Forty-eight Shades of Brown* were adapted as plays by Philip Dean and published by Currency Press. *Zigzag Street* was adapted as a feature film; *Forty-eight Shades of Brown* was optioned for film; *Bachelor Kisses* was adapted as a television pilot in Australia. Several of Earls' books have been adapted as audiobooks, read by the author.

Sidelights

Australian novelist Nick Earls broadened his focus to write for a teen audience with *After January,* which was hailed by both critics and readers after its publication in 1996. Praising Earls' book as "the sort of teenage novel I believe needs to be published," Robyn Sheahan remarked in a *Viewpoint* review that *After January* is "the beginning of a new kind of Australian teenage novel, one which recognises that adolescence does not end at seventeen, that there are still crucial paths to be negotiated between childhood and adulthood." Earls has continued to produce books for teen readers that focus on high schoolers working to make the transition from childhood to adulthood while also negotiating a new romance with a strong and independent young woman, and has been interspersing such novels as *Forty-eight Shades of Brown* and *Making Laws for Clouds* in between his growing list of popular adult fiction.

Born in Northern Ireland, Earls moved to Australia with his parents in 1972, and graduated with a medical de-

After his father takes a job in Switzerland, Dan stays behind to live with his young aunt and soon discovers that life with her is both fascinating and frustrating. (Cover photos by G. K. Hart, Vikki Hart, and Roger Wright.)

gree from the University of Queensland in 1986. After working as a general practitioner for several years, he moved into writing, penning short fiction and advertising copy as a freelancer while also editing a medical journal. Then, "late in 1993, I was asked to write a short story for the fifteen-to-eighteen age group," he once explained to *Something about the Author (SATA).* "I was reluctant to try, because I didn't know the market, but the editor persuaded me. She suggested I come up with a central character in this age group, and approach the story simply as a piece of fiction. 'Remember what you were like when you were that age,' she told me, and I could. Sometimes far too easily." Earls' trip down memory land allowed him to remember "all kinds of insecurities and perceived inadequacies and routine moments of desperation. In fact," he added, "the recollections were so vivid the character wouldn't leave me alone after I'd written the story." As a freelancer, he cast about for other ways of using his new character, and decided to cast him in a novel.

"I couldn't recall anything quite like what I had in mind," Earls noted of his time plotting out *After January.* "I couldn't recall anything that seemed particularly real or relevant to me. . .. So I wondered if I could write the sort of book that I would desperately have wanted to have read at that age, a book that gets inside the head of its central character, and ends up saying 'It's okay. You might feel very undesirable. You might have all these insecurities and improbable dreams. But you're okay. You're normal. You'll be fine. Look at this. . ..'"

After January is the story of seventeen-year-old Alex Delaney, who is poised on the brink of adulthood, still unsure of who he is, and what he needs to do with his life. Having completed his secondary-school education and waiting for notification of acceptance into law school—the Australian school year ends in December, rather than in June as in the United States—Alex spends the month of January in a kind of emotional flux. Smart but shy and timid, he has an introspective nature, and his tall, lanky appearance has always made him feel gawky around girls. Now, as he kills time surfing at the beach or talking to neighbors, he has the sense that his life is about to change, and it does when Alex meets and falls in love with a young woman named Fortuna. The daughter of a Bohemian potter, she is a worldly free spirit, in contrast to Alex's restrained, middle-class self. Calling *After January* "a genuinely witty book," Pam Macintyre wrote in the *Australian Book Review* that Earls' young adult novel "has many of those moments of insight when first love opens new ways of looking at the world." Gillian Swan agreed in *Fiction Focus,* maintaining that in the novel, which is narrated, like all Earls' novels, in the first person by its teen protagonist, "Earls has captured the 'nowhere' feeling that exists when people have finished with one part of life but not yet started on the next; the waiting, the reflection, the looking forward, the not knowing." "In writing *After January,* I wanted to explore contemporary issues, but in a different context," the author explained. "There are no heavy messages, and humour and irony are of great importance. It is a story of the strong feelings and small happenings that, at seventeen, mean a great deal."

Earls has continued to return to the universal feelings and events of the transition time between teen-and adulthood in his other YA novels. In *Forty-eight Shades of Brown* he introduces almost-seventeen-year-old Dan, who is finishing his final year of high school while rooming with his twenty-something, university-going Aunt Jacq and Jacq's housemate, psychology major Naomi. When he begins to crush on the beautiful Naomi, Dan's attentions wander from calculus, and his first year of independence finds his actions dictated more by hormones than free intellectual choice. Praising the novel, a *Publishers Weekly* critic cited Earls' protagonist for his "dry sense of humor and [his] intellectual bent," and wrote that the author "perfectly captures the obsessive, self-conscious, confused state of mind that goes along with adolescence." A *Kirkus Reviews* contributor dubbed the first-person narration in *Forty-eight Shades of Brown* "wickedly funny," while in *School Library Journal* Miranda Doyle praised Dan as a "wonderful, complex character" and the novel as "insightful, appealing, and very funny."

Biographical and Critical Sources

PERIODICALS

Australian, January 27, 1996.
Australian Book Review, February-March, 1996, Pam Macintyre, review of *After January,* p. 56.
Booklist, July, 2004, Gillian Engberg, review of *Forty-eight Shades of Brown,* p. 1833.
Fiction Focus, Volume 10, number 2, Gillian Swan, review of *After January,* 1996.
Kirkus Reviews, June 1, 2004, review of *Forty-eight Shades of Brown,* p. 535.
Magpies, May, 1996, p. 47.
Publishers Weekly, June 28, 2004, review of *Forty-eight Shades of Brown,* p. 51.
School Library Journal, June, 2004, Miranda Doyle, review of *Forty-eight Shades of Brown,* p. 138.
Sydney Morning Herald, February 24, 1996.
Viewpoint, autumn, 1996, pp. 37-38; winter, 1996, Robyn Sheahan, review of *After January* and interview with Earls, pp. 31-33.

ONLINE

Age Online, http://www.theage.com/ (August 14, 2004), Nicola Walker, review of *The Thompson Gunner.*
Nick Earls Web site, http://www.nickearls.com/ (January 17, 2005).*

FLEISCHMAN, Paul 1952-

Personal

Born September 5, 1952, in Monterey, CA; son of Albert Sidney (a children's author) and Beth (Taylor) Fleischman; married (divorced); married second wife, Patty; children: (first marriage) Seth, Dana. *Education:* Attended University of California, Berkeley, 1970-72; University of New Mexico, B.A., 1977.

Addresses

Home—P.O. Box 646, Aromas, CA 95004.

Career

Author. Worked variously as a carpenter, bagel baker, bookstore clerk, library aide, and proofreader.

Member

Authors Guild, Society of Children's Book Writers and Illustrators.

Awards, Honors

Silver Medal, Commonwealth Club of California, Golden Kite Honor Book designation, Society of Children's Book Writers and Illustrators (SCBWI), and outstanding book designation, *New York Times,* all 1980, all for *The Half-a-Moon Inn;* Newbery Honor Book, American Library Association (ALA), 1983, for *Graven Images: Three Stories;* Golden Kite Honor Book designation, and Parents' Choice Award, Parents' Choice Foundation, both 1983, both for *Path of the Pale Horse;* *Boston Globe-Horn Book* Honor Book designation, ALA Best Books for Young Adults nomination, both 1988, and Newbery Medal, 1989, all for *Joyful Noise: Poems for Two Voices; Boston Globe-Horn Book* Honor Book designation, 1990, and ALA Notable Book designation, 1991, both for *Saturnalia;* Golden Kite Honor Book designation, 1992, for *The Borning Room;* Scott O'Dell Award, and Silver Medal, Commonwealth Club of California, both 1994, both for *Bull Run;* Jane Addams Children's Book Awards honor designation, and Golden Kite Honor Book designation, both 1998, both for *Seedfolks;* Golden Kite Honor Book designation, 1999, for *Whirligig;* PEN West Literary Award, 2000, and California Young Reader's Medal, 2002, both for *Weslandia;* National Book Award finalist, 2003, for *Breakout;* Leo Politi Golden Author Award, 2005.

Writings

FOR CHILDREN

The Birthday Tree, illustrated by Marcia Sewall, Harper (New York, NY), 1979.

Paul Fleischman

The Half-a-Moon Inn, illustrated by Kathy Jacobi, Harper (New York, NY), 1980.

Graven Images: Three Stories, illustrated by Andrew Glass, Harper (New York, NY), 1982, Candlewick Press (Cambridge, MA), 2005.

The Animal Hedge (picture book), illustrated by Lydia Dabcovich, Dutton (New York, NY), 1983, illustrated by Bagram Ibatoulline, Candlewick Press (Cambridge, MA), 2003.

Path of the Pale Horse, Harper (New York, NY), 1983.

Phoebe Danger, Detective, in the Case of the Two-Minute Cough, illustrated by Margot Apple, Houghton (Boston, MA), 1983.

Finzel the Farsighted, illustrated by Marcia Sewall, Dutton (New York, NY), 1983.

Coming-and-Going Men: Four Tales, illustrated by Randy Gaul, Harper (New York, NY), 1985.

I Am Phoenix: Poems for Two Voices, illustrated by Ken Nutt, Harper (New York, NY), 1985.

Rear-View Mirrors, Harper (New York, NY), 1986.

Rondo in C, illustrated by Janet Wentworth, Harper (New York, NY), 1988.

Joyful Noise: Poems for Two Voices, illustrated by Eric Beddows, Harper (New York, NY), 1988.

Saturnalia, Harper (New York, NY), 1990.

Shadow Play (picture book), illustrated by Eric Beddows, Harper (New York, NY), 1990.

The Borning Room, HarperCollins (New York, NY), 1991.

Time Train, illustrated by Claire Ewart, HarperCollins (New York, NY), 1991.

Townsend's Warbler (nonfiction), HarperCollins (New York, NY), 1992.

Bull Run, woodcuts by David Frampton, HarperCollins (New York, NY), 1993.

Copier Creations, illustrated by David Cain, HarperCollins (New York, NY), 1993.

A Fate Totally Worse than Death, Candlewick Press (Cambridge, MA), 1995.

Dateline: Troy, illustrated by Gwen Frankfeldt and Glenn Morrow, Candlewick Press (Cambridge, MA), 1996.

Seedfolks, HarperCollins (New York, NY), 1997.

Whirligig, Holt (New York, NY), 1998.

Weslandia, illustrated by Kevin Hawkes, Candlewick Press (Cambridge, MA), 1999.

Mind's Eye, Holt (New York, NY), 1999.

Lost!: A Story in String, illustrated by C. B. Mordan, Holt (New York, NY), 2000.

Big Talk: Poems for Four Voices, illustrated by Beppe Giacobbe, Candlewick Press (Cambridge, MA), 2000.

(Editor) *Cannibal in the Mirror,* photographs by John Whalen, Twenty-first-Century Books (Brookfield, CT), 2000.

Seek, Cricket Books (Chicago, IL), 2001.

Breakout, Cricket Books (Chicago, IL), 2003.

Sidewalk Circus, illustrated by Kevin Hawkes, Candlewick Press (Cambridge, MA), 2004.

Zap (play; produced in New York, NY, 2004), Candlewick Press (Cambridge, MA), 2005.

Contributor to various journals and magazines.

Sidelights

Paul Fleischman is a Newbery Award-winning author of books for both children and young adults. He blends musical language with quirky looks at the world as viewed through the lens of human and natural history. "I'm a maker at heart," Fleischman declared in an essay for *School Library Journal.* By that, Fleischman meant that he creates stories out of the most unlikely found objects: forgotten bits of history, the detritus of bookstores and scrapbooks. Comparing writing to the creation of found sculptures, Fleischman explained the making of his books: "I collect materials, relying heavily on chance. I sort and discard. I envision possible shapes the book might take. . .. A sculpture grows upward; paragraphs grow down."

Fleischman's subject-matter has ranged from the insect world to a bloody U.S. Civil War battle, the limitations of medicine, a world turned upside-down, or a class trip that is transformed into a time-travel expedition. His works, which include novels, picture books, poems, and short stories, "are written with consummate skill," noted Cooki Slone in *Children's Books and Their Creators,* "and his stylistic range is as varied as is his choice of format." With his first book, *The Birthday Tree,* in which a young boy is connected to the tree planted at his birth, Fleischman's talent was recognized, and with each new book he has proven his ability to write supernatural mysteries as well as paeans to nature, consistently paying close attention to the sound of words and the shape of language.

Born in Monterey, California, in 1952, Fleischman grew up in Santa Monica, the son of well-known children's author Sid Fleischman. "Growing up hearing the wonderful works of my father . . . read aloud as they rolled out of the typewriter, I was exposed to books," Fleischman recalled in *School Library Journal,* "but was not a reader and certainly had no plans to be a writer." Instead of holing up in libraries as a youth, Fleischman and his sisters spent time on their bicycles exploring the streets and alleyways of their beach town. These explorations soon became foraging expeditions, as the children gathered other people's castaways from trash cans. However, while growing up in a writer's household the young Fleischman absorbed the elements of story without knowing it. In 1977, when he was about to graduate from college and was casting around for a suitable occupation, writing presented itself to him as a real possibility because he had witnessed his father's success as an author.

Fleischman's first book, *The Birthday Tree,* showed that he had potential as an author, and from that first book he has branched out into a wide range of themes and styles. Early young adult-books include the Edgar Allan Poe-and Nathaniel Hawthorne-inspired *Graven Images* and *The Half-a-Moon Inn,* the former a Newbery honor book. Fleischman blends his love of research and his musical approach to language into these works. "I write only a page or so a day," he explained in his 1989 Newbery acceptance speech, as published in *Horn Book.* "After several books it dawned on me that this was because I was writing prose that scanned, something that makes for slow progress." His "scanned prose," or verse-like writing with rhythm, meter, and occasional internal rhyme, is as close as Fleischman feels he can get to composing music, one of the loves of his life. "All my prose is written in 4/4 time," Fleischman explained.

The author's poet-like concerns for the rhythm of language is apparent in books such as *Joyful Noise: Poems for Two Voices,* in which Fleischman presents fourteen poems that celebrate the insect world, and *Big Talk: Poems for Four Voices.* The poems in *Joyful Noise* are onomatopoeic, their texts echoing the sounds made by the insects themselves, and are intended to be read aloud. Mary M. Burns, reviewing the poetry collection for *Horn Book,* called *Joyful Noise* a "marvelous, lyrical evocation of the insect world" and concluded that "Each selection is a gem, polished to perfection. If Paul Fleischman never wrote another book, his reputation would remain secure with this one." The Newbery committee agreed with Burns and numerous other reviewers, awarding Fleischman the 1989 Newbery Medal for *Joyful Noise.* Interestingly, the author's father, Sid Fleischman, had received that same award just two years previously. In *Big Talk,* which *Booklist* reviewer Gillian Engberg dubbed "perfect for classroom theatre," a color-coded text helps four readers collaborate on reciting the three poetic narratives: "The Quiet Evenings Here," "Seventh-Grade Soap Opera," and "Ghost's Grace."

"The likely cacophony will bring giggles as readers work on getting the hang of all this big talk," quipped Margaret Bush in her review of the book for *School Library Journal.*

In addition to his passion for music, Fleischman is also fascinated by the past. Much of this he credits to his father's own love for research and history; he also noted in *School Library Journal* the serendipity that led him on a cross-country bicycle trip and to live in a 200-year-old house in the New Hampshire woods. It was a time of revelation for Fleischman, long before he thought of becoming a writer. He learned of seasons, of the names for birds and plants, and felt—in the absence of electricity—as if he were living two centuries earlier. Recalling his long list of novels, short stories, poems, and nonfiction books in *School Library Journal,* Fleischman declared that "None of those book would have been written had I not lived in that house."

Fleischman's abiding interest in the past has led him to create an impressive group of historical novels and nonfiction, ranging throughout his earliest fiction and continuing through such novels as *Saturnalia, The Borning Room,* and *Bull Run,* as well as through the nonfiction works *Townsend's Warbler* and *Dateline: Troy.* Focusing on the white man's treatment of both servants and Native Americans, *Saturnalia* is set in Boston in 1681 and plays with the idea of a world turned upside down, as during the Roman festival Saturnalia. The book focuses on a young Narragansett Indian boy in search of his twin brother as well as his heritage, both of which he lost six years earlier when his village was attacked by whites. "The writing is lyrical with somber tones, bright and lively notes, and quiet, thoughtful stretches," commented Amy Kellman in *School Library Journal,* adding that *Saturnalia* is "a very special book for a special audience." *Booklist* reviewer Denise M. Wilms concluded that "this absorbing story exemplifies Fleischman's graceful, finely honed use of the English language," while Raymond E. Houser noted in *Voice of Youth Advocates* that the novel "will challenge the most mature reader with its vocabulary and symbolic approach."

Fleischman deals in first-person narrative in *The Borning Room,* a novel that relates the life story of Georgina Lott. Georgina tells her story to a portrait painter called in to do her picture before she dies, and all of the action takes place in the borning room in which she was brought into the world. Fleischman weaves larger history, such as the U.S. Civil War and the underground railroad, as well as domestic history, into his fictional tapestry. Writing in *Booklist,* Hazel Rochman observed that "Rebirth comes through connection and loving memory and through art. And it comes through stories, like this one." Zena Sutherland concluded in the *Bulletin of the Center for Children's Books* that *The Borning Room* is "smoothly knit" and a "moving family chronicle."

A farmer lovingly trims the hedges of his new home in shapes that remind him of the animals he was forced to sell during a severe drought in Fleischman's tale of grief and acceptance. (From The Animal Hedge, *illustrated by Bagram Ibatoulline.)*

With *Bull Run,* Fleischman highlights that well-known civil war battle, as seen through the eyes of sixteen different men and women. Samantha Hunt, writing in the *Voice of Youth Advocates,* described the novel as a "remarkable series of vignettes," comparing Fleischman's characterization to that employed by twentieth-century writer Edgar Lee Masters in his *Spoon River Anthology.* "Literally, this work stands alone in juvenile and young adult fiction," Hunt remarked, noting that *Bull Run* does for juvenile prose what Fleischman's *Joyful Noise* accomplished for juvenile poetry. A *Publishers Weekly* reviewer observed that, "like a Shaker cabinetmaker, Fleischman creates stories of deceptively simple design . . . that resonate with grace and beauty," and concluded that *Bull Run* "is a tour de force that should not be missed." Carolyn Phelan concluded in *Booklist* that by "abandoning the conventions of narrative fiction, Fleischman tells a vivid, many-sided story in this original and moving book."

Fleischman also serves up nonfiction in his *Townsend's Warbler.* This book tells the story of two nineteenth-century naturalists, John Townsend and Thomas Nuttall, who made their way across the country in search of new plants and animals, including the tiny bird featured in the book's title. Lois Ringquist noted in *Five Owls* that "Fleischman brings to life the adventure" that lies behind the tiny stuffed bird in the natural history display.

In *Dateline: Troy* the author employs a current-newspaper format to bring to life the events surrounding the Trojan War, juxtaposing the war as related by Homer against modern-day headlines. Shirley Wilton, writing in *School Library Journal,* noted that "What comes across in Fleischman's fine retelling is the universality of the human qualities of greed, treachery, and violence." Betsy Hearne concluded in the *Bulletin of the Center for Children's Books* that *Dateline: Troy* is a "thought-provoking book, classically austere in design, with a partnership of text and illustration unusual" in young adult works.

In addition to exploring the past, Fleischman also engages readers with fiction dealing with modern-day themes and problems. In titles such as *A Fate Totally Worse than Death, Seedfolks, Whirligig, Weslandia,* and *Breakout* he demonstrates the range of styles and themes that have made him such a versatile writer. Parodying teen-horror novels, Fleischman serves up a "funny, mocking, and . . . surefire hit" with *A Fate Totally Worse than Death,* according to Julie Cummins in *School Library Journal.* "Lavishly dosed with comic hyperbole, his plot is good for some chuckles—and many groans," noted a reviewer for *Publishers Weekly.* In *Seedfolks* the author once again employs his multi-faceted narrative voice, "arraying voices like threads on a loom," according to a contributor to *Publishers Weekly,* noting that the novel weaves "a seamless tale of the advent of a garden in urban Cleveland and how it unites a community." Susan Dove Lempke, reviewing the same title for *Booklist,* concluded that the "characters' vitality and the sharply delineated details of the neighborhood makes [*Seedfolks*] . . . not merely an exercise in craftsmanship or morality, but an engaging, entertaining novel as well."

Whirligig examines the aftermath of a teen traffic accident. Coming home from a party intoxicated and despondent, Brent tries to commit suicide, but instead kills a stranger—a talented and lovely high-school senior. His atonement for the crime, as set by the dead girl's mother, is to erect four whirligigs with pictures resembling the victim at the four corners of America. Brent's subsequent journey takes him not only across the United States but into his own psyche as well. "The brilliant Fleischman has written a beautifully layered, marvelously constructed novel that spins and circles in numerous directions," commented Miriam Lang Budin in *School Library Journal.*Another book for older readers, *Breakout* focuses on seventeen-year-old Del Thigpen, whose impetuous decision to fake her death and escape from her current foster home is frustrated by a Los Angeles traffic jam. While stuck on the freeway, Del has time to reassess her situation, and Fleischman threads his novel with a parallel narrative that shows an older Del—now a performance artist calling herself Elena Franco—reflecting on the shift caused by these ruminations. A *Publishers Weekly* reviewer explained that the novel, which "explores the way art allows people to re-examine their lives," is structured to "allow . . . the real and imagined events to blend, supplementing and augmenting each other." While noting that *Breakout* "makes demands on its readers," *Booklist* reviewer Ilene Cooper added that the "artful, insightful" novel is "very much worth the effort."

Toddlers and novice readers have also enjoyed Fleischman's work via the author's chapter books and picture books. Among the many titles he has created for younger readers are *Shadow Play, Time Train, Weslandia,* and *The Animal Hedge.* With these volume, as with his poetry and novels for older readers, Fleischman shows himself to be an inventive wordsmith and a spinner of original, often whimsical tales. As Catherine Price noted in the *St. James Guide to Young Adult Writers,* the author "is a master of his craft" whose "lyrical language and remarkable imagery enable him to create convincing characters and time periods. An added appeal of his work is that his protagonists often share young readers' powerful emotional needs, and therefore help them make discoveries about themselves." In *Weslandia* a young outsider grows a garden of strange plants and from it creates a miniature world in his backyard, complete with its own language. In *The Animal Hedge* a farmer who was forced to sell his beloved farm, together with his three sons, cultivate the shrubbery in their new yard, clipping and pruning the images of the things they love most—the farmer shapes his beloved livestock, the sons' images reflect their future dreams. The story, an allegory that reminds readers that "following the dictates of one's heart is the surest path to personal fulfillment," according to Miriam Lang Budin in *School Library Journal,* is told in traditional folk fashion, creating what a *Publishers Weekly* contributor praised as an "inspiring" and "heartwarming story with quiet power."

Biographical and Critical Sources

BOOKS

Children's Books and Their Creators, edited by Anita Silvey, Houghton (Boston, MA), 1995, p. 245.
Children's Literature Review, Volume 20, Gale (Detroit, MI), 1990, pp. 63-70.
Fifth Book of Junior Authors and Illustrators, edited by Sally Holmes Holtze, H. W. Wilson (Bronx, NY), 1983, pp. 114-116.
St. James Guide to Young Adult Writers, edited by Sara Pendergast and Tom Pendergast, St. James Press (Detroit, MI), 1999, pp. 285-286.

PERIODICALS

Booklist, May 1, 1990, Denise M. Wilms, review of *Saturnalia,* p. 1702; October 1, 1990, p. 338; September 1, 1991, pp. 61-62; October 1, 1991, Hazel Rochman, review of *The Borning Room,* p. 328; January 15,

1993, Carolyn Phelan, review of *Bull Run,* p. 898; July, 1993, p. 1960; October 15, 1995, p. 397; May 15, 1997, Susan Dove Lempke, review of *Seedfolks,* p. 1573; April, 1998, p. 1324; April 15, 2000, Randy Meyer, review of *Cannibal in the Mirror,* p. 1536; June 1, 2000, Gillian Engberg, review of *Big Talk: Poems for Four Voices,* p. 1883; July, 2000, Michael Cart, review of *Lost!: A Story in String,* p. 2038; October 15, 2002, Anna Rich, review of *Seek,* p. 438; December 15, 2003, Ilene Cooper, review of *Breakout,* p. 746.

Bulletin of the Center for Children's Books, January, 1991, p. 117; September, 1991, Zena Sutherland, review of *The Borning Room,* pp. 9-10; November, 1991, p. 63; December, 1995, p. 126; March, 1996, Betsy Hearne, review of *Dateline: Troy,* p. 225; July-August, 1997, p. 393; June, 1998, p. 361.

Childhood Education, mid-summer, 2004, Sylvia Loh, review of *Breakout,* p. 273.

Children's Book Awards Annual, 1998, p. 62.

Five Owls, September-October, 1994, Lois Ringquist, review of *Townsend's Warbler,* p. 7.

Horn Book, May-June, 1988, Mary M. Burns, review of *Joyful Noise: Poems for Two Voices,* pp. 366-367; July-August, 1989, Paul Fleischman, "Newbery Medal Acceptance," pp. 442-451; May-June, 1990, pp. 337-338; January-February, 1991, pp. 63-64; July-August, 1996, p. 581; May-June, 1997, p. 320; March-April, 1999, pp. 187-188; May-June, 2004, Joanna Rudge Long, review of *Sidewalk Circus,* p. 311.

Kirkus Reviews, May 15, 1979, review of *The Birthday Tree,* p. 573; August 15, 1990, pp. 1167-68; July 15, 1991, p. 938; June 1, 1993, p. 720; September 15, 1995, p. 1349; May 1, 1997, p. 720; July 1, 1999, p.1053.

Kliatt, January, 2002, Sally M. Tibbetts, review of *Joyful Noise,* p. 51; November, 2002, Miles Klein, review of *Seek,* p. 49; May, 2003, Carol Reich, review of *Seekfolks,* p. 50.

Publishers Weekly, February 1, 1991, p. 81; March 29, 1991, p. 94; July 12, 1991, p. 66; July 19, 1991, p. 57; January 11, 1993, review of *Bull Run,* p. 64; September 18, 1995, review of *A Fate Totally Worse than Death,* p. 133; April 17, 1997, review of *Seedfolks,* p. 93; April 12, 1999, p. 28; May 12, 1999, p. 78; July 12, 1999, pp. 95-96; July 28, 2003, review of *Breakout,* p. 96; September 8, 2003, review of *The Animal Hedge,* p. 76.

School Library Journal, May, 1990, Amy Kellman, review of *Saturnalia,* p. 122; May, 1991, Shirley Wilton, review of *Dateline: Troy,* p. 138; October, 1995, Julie Cummins, review of *A Fate Totally Worse than Death,* p. 152; April, 1998, Miriam Lang Budin, review of *Whirligig,* p. 131; March, 1999, Paul Fleischman, "The Accidental Artist," p. 105; June, 1999, p. 94; August, 1999, p. 155; April, 2000, Steven Engelfried, review of *Cannibal in the Mirror,* p. 147; June, 2000, Grace Oliff, review of *Lost!,* p. 112; Margaret Bush, review of *Big Talk,* p. 163; October, 2003, Miriam Lang Budin, review of *The Animal Hedge,* p. 119; July, 2004, Robin L. Gibson, review of *Sidewalk Circus,* p. 75.

Voice of Youth Advocates, June, 1990, Raymond E. Houser, review of *Saturnalia,* p. 102; June, 1993, Samantha Hunt, review of *Bull Run,* p. 89; February, 1994, p. 393; December, 1996, pp. 285-86; June, 1998, pp. 121-122.

ONLINE

Paul Fleischman's Official Web site, http://www.paul fleischman.net/ (December 2, 2004).

G

GEORGE, Kristine O'Connell 1954-

Personal
Born May 6, 1954, in Denver, CO. *Education:* Colorado State University, B.S., 1976.

Addresses
Agent—c/o Author Mail, Clarion Books, 215 Park Ave., New York, NY 10003. *E-mail*—kristine@kristinegeorge. com.

Career
Writer. Conference speaker and visiting author in schools; poetry consultant for *Storytime* television program, produced by Public Broadcasting System; University of California-Los Angeles Writers' Program, writing instructor for children's poetry, beginning 1999.

Awards, Honors
Lee Bennett Hopkins Promising Poet Award, International Reading Association (IRA), 1998; Lee Bennett Hopkins Poetry Award, 1998; American Booksellers Association (ABA) Pick of the Lists designation, National Council of Teachers of English (NCTE) Notable Book in the Language Arts designation, and *School Library Journal* Best Books designation, all 1998, all for *The Great Frog Race and Other Poems;* New York Public Library's 100 Titles for Reading and Sharing listee, 1998, for *The Great Frog Race* and *Old Elm Speaks: Tree Poems,* and 2001, for *Book!;* Chicago Public Library Best of the Best listee, 1998, for *Old Elm Speaks;* Golden Kite Award, Society of Children's Book Writers and Illustrators, 1999; Myra Cohn Livingston Award for Excellence in Children's Poetry, Southern California Council on Literature for Children and Young People, 1999, and 2002, for *Toasting Marshmallows: Camping Poems;* Oppenheimer Toy Portfolio Gold Award, 2001, for *Book!;* Bank Street College Claudia Lewis Poetry Award, and South Dakota Prairie Bud Award nomina-

tion, both 2002, both for *Little Dog and Duncan;* IRA/Children's Book Council Choice designation, William Alllen White Book Award nomination, and South Carolina Junior Book Award nomination, all 2003, all for *Swimming Upstream: Middle School Poems;* Texas Bluebonnet Master List nomination, 2005, for *Hummingbird Nest: A Journal of Poems.*

Writings

The Great Frog Race and Other Poems, illustrated by Kate Kiesler, introduction by Myra Cohn Livingston, Clarion Books (New York, NY), 1997.

Old Elm Speaks: Tree Poems, illustrated by Kate Kiesler, Clarion Books (New York, NY), 1998.

Little Dog Poems, illustrated by June Otani, Clarion Books (New York, NY), 1999.

Toasting Marshmallows: Camping Poems, illustrated by Kay Kiesler, Clarion Books (New York, NY), 2001.

Book!, illustrated by Maggie Smith, Clarion Books (New York, NY), 2001.

Swimming Upstream: Middle School Poems, illustrated by Debbie Tilley, Clarion Books (New York, NY), 2002.

Little Dog and Duncan, illustrated by June Otani, Clarion Books (New York, NY), 2002.

One Mitten, illustrated by Maggie Smith, Clarion Books (New York, NY), 2004.

Hummingbird Nest: A Journal of Poems, illustrated by Barry Moser, Harcourt (Orlando, IL), 2004.

Up!, illustrated by Hiroe Nakata, Clarion Books (New York, NY), 2005.

Fold Me a Poem, illustrated by Lauren Stringer, Harcourt (Orlando, FL), 2005.

Contributor of stories and poems to anthologies and to periodicals, including *Cricket* and *Spider.* Contributor to *Children's Writers and Illustrators Market,* Writer's Digest Books, 2000.

Sidelights
Kristine O'Connell George is the author of several well-received collections of poetry for young people. In her introduction to George's debut work, *The Great Frog*

Using a variety of poetic forms, George catches the moods and thoughts of a student new to middle school. (Cover illustration by Debbie Tilley.)

Race and Other Poems, Myra Cohn Livingston wrote that it "is not only refreshing but urgent that our children hear poetry resonating with music, keen observation, fresh metaphor and personification, and meaningful flights of imagination. . . .. George promises us that!" Other works by George include the collections *Swimming Upstream: Middle School Poems* and *Toasting Marshmallows: Camping Poems,* as well as several picture books that contain a rhyming text. Praising George's picture book *Little Dog and Duncan,* about a small pup who has to compete for the attention of his young owner when a rambunctious Irish wolfhound comes to play, Joy Fleishhacker noted in *School Library Journal* that the author possesses a talent for focusing on "ordinary moments and describing them in accessible yet lyrical language, transforming the mundane into the magical."

Born and raised in Colorado, George began her career as a poet to the young after a 1989 writing class

taught by author Myra Cohn Livingston. Her first published work was 1997's *The Great Frog Race and Other Poems,* which a *Publishers Weekly* reviewer characterized as "an invitation to experience joy and wonder." Many of George's poems reflect her love of the natural world, and everything from tadpoles and wild birds to horses and trees appear throughout her books. Margaret Bush remarked in *School Library Journal* on the many poetic forms George employs: "Haiku, blank verse, bits of rhyme, and some lovely little bundles of words are sprinkled along in pieces that are descriptive and engaging." Deborah Stevenson likened some of George's "quiet and observant" poems to those of William Carlos Williams in her review for the *Bulletin of the Center for Children's Books,* adding: "The phraseology is fresh and apt, employing tactile as well as visual conceits, and the subjects are kid-appealing ones indeed."

George uses several poetic forms to celebrate the natural world in her second collection, *Old Elm Speaks: Tree Poems,* which Tunie Munson-Benson in *Riverbank Review* described as "beckoning as irresistibly as a basketful of polished stones." Here George's playful use of language makes music of her observations of the knotholes in a wooden fence, squirrels playing in a tree, a tree branch that juts out in such as way as to make it a perfect imaginary horse for a small child, and a fisherman who catches a pine tree rather than a fish. A critic for *Kirkus Reviews* dubbed the book "a lovely, often luminous, collection," while a *Publishers Weekly* contributor described *Old Elm Speaks* as "just the right gift for nature lovers."

"Writing the poems for *Old Elm Speaks* was such a joy!," George noted on her Web site, reflecting the personal connection her writing has for her. "I have always loved trees—their diversity, quiet dignity, and the places they hold in the landscape of my memories. I was the type of child who always noticed trees and I still remember specific trees from homes in Colorado, Texas, Oregon, Ohio, and Idaho. . . .. Many of these poems represent special memories not only of trees, but also places I love." George also draws from her personal experiences in *Hummingbird Nest: A Journal of Poems.* The book follows the author's family as they watch a pair of hummingbirds hatch youngsters and grow them to maturity in a nest the mother bird built in a potted tree on the patio of the George family's home. After nest-building, tiny eggs hatch, and suddenly every waking hour is spent feeding the tiny hatchlings. It is not long until the tiny birds are old enough to take their first flight, and suddenly, they are gone. In addition to poems describing each stage of the family's observations, George includes notes about the hummingbird, making *Hummingbird Nest* useful as a reference tool for budding naturalists. "As in the best nature writing, the excitement here is in the particulars that bring readers close up to a universe," noted Hazel Rochman in *Booklist,* while a *Kirkus Reviews* critic praised the book as a "smooth, easy-reading glimpse into the natural world," enhanced by realistic watercolor illustrations by Barry Moser.

A small girl describes her dog and their canine guest through childlike observations in George's warmhearted poems in Little Dog and Duncan, *illustrated by June Otani.*

In the books *Little Dog Poems* and *Little Dog and Duncan,* George depicts the life of a small puppy. *Little Dog Poems* follows dog and owner on their round of daily activities, including a war between the pup and the vacuum cleaner, watching with hopeful fascination as Mom cooks in the kitchen, and playing a game of catch with his young owner. *Booklist* contributor Stephanie Zvirin viewed the volume as "a charming way to introduce little ones to the form and feeling of poetry," while Joanna Rudge Long, writing in *Horn Book,* asserted that *Little Dog Poems* is especially distinguished by "the author's true understanding of canine behavior and her insight into the happy relationship between dog and child."

Biographical and Critical Sources

BOOKS

George, Kristine O'Connell, *The Great Frog Race and Other Poems,* introduction by Myra Cohn Livingston, Clarion Books (New York, NY), 1997.

PERIODICALS

Appraisal, spring, 1999, pp. 17-18.
Booklist, March 15, 1997, p. 1238; January 1, 1999, review of *Old Elm Speaks: Tree Poems,* p. 784; March 15, 1999 Stephanie Zvirin, review of *Little Dog Po*-

ems; March 15, 2001, Gillian Engberg, review of *Toasting Marshallows: Camping Poems,* p. 1394; January 1, 2003, GraceAnne A. DeCandido, review of *Swimming Upstream: Middle School Poems,* p. 878; February 1, 2004, Hazel Rochman, review of *Hummingbird Nest: A Journal of Poems,* p. 974; November 15, 2004, Ilene Cooper, review of *One Mitten,* p. 590.
Bulletin of the Center for Children's Books, June, 1997, Deborah Stevenson, review of *The Great Frog Race,* p. 358.
Creative Classroom, March-April, 1999, p. 36.
Horn Book, March-April, 1999, Joanna Rudge Long, review of *Little Dog Poems,* p. 216; July-August, 2002, Roger Sutton, review of *Little Dog and Duncan,* p. 478; January-February, 2003, Martha V. Parravano, review of *Swimming Upstream,* p. 89.
Kirkus Reviews, February 15, 1997, p. 299; August 1, 1998, review of *Old Elm Speaks,* p. 1116; September 15, 2001, review of *Book!,* p. 1358; August 1, 2002, review of *Swimming Upstream,* p. 1129; March 1, 2004, review of *Hummingbird Nest,* p. 222.
Publishers Weekly, January 27, 1997, review of *The Great Frog Race,* p. 107: September 14, 1998, review of *Old Elm Speaks,* p. 68; February 22, 1999, review of *Little Dog Poems,* p. 94; March 12, 2001, review of *Toasting Marshmallows,* p. 90; October 1, 2001, review of *Book!,* p. 60; March 11, 2002, review of *Swimming Upstream,* p. 74.
Riverbank Review, fall, 1996, Tunie Munson-Benson, review of *Old Elm Speaks,* p. 41.
School Library Journal, April, 1997, Margaret Bush, review of *The Great Frog Race,* p. 124; September, 1998, pp. 190-191; May, 1999, p. 106; July, 2001, Luann Toth, review of *Toasting Marshmallows,* p. 93; March, 2002, Joy Fleishhacker, review of *Little Dog and Duncan,* p. 212; September, 2002, Kristen Oravec, review of *Swimming Upstream,* p. 244; April, 2004, Susan Scheps, review of *Hummingbird Nest,* p. 111; December, 2004, Laura Scott, review of *One Mitten,* p. 109.

ONLINE

Kristine O'Connell George Web site, http://www.kristine george.com/ (December 2, 2004).*

*   *   *

GLEITZMAN, Morris 1953-

Personal

First syllable of surname rhymes with "light"; born January 9, 1953, in Sleaford, Lincolnshire, England; immigrated to Australia, 1969; son of Phillip (an auditor) and Pamela (Bates) Gleitzman; married Christine McCaul (a film editor), February 9, 1978 (separated January, 1994); children: Sophie, Ben. *Education:* Canberra College of Advanced Education, B.A. (professional writing), 1974. *Hobbies and other interests:* Travel, reading, making lists.

Morris Gleitzman

Addresses

Home—Victoria, Australia. *Agent*—Anthony Williams, 50 Oxford St., Paddington, Sydney, New South Wales 2021, Australia. *E-mail*—morris@morrisgleitzman.com.

Career

Australian Broadcasting Corporation, Sydney, New South Wales, television promotions director, 1973-75, television entertainment script editor and producer, 1975-76, and writer for *The Norman Gunston Show,* 1976-78; Seven Network, Sydney, writer for *The Norman Gunston Show,* 1978-81; freelance writer, 1981—.

Awards, Honors

Awgie Award, Australian Writers Guild, 1985, for television film *The Other Facts of Life;* Family Award, 1990, for *Two Weeks with the Queen;* Book of the Year Younger Honour, Children's Book Council of Australia, 1992, for *Misery Guts,* and 1993, for *Blabber Mouth;* COOL Award (Australia Capital Territory), BILBY Award (Queensland), YABBA Award (Victoria), and KOALA Award shortlist (New South Wales), and *Guardian* Children's Fiction Award shortlist, all 1999, all for *Bumface;* Dymocks Booksellers Children's Choice Awards Favorite Australian Author designation, 1999.

Writings

NOVELS; FOR CHILDREN

The Other Facts of Life (adapted from author's television screenplay of the same title; also see below), Penguin (Ringwood, Victoria, Australia), 1985, reprinted, 2004.

Second Childhood (adapted from author's television screenplay), Puffin (Ringwood, Victoria, Australia), 1990.

Misery Guts, Piper (Sydney, New South Wales, Australia), 1991, Harcourt (San Diego, CA), 1993.

Worry Warts, Pan Macmillan (Sydney, New South Wales, Australia), 1992, Harcourt (San Diego, CA), 1993.

Puppy Fat, Pan Macmillan (Sydney, New South Wales, Australia), 1992, Harcourt (San Diego, CA), 1995.

Blabber Mouth, Pan Macmillan (Sydney, New South Wales, Australia), 1992, Harcourt (San Diego, CA), 1995.

Sticky Beak, Pan Macmillan (Sydney, New South Wales, Australia), 1993, Harcourt (San Diego, CA), 1995.

Belly Flop, Pan Macmillan (Sydney, New South Wales, Australia), 1996.

Water Wings, Pan Macmillan (Sydney, New South Wales, Australia), 1996.

Bumface, Puffin (Ringwood, Victoria, Australia), 1998.

Gift of the Gab, Puffin (Ringwood, Victoria, Australia), 1999.

Toad Rage, Puffin (Ringwood, Victoria, Australia), 1999, Random House (New York, NY), 2004.

Adults Only, Puffin (Ringwood, Victoria, Australia), 2001.

Toad Heaven, Puffin (Ringwood, Victoria, Australia), 2001, Random House (New York, NY), 2005.

Boy Overboard, Puffin (Camberwell, Victoria, Australia), 2002.

Teachers's Pet, Puffin (Camberwell, Victoria, Australia), 2003.

Toad Away, Puffin (Camberwell, Victoria, Australia), 2003.

Girl Underground, Puffin (Camberwell, Victoria, Australia), 2004.

Worm Story, Puffin (Camberwell, Victoria, Australia), 2004.

Gleitzman's books have been translated into French, Japanese, German, Italian, and Spanish.

"WICKED!" SERIES; NOVELS

(With Paul Jennings) *The Slobberers,* Puffin (Ringwood, Victoria, Australia), 1997.

(With Paul Jennings) *Battering Rams,* Puffin (Ringwood, Victoria, Australia), 1997.

(With Paul Jennings) *Croaked,* Puffin (Ringwood, Victoria, Australia), 1997.

(With Paul Jennings) *Dead Ringer,* Puffin (Ringwood, Victoria, Australia), 1997.

(With Paul Jennings) *The Creeper,* Puffin (Ringwood, Victoria, Australia), 1997.

(With Paul Jennings) *Till Death Us Do Part,* Puffin (Ringwood, Victoria, Australia), 1997.

(With Paul Jennings) *Wicked!* (includes six volumes), Puffin (Ringwood, Victoria, Australia), 1998.

"DEADLY!" SERIES; NOVELS

(With Paul Jennings) *Nude,* Puffin (Ringwood, Victoria, Australia), 2000.

(With Paul Jennings) *Brats,* Puffin (Ringwood, Victoria, Australia), 2000.

(With Paul Jennings) *Stiff,* Puffin (Ringwood, Victoria, Australia), 2000.

(With Paul Jennings) *Hunt,* Puffin (Ringwood, Victoria, Australia), 2001.

(With Paul Jennings) *Grope,* Puffin (Ringwood, Victoria, Australia), 2001.

(With Paul Jennings) *Pluck,* Puffin (Ringwood, Victoria, Australia), 2001.

(With Paul Jennings) *Deadly!* (includes all six volumes), Puffin (Ringwood, Victoria, Australia), 2002.

OTHER

Doctors and Nurses (screenplay), Universal Entertainment, 1981.

Melvin Son of Alvin (screenplay), Roadshow, 1984.

The Other Facts of Life (television film), Ten Network, 1985.

Skin Free (two-act play), produced in Sydney, New South Wales, 1986.

(With Trevor Farrant) *Not a Papal Tour* (stage show), produced in Canberra, Australian Capital Territory, at Canberra Theatre, 1987.

Two Weeks with the Queen (adult novel), Blackie & Son, 1989, Putnam (New York, NY), 1991.

Harbour Beat (screenplay), Palm Beach Pictures/Zenith Productions, 1990.

Just Looking: Gleitzman on Television (collected columns), Sun Books (Chippendale, New South Wales, Australia), 1992.

Gleitzman on Saturday (collected columns), Macmillan, 1993.

SelfHelpLess: Fifty-seven Pieces of Crucial Advice for People Who Need a Bit More Time to Get It Right, Penguin (Ringwood, Victoria, Australia), 2000.

Writer of scripts for television series, including *Second Childhood, Crossroads, Bust, Instant TV,* and *The Daryl Somers Show.* Author of weekly television column in *Sydney Morning Herald,* 1987-92; columnist for *Good Weekend* (magazine supplement to *Sydney Morning Herald* and *Melbourne Age*), beginning 1990.

Adaptations

Gleitzman's novel *Two Weeks with the Queen* was adapted as a play by Mary Morris, Piper, 1994.

Sidelights

Although he started out his writing career as a television scriptwriter, Morris Gleitzman has earned a reputation in his adopted home of Australia for creating humorous, evocative young-adult novels as well as penning entertaining novel series such as *Wicked!* and *Deadly!* with fellow writer Paul Jennings. The "cheeky brand of humor" and "sensible, tolerant attitude" toward family life that a *Publishers Weekly* reviewer noticed in Gleitzman's early novels, has continued to be honed by the author, and his dry humor continues to find an appreciative audience with children and critics alike. "One looks forward to a Gleitzman title," wrote Trevor Carey in *Magpies;* and according to *Horn Book* critic Karen Jameyson, the award-winning writer's name "has been steadily edging its way into cult territory." By 1999 Gleitzman was considered one of the most popular children's writers in Australia, and the majority of his books have been translated into several languages.

The secret of Gleitzman's success, according to some critics, is his ability to couch highly sensitive topics and conflicts in chaotic situations peppered with amusing dialogues. Readers may find themselves laughing through stories about divorce, alienation, and physical challenges as these crises are encountered by the author's young protagonists. In his book *Boy Overboard* he addresses a broader concern facing young people while still employing his trademark humor, creating a likeable protagonist who lives in Afghanistan with his family and must face intolerance and the problems faced by refugees when his family is forced to flee to Australia. Gleitzman once explained that, when writing for a young audience, he uses "humor to explore the big subjects. I like characters who find themselves face to face with The Biggies unequipped with the adult armory of evasion, rationalization, and red wine."

Born and raised in the south of London, Gleitzman immigrated to Australia at age sixteen and quickly decided to become a writer. "I thought I'd better do some of those colorful jobs writers always seem to have done," he once commented. "I worked for a bit as a frozen chicken-thawer, a department store Santa Claus, an assistant to a fashion designer, and a rolling-stock unhooker in a sugar mill. I applied for whaling, but they rejected me because I said I'd only do it if I could throw the whales back." After enrolling in a college program in professional writing, Gleitzman established himself as a writer in the film and television industry in Australia. He worked as a promotions director and script editor and producer for the Australian Broadcasting Corporation, and wrote for *The Norman Gunston Show* for several years before becoming a freelance writer.

Gleitzman's first two books were adapted from his screenplays, and these projects gave him the confidence to make the career move from playwright to novelist. His most widely known novel, the award-winning *Two Weeks with the Queen,* was conceived as a novel "in a flash," as the writer once explained. "As I was writing it, I realized it was, in part, a story about the tendency of loving parents to overprotect their kids from difficult realities, both domestic and global. I was pleased to discover this, as I do it all the time myself."

"The things that happen in my books are almost all made up," Gleitzman admitted in a question-and-answer on his Web site. "For me, imagination makes much better stories than memory. Specially as my memory isn't very good. I can't remember many of the adventures of my childhood, so it's easier for me to make them up. Occasionally, though, a bit of my real life creeps into a story. I emigrated from England with my folks when I was 16, and that experience helped me write *Misery Guts.*"

Misery Guts and its sequel, *Worry Warts,* Gleitzman's two novels about nervous teen Keith Shipley, describe the effects of parents' attempts to protect their children, and also of children's efforts to protect their parents. Keith is troubled by his worried parents, a couple of "misery guts." His attempt to pick up their business—as well as their spirits—by painting their shop in the south of London a glossy mango color fails. Keith's parents show no interest in his plans for a tropical vacation or a move to Australia. When Keith finally persuades them to take a day trip to the beach, he forgets to turn the fryer at the fish and chips shop off. As a result, the shop burns down, and the family's business is ruined. To Keith's delight, his parents decide to begin another business in sunny Australia. As *Misery Guts* closes, readers find Keith content and the misery guts hopeful.

The Shipley family drama continues in *Worry Warts,* as money problems keep Keith's parents quarreling. Keith paints their car to cheer them up but it doesn't help; they announce that they want to divorce. Thinking that money will keep his parents together, Keith runs away to the opal fields. Although he manages to find an opal, he becomes trapped in a mine and his parents are forced into a costly rescue effort to bring their son home safely. While Keith eventually convinces his parents to stay together for him, he eventually puts his own desires aside for the good of all. While Ilene Cooper noted in *Booklist* that the conclusion of *Worry Warts* may be "unsatisfying" for those who applauded the boy's "efforts to keep his family together," a *Kirkus Reviews* critic found the same conclusion "surprising but appropriate."

Keith and his family return in several more novels by Gleitzman, including *Puppy Fat,* which finds Keith still at work solving his separated and now-single parents' problems for them. Worried that, in their mid-thirties, they have both become overweight and doddery and need to find new partners, he channels his artistic talents into finding ways to advertise their availability for dating. However, painting them in skimpy bathing suits on a wall in his South London neighborhood proves unsuccessful, so he calls in help, with predictably humorous results. A *Publishers Weekly* contributor wrote that Gleitzman's "punchy narrative, droll characters, and original plot" make *Puppy Fat* a "real page-turner," while in *Booklist* Ilene Cooper noted that the author characteristically "turns everyday situations upside down with his humor and off-the-wall take on life." *Blabber Mouth, Sticky Beak,* and *Gift of the Gab* all feature Rowena Batts, a girl who was born without the ability to speak. Although she is dumb, Rowena manages to express her opinion with signs, written words, and actions. While in *Blabber Mouth* the central problems revolve around Rowena's relationship with her flamboyant father, his decision to remarry causes new problems in *Sticky Beak,* In this novel Rowena expands her communication tools, throwing a Jelly Custard Surprise during a party for her teacher, who has married Rowena's father and is pregnant with Rowena's half-sibling. Despite Rowena's speech problem and

A cane toad named Limpy leaves his family home in the swamp and travels to Sydney during the Olympics to try to cement the relationship between his species and humans in Gleitzman's adventurous, humorous book for young readers. (Cover illustration by Rod Clement.)

sometimes-outlandish behavior, she is a resilient protagonist. By the end of *Sticky Beak,* for example, she has learned new ways of coping with her outrageous yet loving father, her new stepmother, the new baby, and even the class bully. *Gift of the Gab* finds her reconciling with her father while attempting to uncover the reason for her speech problem, which takes the family to France in search of answers. According to *Magpies* contributor Cathryn Crowe, Gleitzman "wraps" themes involving rejection and insecurity into "a tight bundle with plenty of zany humour."

In an unusual step for Gleitzman, he takes on an animal protagonist in *Toad Rage* and its sequels, *Toad Heaven* and *Toad Away.* In *Toad Rage* readers meet Australian cane toad Limpy, who is angered over the number of relatives who have ended up as road kill. In an effort to end the needless slaughter of amphibians, Limpy begins a public relations campaign, trying to sell humans on the notion that cane toads are truly man's best friend and ultimately hoping to become the next Olympic mascot. *Toad Away* finds Limpy still searching for a safe haven for cane toads, and joining with two friends to travel to the mythical Amazon, which is rumored to be such a place. Praising *Toad Rage* as a "hilarous dark comedy," a *Publishers Weekly* writer noted that Gleitzman originally wrote the novel for the 2000 Sydney Olympics as a tongue-in-cheek commentary on the country's animal-mascot selection process. Whatever its origins, the novel works on its own merits; as Ed Sullivan wrote in *Booklist,* Gleitzman's saga of "one toad's bold quest to reach out to another species will give readers plenty of laughs." "This toad's-eye view of human society provides both solid entertainment and a barbed commentary on the importance of looks," added a *Kirkus Reviews* contributor.

Biographical and Critical Sources

PERIODICALS

Booklist, July, 1993, Ilene Cooper, review of *Worry Warts,* p. 1958; May 1, 1995, Mary Harris Veeder, review of *Blabber Mouth,* p. 1561; June 1, 1995, Mary Harris Veeder, review of *Sticky Beak,* p. 1770; June 1, 1996, Ilene Cooper, review of *Puppy Fat,* p. 171; March 1, 2004, Ed Sullivan, review of *Toad Rage,* p. 1188.

Horn Book, July, 1993, Karen Jameyson, "News from down Under," pp. 496-498; July-August, 1995, Elizabeth S. Watson, review of *Blabber Mouth,* p. 458.

Junior Bookshelf, November, 1993, review of *Sticky Beak,* pp. 65-66.

Kirkus Reviews, February 1, 1993, review of *Misery Guts,* p. 146; April 1, 2004, review of *Toad Rage,* p. 329.

Magpies, November, 1991, p. 29; November, 1992, Trevor Carey, review of *Blabber Mouth,* p. 30; November, 1993, Cathryn Crowe, review of *Sticky Beak,* p. 32.

Publishers Weekly, January 11, 1991, review of *Two Weeks with the Queen,* p. 105; February 8, 1993, review of *Misery Guts* and *Worry Warts,* p. 87; May 6, 1996, review of *Puppy Fat,* p. 8; March 22, 2004, review of *Toad Rage,* p. 86.

School Library Journal, May, 1993, pp. 104-105.

ONLINE

Morris Gleitzman Web site, http://www.morrisgleitzman. com/ (January 17, 2005).*

*   *   *

GOING, K(elly) L.

Personal

Female. *Education:* Graduated from college. *Hobbies and other interests:* Music, reading, travel.

Addresses

Home—Beacon, NY. *Agent*—c/o Author Mail, G. P. Putnam, 375 Hudson St., New York, NY 10014. *E-mail*—kl@klgoing.com.

Career

Writer. Has worked variously as an adult literacy tutor, airline ticket agent, resort hotel desk clerk, and assistant to a literary agent; Merritt Bookstore, Cold Spring, NY, part-time clerk.

Awards, Honors

Michael L. Printz Honor, American Library Association, 2004, for *Fat Kid Rules the World.*

Writings

Fat Kid Rules the World, Putnam (New York, NY), 2003.
The Liberation of Gabriel King, Putnam (New York, NY), 2005.

Contributor of short fiction to periodicals, including *Rush Hour.*

Sidelights

Author K. L. Going made her writing debut, and also earned the American Library Association's Michael L. Printz Award, with *Fat Kid Rules the World,* the story

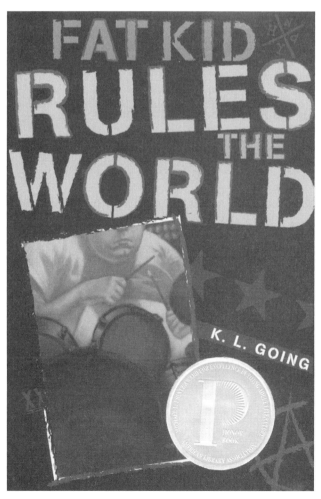

Troy Billings is an obese and suicidal teenager who is brought back from the edge by a young, homeless, and musically talented legend, who inspires Troy to join a rock band. (Cover illustration by Sterling Hundley.)

of a dejected 6' 1″, 300-pound Watson High School senior named Troy Billings. Through the development of a rather unlikely friendship with local rock musician Curt MacCrae, Troy becomes a drummer in his new friend's band, and begins to deal with his depression, while simultaneously working through numerous other personal issues as well. A reviewer for *Publishers Weekly* called the debut novel "savvy and fast-paced," while Ilene Cooper commented in *Booklist* that while Going's "narrative could have been tighter in places, *Fat Kid Rules the World* "is an impressive debut that offers hope for all kids." Renee Steinberg stated in a *School Library Journal* review that because the novel contains "many unexpected twists and turns," readers "will love [Going's] . . . wonderful, engrossing tale."

Going makes her home in New York state, where she lives with two cats and works part time in a nearby bookstore. Her second novel, this time for middle-grade readers, is titled *The Liberation of Gabriel King* and was published in 2005. On her Web site, Going explained that her fiction is based on the feelings she experienced while growing up. "I've always been small and thin (4'11 and 3/4"!), but I've spent a vast amount of my life feeling like the 'fat kid'—namely, self-conscious. I try to tap into the extreme ends of the emotional spectrum. I'm not as interested in the stable feelings in the middle. I take the best and worst feelings and try to make those emotions come alive through my characters."

Biographical and Critical Sources

PERIODICALS

Booklist, May 15, 2003, Ilene Cooper, review of *Fat Kid Rules the World,* p. 1659.
Horn Book, July-August, 2003, Peter D. Sieruta, review of *Fat Kid Rules the World,* p. 456.
Kirkus Reviews, May 1, 2003, review of *Fat Kid Rules the World,* p. 676.
Publishers Weekly, June 23, 2003, review of *Fat Kid Rules the World,* p. 69.
School Library Journal, May, 2003, Renee Steinberg, review of *Fat Kid Rules the World,* p. 152.

ONLINE

K. L. Going Web site, http://www.klgoing.com/ (January 5, 2005).

* * *

GORDON, Amy 1949-
(Amy Lawson)

Personal

Born January 22, 1949, in Boston, MA; daughter of Lincoln (a professor, diplomat, and economist) and Allison (an artist, writer, and mother; maiden name, Wright), Gordon; married Richard Lawson (divorced 1995); children: Nicholas Lawson, Hugh Lawson. *Education:* Bard College, graduated, 1972. *Politics:* "Eclectic." *Religion:* "Eclectic." *Hobbies and other interests:* "Writing, reading, mountain climbing, sailing, spending time with people I like, traveling."

Addresses

Home—P.O. Box 186, 2 Old Sunderland Rd., Montague, MA 01351. *Agent*—George Nicholson, Sterling Lord Literistic, 65 Bleecker St., New York, NY 10012.

Career

Bement School (K-9 boarding school), Deerfield, MA, drama teacher and director, chair of fine arts program, 1980—.

Awards, Honors

Texas Blue Bonnet Award nomination, 2004, and Missouri Association of Librarians award, both for *The Gorillas of Gill Park.*

Writings

(Under name Amy Lawson) *The Talking Bird and the Story Pouch,* illustrated by Craig McFarland Brown, Harper (New York, NY), 1983.
(Under name Amy Lawson) *Star Baby,* illustrated by Margot Apple, Harcourt Brace Jovanovich (San Diego, CA), 1991.
Midnight Magic, illustrated by Judy Clifford, BridgeWater (Mahwah, NJ), 1995.
When JFK Was My Father, Houghton Mifflin (Boston, MA), 1999.
The Gorillas of Gill Park, Holiday House (New York, NY), 2003.
The Secret Life of a Boarding School Brat, Holiday House (New York, NY), 2004.

Work in Progress

The Blue Gang of Gill Park, for Holiday House.

Sidelights

Amy Gordon's books for young people reflect their author's belief in the positive power of imagination. While her 1995 chapter book *Midnight Magic* extols the value and fun of imagination for beginning readers, Gordon's teen novel *When JFK Was My Father* asserts the power of a fantasy life for adolescents. Harnessing imagination through the creative act of writing is at the core of Gordon's 2004 novel, *The Secret Life of a Boarding School Brat,* a book that had its basis in the author's own experiences. As Gordon recalled, after two years living in Rio de Janeiro, Brazil, with her family, "I was sent back to the United States for a more serious education at a girls' boarding school. I went there for five years—five years of a blue uniform skirt, a white blouse, sensible shoes, and crazy housemothers. In the fall of my first year, John F. Kennedy was shot; in the spring of my last year, Bobby Kennedy was shot." After attending Bard College "during the turbulent years of the late '60s and early '70s," Gordon explained: "I found my way to teaching; I was a camp counselor for many years and knew that I loved working with kids. Now I teach drama and put on plays with kids and write as much as I can between teaching and raising my two sons." *Midnight Magic* finds Uncle Harry babysitting Jake and Sam during a weekend of crises: Sam has lost a tooth and Jake's pet hamsters are missing. Uncle Harry distracts the children by enacting their favorite story, "Puss in Boots," and when they wake up on Saturday morning, Sam finds a golden key left under his pillow by the Tooth Fairy. When Sam and Jake begin a search for the evil ogre of the "Puss in Boots" story, hoping to return the golden key to him, they somehow end up on the hamster's trail. *School Library Journal* reviewer Mary Jo Drungil singled out Gordon's "utterly realistic" portrait of two likeable young boys, as well as their "ideal" uncle, for special praise, and predicted that *Midnight Magic* is "certain to be appreciated by young fairy-tale fans."

Geared for middle-grade readers, *The Gorillas of Gill Park* is a humorous novel that focuses on Willy, a lonely middle-schooler who finds a world of new friends while spending the summer with his widowed aunt. The practical-minded Willy is instantly set at ease by his quirky Aunt Bridget, whose job as a costume designer now keeps her busy sewing gorilla costumes in her small urban apartment. Nearby, Willy discovers a small park run by an equally eccentric wealthy musician, and when the park is threatened by land developers the boy's practical sense helps win the day. In *Booklist* Gillian Engberg praised *The Gorillas of Gill Park* as a "suspenseful, winning story" in which "delicious words, clever dialogue, and endearing characters" retain reader attention. Noting that Gordon draws her cast of characters from among "folk of varying degrees of eccentricity," a *Publishers Weekly* critic added that the young protagonist's "gradual discovery of his own worth is satisfying" and the storyline "often funny."

Taking place in the 1960s, Gordon's novel *When JFK Was My Father* centers on fourteen-year-old Georgia Hughes, who lives in Brazil with her emotionally remote parents. When her parents get divorced, Georgia and her mother move back to the United States, and Georgia is deposited in a boarding school. The highly inventive Georgia feels abandoned by both parents, particularly her father, and she compensates for her loneliness as she did in Brazil: by pretending that recently assassinated U.S. president John F. Kennedy is her real father. When Tim, a friend from Brazil who has run away from his boarding school, invites Georgia to hit the road with him, she suddenly realizes that her school, and the friends she has made there, may have filled an

During the summer before seventh grade, Willy experiences big-city life through his relationships with several offbeat people who frequent the neighborhood park. (Cover illustration by Matthew Cordell.)

important void in her life. "Georgia's account of her virtual abandonment at school by her parents and her barely conscious search for a home is both poignant and gently funny," contended Lauren Adams, reviewing *When JFK Was My Father* for *Horn Book*. Praising Gordon's novel as "well paced with moments of dramatic tension," the critic added that "Georgia's refreshing narrative" ably reveals the cast of interesting secondary characters. "Gordon writes in a vivid, defining style that allows Georgia to emerge as a fresh, fully realized character," attested Ilene Cooper in *Booklist,* while Connie Tyrrell Burns wrote in *School Library Journal* that the success of *When JFK Was My Father* rests on Gordon's creation of a "likable and well-drawn character" with whom readers can identify. The gift of a diary by her grandmother proves to be Lydia's salvation in *The Secret Life of a Boarding School Brat*. Also taking place in the 1960s, the novel follows Lydia Rice, a seventh grader who feels isolated, not only because of her parents' divorce and their decision to ship her off to boarding school, but also because of the recent death of a beloved grandmother. Written in the form of the diary

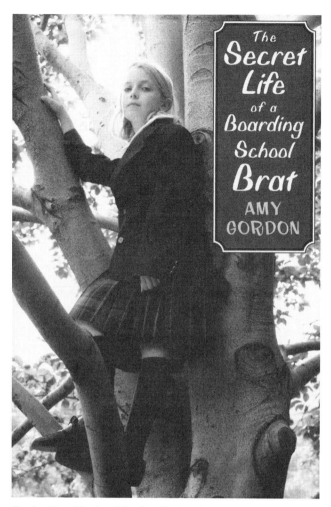

Set in New England in the 1960s, Gordon's novel portrays seventh-grader Lydia, who is sent to a boarding school and loathes it until an inventive night watchman entices her with an intriguing puzzle to solve. (Cover photo by Marc Tauss.)

Lydia starts while at Miss Pocket's Boarding School, the novel follows the girl's efforts to solve a puzzle from the past, a task put to the lonely girl by the school's kind-hearted maintenance man. Noting the novel's "lively pacing and appealing if improbable . . . characters," a *Publishers Weekly* contributor predicted that "many readers will be caught up in the mystery" like Lydia. In *Horn Book* Susan Dove Lempke had special praise for the young protagonist's "lively personality" and Gordon's depiction of "the intergenerational friendship she forms" with the school handyman, while a *Kirkus Reviews* critic dubbed *The Secret Life of a Boarding School Brat* a "pleasant read."

Gordon once told *Something about the Author:* "When I was young, I was a shy person in a verbal, intellectual, talkative family. I discovered that if I *wrote* entertaining stories as Christmas presents, then I could get the entire family to stop talking and pay attention to me. The written word allowed me to have a voice.

"I loved to read when I was young, and spent quite a lot of time pretending. I loved the world of childhood and left it reluctantly. In my adult life, I am very lucky to have a career (teaching drama and directing plays with 6th-9th graders) which allows me to encourage pretending. The creative problem-solving involved in teaching helps my writing, and the kids I teach, also, of course, inspire me. I am a lot less shy, now, but I still feel the written word is my best tool for expressing and sharing my real self."

Biographical and Critical Sources

PERIODICALS

Booklist, June 1, 1999, Ilene Cooper, review of *When JFK Was My Father,* p. 1813; June 1, 2003, Gillian Engberg, review of *The Gorillas of Gill Park,* p. 1776.
Horn Book, July-August, 1999, Lauren Adams, review of *When JFK Was My Father,* pp. 463-464; July-August, 2004, Susan Dove Lempke, review of *The Secret Life of a Boarding School Brat,* p. 452.
Kirkus Reviews, April 15, 2004, review of *The Secret Life of a Boarding School Brat,* p. 394.
New York Times Book Review, October 17, 1999, Patricia McCormick, review of *When JFK Was My Father,* p.31.
Publishers Weekly, May 26, 2003, review of *The Gorillas of Gill Park,* p. 70; March 22, 2004, review of *The Secret Life of a Boarding School Brat,* p. 86.
School Library Journal, December, 1995, Mary Jo Drungil, review of *Midnight Magic,* pp. 80-81; April, 1999, Connie Tyrrell Burns, review of *When JFK Was My Father,* p. 134.

* * *

GOWEN, L. Kris 1968-

Personal

Born October 23, 1968, in Mountain Lakes, NJ. *Education:* Stanford University, B.A., 1990; Harvard Graduate School of Education, Ed.M., 1994; Stanford University School of Education, Ph.D., 1998. *Hobbies and other interests:* Hockey, being a dog owner, home restoration.

Addresses

Home—3617 Northeast Sixth Ave., Portland, OR 97212. *Agent*—Andrea Pedolsky, Altair Literary Agency, P.O. Box 11656, Washington, DC 20008.

Career

Womensforum.com, San Francisco, CA, senior channel producer, 1998-2000; Foundation for Accountability, Portland, OR, senior research associate, 2000-04; Portland State University, Portland, OR, member of adjunct faculty, 2000—. OMPRO, project coordinator, 2004—.

Member

Oregon Public Health Association, American Psychological Association, SIECUS.

Writings

Making Sexual Decisions: The Ultimate Teen Guide, Scarecrow Press (Lanham, MD), 2003.
Image and Identity: Becoming the Person You Are, for Scarecrow Press (Lanham, MD).2003.

Contributor of articles to professional journals, including *Journal of Adolescence, Journal of Youth and Adolescence, Sex Roles,* and *Health Education and Behavior.*

Sidelights

L. Kris Gowen told *Something about the Author:* "I was happy and excited when I was asked to write a book on sex education. It was nothing short of a dream come true. Sex education—and other types of health education—is a main interest of mine. I've taught it, thought about it, and researched it quite a bit. Why? Because I think it's important. I want to help teens make educated decisions about their sexual behaviors. I want to help them fill in some of the blanks in their knowledge about sex and relationships. I also want to provide them some things to think about when it comes to the feelings and emotions that surround sex. In short, I want to help them make their own decisions when it comes to relationships and being sexual with others. Because I believe, that given the right information and a good amount of support, teens can be trusted to choose wisely."

Biographical and Critical Sources

PERIODICALS

School Library Journal, November, 2003, review of *Making Sexual Decisions: The Ultimate Teen Guide,* p.158.

*   *   *

GRAVES, Keith

Personal

Married; wife's name Nancy; children: Max, Emma (twins). *Hobbies and other interests:* Befriending armadillos.

Addresses

Home—Austin, TX. *Agent*—c/o Author Mail, Philomel, Putnam Berkley Group, 200 Madison Ave., New York, NY 10016. *E-mail*—kgraves@austin.rr.com.

Career

Artist, illustrator, and writer.

Writings

Frank Was a Monster Who Wanted to Dance, Chronicle Books (San Francisco, CA), 1999.
Pet Boy, Chronicle Books (San Francisco, CA), 2000.
Uncle Blubbafink's Seriously Ridiculous Stories, Scholastic Press (New York, NY), 2001.
Loretta: Ace Pinky Scout, Scholastic (New York, NY), 2002.
Down in the Dumps with the Three Nasty Gnarlies, Scholastic (New York, NY), 2003.

ILLUSTRATOR

Mary Alice Fontenot, *Clove Crawfish and Petit Papillon,* Pelican Pub. Co. (Grenta, LA), 1984.
Mary Alice Fontenot, *Clovis Crawfish and His Friends,* Pelican Pub. Co. (Gretna, LA), 1985.
Helen Ketteman, *Armadillo Tatletale,* Scholastic Press (New York, NY), 2000.
Margie Palatini, *Moo Who?,* Katherine Tegen Books (New York, NY), 2004.
Sandy Asher, *Too Many Frogs!,* Philomel Books (New York, NY), 2005.

Sidelights

Texas-based artist Keith Graves is the author and illustrator of several children's books, among them *Down in the Dumps with the Three Nasty Gnarlies, Loretta: Ace Pinky Scout,* and *Frank Was a Monster Who Wanted to Dance.* Describing *Down in the Dumps with the Three Nasty Gnarlies,* the story of three singing, stinking, and sublimely satisfied dump dwellers, Jennifer Mattson wrote in *Booklist* that "kids will relish these stinkers' gleeful unconcern for matters of personal hygiene, along with Graves' infectiously silly verses and his irreverent spin on the just-be-yourself message." Liza Graybill shared Mattson's enthusiasm in her *School Library Journal* review, writing of *Down in the Dumps with the Three Nasty Gnarlies* that the book's "illustrations, concept and rhyming text . . . mesh to form a unified stinky nest of fun."

Another of Graves' silly children's fictions, *Loretta: Ace Pinky Scout,* finds a young perfectionist crushed when she does not come out on top in a scouting contest. In *Kirkus Reviews* a critic stated that while the book's "message isn't new, and the snarky smirk on Loretta's face is perfectly annoying, . . . Graves adds some levity by exaggerating the quest for merit badges among Scouts to the level of caricature." Classing the picture book as a "great read-aloud and praising "the colorful, rowdy illustrations," *School Library Journal* critic Leslie Barban enjoyed Graves' saucy protagonist, writing that "Loretta's can-do attitude, humor, and enthusiasm for life make her a heroine whom readers will admire."

Biographical and Critical Sources

PERIODICALS

Booklist, March 15, 2001, John Peters, review of *Pet Boy,* p. 1404; October 15, 2002, GraceAnne A. DeCandido, review of *Loretta: Ace Pinky Scout,* p. 412; November 15, 2003, Jennifer Mattson, review of *Down in the Dumps with the Three Nasty Gnarlies,* p. 600.

Kirkus Reviews, August 15, 2002, review of *Loretta: Ace Pinky Scout,* p. 1223.

Publishers Weekly, March 26, 2001, review of *Pet Boy,* p. 92; September 9, 2002, review of *Loretta: Ace Pinky Scout,* p. 68.

School Library Journal, September, 2000, Judith Constantinides, review of *Armadillo Tattletale,* p. 201; January, 2002, Barbara Bunkley, review of *Uncle Blubbafink's Seriously Ridiculous Stories,* p. 98; December, 2002, Leslie Barban, review of *Loretta: Ace Pinky Scout,* p. 96; December, 2003, Liza Graybill, review of *Down in the Dumps with the Three Nasty Gnarlies,* p. 113.

ONLINE

Keith Graves Web site, http://www.keithgravesart.com/ (January 5, 2005).*

*　　*　　*

GRINSPOON, David H. 1959-

Personal

Born December 21, 1959, in Boston, MA; son of Lester (a physician) and Evelyn (a mathematics professor) Grinspoon; married Tory Read (a photographer), May 13, 1995. *Education:* Brown University, Sc.B. (planetary science), 1982, B.A. (philosophy of science), 1982; postgraduate work at University of Arizona, 1989. *Religion:* "Cosmist." *Hobbies and other interests:* Performing rock music.

Addresses

Office—Funky Science, 1836 Blake St., Suite 100A, Denver, CO 80211. *Agent*—Tina Bennett, Janklow & Nesbit, 445 Park Ave., New York, NY 10022. *E-mail*—david@funkyscience.net.

Career

NASA/Ames Research Center, Mountain View, CA, postdoctoral research associate, 1989-91; University of Colorado, Boulder, assistant professor, 1991-99, adjunct professor, 2000—; Southwest Research Institute, Boulder, CO, planetary scientist, beginning 2000.

Member

American Astronomical Society, American Association for the Advancement of Science, Authors Guild, Authors League.

Awards, Honors

Los Angeles Times Book Prize, 1998, for *Venus Revealed;* Gerard Kuiper Memorial Award for outstanding scholarship, University of Arizona, 1, 1989.

Writings

Venus Revealed: A New Look below the Clouds of Our Mysterious Twin Planet, Addison-Wesley Pub. (Reading, MA), 1997.

(With Mikhail Iakovlevich Marov) *The Planet Venus,* Yale University Press (New Haven, CT), 1998.

Lonely Planets: The Natural Philosophy of Alien Life, Ecco Press (New York, NY), 2003.

Contributor to periodicals, including *Scientific American, New York Times, Boston Globe, Astronomy,* and *Slate.*

Sidelights

Planetary scientist and educator David H. Grinspoon is the author of *Lonely Planets: The Natural Philosophy of Alien Life,* a book referred to by a *Publishers Weekly* reviewer as "an up-to-date picture of the search for extraterrestrial life and the prospects of finding it in a universe that we now know contains other solar systems." The well-organized book begins with a recap of astronomical and social history that extends back nearly four centuries. Grinspoon discusses hypotheses about far-off worlds and the possibility that other forms of life exist in the solar system. He then continues on with a discussion of more modern topics, including updates regarding the knowledge gained through recent scientific discoveries. Noting that the author "comes across like a buddy in a bar, trying out ideas over a beer or few," *Booklist* contributor Frieda Murray added that Grinspoon "seasons the discussion with witty anecdotes, personal experiences . . . and reminders of what has been demonstrated and what is still theoretical fun to read." Reviewing *Lonely Planets* for *Astronomy,* Glenn Muller added that Grinspoon's relaxed approach to a technical subject makes his book particularly accessible to "young people contemplating an astrobiology career," who "will sense Grinspoon's delight (and sometimes repulsion) and his realization that he still has much to learn."

Biographical and Critical Sources

PERIODICALS

Astronomy March, 2004, Glenn Muller, "Are We Alone? Perhaps Not.," p. 96.

Booklist, November 1, 2003, Frieda Murray, review of *Lonely Planets: The Natural Philosophy of Alien Life,* p. 466.

Entertainment Weekly, November 14, 2003, Wook Kim, review of *Lonely Planets,* p. 134.

Publishers Weekly, October 27, 2003, review of *Lonely Planets,* p. 56.

H

HALPERIN, Michael

Personal
Male.

Addresses
Agent—George Nicholson, Sterling Lord Literistic, 65 Bleecker St., New York, NY 10012. *E-mail*—michaelhalperin@sprintmail.com.

Career
Screenwriter and children's book author.

Awards, Honors
Best Book designation, American Bookseller's Association, 1993, and Teachers Choice award, International Reading Association, and Notable Children's Trade Book designation, Childrens Book Council/National Council for Social Studies, both 1994, all for *Jacob's Rescue: A Holocaust Story.*

Writings

FOR CHLDREN

(With Malka Drucker) *Jacob's Rescue: A Holocaust Story,* Doubleday (New York, NY), 1993.
Black Wheels, XLibris (Philadelphia, PA), 2003.

OTHER

Writing Great Characters: The Psychology of Character Development in Screenplays, Lone Eagle (Los Angeles, CA), 1996.
Writing the Second Act: Building Conflict and Tension in Your Film Script, Michael Wiese Productions (Studio City, CA), 2000.

Writing the Killer Treatment: Selling Your Story without a Script, Michael Wiese Production (Studio City, CA), 2002.

Also author of numerous television-series screenplays.

Sidelights
Taking a break from his career as a television screenwriter, Michael Halperin has collaborated with coauthor Malka Drucker on *Jacob's Rescue,* an award winning children's story that focuses on the Holocaust. In the 1993 novel, eight-year-old Marissa learns the story of her father Jacob and her uncle David's experiences under the Nazi occupation of Poland during World War II. While living in a Warsaw ghetto as children, and fearing deportation and death from starvation, the two young brothers are smuggled out of the ghetto and taken in by a non-Jewish couple who risk their own lives in order to save the boys. "This is a heartening story of great courage in the midst of the madness of war," commented *Horn Book* reviewer Hanna B. Zeiger, explaining that the novel is based on a true story. While noting that "the most heroic gestures don't quite ring true," a *Publishers Weekly* critic nonetheless had praise for *Jacob's Rescue,* writing that Halperin and Drucker "are much better at the smaller moments," enough of which "exist to engage the reader's imagination, if not to infuse the story with unflappable authenticity."

Halperin's book *Black Wheels* is also based on a true story. The book follows an African-American teen living during the late nineteenth century who runs away from home. Joining the U.S. Army's all-black Twenty-fifth Infantry, he soon finds himself trekking across North America on a bicycle, in a novel that *Voice of Youth Advocates* contributor Susan Allen dubbed "a gem." Praising the story as "well told," Allen added that *Black Wheels* contains "real nuggets of irony throughout" and predicted that the book would be a hit with teen readers.

Biographical and Critical Sources

PERIODICALS

Horn Book, September-October, 1993, Hanna B. Zeiger, review of *Jacob's Rescue: A Holocaust Story,* p. 596.

Publishers Weekly, May 10, 1993, review of *Jacob's Rescue,* p. 72.

Voice of Youth Advocates, December, 2003, Susan Allen, review of *Black Wheels,* p. 393.

Writer, March, 2003, Chuck Leddy, "Hollywood Veterans Share Writing, Marketing Tips," p. 50.

* * *

HAMPTON, Wilborn

Personal

Born in Dallas, TX; married an editor. *Education:* University of Texas at Austin, B.A. (English literature), c. 1963.

Addresses

Home—New York, NY. *Agent*—c/o Author Mail, Candlewick Press, 2067 Massachusetts Ave., 5th Floor, Cambridge, MA 02140.

Career

Journalist and author. United Press International (UPI), cub reporter in Dallas, TX, 1963, then foreign correspondent; *New York Times,* New York, NY, editor.

Awards, Honors

Blue Ribbon Award, 1997, Young Adult Library Services Association Editor's Picks for Reluctant Readers designation, 1998, and Texas Bluebonnet Award nomination, 1999, all for *Kennedy Assassinated!*

Writings

Kennedy Assassinated!: The World Mourns: A Reporter's Story, Candlewick Press (Cambridge, MA), 1997.

Meltdown: A Race against Nuclear Disaster at Three Mile Island: A Reporter's Story, Candlewick Press (Cambridge, MA), 2001.

September 11, 2001: Attack on New York City, Candlewick Press (Cambridge, MA), 2003.

Sidelights

In *Kennedy Assassinated!: The World Mourns: A Reporter's Story,* journalist Wilborn Hampton tells the story of how, as a rookie reporter, he happened to be

Wilborn Hampton details the 2001 attacks on the World Trade Center and provides personal stories from New York residents who survived and witnessed the tragedy. (From September 11, 2001: Attack on New York City.*)*

the first employee at United Press International's Dallas, Texas, offices to receive an incoming telephone call reporting that President John F. Kennedy had just been shot. Ironically, the 1963 assassination launched Hampton's career in a new direction: an English literature major, he proved that he had journalistic savvy and fortitude in the hours that ensued as he covered the unfolding story. With what reviewer Elizabeth Bush, writing in the *Bulletin of the Center for Children's Books,* called "journalistic flair and raw, edge-of-the-seat urgency," Hampton describes the pandemonium in covering the breaking story of the successful assassination attempt, as reporters attempted to out-scoop each other for the latest developments and wrestle for use of the press phone. In one case, Hampton tells of purposefully tying up a hospital phone line so that UPI could have direct and instant access to ongoing events. He also moves beyond the assassination and describes related historical events, such as the inauguration of Vice President Lyndon Johnson and the murder of Lee Harvey Oswald at the hands of Jack Ruby, highlighting his text with photos that lend historical perspective. A reviewer for *Publishers Weekly* claimed that the journalist's "taut narrative is absorbing enough to keep pages turning." Hampton does not neglect the emotional impact of the event either, and describes breaking down and crying at Kennedy's death. During his career as a reporter, Hampton has come face to face with other momentous turns of fate. In *Meltdown: A Race against Nuclear Disaster at Three Mile Island,* he describes one of the worst nuclear power plant accidents in the United States, narrating the story in hour-by-hour chronology. In what a *Publishers Weekly* reviewer described as an "engaging, personal, behind-the-scenes viewpoint," Hampton moves from a discussion of Hiroshima, Japan, as it came under nuclear attack during World War II through the development of nuclear energy to the problems of the Three Mile Island nuclear plant in Harrisburg, Pennsylvania, in 1979. By ending his book with a discussion of the nuclear tragedy at the Soviet plant at Chernobyl in the mid-1980s, Hampton encourages readers to consider "weighty ethical questions about the future of atomic power," the *Publishers Weekly* reviewer added. *Meltdown* provides information regarding the basic operation of a nuclear plant and how the U.S. government dealt with the tragedy as well as presenting readers with "a glimpse into the workings of an experienced journalist," according to *Horn Book* contributor Betty Carter, who praised the book as a "dramatic narrative."

Hampton was living and working in New York City the day the United States came under attack by terrorists, and his book *September 11, 2001: Attack on New York City* presents his experiences. His book takes the form of a collection of vignettes that focus on the way individual people—including those who lost family members, those who lived through the ordeal, and those who helped in clean-up efforts—coped with tragedy. "Without sentimentalizing or sensationalizing, Hampton connects all these stories into a cohesive narrative," noted *Horn Book* contributor Betty Carter, praising the book

as "accessible and informative." A *Publishers Weekly* reviewer noted that Hampton's "strong, and occasionally rawly emotional, reporting" is compelling, while in *Booklist* GraceAnne A. DeCandido dubbed *September 11, 2001* "one of the best" books written to explain that fateful day to younger readers.

Biographical and Critical Sources

PERIODICALS

Booklist, September 15, 1997, Ilene Cooper, review of *Kennedy Assassinated!: The World Mourns: A Reporter's Story,* p. 230; January 1, 2002, Randy Meyer, review of *Meltdown: A Race against Nuclear Disaster at Three Mile Island: A Reporter's Story,* p. 835; July, 2003, GraceAnne A. DeCandido, review of *September 11, 2001: Attack on New York City,* p. 1878.
Bulletin of the Center for Children's Books, October, 1997, pp. 52-53.
Horn Book, January-February, 2003, Betty Carter, review of *Meltdown,* p. 98; September-October, 2003, Betty Carter, review of *September 11, 2001,* p. 629.
New York Times Book Review, November 16, 1997, p. 28.
Publishers Weekly, July 28, 1997, review of *Kennedy Assassinated!,* p. 75; November 3, 1997, p. 60; October 15, 2001, review of *Meltdown,* p. 73; August 18, 2003, review of *September 11, 2001,* p. 81.
School Library Journal, October, 1997, review of *Kennedy Assassinated!,* p. 147; July, 2003, Wendy Lukehart, review of *September 11, 2001,* p. 141.

ONLINE

Candlewick Press Web site, http://www.candlewick.com/ (January 23, 2005), "Wilborn Hampton."*

*   *   *

HANSEN, Jennifer 1972-

Personal

Born September 7, 1972, in Heidelberg, Germany; daughter of Laurence A. Partan and Karleen Leinemann Escobar; married Chris Hansen, August 12, 1994; children: Sterling, Siena. *Education:* Middlebury College, B.A., 1994. *Religion:* "Christian." *Hobbies and other interests:* Baking.

Addresses

Home—714 Poinsettia Ave., Corona Del Mar, CA, 92625. *E-mail*—chefjhansen@yahoo.com.

Career

Writer.

Writings

(Editor) *Anne Frank* (essays; "People Who Made History" series), Greenhaven Press (San Diego, CA), 2003.

Work in Progress

For Love of Bread, a novel.

Biographical and Critical Sources

PERIODICALS

Kliatt, November, 2003, Paula Rohrlick, review of *Anne Frank,* p. 32.

*   *   *

HATHORN, Elizabeth
See HATHORN, Libby

*   *   *

HATHORN, Libby 1943-
(Elizabeth Hathorn)

Personal

Full name, Elizabeth Helen Hathorn; surname is pronounced "hay-thorn"; born September 26, 1943, in Newcastle, New South Wales, Australia; married John Hathorn (a teacher, deceased 1998); children: Lisa, Keiran. *Education:* Attended Balmain Teachers' College (now University of Technology).

Addresses

Agent—Fran Moore, Curtis Brown, Level 1/2 Boundary Street, Paddington 2021 Australia; fax: 612-93616161.

Career

Teacher and librarian in schools in Sydney, Australia, 1965-81; worked as a deputy principal, 1977; consultant and senior education officer for government adult education programs, 1981-86; full-time writer, 1987—; writer in residence at the University of Technology, Sydney, 1990, Woollahra Library, 1992, and at Edith Cowan University, 1992. Consultant to the Dorothea Mackellar National Poetry Competition/Festival for children; speaker for student, teacher, and parent groups; Australia Day Amabassador, 1992—.

Awards, Honors

The Tram to Bondi Beach was highly commended by the Children's Book Council of Australia, 1982; *Paolo's Secret* was shortlisted for the Children's Book of the

Year Award and for the New South Wales Premier's Literary Awards, both 1986; Honour Award, Children's Book Council of Australia, 1987, Kids Own Australian Literary Award (KOALA) shortlist, 1988, Young Australians Best Book Award (YABBA) shortlist, 1989 and 1990, all for *All about Anna;* Literature Board of the Australia Council fellowships, 1987 and 1988; Honour Award, Children's Book Council of Australia, 1988, for *Looking out for Sampson;* Children's Book of the Year Award shortlist, 1990, for *The Extraordinary Magics of Emma McDade;* Society of Women Writers honors, 1990, for the body of her work during 1987-89; Honour Book of the Year for older readers, Children's Book Council of Australia, 1990, American Library Association Best Book for Young Adults citation, 1991, Canberra's Own Outstanding List shortlist, all 1991, and award from Stichting Collectieve Propaganda van het Nederlands Boek (Foundation for the Promotion of Dutch Books; Dutch translation), 1992, all for *Thunderwith;* Children's Book Council of Australia notable book ciations, 1991, for *So Who Needs Lotto?* and *Jezza Says;* New South Wales Children's Week Medal for literature, 1992; Kate Greenaway Award, United Kingdom, 1995, for *Way Home;* Australian Violence Prevention Certificate Award, 1995, for *Feral Kid* and *Way Home;* Parent's Choice Award and Society of Women Writers (New South Wales, Australia) award, both for *Way Home;* Society of Women Writers award, 1995, for *Feral Kid* and *The Climb,* 1997, for *Rift,* 2001, for *Grandma's Shoes,* and 2003, for *The River;* Notable Book citations from the Children's Book Council of Australia, 1993, 1996, 1997, and 2003; White Raven citation, Bologna Children's Book Fair, 2001, for *The Gift;* best adaptation citation, Australian Writers' Guild, 2001, for the libretto of *Grandma's Shoes;* Australian Interactive Media Industry Award for Best New Children's Product, for *Weirdstop 2003;* Prime Minister's Centenary Medal, 2003.

Writings

FOR CHILDREN AND YOUNG ADULTS

(Under name Elizabeth Hathorn, with John Hathorn) *Go Lightly: Creative Writing through Poetry,* illustrated by Joan Saint, Boden (Sydney, Australia), 1974.
Stephen's Tree (storybook), illustrated by Sandra Laroche, Methuen, 1979.
Lachlan's Walk (picture book), illustrated by Sandra Laroche, Heinemann, 1980.
The Tram to Bondi Beach (picture book), illustrated by Julie Vivas, Collins, 1981, Kane/Miller (Brooklyn, NY), 1989.
Paolo's Secret (novella), illustrated by Lorraine Hannay, Heinemann, 1985.
All about Anna (novel), Heinemann, 1986.
Looking out for Sampson (storybook), Oxford University Press, 1987.

Freya's Fantastic Surprise (picture book), illustrated by Sharon Thompson, Scholastic (New York, NY), 1988.

The Extraordinary Magics of Emma McDade (storybook), illustrated by Maya, Oxford University Press (New York, NY), 1989.

Stuntumble Monday (picture book), illustrated by Melissa Web, Collins Dove, 1989.

The Garden of the World (picture book), illustrated by Tricia Oktober, Margaret Hamilton Books, 1989.

Thunderwith (novel), Heinemann, 1989, Little, Brown (Boston, MA), 1991.

Jezza Says (novel), illustrated by Donna Rawlins, Angus & Robertson, 1990.

So Who Needs Lotto? (novella), illustrated by Simon Kneebone, Penguin, 1990.

Talks with My Skateboard (poetry), Australian Broadcasting Corp., 1991.

(Editor) *The Blue Dress* (stories), Heinemann, 1991.

Help for Young Writers (nonfiction), Nelson, 1991.

Good to Read (textbook), Nelson, 1991.

Who? (stories), Heinemann, 1992.

Love Me Tender (novel), Oxford University Press (New York, NY), 1992, reprinted as *Juke-box Jive* (novel), Hodder, 1996.

The Lenski Kids and Dracula (novella), Penguin, 1992.

Valley under the Rock (novel), Reed Heinemann, 1993.

Way Home (picture book), illustrated by Greg Rogers, Crown (New York), 1993.

There and Back (poetry), Macmillan/McGraw Hill (Santa Rosa, CA), 1993.

The Surprise Box, illustrated by Priscilla Cutter, SRA School Group (Santa Rosa, CA), 1994.

Feral Kid (novel), Hodder & Stoughton, 1994.

Looking for Felix, illustrated by Ned Culio, SRA School Group (Santa Rosa, CA), 1994.

Grandma's Shoes (picture book), illustrated by Elivia Savadier, Little, Brown (Boston, MA), 1994, reissued, illustrated by Caroline Magerl, Hodder, 2000.

What a Star (novel), HarperCollins, 1994.

The Wonder Thing (picture book), illustrated by Peter Gouldthorpe, Penguin, 1995.

The Climb (novel), Penguin, 1996.

Chrysalis (novel), Reed, 1997.

Rift (novel), Hodder Headline, 1998.

Sky Sash So Blue (picture book), illustrated by Benny Andrews, Simon & Schuster (New York, NY), 1998.

Magical Ride, Hodder Headline (Australia), 1999.

(With Gary Crew) *Dear Venny, Dear Saffron* (novel), Lothian, 1999.

Ghostop Book 1: Double Sorrow (novel), Hodder Headline, 1999.

Ghostop Book 2: Twice the Ring of Fire (novel), Hodder Headline, 1999.

Ghostop Book 3: For Love to Conquer All (novel), Hodder Headline, 1999.

The Gift, illustrated by Greg Rogers, Random House (New York, NY), 2000.

A Face in the Water, illustrated by Uma Krishnaswamy, Goodbooks, 2000.

The River (picture book), Curriculum Corporation, 2001.

Okra and Acacia: The Story of the Wattle Pattern Plate (picture book), illustrated by Brigitte Stoddart, Curriculum Corporation, 2001.

The Painter (novel), Hodder Headline, 2001.

Volcano Boy (verse novel), Lothian, 2002.

The Wishing Cupboard (picture book), illustrated by Libby Stanley, Lothian, 2002.

Over the Moon (picture book), illustrated Caroline Magerl, Lothian, 2003.

The Great Big Animal Ask (picture book), illustrated Anna Pignato, Lothian, 2004.

Author of the limited edition poetry anthology *Heard Singing,* Out of India Press, 1998. Also author of a libretto for a children's opera, composed by Grahame Koehne, based on *Grandma's Shoes,* that was first performed in 2000 at the Australian Opera and Theatre of Image, Sydney, Australia; author of libretto for *Sky Sash So Blue,* composed by Phillip Ratliff and first performed at Miles College, Alabama, 2004; writer and producer for interactive storytelling series *Weirdstop 2003, Coolstop 2004,* and *Wonderstop 2005.*

FOR ADULTS

(With G. Bates) *Half-Time: Perspectives on Mid-life,* Fontana Collins, 1987.

Better Strangers (stories), Millennium Books, 1989.

Damascus, a Rooming House (libretto), performed by the Australian Opera at Performance Space, Sydney, 1990.

The Maroubra Cycle: A Journey around Childhood (performance poetry), University of Technology, Sydney, Australia, 1990.

(And director) *The Blue Dress Suite* (music theater piece), produced at Melbourne International Festival, Melbourne, Australia, 1991.

Author of the series *On Course!: Today's English for Young Writers,* Macmillan, and *Help for Young Writers,* Nelson.

Some of Hathorn's works have been translated into Greek, Italian, Dutch, German, French, Norwegian, Danish, Swedish, Portuguese, and Korean.

Adaptations

Thunderwith was produced as a "Hallmark Hall of Fame" television movie titled *The Echo of Thunder; Songs with My Skateboard* features Hathorn's poems set to music by Stephen Lalor. *Grandma's Shoes* and *Sky Sash So Blue* were produced as children's operas. Barking Gecko produced a play that Hathorn wrote based on *Way Home* with music by Stephen Lalor.

Work in Progress

Georgiana, a historic novel; a picture book.

Sidelights

Libby Hathorn is an Australian writer who produces poetry, picture books, drama, novels, short stories, and nonfiction for children, young adults, and adults. Best known in the United States for her critically acclaimed novel *Thunderwith,* Hathorn has created works ranging from serious stories of troubled youth to lighthearted, fast-paced comedies. She writes of powerful female characters in her novels for junior readers, such as the protagonists in *All about Anna* and *The Extraordinary Magics of Emma McDade*; or of lonely, misunderstood teenagers in novels such as *Feral Kid, Love Me Tender,* and *Valley under the Rock.* As Maurice Saxby noted in *St. James Guide to Children's Writers,* "In her novels for teenagers especially, Hathorn exposes, with compassion, sensitivity, and poetry the universal and ongoing struggle of humanity to heal hurts, establish meaningful relationships, and to learn to accept one's self—and ultimately—those who have wronged us."

"I must have been very young indeed when I decided to become a writer," Hathorn once commented. "My grandmother always kept my stories in her best black handbag and read them out loud to long-suffering relatives and told me over and over that I'd be a writer when I grew up." Though Hathorn started her career as a teacher and librarian, she did eventually become a writer. "Libby Hathorn knows exactly how today's children think and feel," observed Maurice Saxby in *The Proof of the Puddin': Australian Children's Literature, 1970-1990.* "She has an uncanny ear for the speech nuances of the classroom, playground and home. . .. [She] is always able to penetrate the facade of her characters and with skill and subtlety reveal what they are really like inside."

Hathorn grew up near Sydney, Australia, and recalled that at that time her parents did not own a car. "In fact, not many people on the street where I lived in the early 1950s owned cars. We had no television, either. We amused ourselves with storytelling and reading out loud and lots of games." Hathorn often read and told stories to her sisters and brother; she was encouraged by her parents, who "loved books" and had bookcases crammed with them. "Books were pretty central in our lives," she stated. "My father in particular read to us at night when he could get home in time. He was a detective and had long shifts at night that often kept him late. When he read we didn't interrupt, in fact we'd never dream of it as his voice filled the room because it seemed so obviously important to him—the ebb and flow of the language. My mother—who was very proud of her Irish ancestry—told us lots of true stories about the history of our family and also about her own girlhood."

As a child, Hathorn read "adventure books set in the Australian bush, like *Seven Little Australians,* as well as classics like *Black Beauty, The Secret Garden, Little Women,* and books by Emily and Charlotte Brontë," she once explained. She also read works by Australian authors "with considerable delight at finding Australian settings and people in print." Later, Hathorn would lend her own work an Australian flavor after noticing "the need for more books that told Australian kids about themselves."

Hathorn began writing her own stories and poems when she was still a girl. Though she was often shy and quiet, Hathorn once noted that she could keep company "entertained with strings of stories that I made up as I went along." Her family encouraged her, and Hathorn "loved being at center stage—so I couldn't have been altogether a shy little buttercup." At school, she enjoyed reading and creative writing, and was disappointed in later years when "we had to write essays and commentaries but never, never stories or poems. I was extremely bored in my final years at school." Hathorn has also acknowledged that her high school years weren't all bad: "After all, I was introduced to the works of William Shakespeare, and particularly in my later years the poetic nature of his work touched me deeply. And best of all we studied the Romantic poets and I fell in love with John Keats and Samuel Coleridge as well as Percy Bysshe Shelley, Lord Byron, and William Wordsworth."

After graduating from high school, Hathorn worked in a laboratory and studied at night for a year before attending college full-time. Despite her parents' objections, she contemplated a career in journalism, hoping that she could learn "the art and craft of novel writing." "Anyway, my parents thought it important that I have a profession where I could earn a reasonable living—writers being notoriously underpaid," Hathorn remarked. "I was drawn to teaching; so after a year of broken specimen flasks and test tubes and discovering that my science courses did not enthrall me, I left the laboratory."

Hathorn attended Balmain Teachers' College (now the University of Technology, Sydney). "I must admit that I found the regulations of the place quite hard," she recalled. "Many of the lectures of those days seemed so dull to me that I wondered whether indeed I would last as a teacher for very long." Hathorn did enjoy her literature classes and was surprised to find that "when I came out of the rather dull years at college, I not only liked classroom teaching, but I also discovered that it was the most thrilling, absorbing, rewarding, and wonderful job anyone could have!"

After teaching for several years in Sydney, Hathorn applied for a position as a school librarian. "Although I was sorry to leave the intimacy of family that a classroom teacher has with her own class, the library was a new and exciting chapter for me," Hathorn once commented. "I had books, books, and more books to explore and the amazingly enjoyable job of bringing stories to every child in the school!" Her job as a librarian, the author added, "had a major influence on my decision to seriously try to publish my stories."

Hathorn's first book for children was *Stephen's Tree,* which was published in 1979. She followed this with two picture books: *Lachlan's Walk* and *The Tram to Bondi Beach.* In the genre of children's picture books, Hathorn discovered, as she explained, "such a scarcity of Australian material! I wanted to talk about our place, here and now, and have pictures that Australian children would instantly recognize. *Stephen's Tree* was a breakthrough in publishing. I had to fight with my publisher to have a gum tree on the cover. They wanted an ash or elm or oak so it would sell in England and Europe! Similarly, I was told *The Tram to Bondi Beach* should not mention Bondi. I won those fights and I must say *The Tram to Bondi Beach* has made its way onto the American market and American children didn't seem to have much trouble at all."

The Tram to Bondi Beach tells the story of Keiran, a nine-year-old boy who longs for a job selling newspapers to passengers on the trams that travel through Sydney. Keiran wants to be like Saxon, an older boy, who is an experienced newspaper seller. Reviewers commented on the nostalgic quality of the story, which is set in the 1930s. Marianne Pilla of the *School Library Journal* complimented its "smooth" narrative and "vivid" passages. *Times Literary Supplement* contributor Ann Martin called it "a simple but appealing tale," and Karen Jameyson wrote in *Horn Book* that the book "will undoubtedly hold readers' interest."

Hathorn followed *The Tram to Bondi Beach* with *Paolo's Secret, All about Anna,* and *Looking out for Sampson.* As Hathorn once noted, *All about Anna,* her first novel, "is based on a wild, naughty cousin I had who drove her mother's car down the road at ten years of age and did other wild deeds—a perfect subject to write about." The book details the comic adventures of Lizzie, Harriet, Christopher, and their energetic, imaginative cousin, Anna. Lizzie, the narrator, explains that "I like being with Anna because somehow things always seem fast and furious and funny when she's around—and well, she's just a very unusual person."

Like *All about Anna, Looking out for Sampson* touches on family themes. Bronwyn wishes that her younger brother, Sampson, were older so that she could have a friend instead of someone to babysit. And when Cheryl and her mother come to stay with Bronwyn's family, Bronwyn's situation worsens. A disagreeable girl, Cheryl hints that Bronwyn's parents must care more about Sampson, since they give the toddler so much attention. After Sampson is lost briefly at the beach, however, Cheryl and Bronwyn reconcile and Bronwyn's parents express their appreciation of her.

Around the time *All about Anna* was published in 1986, Hathorn decided to give up her job and become a full-time writer. "I wanted to be a full-time writer secretly all my life but when I began my working life as a teacher this dream seemed to recede," the author once explained. "And once I was married and with two children I felt I had to keep up my contribution to our lifestyle. My husband is also a teacher and I thought it would be unfair if he had to work every day while I was home writing. It was as if in the eyes of the world writing was not work! And I'm to blame for allowing myself to think like that too.

"I've changed my mind now and I wish I had had the courage to do so much sooner. While I loved teaching, after some years of it I was ready for change. I was already writing short stories but I was aching to tell longer stories, to produce a novel for older readers. This was very hard when I was working full-time and had young children—so the stories I chose to write at that time were for younger children and were either picture books or junior novels like *All about Anna* and *Looking out for Sampson.*"

Among Hathorn's other books for young readers is *The Extraordinary Magics of Emma McDade.* The story describes the adventures of the title character, whose superhuman powers include incredible strength, the ability to call thousands of birds by whistling, and control over the weather. Another of Hathorn's books geared towards beginning readers is *Freya's Fantastic Surprise.* In it Miriam tells the class at news time that her parents bought her a tent, a surprise that Freya attempts to top by making up fantastic stories that her classmates realize are false. Freya eventually has a real surprise to share, however, when her mother announces that Freya will soon have a new sister. Published in the United States as well as Australia, *Freya's Fantastic Surprise* was praised by critics. Louise L. Sherman noted in *School Library Journal* that "Freya's concern about impressing her classmates . . . is on target." In a *Horn Book* review, Elizabeth S. Watson called the book "a winner" and commented that "the text and pictures combine to produce a tale that proves truth is best."

Hathorn began writing her first novel for young adults, *Thunderwith,* after receiving an Australia Council grant in 1987. "At home writing for a year, I realized that this was to be my job for the rest of my life," Hathorn once remarked. "And since I have been able to give full-time attention to my writing it has certainly flowered in many new directions. I have begun writing longer novels for young adults and I have been able to take on more ambitious projects like libretti and music theatre pieces, which I enjoy tremendously."

Thunderwith, published in 1989, is the story of fourteen-year-old Lara, who begins living with the father she barely knows after her mother dies of cancer. Lara's new home is in the remote Wallingat Forest in New South Wales, Australia. Though Lara's relationship with her father develops smoothly, he is often away on business and Lara's stepmother is openly antagonistic towards her. Lonely and grief-stricken, Lara finds solace in her bond with a mysterious dog that appears during a storm. She names the dog Thunderwith and keeps his existence a secret; she only tells the aboriginal storyteller she has befriended at school. Eventually, Lara realizes that Thunderwith has filled the space that her mother's death created, enabling her to come to terms with her loss. Lara is also able to slowly win over her stepmother and to adjust to her new home and family life.

The setting of *Thunderwith* is one with which Hathorn is intimately acquainted. As a child, she had relatives who lived in the Australian bush, and she spent many holidays in the country. "This was to prove very important to me," Hathorn once stated. "The bush weaves its own magic and it's something you cannot experience from a book or television show in a suburban setting. My holidays, especially those on my grandmother's farm in the Blue Mountains, created in me an enduring love for the Australian bush. As a writer, however, up until a few years ago the settings I chose to write about were in the hub of the family and quite often in suburbia."

Hathorn came upon the idea for *Thunderwith* after her brother bought land in Wallingat Forest. "During the first holiday there a huge storm blew up at about midnight and such was the noise and intensity of it we all rose from our beds to watch it," Hathorn once said. "You can imagine how vulnerable you'd feel way out in the bush with thunder booming and lightning raging and trees whipping and bending . . . and in the midst of this fury suddenly I saw a dog. A huge dark dog dashed across the place where some hours earlier we'd had a campfire and eaten our evening meal under the stars—a lovely looking half-dingo creature.

"When I lay down again I had the image of the dog in my mind, against the landscape of the bush and storm. Again and again I saw the dog and a line of a poem seemed to fall into my head from the storm clouds above. 'With thunder you'll come—and with thunder you'll go.' What did it mean? What could it mean? By morning I had unraveled the mystery of the lines of poetry and I had a story about a girl called Lara whose mother dies in the first chapter and who comes to live on the farm in a forest with her dad and a new family."

The dog that Hathorn had seen became *Thunderwith,* "Lara's friend, her escape, and her link to her mother," as Hathorn explained. Lara's mother was modeled after Hathorn's friend Cheryl, who died of cancer before the book was finished. "I feel that Cheryl's spirit leaps and bounds all through it," the author once noted. "So you see for me there are many emotions through many experiences that weave themselves into my stories and into this story in particular—happiness in being together, the joy one feels in being surrounded by natural beauty, a dark sadness at loss, and the pain in hardships that must be endured. And the way people can change and grow even through dark and mystifyingly sad experiences. But you may be pleased to know that love and hope win out in Thunderwith. They have to—as I believe eventually they have to in life itself."

Thunderwith garnered praise as a sensitive and realistic young adult novel. A *Publishers Weekly* reviewer commented that "Hathorn deftly injects a sense of wonderment into this intense, very real story." According to *Horn Book* contributor Watson, *Thunderwith* possesses "a believable plot featuring a shattering climax and a satisfyingly realistic resolution." Robert Strang, writing in *Bulletin of the Center for Children's Books,* commended Hathorn's "especially expert weaving of story and setting." Similarly, *Magpies* contributor Karen Jameyson noted that Hathorn's "control over her complex subject is admirable; her insight into character sure and true; her ear for dialogue keen." Jameyson added that the author's "nimble detour from the usual route will leave readers surprised, even breathless."

Hathorn has also published poems for children and a story collection for young adults. Her poetry book *Talks with My Skateboard,* is divided into several sections and includes poems about outdoor activities, school, family life, cats, and nature. The poem "Skateboard" is written from a child's perspective: "My sister has a skateboard / and you should see her go . . . She can jump and twirl / Do a twist and turn, / What I want to know / Is why I can't learn?" *Who?,* published in 1992, contains stories about ghosts, love and friendship, and mysteries, some of which are based on tales that Hathorn's mother told her. The collection includes "Who?," in which a pitiful ghost awakens a family from their beds; "An Act of Kindness," in which a family mysteriously loses their ability to remember the names of objects; and "Jethro Was My Friend," where a young girl attempts to save her beloved bird from rapidly rising floodwaters.

Hathorn published more novels, including the young adult book *Love Me Tender* and a comic work for junior readers, *The Lenski Kids and Dracula.* Hathorn once commented that "*Love Me Tender* was a story I circled for a few years. It drew on my girlhood experiences although it's about a boy called Alan. It's a gentle story set in the days of rock and roll." In the novel, Alan and his sister and brothers are abandoned by their mother and sent to live with various relatives. Alan is taken in by his bossy, unsmiling Aunt Jessie, and the story chronicles his "interior journey as hope fades that he will ever see his Mum and his family again," Hathorn explained. "Alan changes but more importantly he causes people around him—including his old aunt—to change too. Self-growth is a very important message for young people today—looking inside and finding that strength to go on." *Love Me Tender* is among Hathorn's favorite creations; the book "has a place in my heart," she once commented, because it captures the atmosphere of the author's girlhood in the 1950s. Reviewing the book, which was reprinted in 1996 as *Jukebox Jive, School Librarian*'s Mary Hoffman commented that "this could so easily have been just a collection of cliches [but] what raises it is Libby Hathorn's honesty about Alan's feelings for his mother and his aching realization that the family will never all live together again."

A common thread in several of Hathorn's works is the author's belief in love, hope, and the resiliency of the human spirit. "With all the faults in the world, the injustices, the suffering, and the sheer violence that I am forced to acknowledge though not accept, I still have a great sense of hope," Hathorn once noted. "Human beings never cease to surprise me with their unexpectedness, their kindness, their cheerfulness, their will to go on against the odds. That's inspiring. And I feel a sense of hope should be nurtured in young people, for they are the hope of the world. My stories may sometimes have sad endings but they are never without some hope for the future."

In several books Hathorn has combined her interest in young people with her concerns about the environment, poverty, and homelessness. "My picture book *The Wonder Thing,* written after a visit to a rainforest to 'sing' about the beauty of the place, is also a plea for the survival of the earth's riches—trees, forests, mountains, and rivers," the author once explained. "There are only four to five words per page and it is a prose poem; I try to make those words the most delicately beautiful and evocative that I can. Both her picture book, *Way Home,* and her novel, *Feral Kid,* take up the theme of the homelessness of young people. I feel strongly that we should never accept the fact of homeless children on our streets. A society that allows this sort of thing is not a responsible and caring society to my mind; I very much want people to look closely at stories like mine and begin asking questions about something that is becoming all too common a sight in all cities of the world."

An abandoned adolescent figures in the 1998 novel, *Rift.* Vaughan Jasper Roberts is stuck with his grandmother in an isolated coastal town when his parents take off. "At times ponderous and confusing, this is a complex novel in which Hathorn explores human fragility and courage, manipulation and madness and the comfort of habit and ritual," noted Jane Connolly in a *Magpies* review.

Hathorn also teamed up with writer Gary Crew to produce an epistolary novel between two teenagers in *Dear Venny, Dear Saffron,* and has experimented with online storytelling on her web site, adapting the novel *Ghostop* from that format. Despite the diversity of publications, Hathorn has not neglected her interest in picture books. Her 1998 *Sky Sash So Blue* tells the story of a young slave, Susannah, who is willing to give up her one bit of ornament—her scrap of sky-blue sash, to ensure that her sister has a lovely wedding dress. A writer for *Children's Book Review Service* called this book a "lovely story of hardship, perseverance and love," while reviewer Carol Ann Wilson pointed out in *School Library Journal* that Hathorn employed an article of clothing, as she did in *Grandma's Shoes,* "to symbolize the indomitable spirit of family." Wilson concluded that "Susannah's narrative makes human and accessible the poignant struggles of a people, a family, and one little girl." Hathorn collaborated with American composer Phillip Ratliff to adapt *Sky Sash So Blue* as a children's opera, which was produced at Miles College in Birmingham, Alabama, in 2004 and 2005.

Hathorn acknowledged that though her writings often contain messages, "I don't ever want to write didactic books that berate people, young or old, with messages. I don't think you can really write a successful book by setting out with a 'do-good' or any other kind of message in mind. I can only write what moves me in some way to laugh or to cry or to wonder. I don't know what I'll be writing about a few years hence. There is a great sense of adventure in this—and a sense of mystery about what will find me."

As for advice to aspiring young writers, Hathorn has said: "The more you write the better you write. It's as simple and as difficult as that. To write well you must develop an ease with the pen and paper or the word processor or whatever—but most of all an ease with words. To do this you must be immersed in words; they should be your friends and your playthings as well as your tools. So, young writers, write a lot and love what you write so much that you work over it and shine it up to be the best you can possibly do—and then SHARE IT WITH SOMEONE."

Biographical and Critical Sources

BOOKS

Hathorn, Libby, *Talks with My Skateboard,* Australian Broadcasting Corp., 1991.
St. James Guide to Children's Writers, 5th edition, edited by Sara Pendergast and Tom Pendergast, St. James Press (Detroit, MI), 1999, pp. 482-483.
Saxby, Maurice, *The Proof of the Puddin': Australian Children's Literature, 1970-1990,* Ashton Scholastic, 1993, pp. 219-221.

PERIODICALS

Australian Bookseller and Publisher, March, 1992, p. 26.
Booklist, February 15, 1998, p. 1019.
Books for Keeps, November, 1996, p. 10.
Bulletin of the Center for Children's Books, April, 1991, Robert Strang, review of *Thunderwith,* p. 194; May, 1998, pp. 322-323.
Children's Book Review Service, August, 1998, review of *Sky Sash So Blue,* pp. 164-165.
Horn Book, March-April, 1989, Elizabeth S. Watson, review of *Freya's Fantastic Surprise,* p. 199; July, 1989, Karen Jameyson, review of *The Tram to Bondi Beach,* p. 474; July, 1991, Elizabeth S. Watson, review of *Thunderwith,* p. 462; July-August, 1998, p. 472.
Junior Bookshelf, October, 1990, p. 232.
Magpies, March, 1990, Karen Jameyson, review of *Thunderwith,* p. 4; March, 1993, p. 31; July, 1998, Jane Connolly, review of *Rift,* p. 38; November, 1999, p. 38; November, 1999, Annette Dale Meiklejohn, "Know the Author: Libby Hathorn," pp.10-13.
Publishers Weekly, May 17, 1991, review of *Thunderwith,* p. 65; August 1, 1994, p. 79; December 18, 1995, p.53; June 22, 1998, p. 91.

School Librarian, August, 1996, Mary Hoffman, review of *Juke-box Jive,* p. 105.

School Library Journal, July, 1989, Marianne Pilla, review of *The Tram to Bondi Beach,* p. 66; August, 1989, Louise L. Sherman, review of *Freya's Fantastic Surprise,* p. 120; May, 1991, p. 111; October, 1994, p. 123; March, 1996, p. 189; June, 1998, Carol Ann Wilson, review of *Sky Sash So Blue,* p. 108.

Times Literary Supplement, July 23, 1982, Ann Martin, "Encouraging the Excellent," p. 792.

Voice of Youth Advocates, June, 1991.

OTHER

Libby Hathorn Web site, http://www.libbyhathorn.com/ (January 26, 2005).*

Autobiography Feature

Libby Hathorn

L ibby Hathorn contributed the following autobiographical essay to *SATA:* I wish I could say I was born abroad, in far off Africa or deep in Papua New Guinea, and it was my exotic, isolated childhood that fed my imagination so that I was destined to be a writer. Or that I was raised on a remote, sprawling cattle station in the outback of Australia, where books and radio were my only friends. But no! Mine was a suburban childhood, busy with two sisters and a brother for company, spent in Sydney, Australia. And this is where I have spent most of my life, despite traveling widely as an adult, and is a place that has had its significance in all my writing life.

In fact, I was born in the city of Newcastle, some two hours north of Sydney, where my father had been posted for two years during the Second World War. However, most of my early childhood was in the eastern suburbs of Sydney, at Maroubra where we lived, a little too far from Maroubra Beach; and my adolescence was spent at Tamarama, a more picturesque suburb. Our house, in a tiny but verdant valley park, was a stone's throw from the small (and later to become highly fashionable), treacherous, and yet quite lovely city beach. We could look out the kitchen window and see the breakers of the Pacific Ocean crash onto the fine yellow sand of Tamarama Beach any time of day, and I remember going to sleep strangely calmed by the rhythm and roar of that surf. And we could take the walk along rugged cliffs to the much loved expanse of nearby Bondi Beach. One of my early books, *The Tram to Bondi Beach,* celebrates this beach, albeit as it was way back in the 1930s. Even now I don't like to be inland, to be too far from the edge that's been part and parcel of my whole life.

And yet how I longed for Europe and England during my adolescent years, a desire fed by the books and movies I'd seen, that perpetuated the idea that "real

Young Libby, ready for Sunday school, c. 1950s.

life" was elsewhere. I was to discover much later certain riches were to be discovered "in my own backyard," so to speak, when I began writing stories. In fact, I'd written poetry since my early childhood, completing a rhyming alphabet when I was in second grade—a first remembered "publication" because of the praise my grandmother, in particular, gave it. I'd read every book I could lay my hands on in our house, many of them with English backgrounds, and many way beyond my years, so that I felt I knew England, country and city, as if it were my place. But at the same time, I was listening to many a story by different members of our large, extended family, set firmly in an Aussie setting.

Despite a lack of romantic origins, my childhood was rich—filled with the busy-ness of being part of a largish family of four children and countless aunts and uncles, some of whom came and went. It wasn't without its trials of course—a small house, too many people, and certain tensions between family members at times, but it was a household that shared stories and poetry, and valued books, all the stuff of feeding the imagination. From our parents, who—especially my mother—quoted long tracts of poetry, to a father fond of recounting gritty tales of his country boyhood, to an uncle who was a fabulist, to a grandmother who read poetry aloud, our childhood was immersed and flavoured by story and poem. Another grandmother lived in the Blue Mountains, running tearooms there, and this was a marvelous contrast to city living. Megalong Valley was the setting for many of my early "rapturous" nature poems. To wake to the smell of the eucalypt with overtones of last night's open fire, to hear the raucous song of the kookaburra and other native birds, and to look out onto the green and more green and rugged, yellowy brown steep cliffs lit by morning sun . . . no wonder my sisters and I delighted in our holidays there.

It was a life to which books and story were intrinsic. Our father, a young detective at the time, told bedtime stories of his boyhood whenever he was home on time to do so, but also and, maybe even more importantly for me, he was fond of reading from our old grey-covered, much loved *A Treasury of Verse.* In those days kids went to bed early, with the ritual of being dosed with something called Fry's Emulsion which, we were told—though we didn't believe a word of it—"was good for your system," whatever that meant. The poetry did far more good than the ghastly tasting medicine. Who would not thrill to strange, entrancing, yet incomprehensible to a small child, words like Coleridge's?

In Xanadu did Kubla Khan

A stately pleasure-dome decree

Or the opening lines of the famous Australian ballad by Henry Kendall,

By channels of coolness the echoes are calling,

And down the dim gorges I hear the creek falling

My father's readings booked no interruption and we listened intently. We would shed a tear sometimes for the dog that drowned in *The Ballad of the Drover,* hugely enjoyed his more light-hearted reading of a poem such as *The Jackdaw of Rheims,* and we wondered at the mysterious story of *Abou Ben Adhem.* But we never spoke a word when he gave forth those heartfelt readings.

I think my love affair with words began right there, if it didn't with mother's recitation, word perfect, of "The Slip-rails and the Spur." And of course, her singing—the truly melancholy rendition of "Come to me My Melancholy Baby" or the more light-hearted "Little Mister Baggy Britches" when our baby brother was a bit fractious. I loved this quiet time in our house but best of all I loved to hear the poetry that seemed so natural to her or so important to my dad. Something was "lit up" so that the words seemed alive and singing and powerful or playful, like the surf of Maroubra Beach or Bondi that beat out a rhythm that dramatically pounded in my bones and in my blood. Even a disliked teacher, primly reading the famous Australian ballad by Banjo Patterson, "The Man From Snowy River" (later to become a movie), had its own inexorable charm. It all lay in the poetry itself! The power of words to evoke images, to make music and to make you feel so many emotions just by their saying, the way it did, was extraordinary to me. And still is. And the particular cadence and "truth" a good poem seems to hold in some magical way.

During my lifetime—as a child of the forties, an adolescent of the fifties and sixties—I was lucky to see Australian children's literature come into full flower. In fact, the seventies and eighties, as our publishing houses began publishing local voices, is a time described as the "Golden Age" of Australian children's literature by critic and revered elder in the field, Maurie Saxby. My library teacher at Maroubra Junction Girl's School in Sydney in the early 1950s would never have dreamed of such a thing, ever tidying those shelves of largely English adventure stories such as Enid Blyton's Famous Five. Classics like *Black Beauty, Anne of Green Gables,* and *The Secret Garden* rubbed spines with only a few Australian children's texts, among them such memorable names as Patricia Wrightson, Joan Phipson, and Nan Chauncy.

But it was really the well-worn "Billabong" series by Mary Grant Bruce and the equally well-worn work of Ethel Turner's series that I read over and over, attracted by serial narratives in an Australian setting. Television was something that had happened in America and had no bearing on our lives yet. So the characters of those books peopled our childhood. Reading was all-important and we could simply never have enough books. To this day I have several books on my bedside table and always travel "heavy," taking old friends that I might need near me and a clutch of new to some far-off city or country town that may not sport a bookshop.

But harking back, we lived in a small two bedroom house in Maroubra during my early childhood, a family of four children: Margaret, Elizabeth, Suzanne and Stephen. Everything was done at the old oak kitchen table, from homework to ironing to shelling peas. It wasn't until my older sister Margi went to high school that my mother bought us our first desk, which was to be communally owned, of course, and which fitted miraculously in the verandah sleep-out my sister and I shared. To me, it was luxury to have a place set apart specially for writing, not to mention the added pleasure of a set of drawers in the desk to be filled just with the accoutrements of writing. I loved touching the packet of envelopes, the writing pads (loose sheets of paper were a rarity), the floral stationery set I had been lucky enough to get for Christmas, the HB pencils, and opening the special spotted black-and-white case that housed my precious Conway Stewart fountain pen and matching propelling pencil.

When we reached high school, each child was given a 'good' pen and pencil set, instructed that it had been expensive to purchase and was expected to last us through all our high school days. My father owned a treasured maroon and silver Parker pen and I don't remember ever seeing him with another writing implement. We never shared pens, as we understood it could damage the unique way the user had shaped the nib. But I remember practising his distinctive signature and wishing I could use his fine pen to replicate the downstroke. "Light on the upstroke and heavy on the downstroke," our teachers endlessly instructed us, endeavouring for each and every child to achieve a "copperplate" writing style.

We were all readers in that house, though I was the only writer. That is, the only child that crept away to write her own stories or poems, finding a private though darkish space behind the big tapestry lounge chair in the lounge room, in our busy and noisy household.

In infants school, we were supplied readers, each child with the same one. I'd wrestled in Grade 1 with the boredom of Fay and Don, walking down English-style streets in English-type clothes and living in smart English-type bungalows with never a gum tree in sight. However, my Grade 2 reader remains in mind as a pleasurable compilation of poems and stories, well-thumbed and well-loved. Dramatic stories about girls like Grace Darling, whose daring rescue of shipwrecked souls intrigued me, especially the idea that a girl could ride a horse into the surf and save people! And then the poems that were read aloud and "performed" in what was known as Verse Speaking—a lesson I found thrilling. Fragments of verse, and the particular intonation of my Grade 2 teacher Miss Hinder, have stayed with me a lifetime. "I shall lie in the reeds and hoooowl for your green glass beads, I love them so . . . give them me," and so on.

The readers were exhausted after a term and yet we were obliged to re-read around the class on a regular basis. And often the teacher requested we keep to the place, "finger on the word please" of the poor stumbling child selected to read aloud.

The introduction at home to Australian storybooks such as *Blinky Bill* and *Snugglepot and Cuddlepie* and the beloved Gumnutland host of characters was significant. Books that speak to children about the place they themselves know well, as Dorothy Wall and May Gibbs did for me as young child, must have a lasting

impression, and a lifelong significance. Here among Peter Rabbit and friends, Pooh Bear and friends, and a host of Disney characters in far-flung settings, which were loved too, were stories of our own land, our bush, our city, our animals, and our flora, very much our place.

I distinctly remember the thrill of pleasure at May Gibbs' gentle and environmentally friendly Gumnutland stories, coupled with her charming Australian artwork of our own bottlebrush and gum trees and bush creatures. British books and British influence were still so strong in the 1950s, though things were slowly beginning to change in that regard, and the arts were reflecting this change, our burgeoning literature at the forefront in the naming (and thus the possessing) of things in our own landscape. This was a gradual process of relinquishing Britain and Europe as the centre of our world, and recognising our own country as an entity in itself, and Asian countries as our closest neighbours.

Having said that, much later in the 1990s it was still not easy to have children's books with an Asian theme published. I'd made plans to write a series I'd called Asiastory—six stories set in various Asian countries close to home—as a kind of interesting challenge. But it was to be more difficult than I'd imagined. The first one, a picture storybook set in Vietnam, *The Wishing Cupboard,* which was the first published story to go online in Australia, took six or seven years to find a publisher at Lothian. And it was only in 1999 that I had my book *The River,* which is set in China, launched in Shanghai through an educational publishing house, Curriculum Corporation. I've had four of the stories published to date, and am currently determinedly working on a Korean story.

*

In high school, we were steeped in English literature—from John Donne to the Romantics, our Shakespeare texts studied thoroughly over a whole year, so thoroughly we could quote whole tracts of it. There was not much modern poetry taught at school so I had to find that elsewhere. It was years later I was to discover the charms of other cultures. Translations of Spanish Lorca and Pablo Neruda, American poets like William Carlos Williams, Monica Dickens, and Hugh Langston, the Welsh poet Dylan Thomas, to mention a few.

Teachers had an enormous impact on my life right through my schooling. The shy and beautiful Miss Miller in Grade 1 (who, incidentally, I remember to this day never returned the book on China that my German grandfather gave the family and I proudly took to school, a beautiful book with the unusual treat of coloured pictures). It was important to actually own books but they were a rare treat as gifts.The ample and warm Mrs. Tanner (Grade 3) who always delayed to chat and laugh when my handsome father called to pick us up from school (a really unusual event) and who relentlessly encouraged the use of "good words." A memorable lesson was writing the words "got" and "said" on a piece of paper, going into the school garden which the kids attended to in Nature study lessons, and burying the words. "You can think of a better one to use in your compositions, girls!"

Then there was the principal, the chaotic Miss Swain (Grade 6) who loved to see the whole school march from assembly—where we saluted the flag and swore allegiance to the King of England and later the Queen—to military style music like "Colonel Bogey's March." She was generally a good-natured teacher, despite having the dual role of running the whole school. But she made what she called 'a terrible mistake' that we kids all paid for.

Every week we had to write a tightly structured two-page composition: opening paragraph, two more paragraphs using adverbial or adjectival phrases that were listed on the blackboard, and a closing paragraph that "tied off" all ends neatly. One memorable day, when she obviously hadn't had time to prepare the "straitjacket," we were told, "Today girls, you may write an adventure story!" It was music to our ears. She did not mention any length at all, let alone an adverbial phrase.

Forty-five twelve-year-old girls, well schooled on Enid Blyton and her Famous Five adventure books and Ethel Turner's heart-rending *Seven Little Australians,* went to town. It was a black afternoon when our work was handed back to the class with cold and disapproving comments for each and every one of us.

At least half of us, wild with freedom, had written six or eight or even ten pages of story! She told us she refused to read beyond page three of any of them, that they were generally poor, undisciplined and imitative— well, yes! But then followed a diatribe when poor, hapless, overweight, unpopular, super-bright classmate Judith Meakin was made to stand up and explain why her "disgusting" story had featured something as horrific as murder. And not just one, this vile child had included three murders on board a launch in Sydney Harbour. She laboured the girl's inappropriate subject matter in a rage of disapproval, so humiliating that I'd have been reduced to tears. But Judith stood there, clutching the desk red-faced and, I'm certain, not understanding what all the fuss was about.

It seems laughable in this day and age of violence and death depicted on film and TV, including the news of the day, that a child writing a murder story could be so castigated. But the 1950s were the days before television in Australia, and straightlaced was the way you would describe suburban Maroubra. In any case, there was censorship about what books were allowed into the country (for example, D. H. Lawrence's *Lady Chatterly's Lover* could be read only by university professors even in my adolescence) and the press of the day could not refer directly to things such as a pregnancy. Poor Judith had no doubt read a diet of cheap thrillers and, in reflecting them in her own way,

Libby (center), with her sisters Suzanne (left) and Margaret.

took the full fury of our teacher's annoyance at the outpourings of frustrated writers. I remember thinking then that Judith had been daring and that there was surely a power in a story that could make an adult so mad!

Endorsements for budding writers must have been important. I was in Year 4 when I received my first award, a purplish certificate for my penned (this was a dip pen and ink-penned story) from a large department store, Farmer's, that for some mysterious reason encouraged young Sydney writers. I believe I still have that certificate. But it was not for certificates I wrote the poems and stories that seemed to come from some mysterious source, poured out into precious exercise books where every page was covered, paper being in short supply and thus prized.

In the incredible paper affluence of my adulthood it's almost unimaginable to think how paper and pencils and pens were prized possessions. It was a luxury to have a Woolworth's Jumbo-sized writing pad. Single sheets such as our fax and computer paper were simply not available. I knew more of British history at ten, twelve, fourteen years of age than I did of Australian history. Aboriginal history was for the most part shamefully ignored or, what little there was, often quite inaccurately presented. This was all to change dramatically when I reached college. But I must say I'm grateful to this day for that rich literary background afforded by our schools, which set up a continual love affair with writers of the stature of William Shakespeare and the Romantic poets, to mention but a few.

My sisters and I haunted libraries like the one in Maroubra with the unlikely and agreeable name of

Quandong, where one paid, say, a shilling to borrow two books for a week. Later we traveled by bus a few suburbs away to the Randwick Public Library to take out our precious one book each. I was ten or eleven before Maroubra had a public library in the guise of the Mobile Library—a wondrous caravan of books that traveled some of the library-less suburbs of our area, hooking into the powerline to light up its intriguing interior and the eager knot of readers—and thus bring the demise of private libraries.

The brightness of some of those childhood memories may be somewhat enhanced by time, but images of us just being around books and readers are especially clear. Lying on the beds, long sunny afternoons totally immersed in Mary Grant Bruce's "Billabong" series, my big sister, head in a book, occasionally making a comment about the outback world and the characters we knew and loved. "I think I have a bit of crush on Wally," she might say.

"Well, I think I'm in love with Jim and I want to be Norah," I'd reflect.

"But they're brother and sister!" she'd tell me, usually having the last word.

I know as a big sister to Suzanne, three years my junior, I'd often read aloud to her. She always attests to my improving her reading comprehension, as I'd read some of our school-set novels (not my choice of fiction) such as *Black Arrow* or *The Hill,* and then each three pages or so I'd quiz her on what I'd read. "You really have to listen!" I'd threaten, "or I won't read to you anymore." Thus improving her concentration.

I love that idea of sharing other worlds and I believe that the act of reading allows us to share the dream. We can enter into another's thoughts and another's world as if it were our own.

It's strange how certain memories of a less happy kind remain imprinted. There was a procession of pets who had a great impact on the family. Though we longed to own a dog and my little sister Suzanne arrived home occasionally with a stray, we had cats and kittens! A series of cats were called variously Tiddles if male, or Skinny Minny if female. There was no commercially prepared petfood at the time, and the pets always ate the scraps from the family table and were generally more on the lean side compared to the cats I've owned since the advent of tinned petfood. With the birth of several batches of kittens, we ran out of willing recipients. Vets were not plentiful and the drowning of kittens was not unusual in our street, and was by far more merciful than dumping those hapless kittens in back lanes. But somehow neither of our parents could bring themselves to do the deed when we'd done our best but had clearly run out of prospective owners.

My mother's brother, Uncle Allen, was called to do the job. Not a particularly aggressive or bold man, he must nonetheless have had the requisite skills for kitten-drowning. It was done on the back step where all the children gathered and I remember watching with a certain amount of fear mixed with an awful curiosity. We knew it was inevitable the kittens must go or became strays, uncared for, but how could you actually kill something that was alive and soft and warm? The dark, the cluster of children, the metal bucket, the tiny squirming still blind soft little creatures, Uncle Allen grim but resolute. The hapless mother, Skinny Minny, being cuddled somewhere else, the thought of death in the air, the realization of utter powerlessness. That's a vivid memory for me.

Another stark memory was being locked in. This was a holiday with my older sister Margaret, on a farm on the Nepean River at the foot of the Blue Mountains, where boy cousins were good company for most of the time. It was a dairy farm and magical to us city girls. I didn't realize the grind of 200 cows having to be milked morning and night and the effort this must have cost my uncle and his older son. We loved to come here as the days were long and filled with fun. We learned boys' sports, bows and arrows, the wonder of an air rifle and the game of mice trapping in a recently ploughed field. Then there was riding a tractor to the Nepean River and discovering the wonder of the fact that potatoes didn't grow on bushes but were grown under the ground.

The milking sheds were fascinating and to be visited most afternoons. The cows were always docile, there was a certain exciting smell, milky in the shed and overlain with the cow manure in the yard, the sound of the milking machines sucking away at so many cows' teats—probably thirty cows milked at a time. There was the added wonder of the separation room, and then the cold room, where huge metal milk drums were stored, waiting for pickup. Bruce, my cousin, was a good-natured boy, a year or so older, but he seized the opportunity one afternoon as we two visited the cold room to experience the shiveriness once again, to heave closed the thick metal door and leave us not only shivering in the cold, but marooned in the terror of utter darkness.

Screams were to no avail it seemed, and the few minutes we were incarcerated there seared some memory of terror forever. When he gleefully opened the door and we emerged, I was changed. I was shaking and couldn't speak and remained so, despite the sun on my arms and that comforting ordinary odour of cow manure, for some time. Once again it was the notion of facing death and knowing you were powerless. And worse still, not brave. Not in the least brave. Ever since then, I have felt a kind of panic at the idea of being closed in, and like at least a sliver of light at night when asleep.

*

My first year in high school I made a very special friend in Pat who had laughing eyes, a mop of black curly hair and an outrageous sense of humour. She also just happened to live not far around the corner from my house in Maroubra—a wonderful accident of fate. Some

As a young teacher, 1965.

fifty years later we are still friends and still discussing some of the same issues about the arts, despite both having brought up our families separately. Ten years ago I tried to set down something of the preciousness of this relationship in my poem "Childhood Friend" from *Maroubra Cycle*. (*Maroubra Cycle* has been set to music by composer Stephen Lalor and was later performed under the direction of Paul Weingott at UTS as a musical, when I was writer in residence there).

> You were farewelling me,
> I saw you there
> Standing by the gate
> And heard your laughter
> Down the midnight road
> And thought
> A poem is there in you
> Standing, laughing
> Talking, delaying, beside
> The darkened paling fence
> So reminiscent of our childhood. . ..
> Where we plotted our bright futures.
>
> —"Childhood Friend"

Pat was "artistic" and dreamed of becoming a painter and our conversations over the adolescent years were always of the arts: debates, musings as we fledgling art-

ists tested our own theories in painting and writing in a world not much interested in two Maroubra lasses and their dreams. Pat illustrated my first picture storybook *Kyo,* which was the story of a much-loved dog of my mother's. Kyo, who gained this name from the New South Wales country town Kyogle, was a wonderful black and white terrier my mother swore could smile—at her, of course. Kyo was picked up by the RSPCA when she wandered off one day from Tamarama Beach; we never saw her again. My mother was inconsolable and in fact never had another dog, so Pat and I wrote a story about Kyo's wandering with a very happy ending. She was found! It wasn't even published but I have the original artwork to this day among my treasures.

I attended Teachers' College after an unsuccessful stint as a laboratory assistant in the Medical School at the University of Sydney. Two lecturers at Balmain Teachers' College—as it was then called before becoming part of UTS (University of Technology)—greatly influenced my writing: Ray Cattell who moved to University of New South Wales as I arrived) and the principal, a tall forbidding looking gentleman, Mr. Greenhalgh. It was the English lecturer at Balmain who introduced me to Ray Cattell after my poem won the College Poetry Prize. Ray in turn introduced me to the works of W. B. Yeats when I unwittingly cautioned him to "tread softly" on his criticisms of my own poetry. "Tread softly for you tread on my dreams" he quoted immediately and there began a love affair with works of Yeats. Visits to his home gave timely insight to my passionate but sometimes rambling first poetry, and he insisting I could make poetry my life's work. If only I didn't have to earn a living, I thought, though poetry I knew even then would remain central to my life and inform all my writing.

The other lecturer, the principal of the college, also stands out in my mind impressing me with his far too short series of lectures on philosophy and imploring us, the young students about to embark on our teaching lives, not to "walk through the fields with our gloves on" referring to a famous poem whose name eludes me. I remember buying Will Durant's *The Story of Philosophy* and a whole world opening up to me.

This was intensified by the advent of a soulful and totally engaging person in my life. It's true he was a man, several years older and much more sophisticated than I, but this seemed incredibly attractive to me in itself. With him I could discuss poetry and philosophy and many an evening we sat in the rose garden in Hyde Park; he was too poor to take me to dinner and I was but a poor college student. I listened to the wisdom of John C. It didn't occur to me that when we did go out to the movies or even to coffee that it was I who paid, and it was only years later that I understood why John became attracted to a woman closer to his age who had a smart apartment and a high-paying job. Still, I never regretted his flair for romance and his rather Oscar Wildish take on life.

My school friend Pat and I had discussed classical music but were introduced to the joys of ownership through a friend's dad who'd joined something called The World Record Club. *Brahms' Hungarian Dances* was the first 45 classical record that I ever purchased. Dad was mad about *The Student Prince,* as we all were, and I played it along with Beethoven symphonies. Later came admiration for Bach—I even purchased a small harmonium from a friend, Wendy's dad, who worked at the music shop Paling's, so I could learn to play Bach's Toccata and Fugue.

Saturday mornings, the three girls were expected to do the housework which consisted of vacuuming the house, scrubbing, polishing and—as custom had it in summertime—give the whole house a good spray of Mortein Plus, which had just come onto the market, with a bright red large pump flyspray. Our work was made lighter by the stereogram, a large polished wood affair with a lid that was raised to reveal the turntable, a side compartment for 33s and another for 78s and the smaller 45s. We'd put on the long playing 33s (LPs) of which our parents had such delights as *Oklahoma, Carousel, South Pacific,* and *Showboat.* A favourite was an LP called *The Merry Widow,* considered classical music.

This didn't mean I wasn't in love with Elvis Presley or didn't dance to the new rock and roll and later

favour the magical Beatles! My novel, *Love Me Tender,* reflects this time through the eyes of a young boy, Alan.

Round the corner at Pat's house, her mother had secured a real treasure of an LP, sent all the way from England, of Emlyn Williams reading Charles Dickens. Though I'd read *A Tale of Two Cities* I was delighted by excerpts from *Pickwick Papers* and *Oliver Twist* read aloud to us as we gathered in the lounge room around the precious record player to listen before the advent of television in Australia of course.

The bookcase in the small lounge room of our house at Maroubra was cram-packed. My parents had sets of books alongside the novels, encyclopedias, and dictionary (Webster's), a huge tome. Sets of science and philosophy (The Living Thoughts Library: of Thoreau, Descarts, Spinoza, etc.) alongside *Readers' Digest* series books and World War II books. These I remember were large clothbound with firm spines: *Soldiering On,* Army, Navy, and Air Force accounts of the returned men, anxious to somehow tell something of their disquieting stories.

Arthur Mees' *Book of Everlasting Things* seems such a quaint idea in a world of computers with knowledge at your fingertips. But it was a much loved tome, a book of wonder, despite its rather smudgy black and white photographs of sights such as the pyramids, or the Amazon River.

An aunt of mine was housekeeper for a very well-off family in nearby Dover Heights and this was rather fortunate for us. The Rusten girls were readers, and we only imagined their life, as we never met them. But in a way I thought we had, for their names were often inscribed in the books that came our way. The Rustens gave our aunt the entire set of Billabong books by Mary Grant Bruce, doled out on birthdays and Christmases to eager recipients; twelve or fourteen of them that were published in Great Britain by Ward Lock. Some rather trashy love stories such as *Broken Wings* by F. J. Thwaites found their way onto our shelves, made all the more meaningful because of the fact that our mother admitted she had once or twice gone out with him when he was a young man.

Shy the Platypus by Lesley Reece was another treasure. I was to later meet Lesley at the Fremantle Children's Literary Centre in 1997, and to learn that as a young journalist he'd actually interviewed James Joyce in Paris.

My story *The Day TV Came* was published by the Museum of Contemporary Art when it opened to an exhibition celebrating the coming of television to Australia in the 1950s; though fictional, it tried to capture some of the wonder of film on tap in one's own house. Our television, like our record player, was a substantial piece of furniture—two wooden doors in a cabinet with fake gold handles, opening to reveal a screen below which giant knobs conveyed us to worlds beyond our world, albeit in black and white. When our family bought a television in 1959, we were transfixed by any and every program. Sunday nights were family occasions when we gathered for a TV dinner generally, toasted tomato and cheese on specially designed TV plates, either made in a waffle iron or in our Dad's new-fangled griller. Bought from a door-to-door salesman, the Spaceship, so named for its shape, could grill anything to a crisp, from sausages to sandwiches. One of the features of Sunday evening viewing was Disney World and eating toasted "samos" as our Dad called them, toasted to perfection on the Spaceship. Or during the week watching exciting American shows like *77 Sunset Strip, The Fugitive, Maverick, I Love Lucy,* or *Father Knows Best.* There were very few Australian shows. *Homicide,* the first cop show, comes to mind as well as a copycat Saturday afternoon Bandstand where you could watch people your own age rock and rolling—and even get a ticket to go out to Gore Hill and become part of the audience that was filmed! If you were brave enough.

*

As a young woman I began writing poetry, hesitatingly at first given the models of such accomplishment I'd had. I was drawn to write about what I knew, events and landscapes and people and all the strange yet somehow "ordinary" miracles that Walt Whitman so cleverly describes in his poem of that name. Poetry writing was a major pastime but I began keeping notebooks, fragments of conversation, dreams, reflections. I remember a line of poetry I wrote when I was eighteen years old that said though I, too, longed for Europe, I wanted to know my own country and that henceforth I was "stepping out into Australian times."

In a lustful search for a diversity of texts after my school years and whilst at college, I began consciously exploring Australian literature, particularly poetry. The work of Judith Wright, David Campbell, John Shaw Neilsen, Chrisopher Brennan. I still keep a raggedy copy of that very first *Penguin Anthology of Australian Verse* that introduced to me to the wealth of Australian voices. Later at college I began to explore more contemporary voices, the likes of Les Murray, Gwen Harwood, Elizabeth Riddell, and Peter Porter. The wonderful old bookshop on Pitt Street in Sydney, Angus and Robertson's with its polished linoleum covered basement where poetry and plays resided, became a place of miraculous discoveries. As did the magical little Rowe Street with its first coffee shops and book shops and records imported from overseas for which you'd have to save to buy.

Translations by Arthur Waley and Ezra Pound of Chinese poetry, and that extreme jewel of verse, the Japanese haiku, were discovered in Rome Street. This largesse, along with the newly translated novels of European authors such as Gide and Mann, Camus, and a whole range of Russian novels from Tolstoy to Chekov Dostoyovsky. My head was hardly ever out of a book and it was a wonder I graduated from college at all. When I did I was to discover the real joys of teaching

and must say that my first year at Bankstown Primary School was a year of wonders. Despite the rigours of the timetable imposed then (thirty minutes for this and twenty-five for that, and woe betide you if you didn't teach the said subject at the said hour) I found I could encourage poetry writing with my nine-year-olds—45 of them in a room designed to take up to fifty pupils! This was 1964 and classes were large.

I remember distinctly the exciting drives to Bankstown Primary School (a long train and bus ride from my home at Tamarama Beach) with my new friend Wendy Stites. She was a young teacher at Bankstown Infants who was lucky enough to own a car, a VW Beetle, with whom I shared petrol money and long conversations. We talked of life and love at length being young women at the time, alongside the joys of art and poetry, and how we could influence the kids we taught. She was later to marry Australian filmmaker Peter Weir and devote all her creative passion to design and wardrobe for movies.

At this time I was going out with a young medical student, Ron Gray, of Polish parentage (his mother had promptly changed their name on arrival as a migrant to Australia) who shared this love of the arts and especially of poetry, and gave into my hands some treasure tomes from his own bookcase. I still have the poetical works of Rainer Maria Rilke he parted with somewhat reluctantly, because I'd told him the book was not to be had in any Sydney bookshop and I loved the work so much. Forbidden movies in Trade Union Hall (*Quiet Flows the Don*) or "continental movies" as we called them, like *Virgin Spring* or *La Dolce Vita* at Savoy, Lido, or the Paris Theatre, where at interval there was the luxury of buying Italian coffee, were part and parcel of the discovery of "other times." Ron was an extraordinarily clever fellow academically, but I remember his frustration at not being able to paint or write poetry and sometime a flash of annoyance when I'd produce some writing about a place we'd visited together—the fir forest where we'd camped or the Blue Mountains where we'd taken long bracing walks. He was a loving person to me and I am glad to have had such a strong and tender relationship over three or four years of growing up time. But it was through him I realised that understanding and loving poetry or fiction was not enough, that there was another dimension that has nothing to do with the will, and that perhaps in some miraculous and inexplicable way, writing had chosen me!

I broke my medical student's heart when after four years and with our inevitable marriage in sight, I met John Hathorn, a teacher seven years my senior, dashing, romantic and persuasive. But there was grief for me too, in that break, as I felt Ron was part of my most formative years and intoxicated though I was with John's energy and excitement, there were moments of real longing to see Ron again.

My own writing in that time consisted of largely unpublished poetry. I remember the thrill of first acceptance in *The Poetry Journal,* then managed by poet

Grace Perry, of my first poem. This coincided with meeting John, my husband to be, at the school I'd been transferred to, Bellevue Hill Primary School. In those first heady days of our relationship I expressed my desire to be a writer—and a published writer at that!—and explained that it was central to my life. After we were married in 1968, John Hathorn, being a practical soul, suggested that I begin my foray into publishing by writing textbooks. We worked together on the first little books for infants and then I decided I'd write up all the marvelous work the children were capable of in poetry, and *Go Lightly,* my first substantial book, was published. As I was not fully confident to "go it alone," John was actually listed as co-author. He had, after all, I reasoned, trialed all the poetry techniques written up in the book.

The birth of my children, daughter Lisa in 1970 and then Keiran in 1973, changed our lives once again. I could not think about writing, especially children's books, in the same way. Bringing up children enlivens your perceptions and memories of your own childhood, feeding the fires.

The seventies saw a new confidence in the arts that we all responded to. We'd left behind to some extent the "outback image" that had been promulgated through books and movies, and began to record our urban and indeed our multicultural experiences as wave after wave of migrants settled into the cities, impacting on the Australian way of life. It seemed to young artists unburdened by the weight of a long European history that we were free to go in any direction. But Australian children were still largely invisible in the body of literature available to them and I think myself lucky to have been writing at the time that publishers acknowledged that "gap."

I had been a classroom teacher but moved into the role of librarian in the primary school where I worked now at Drummoyne, a significant move on my part. Librarianship suited my addiction to books and story and gave me an up-to-the-minute overview of what children were reading. I was very much aware that we needed books about our place, the city as well as the country. I read hundreds of books and was delighted by some Australian novels by Colin Thiele and Ivan Southall, some early Australian picture storybooks like Lydia Pender's *Barnaby's Rocket,* and the Aboriginal tales *The Rainbow Serpent* by Dick Roughsey.

Engaged to John Hathorn, 1966.

Looking back, there were two particular writers I discovered in well-stacked shelves who I think deeply influenced my own writing. A series of readers by the English writer Leila Berg, which told hilarious stories of working class kids and their parents, opened my eyes to the way ordinary folk could be written about and also to the fact that ordinary folk were not really well represented in Australian children's literature. And then the work of the Dutch writer Meindert de Jong with his wonderful novel, *Journey from Peppermint Street,* and for younger readers *Nobody Plays with a Cabbage.* These were sensitive stories written in spare and beautiful prose and they truly inspired me. I also noticed at this time some very "cool" paperbacks books for struggling readers by a certain Paul Jennings were being very well borrowed from the library. Paul was to become a legend in his own lifetime with a series of hilarious novels some years later.

*

It all happened at a party, whose I don't recall, but I was introduced to a young man who worked for an English publishing company, Methuen, who had an office in Sydney. And yes, he'd talk to the children's editor there about a book I was writing.

Stephen's Tree was my first picture storybook. It was set at my brother's then garden market in Waverley, a veritable rainforest of ferns and trees and Australian plants right in the heart of the suburbs. I was thrilled to have a work of fiction underway but I had to debate long and hard with Methuen about having a gum tree central to the story. They strongly advised a beech, ash or elm so the work would sell better in England! It was important for me to have the gum tree but it was equally important to be published.

My first children's book editor, the gentle but resolute Liz Fulton, must have argued well, for a gum tree it was! The book was launched at our local Waverley Library by Peter Weir, who'd already begun to make his name with his first movie, *Picnic at Hanging Rock,* and all Sandra Laroche's delicate depictions of gum trees and kids were exhibited. The book attracted much media attention not only because it was about an Australian tree but also because *Stephen's Tree* was a publishing experiment. The publisher, responsive to our multicultural society of largely Greek and Italian migrants, published *Stephen's Tree* in dual text versions, both Greek and Italian! This experiment was repeated with *Lachlan's Walk.* Though the books sold well in the English version, the dual language was not a great seller and sad to say, the idea of dual texts was canned!

This connection to Waverley Library for my first-ever book launch was auspicious. Sandra illustrated my next children's picture storybook *Lachlan's Walk,* set at Watson's Bay and based on a true story about my sister's son Lachlan wandering away from home towards a dangerous cliffside park. It too, was launched

at Waverley Library by cartoonist Bruce Petty. And it was to be there at the library that I became aware of the outstanding work of illustrator Julie Vivas through enthusiastic children's librarian, Roniet Myerthal. Julie had an exhibition of her watercolours and after I'd seen her work, Roniet arranged a meeting where I invited Julie to illustrate my next book *The Tram to Bondi Beach,* to be set in the 1930s, the time of paperboys and trams in Sydney. Julie assured me that her art was not suitable for children's literature, but I thought differently and asked to show some of her work to my Methuen publishers, who immediately agreed with me that she would make a fine partner for the text. Julie had a tough time of it family-wise the year she undertook her superb illustrations for the story, her first picture book, for her husband was away in Spain and she had two small children to look after. We visited the Loftus, the Tram Museum south of Sydney, to get reference photographs because by that time, in 1980s, trams had disappeared from the Sydney streets. Here the children Ana and Kate, along with my children Lisa and Keiran, acted as models for paperboys and passengers. *The Tram to Bondi Beach,* launched by Maurie Saxby, was highly commended by the Children's Book Council of Australia, and Julie's new career was begun. The then NSW Film and Television group wanted to make a movie of *Tram* with its setting in the Depression in Bondi. I wrote the first filmscript filled with hope about the possibility of Julie's marvellous artwork and my story, but it was to be one of those many movie projects that only "almost" came off.

During this time in the seventies with two children and a teacher-librarian career, I was fortunate on the home front to have the help of a wonderful woman my mother's age who came to stay for three weeks and stayed instead over a period of twenty years. Without Paddy's help, her organisation of household matters, her sense of humour and her winning ways with little children, I could not have given such time to my own writing. She became a treasured family member at our house and though elderly now, is still interested to hear every scrap of information about our children, Lisa and Keiran.

Back in the eighties as my own children were growing older—though it's true I'm forever interested in picture storybooks—I began to write "chapter books," or what we called junior novels, for young readers. *All about Anna,* which recalled my Maroubra childhood and was where I consciously placed a girl as an adventurous main character, won honours in the CBA awards. This was followed by a fantasy, *The Extraordinary Magics of Emma McDade,* the first of my short novels to be translated into Korean, and was similarly shortlisted for awards. *Paolo's Secret* in 1985 was written to portray the loneliness of some children in the school yard when limited by language. As a teacher-librarian in an inner city school I was very much aware of this situation for shy children who found the prospect of the playground daunting. But the novel that was to change

The author's children, Christmas, 1979: (front) Lisa and (back, right) Keiran, with their friend Isabelle.

my life in the late eighties, and indeed take me all the way to Hollywood, was written for young adult readers and was strongly inspired by the bushland setting of the central coast of NSW.

Thunderwith was written in 1988 on my brother's farm in the Wallingat Forest, which is north of Sydney. This is the story of the loss and alienation of a young girl Lara, as she has to come to terms not only with the death of a beloved mother, but with a dad she barely remembers and a hostile new mother. Its setting is uniquely Australian and when my agents Curtis Brown offered it for publication, in 1988, the $10,000 advance paid by the publisher Heinneman was then considered the largest ever given in Australia for a children's book.

Immediately there were offers for movie options from three Australian companies and it was finally optioned to Southern Star Xanadu. Sandra Levy (currently the head of the Australian Broadcasting Company) was the producer of Xanadu then, and I would have been more than happy to work with her as she had such a sensitivity to the story, but there was to be a lull in movie-making which meant it was difficult to get finances together. In the meantime, *Thunderwith* the novel travelled well into Europe, being bought in Holland and Denmark, Sweden and Great Britain, then was

also published in the United States and was serialized in India. It went into reprint several times in its first year, picking up honours in the CBA awards, too. But it was the offer by Hallmark Hall of Fame in the United States in the late nineties to make a television movie, and to have me as the writer, that was the most exciting news for this story. Several meetings in Hollywood with producer Dick Welsh indicated that they wanted me to write a treatment for the movie placing Gladwyn, the mother, central to the story. This was because their demographic was largely adult females, they told me, and for family viewing. Armed with some how-to-write-movies guidebooks back home, I took off to Seal Rocks and the Wallingat and began the arduous task of writing a movie script to please my producers. Later, American writers were brought on to finish the script and though I was disappointed, I knew I'd reached a time when I simply couldn't make any more changes and still feel it was my story.

Simon Wincer, as director, had chosen Victoria, his home state, rather than NSW where the story is actually set. My husband John, who had become ill with leukemia, had been under heavy treatment and though in remission, had little energy at this time. He encouraged me to take our daughter Lisa and visit the set. It was amazing to go on the set at Mt. Beauty in Victoria to see a whole property changed, roads built, a farmhouse and outhouses constructed, palms planted to create a plantation, a dam built, to mention just a few of the wonders that happened. Judy Davis played a marvelous Gladwyn and was nominated for an Emmy for her performance in *The Echo of Thunder,* as it was called. Lauren Hewitt made a strong Lara and Emily Browning (later starring in *Lemony Snicket*) made her film debut as an engaging young Opal. *Thunderwith* today is still one of my best-selling novels and is a set text in many schools across Australia.

*

In the mid-nineties John had retired from school and we traveled widely, including living in a loft in Mulberry Street in New York, whilst I made better contact with my then agent Laura Blake at Curtis Brown. During that time I met Little Brown's Maria Modugno who had taken both *Thunderwith* and *Grandma's Shoes,* and later Simon & Schuster's Virginia Duncan who had taken *Sky Sash So Blue.* Virginia, moving to Greenwillow, was to hand over to Stephanie Owens Lurie but told me in a farewell letter that *Sky Sash* was the best children's story she'd ever worked on! Stephanie was incredibly enthused and put Benny Andrews' wonderful artwork for the cover of *Sky Sash* on their S & S catalogue. Whilst in New York I also visited the office of the legendary Margaret McElderry who told me how she'd enjoyed reading *Thunderwith.* It was a great visit, at the end of which came the American offers for the movie of *Thunderwith.*

Another book that had a huge impact was my picture storybook *Way Home.* It was inspired by the sight of a boy in the underground in London who was begging at the bottom of the giant escalators. He seemed incredibly young to be there alone. I boarded the train and began thinking of my own children safe and sound in a Midland farmhouse, and wrote a poem about a boy called Shane that was to become the basis of the text of *Way Home.* Mark McLeod, who was a publisher with Random House then, loved the text and magically brought the illustrator Greg Rogers and me together. We traversed the streets of Sydney taking photographs as source material and then Greg returned to Brisbane, where he worked over his amazing artwork that was to win the much-coveted Kate Greenaway Medal in the United Kingdom.

That it was an Australian artist illustrating and Australian text has always amazed and pleased me. It also won a Parents' Choice in America. Praise for the book in Britain and the United States, where it was also published, was high. Luminaries such as Jeremy Briggs and Anthony Browne had positive things to say about it, and after meeting Anthony at an Australian conference, he invited me to send a text I might think suitable for his work. The reviews for *Way Home* in Australia were not generally good, and it garnered no honours here in any award. But the book has remained in print ever since and is a set text in many schools. The theatre company Barking Gecko produced a play I'd written

based on the book with music by a composer Stephen Lalor, whom I'd worked with over the years and who has set much of my children's poetry to music. It remains one of my favourites. At the same time, taken up with the reports I was reading on homeless kids around the world, and surprised at the number in Australia, I wrote *Feral Kid.* This is a young adult novel about an older boy who is homeless, and it was to be optioned by Hallmark Hall of Fame, as well.

On our travels, John and I lived in Holland for a few months in a wonderful apartment on the Prinsengracht found by my Dutch publishers at Ploegsma. There we met the delightful Nanny Brinkman, at this time still the head of the company, and her husband Paul, who gave us much of his time in showing us Holland. Nanny had taken my novels *Thunderwith* and *Feral Kid* and later *The Climb.* Their own house on the Kaisergracht, a huge former merchant's home, was a wonder to us with its ample beautifully furnished rooms and its rooftop garden with views of Amsterdam all around.

I was inspired at the Vincent Van Gogh Museum in Amsterdam to write my novel *The Painter,* based on the imagined life of an adolescent would-be painter, Bernard, who meets Vincent in Arles and whose life is changed by this encounter. Every morning I'd get on

Writing Thunderwith *in the Wallingat Forest, 1998.*

The author with her husband, John, in Monet's garden, Giverny, 1996.

the tram to the museum whilst John hunted antiques and, in the library there, undertake the delightful task of reading Vincent's letters, and then viewing letters that the offspring of his models had written and so on. John and I felt we could have stayed in Amsterdam forever. I had previously signed a six-book contract with publishers Hodder Headline in Australia, and my novels were in the hands of a wonderful children's publisher Belinda Bolliger. I still consult with Belinda on all my work and trust her judgment particularly when it comes to editing.

Picture storybook texts are the closest thing to poetry for me and I'll always want to write them. But it is a pretty amazing thing when they move from picture storybook to opera. *Grandma's Shoes,* which was published in Great Britain and the United States and has been published twice in Australia with two different artists (one of Belinda's choice), was to become the first children's opera performed in Australia in the new millennium. This is the story of a young girl's search for her grandmother, wearing her precious shoes, and deals with the loss of a beloved family member in a consoling way. There is even an air of triumph for the little girl as she pledges to take up her grandma's story-telling skills.

Not only did I approach Opera Australia with the story text and the idea for an opera, but through my editor at Oxford University Press, Rita Scharf, I had an auspicious meeting with Kim Carpenter, director of Theatre of Image. Kim loved the text and encouraged me to write the libretto. He introduced me to Graeme Koehne, an Adelaide composer whose work is known world-wide. We gained support from Opera Australia by way of musicians and singers, rehearsal spaces and advertising. *Grandma's Shoes* had a Kim Carpenter setting of a giant book out of which stepped all the characters, and his puppets and backdrop of animations made it a truly wonderful performance. It played to full houses and later I was thrilled to receive an award from the AWGIE (Australian Writers Guild) for this libretto. And later to receive a Prime Minister's Millennium Award for 2000.

Opera is expensive and difficult to mount so it was with some delight in 2003 that I received an invitation from Alabama to have my text for my picture storybook *Sky Sash So Blue,* published by Simon and Schuster in 1998 in the States, used as libretto. This picture storybook, embellished so lovingly by the artwork of Benny Andrews, is a celebration of freedom; it was inspired by reading Toni Morrison's powerful novel *Beloved* and is set in the same period of slavery in the deep south. The invitation was from a music lecturer at Miles, an all black college, in Birmingham, Alabama. Phillip Ratliffe had plans for a children's opera using the text already written in verse.

We undertook a long correspondence by e-mail and eventually Philip announced that not only had he almost completed the opera but that he'd secured the funds for its performance in November, 2004. The visit, which enabled me to see the rehearsals and the calibre of opera singers and chamber orchestra, was an exciting one, for it was my first experience of the south. But I must admit that on first hearing Philip's startling atonal music I wondered how young people—some as young as Grade 2—would respond. However, a group of teachers using Maxine Green's music, of the Lincoln Centre reputation, as an inspirational aesthetic education model had fully prepared their students.

So on the day of performance around 700 African-American students enjoyed the opera with its sparse set and accomplished singers and the use of a long, trailing sky sash of deep blue. In 2005, I had more correspondence from Phillip, to indicate *Sky Sash* will be performed again. This has been made possible by the Cultural Alliance and the Division of Humanities at Miles College, with in-kind donations from the Birmingham Museum of Art, UAB, Midfield Schools, and the Alabama School of Fine Arts. Miracles do happen!

With authors David Malouf and Gillian Mears, Chennai, India, 1997.

*

I have been fortunate over the years in invitations to speak in other countries and often am asked if this is the stuff of inspiration. If it's true that settings do have a huge impact, you never know whether you are going to be found by a story no matter how dramatic or how different the landscape. My initial visit to Papua New Guinea visit was to launch the first ever PNG Children's Book Fair in 1994. After a tour of some of the schools in Port Moresby, accompanied by an Australian journalist who lived there, I was taken to various island schools and touched by the enthusiasm with which a writer was greeted in schools that often lacked libraries and were even sometimes short of notepaper. On the volcanic island of Rabaul, viewing the terrifying outcome of the 1993 eruption and talking to the locals, I was inspired for my verse novel *Volcano Boy,* though it wasn't to be written until many years later. The following year in 1995, I was invited to run a writing course on the marvelous island of Madang in Papua, New Guinea, and had my first experience of snorkeling in a truly tropical place. I couldn't wait for my workshops to be over, to run helter skelter to my cabin, change into swimming gear, and spend hours, head in the water, in a world that was dramatically lovely, strange, and inspirational. At home, my son, who had undertaken a scuba diving course, had enthused about the underwater world being a great subject for a novel. And it was strange that after a cult leader in California had enticed a group of his followers, some of them quite young, to commit suicide together, and I'd seen a video of his "explanation" to them, that all these things came together in the novel *Rift.*

An author tour organized by the Australia Council in 1997 took revered Australian writer David Malouf and Gillian Mears and me to India for a marvelous three weeks. Visiting bookshops and universities, we had speaking engagements in New Delhi, Bangalore, Madras (now Chennai) and Bombay (now Mumbai). We were met by writers in each of these places and had two each of our own books launched there by Senator Alston, the then Minister for the Arts. The impact of India on the tourist has been attested to many times. Suffice to say we were enthralled by the diversity, delighted by our hosts, upset by the poverty that was so apparent, and yet charmed by the generosity of those we met. However, we were so programmed as to never get to see the Taj Mahal, something I'd always dreamt of visiting, and where I was sure a story would be lurking. One fortunate connection I'd made was with a printer at an ashram at Pondicherry famous for the quality of the paper it produced. To and fro communication indicated they'd do a limited edition of a book of my poems on specially chosen paper of a generous thickness, with petal impressed endpapers and a handmade binding in Hablik cloth.

Invited to speak at the prestigious IBBY (International Board of Books for Young People) Conference, which was to be held in New Delhi, India, I returned the next year in 1998, this time with my friend Pat and my two sisters Margaret and Suzanne, who had heard my enthusiastic descriptions of this exotic culture. This time, after IBBY, I determined to make the journey to Agra as well as one to the equally famed Lake Palace. India simply seduced us as we moved from place to place, dazzled by all we saw and especially the Taj Mahal which was all and more than I'd expected.

I'd met a charming publisher at IBBY and was invited to present my text set at the Taj Mahal to her

Libby Hathorn with her son, Kieran, and daughter, Lisa (holding baby Ruby Rose), Dorrigo, New South Wales, 2004.

small, brave children's publishing house, Tulika Books, just getting underway in Chennai. *A Face in the Water* is a timeslip story which takes a historic view of the building of the Taj and stars the daughter of the emperor Shah Jahan and two present-day Australian kids. It was illustrated by a young Indian artist Uma Krishnaswamy and published in India in 2000.

We visited Pondicherry and the ashram where *Heard Singing* was to be printed on hand-made paper. Australian paper-cutting artist Brigitte Stoddard's delicate work in Australian wildflowers graced this limited edition. Brigitte eventually illustrated my junior novel, *Okra and Acacia: The Story of the Wattle Pattern Plate*, based on the Chinese legend "The Story of the Willow Patter Plate," which was published by Hodder Headline. A wonderful hand-sewn hessian wrapped bundle of poetry books eventually arrived in Sydney from India and it gave me a great deal of pleasure to have seen the whole process and to know that I had been able to influence the look and feel of *Heard Singing*. Gifts were made of the book, some were sold and it remains a favourite book on my own shelves.

My husband John died in 1998 when leukemia he'd contracted in 1996 re-occurred. He had been fighting it for two years and his bravery in the face of a bone marrow transplant was amazing, though so difficult to witness, even though he remained positive in the face of all his trials. I've tried to write a book about our last overseas journey together in 1997 between his treatments, where we lived for a short time in a magical chateau in Normandy, John collecting antiques whilst I wrote a filmscript; but somehow that book is still unfinished.

There have been some big life changes in that time both at home and in my work. Both my children are with partners and in fact I'm a grandmother to a baby girl, Ruby Rose (inspiration for storybooks of course). My son Keiran working in Information Technology has inspired me to work on interactive stories. Our small company has released two CD-ROMs thus far. The first one, *Weirdstop*, which comprises stories of the weird variety for ten-to fourteen-year-olds, immediately won the Australian Interactive Media Industry Award for Best New Children's Product in 2003. *Coolstop* which links sport and literacy was launched by an Olympic medallist in late 2004, and we're currently working on a game and story for younger readers we've called *Won-*

derstop, which is environmental in approach. A whole new world of writing and producing has opened up.

This does not mean that I'm not writing story books. My historic novel *Georgiana* is still underway, as is a new picture storybook; whilst last year saw the launch of children's picture storybook *The Great Big Animal Ask* by film producer Rebel Penfold Russell. I'm also working on a poetry Web site, which is a long overdue project with notes for parents and teachers as to how to "turn kids on to poetry!" You see, poetry has rewarded me in every possible way. Writer Shirley Hazzard has attested that poetry changes things. And there's no doubt in my mind that those early poetry sessions with our parents, the reading and the reciting, always having poetry books to hand that illuminated my world, and taking on poetry as a significant companion has been the greatest influence on my writing, and indeed on all of my life.

HERRICK, Steven 1958-

Personal

Born December 31, 1958, in Brisbane, Australia; son of William (a factory worker) and May (a homemaker; maiden name Clulow) Herrick; married Catherine Gorman (a bank officer); children: Jack Gorman, Joe Gorman. *Education:* University of Queensland, B.A., 1982. *Hobbies and other interests:* Playing soccer, coaching youth soccer.

Addresses

Home—Katoomba, New South Wales, Australia. *Office*—P.O. Box 116, Hazelbrook, 2779, Australia. *Agent*—Glen Leitch Management, 332 Victoria St., Darlinghurst, 2010, Australia. *E-mail*—sherrick@acay.com.au.

Career

Poet, 1988—. Presenter and readers at numerous schools throughout Australia.

Member

Poets Union.

Awards, Honors

Australian Children's Book of the Year for Older Readers shortlist, Australian Children' Book Council (CBC), and New South Wales Premier's Literary Award shortlist, both 1997, both for *Love, Ghosts, & Nose Hair;* Victorian Premier's Literary Award commendation, 1998, and CBC book of the Year shortlist, and New South Wales Premier's Literary Award shortlist, both 1999, all for *A Place like This;* New South Wales Premier's Literary Award, 2000, for *The Spangled Drongo;* KOALA/YABBA Book of the Year Award shortlist, 2000, for *My Life, My Love, My Lasagna;* CBC Book of the Year shortlist, and New South Wales Premier's Literary Award shortlist, both 2001, both for *The Simple Gift;* CBC Book of the Year shortlist, 2003, for *Tom Jones Saves the World,* and 2004, for *Do-wrong Ron;* Children's Literature Peace Prize highly commended designation, for *The Simple Gift* and *Tom Jones Saves the World.*

Steven Herrick

Writings

POETRY; FOR CHILDREN

My Life, My Love, My Lasagne, illustrated by Annmarie Scott, University of Queensland Press (St. Lucia, Queensland, Australia), 1997.

Poetry to the Rescue, illustrated by Catherine Gorman, University of Queensland Press (St. Lucia, Queensland, Australia), 1998.

Love Poems and Leg Spinners: A Month in the Life of Class 5B, illustrated by Joe Gorman, University of Queensland Press (St. Lucia, Queensland, Australia), 2001.

PICTURE BOOKS

The Place Where the Planes Take Off, illustrated by Annmarie Scott, University of Queensland Press (St. Lucia, Queensland, Australia), 1995.

POETRY; FOR YOUNG ADULTS

Caboolture, Five Islands, 1990.
Water Bombs: A Book of Poems for Teenagers, Jam Roll Press (Nundah, Queensland, Australia), 1992.

NOVELS IN VERSE; FOR CHILDREN AND YOUNG ADULTS

Love, Ghosts, & Nose Hair, University of Queensland Press (St. Lucia, Queensland, Australia), 1996, published as *Love, Ghosts, & Facial Hair,* Simon & Schuster (New York, NY), 2004.
A Place like This, University of Queensland Press (St. Lucia, Queensland, Australia), 1998, Simon & Schuster (New York, NY), 2004.
The Spangled Drongo, University of Queensland Press (St. Lucia, Queensland, Australia), 1999.
The Simple Gift, University of Queensland Press (St. Lucia, Queensland, Australia), 2001, Simon & Schuster (New York, NY), 2004.
Tom Jones Saves the World, University of Queensland Press (St. Lucia, Queensland, Australia), 2002.
Do-wrong Ron,, illustrated by Caroline Magerl, Allen & Unwin (Crows Nest, New South Wales, Australia), 2003.
By the River, Allen & Unwin (Crows Nest, New South Wales, Australia), 2004.

POETRY; FOR ADULTS

The Esoteric Herrick: Poems and Things, illustrated by Roger Norris, Red Hill, 1982.
The Sound of Chopping, Five Islands, 1994.

Sidelights

Steven Herrick is an Australian poet who is dedicated to spreading the word about the magic of language to young people. Through his popular verse novels, which carry such compelling titles as *Love, Ghosts, & Nose Hair* and *Tom Jones Saves the World,* Herrick has captivated young readers in his native country as well as Great Britain and North America, where his books have also been published. As Herrick once explained to *Something about the Author,* "I love the power of poetry and the potential of poetry. I've always believed that poetry can talk to an audience or reader in the most concise, direct, and thought-provoking way."

With his 1992 poetry collection *Water Bombs: A Book of Poems for Teenagers*—his second book of verse for teen readers—Herrick uses his frank style to mark the milestones of two lives through a group of stand-alone poems that collectively reveal the cyclical nature of life. The reader glimpses verbal snapshots of Joe and Debbie's lives, from their own childhood dreams to their hopes for their children. In "almost everyday speech," observed Felicity Norman in a *Magpies* review, *Water Bombs* "speaks easily to its audience and will be very popular."

Herrick's verse-novel *Love, Ghosts, & Nose Hair,* which was published in the United States as *Love, Ghosts, & Facial Hair,* exemplifies Herrick's preferred writing format. Comprised of a series of first-person poems, the novel looks at how a family copes with the death of a loved one. Each voice examines the loss from its own perspective, like one of several cameras set to catch the same action from its own unique angle. While the predominant perspective belongs to Jack, a sixteen year old writer who is preoccupied with his girlfriend, Annabel, sports, and the death of his mother to cancer seven years ago, the reader see Jack through the eyes of his sister and now-widowed father. In the companion novel *A Place like This* Jack and Annabel decide to take a year off before college and, despite their plans of a motor tour around Australia, wind up working long hours as apple pickers for a family with troubles of their own. *Magpies* critic Anne Hanzl commented that *Love, Ghosts, & Nose Hair* is a "sad, funny, moving, and thoughtful" book, while in *Booklist* Jennifer Mattson praised Herrick's "rich, layered verse" and noted that the two novels "speak with sincerity and sensitivity" to the trauma of family upheavals, and *A Place like This* includes "a Kerouacian fantasy that will resonate with many teens."

Other verse novels by Herrick include *Tom Jones Saves the World,* about a boy frustrated by his stuffy parents who escapes from his gated community and has a series of adventures that connect him to his family's past and make him appreciate his advantages in life. Another boy escapes from his family in *The Simple Gift,* although this time his family life is a bit more daunting. Sixteen-year-old Billy makes a new home for himself in an abandoned railway freight car, and meets a new community of friends that sustain him in a novel that *Booklist* contributor Jennifer Mattson called "tender [and] uplifting," adding that the book is characteristic Herrick: "crowd-pleasing" and "swift-reading."

In addition to his writing, Herrick visits hundreds of schools each year in his capacity as a self-appointed ambassador of verse, and has even traveled to Canada, the United Kingdom, the United States, and Singapore. "I have a touch of the evangelist in me when it comes to poetry," the poet once admitted—"I want the public to recognize poetry as an enjoyable, entertaining medium. That's why I not only write poetry, but I also read it in front of an audience. I believe writers need to see (and hear) how an audience reacts to their writing. Performing my poetry allows me that luxury." "One of the great joys I feel in visiting so many schools is talking to children and young adults," Herrick added. "I listen to what they say and how they say it. I hope my books reflect some of what I've heard over the years. I hope they get more people of all ages reading poetry and believing that poetry, as a medium, can tell a story as well as prose." An entertaining performer—Herrick has been a frequent guest on live radio shows and has appeared on various Australian television programs—his writing and performance styles are similar, reported *Sydney Morning Herald* critic Shelli-Anne Couch: they are "extraordinarily simple on the surface but spliced with subtle bites and small twists." The straightforward quality common to Herrick's spoken and written word, was also noted by Norman, who wrote in *Magpies* that the poet's writings reflect the "directness and immediate impact" required of performance poetry.

Explaining his reason for writing verse-novels in addition to "straight" poetry, Herrick noted that a free-verse text "allows me into the personality of each character—his or her thoughts, emotions, insecurities, and ambitions. The verse-novel form lets me tell the story from a number of perspectives, and, hopefully, with an economy of words. In short, it allows each character to tell the story in his or her own language, from his or her own angle."

Biographical and Critical Sources

PERIODICALS

Australian Book Review, June, 1994, p. 53; September, 1998, p. 44.

Booklist, March 15, 2004, Jennifer Mattson, review of *Love, Ghosts, & Facial Hair* and *A Place like This,* p.1299; August, 2004, Jennifer Mattson, review of *The Simple Gift,* p. 1919.

Kliatt, May, 2004, Nancy Zachary, review of *The Simple Gift,* p. 18; July, 2004, Heather Lisowski, review of *Love, Ghosts, & Facial Hair,* p. 18.

Magpies, September, 1992, Felicity Norman, review of *Water Bombs: A Book of Poems for Teenagers,* p. 24; July, 1996, Anne Hanzl, review of *Love, Ghosts, & Nose Hair,* p. 33.

School Library Journal, March, 2004, Sharon Korbeck, review of *Love, Ghosts, & Facial Hair,* p. 213.

Sydney Morning Herald, April 26, 1994, Shelli-Anne Couch, "When There's Pure Poetry in the Making," p.23.

ONLINE

Steven Herrick Web site, http://www.acay.com.au/~sherrick/ (December 2, 2004).

*   *   *

HOSSEINI, Khaled 1965-

Personal

Born 1965, in Kabul, Afghanistan; son of a diplomat and a teacher; immigrated to the United States, 1980; married; children: Haris, Farah. *Education:* Santa Clara University, B.A. (biology), 1988; University of San Diego, M.D., 1993. *Hobbies and other interests:* Soccer, racquetball, writing, involved in charities Paralyzed Vets of America and Aid the Afghan Children.

Addresses

Home—CA. *Agent*—c/o Author Mail, Riverhead Books, 375 Hudson St., New York, NY 10014.

Career

Practicing physician specializing in internal medicine, 1996–; The Permanente Medical Group, Mountain View, CA, physician, beginning 1999.

Awards, Honors

Original Voices Award, Borders Group, and Alex Award, YALSA, both 2004, both for *The Kite Runner.*

Writings

The Kite Runner, Riverhead Books (New York, NY), 2003.

Adaptations

The Kite Runner was adapted for audio, read by the author, Simon & Schuster, 2003, and was slated for adaptation as a feature film to be produced by Dreamworks.

Sidelights

Khaled Hosseini's debut novel, *The Kite Runner,* spans four decades and returns readers to pre-Soviet Afghanistan. The tale is narrated by Amir, an adult writer living in California. Amir's story recalls his childhood in Kabul, when the quiet, motherless boy yearns for attention from his successful father, Bapa, but finds a friend in Hassan, the son of his father's servant. Amir resents sharing his father's affection with the loyal and talented Hassan, but when Amir wins a kite-flying contest, his father finally gives him the praise he craves. In that single incident, however, he also loses Hassan, who is attacked and raped by Assef, the town bully, while attempting to retrieve a downed kite. Because of his feelings of guilt for not helping his friend, Amir pushes Hassan away, even accusing his former friend of theft. Years later, an associate of Amir's now-deceased father, who knows the history of Amir and Hassan, calls from Pakistan. He tells Amir that Hassan and Hassan's wife have been executed by the terrorist Taliban, leaving their son, Sohrab, orphaned and without care. Realizing that he owes a debt to Hassan, Amir returns to Afghanistan to find Sohrab, only to come across the boy in the custody of the criminal Assef.

Reviewing *The Kite Runner* in the *New York Times Book Review,* Edward Hower wrote that "Hosseini's depiction of pre-revolutionary Afghanistan is rich in warmth and humor but also tense with the friction between the nation's different ethnic groups." The critic added that the story "turns dark when Hosseini describes the suffering of his country under the tyranny of the Taliban. . .. The final third of the book is full of haunting images." *School Library Journal* reviewer Penny Stevens called *The Kite Runner* a "beautifully written first novel," and a *Publishers Weekly* contributor dubbed it "stunning," adding that "it is rare that a book is at once so timely and of such high literary quality."

While fiction, *The Kite Runner* draws on parts of its author's own past. Hosseini was born in Kabul, Afghanistan, the son of a diplomat whose wife, Hosseini's mother, taught Farsi and history at a private girls' school in the city. In 1976 the family was relocated to Paris, France, where Hosseini's father was assigned to the Afghan embassy, and they remained there until 1980. Because of the Soviet takeover of Afghanistan following a bloody military coup, the Hosseini family was granted political asylum in the United States, and they made a new home for themselves in San Jose, California. By leaving Afghanistan, Hosseini's parents were forced to leave everything they owned behind, and the family relied on welfare until the author's father and mother were able to get back on their feet. Self-reliant and determined due to his childhood experiences, Hosseini attended college and became a physician; while working and raising his family of two children, he also tapped into a lifelong love of writing by penning *The Kite Runner.*

Biographical and Critical Sources

PERIODICALS

Booklist, July, 2003, Kristine Huntley, review of *The Kite Runner,* p. 1864.

Kirkus Reviews, May 1, 2003, review of *The Kite Runner,* p. 630.

Library Journal, April 15, 2003, Rebecca Stuhr, review of *The Kite Runner,* p. 122; November 15, 2003, Michael Adams, review of *The Kite Runner* (audio version), p.114.

New York Times Book Review, August 3, 2003, Edward Hower, review of *The Kite Runner,* p. 4.

Publishers Weekly, May 12, 2003, review of *The Kite Runner,* p. 43.

School Library Journal, November, 2003, Penny Stevens, review of *The Kite Runner,* p. 171.

Times (London, England), August 30, 2003, review of *The Kite Runner,* p. 17.

ONLINE

Khaled Hosseini Home Page, http://www.khaledhosseini.com/ (January 13, 2005).

National Public Radio Web site, http://www.npr.org/ (July 27, 2003), Liane Hansen, *Weekend Edition Sunday* interview with Hosseini.*

I

IBBOTSON, Eva 1925-

Personal
Born January 21, 1925, in Vienna, Austria; daughter of B. P. (a physiologist) and Anna (a writer; maiden name, Gmeyner) Wiesner; married Alan Ibbotson (a university lecturer), June 21, 1948; children: Lalage Ann, Tobias John, Piers David, Justin Paul. *Education:* Bedford College, London, B.Sc., 1945; attended Cambridge University, 1946-47; University of Durham, diploma in education, 1965. *Hobbies and other interests:* Ecology and environmental preservation, music, continental literature, history ("My favorite period is 1904!").

Addresses
Home—2 Collingwood Terrace, Jesmond, Newcastle upon Tyne NE2 2JP, England. *Agent*—Curtis Brown, 162-168 Regent St., London W1R 5TA, England; John Cushman Associates Inc., 25 West 42nd St., New York, NY 10036.

Career
Full-time writer. Former research worker, university teacher, and schoolteacher.

Awards, Honors
Carnegie Medal shortlist, British Library Association, 1979, for *Which Witch?,* and 2001, for *Journey to the River Sea;* Best Romantic Novel of the Year Published in England, Romantic Novelists Association, 1983, for *Magic Flutes;* Smarties Prize Shortlist, and Best Books designation, *School Library Journal,* 1998, for *The Secret of Platform 13; Guardian* Children's Fiction Award runner-up, and Whitbread Children's Book of the Year award shortlist, and Smarties Prize shortlist, all 2001, all for *Journey to the River Sea.*

Writings

FOR CHILDREN

The Great Ghost Rescue, illustrated by Simon Stern, Macmillan (London, England), 1975, illustrated by Giulio

Eva Ibbotson

Maestro, Walck, 1975, illustrated by Kevin Hawkes, Dutton (New York, NY), 2002.

Which Witch?, illustrated by Annabel Large, Macmillan (London, England), 1979, Scholastic (New York, NY), 1988.

The Worm and the Toffee-nosed Princess, and Other Stories of Monsters (folklore), illustrated by Margaret Chamberlain, Macmillan (London, England), 1983, illustrated by Russell Ayto, Hodder Children's (London, England), 1997.

The Haunting of Hiram C. Hopgood, Macmillan (London, England), 1987, published as *The Haunting of Granite Falls,* Dutton (New York, NY), 2004.

Not Just a Witch, illustrated by Alice Englander, Macmillan (London, England), 1989, Chivers North America, 1992.

The Secret of Platform 13, illustrated by Sue Porter, Macmillan (London, England), 1994, Dutton (New York, NY), 1998.

Dial-a-Ghost, illustrated by Kirsten Meyer, Macmillan (London, England), 1996, illustrated by Kevin Hawkes, Dutton (New York, NY), 2001.

Monster Mission, illustrated by Teresa Sdralevich, Macmillan (London, England), 1999, published as *Island of the Aunts,* illustrated by Kevin Hawkes, Dutton (New York, NY), 2000.

Journey to the River Sea, illustrated by Kevin Hawkes, Dutton (New York, NY), 2001.

The Star of Kazan, illustrated by Kevin Hawkes, Dutton (New York, NY), 2004.

ROMANCE NOVELS

A Countess below Stairs, MacDonald (London, England), 1981, Avon (New York, NY), 1982.

Magic Flutes, St. Martin's Press (New York, NY), 1982.

A Glove Shop in Vienna and Other Stories, Century (London, England), 1984, St. Martin's Press (New York, NY), 1992.

A Company of Swans, St. Martin's Press (New York, NY), 1985.

Madensky Square, St. Martin's Press (New York, NY), 1988.

The Morning Gift, St. Martin's Press (New York, NY), 1993.

A Song for Summer, Arrow (London, England), 1997, St. Martin's Press (New York, NY), 1998.

OTHER

Linda Came Today (television drama), ATV, 1965.

Contributor of hundreds of articles and stories to periodicals. Works have been anthologized in books, including *Yearbook of the American Short Story.*

Adaptations

Dial-a-Ghost, The Great Ghost Rescue, The Haunting of Hiram C. Hopgood, Not Just a Witch, The Secret of Platform 13, and *Which Witch?* have all been released on audiocassette.

Sidelights

Vienna-born British writer Eva Ibbotson works in two markedly different areas of fiction: tongue-in-cheek ghost stories for a young-adult audience; and adult romances that are frequently set in her hometown during the early part of the twentieth century. Of this dual ca-

reer, she herself once said, "After years of writing magazine stories and books for children, I am trying hard to break down the barrier between 'romantic novels' and 'serious novels' which are respectfully reviewed." Certainly no one would accuse her of being too serious in her ghost stories, which are written in a "spirit" of great fun. As *Horn Book* reviewer Kitty Flynn explained, "Ibbotson's vivid descriptions of the gruesome and grotesque will delight readers, and even the ghastliest of her spectral characters manages to be likable." Still, the smooth, easy flow of her supernatural tales, which has won Ibbotson praise from many critics, fits well with the second half of her stated desires as a novelist: "My aim is to produce books that are light, humorous, even a little erudite, but secure in their happy endings. One could call it an attempt to write, in words, a good Viennese waltz!"

Growing up in Austria, Ibbotson moved with her family to England after the Nazis took power during the 1940s. She got her degree at the University of London and intended to become a physiologist, although the amount of animal experimentation required of this career path soon caused her to change her mind. Instead, she got married and raised a family. She returned to school and earned a degree in education in the mid-1960s. One of her first written works was the television play *Linda Came Today,* produced by ATV in 1965; her first children's book *The Great Ghost Rescue,* was published a decade later, in 1975, and she has been writing ever since.

Ibbotson's books for younger readers have gained her a large following among both British and American readers due to her imaginative plots and clever dialogue. Reviewing *The Great Ghost Rescue,* a critic noted in *Growing Point* that the author develops "a gloriously improbable situation with an inexhaustible provision of verbal wit." Noting Ibbotson's penchant for flouting "political correctness," the contributor also noted that she pokes fun at "some of the more lumbering conservation-sermons disguised as fiction which are currently being offered to young readers." The novel focuses on Rick Henderson, a serious-minded boarding-school student concerned about the environment, who sees the ghosts in the story as something of an endangered species and sets about to help them. Humphrey the Horrible, in particular, needs help, because he lacks the ability to frighten the students at Rick's boarding school, and he is joined in seeking Rick's help by family members Headless Aunt Hortensia and George the Screaming Skull, among others. Noting that the story has "considerable appeal," *School Library Journal* contributor Steven Engelfried added that the novel benefits from Ibbotson's "deliciously consistent macabre humor and the entertaining ensemble of ghosts" she conjures up with her pen. According to Ann A. Flowers in *Horn Book,* "The delightfully horrid details and the richly comic assortment of ghosts make [*The Great Ghost Rescue*] an amusing and satisfying story."

Which Witch? is the story of a competition between witches eager to become the bride of the wicked wizard of the North, Arridian. A reviewer in *Junior Bookshelf* praised the novel, noting that Ibbotson's writing is so visual and evocative that, "With all respect to [illustrator] Annabel Large, illustrations are superfluous." *Dial-a-Ghost* finds Ibbotson on similar ground as it relates the activities surrounding a ghost placement agency. "There are plenty of bloodstains and creepy crawlies," promised a reviewer in *Junior Bookshelf,* "and many rather grotesque humans who help to make the ghosts seem normal."

Ghosts faced the problem of relocation in *The Great Ghost Rescue* and they encounter a similar situation in *The Haunting of Hiram C. Hopgood,* published in the United States as *The Haunting of Granite Falls.* Hopgood, a Texas oil magnate, wants to buy an English castle and bring it home with him, and twelve-year-old Alex MacBuff, an orphan who can no longer afford to keep up his ancestral home, is happy to sell it. The only problem is that Hopgood demands that the castle arrive in Texas ghost-free, and Alex has to figure out a way to negotiate with the ghosts, which include a Viking warrior, a toothless vampire named Stanislaus, and a hellhound. Along the way, he has an innocent romance with Hopgood's ten-year-old daughter Helen, whom the ghosts assist when she is kidnapped. "This combination of farce and fantasy," wrote Elizabeth Finlayson in *School Librarian,* "has much to offer besides a thoroughly enjoyable story." Noting that the story "gives new meaning to the term 'blended family,'" *Horn Book* contributor Kristi Elle Jemtegaard praised the author's "knack for vivid detail" and noted that in *The Haunting of Granite Falls* "The comfort of a happy ending is never in doubt."

Not Just a Witch, like *Which Witch?,* concerns a competition between witches, but this time the rivalry is between two former friends who have a silly falling out over a hat. Dora and Heckie—short for Hecate—compete with each other to see who can rid a town of the most evil. Employing a classic remedy, Dora turns problem personalities into stone, but Heckie is more imaginative: she transforms her town's evildoers into caged zoo animals. When their private competition is discovered by an entrepreneurial furrier named Lionel Knapsack, the battle between the witches is cooperated: wooing Heckie with chocolate, Lionel plans to turn a whole prison full of inmates into snow leopards, a creature whose fur is highly marketable. Noting that *Not Just a Witch* deals with the perennial battle between good and evil, a *Publishers Weekly* contributor wrote that "Ibbotson again blends hilarious social commentary . . . into a potent recipe for fun." Most of Ibbotson's early supernatural tales involve ghosts or witches, but *The Secret of Platform 13* constitutes somewhat of a departure. Next to Platform 13, in an old subway station—or Tube station, as they are called in London—is a gate into a mythic underworld of wizards and fairies. The gate

Maia is an orphan who is sent to live with her spoiled cousins in Brazil, where she vies to escape the drab walls of her cousins' bungalow to explore the adventures of the Amazon River. (From Journey to the River Sea, *written by Ibbotson and illustrated by Kevin Hawkes.)*

only opens once every nine years, and a spoiled, selfish woman named Larina Trottle takes advantage of this opportunity to kidnap the child prince from the other world and bring him back to London. The denizens of the underworld have to come up to the surface and find their boy and rescue him, which they do with the help of Larina's son Ben. Ben, as it turns out, is lovable and kind, whereas Raymond, the boy they are searching for, has become a little tyrant under Larina's care. Praising the book as "Fast, fun," and "full of bizarre characters and ideas," a reviewer in *Books for Keeps* dubbed *The Secret of Platform 13* "a real imagination tickler" with a surprise ending.

In contrast to Ibbotson's ghost stories, her adult novels, such as *Magic Flutes, Madensky Square,* and *The Morning Gift,* are much "quieter" books, though nonetheless imbued with the author's good humor and wit. *Madensky Square,* like most of the others, takes place in Vienna—in this case, the Vienna of 1911, which is yet unsullied by World War I. The story of Susanna, a dressmaker whose shop opens onto the quiet square, is told through her diary, in which she reveals a number of surprising details, including an ongoing affair with a nobleman. "This refreshing novel in which the heroine overcomes hardship [and] sticks to her ideals, [is] carried off without sticky sentimentality," wrote a critic in *Publishers Weekly*. In a similar vein, Ibbotson's children's book *Journey to the River Sea* takes place in 1910 and focuses on a young girl who is un-haunted by ghosts of any kind. Instead of spectres, orphaned Maia Fielding is troubled by her new guardians, the Carters, who bring her to live with them on their poorly run rubber plantation in Brazil, where they live while pretending they are back in England. Escaping the confines of the Carter's home, Maia meets new friends and discovers a new world in the exotic Amazon rainforest around her. In addition to becoming enmeshed in the investigations of a pair of British detectives, Maia also discovers her life's calling: to be an explorer. Noting that the author "does a wonderful job of turning genre themes topsy-turvy," *Booklist* contributor Jean Franklin praised Ibbotson's "plucky" protagonist and her "delightfully humorous style." *Journey to the River Sea* is

a novel "rich in drama, suspense, hints of romance, and a sense of justice," added Jean Gaffney in a review for *School Library Journal,* the critic going on to praise Ibbotson for bringing Brazil's "natural beauty and the time period . . . to life."

In addition to humor and a fast-moving story, all of Ibbotson's books are united by her creation of a spirited protagonists, many of whom have talents that are overlooked by those around them. "Every kid wants to believe that he or she is special and hopes that someone out there will recognize their hidden talents and uniqueness, qualities that, too often, adults do fail to see," commented Jeannette Hulick in a profile of Ibbotson for the *Bulletin of the Center for Children's Books Online*. "In the words of Aunt Etta of *Island of the Aunts,* 'You'd be surprised. There are children all over the place whose parents don't know how lucky they are.' Fortunately, in Ibbotson's worlds, kids do find confirmation that they are, in fact, extraordinary people."

Biographical and Critical Sources

BOOKS

Ibbotson, Eva, *Island of the Aunts,* Dutton (New York, NY), 2000.

PERIODICALS

Booklist, January 1, 1985, p. 620; June 15, 1985, p. 1435; September 15, 1988, p. 120; August, 1993, p. 2036; December 15, 2001, Jean Franklin, review of *Journey to the River Sea,* p. 727; May 1, 2004, Kay Weisman, review of *The Haunting of Granite Falls,* p. 1559.
Books for Keeps, November, 1995, review of *The Secret of Platform 13,* p. 11.
Growing Point, November, 1979, p. 3598; April, 1975, review of *The Great Ghost Rescue,* p. 2599.
Horn Book, December, 1975, Ann A. Flowers, review of *The Great Ghost Rescue,* pp. 593-594; January-February, 2002, Christine M. Heppermann, review of *Journey to the River Sea,* p. 78; September-October, 2002, Kitty Flynn, review of *The Great Ghost Rescue,* p. 574; July-August, 2004, Kristi Elle Jemtegaard, review of *The Haunting of Granite Falls,* p. 453.
Junior Bookshelf, October, 1979, review of *Which Witch?,* p. 279; October, 1987, p. 235; February, 1990, review of *Not Just a Witch,* p. 27; October, 1996, review of *Dial-a-Ghost,* pp. 202-203.
Kirkus Reviews, June 1, 1985, p. 492; June 1, 1993, pp. 678-679; January 1, 1998, p. 57; June 15, 2003, review of *Not Just a Witch,* p. 859.
Publishers Weekly, October 13, 1975, p. 111; October 26, 1984, p. 96; May 31, 1985, p. 46; September 2, 1988, review of *Madensky Square,* p. 86; July 19, 1993, p.238; July 21, 2003, review of *Not Just a Witch,* p. 195.

Realizing their mortality, three aging sisters secluded on an island devise a plan to kidnap children in order to perpetuate the care giving of their unusual collection of sea creatures and ghosts. (From Island of the Aunts, *written by Eva Ibbotson and illustrated by Kevin Hawkes.)*

School Librarian, September, 1980, p. 266; February, 1988, Elizabeth Finlayson, review of *The Haunting of Hiram C. Hopgood,* p. 28.

School Library Journal, May, 1975, p. 70; January, 2002, Jean Gaffney, review of *Journey to the River Sea,* p.132; August, 2002, Steven Engelfried, review of *The Great Ghost Rescue,* p. 189.

ONLINE

Bulletin of the Center for Children's Books Online, http://www.lis.uiuc.edu/puboff/bccb/ (March 1, 2002), Jeannette Hulick, "Eva Ibbotson."

Penguin Putnam Web site, http://www.penguinputnam.com/ (December 2, 2004).*

J-K

JUBY, Susan 1969-

Personal

Born 1969; married, 2001; husband's name James. *Education:* Attended University of Toronto; University of British Columbia, B.A. (English literature).

Addresses

Home—Vancouver Island, Canada. *Agent*—c/o author Mail, HarperCollins, 1350 Avenue of the Americas, New York, NY, 10019-4703. *E-mail*—andfurthermore@ shaw.ca.

Career

Editor at publishing company in Vancouver, British Columbia, Canada, c. 1992; writer, beginning 1995.

Writings

Alice, I Think, Thistledown Press (Saskatoon, Saskatchewan, Canada), 2000, revised edition, HarperTempest (New York, NY), 2003.
Miss Smithers, HarperTempest (New York, NY), 2004.
Alice Macleod, Realist at Last, HarperTempest (New York, NY), 2005.

Adaptations

Alice, I Think was adapted as an audiobook by Harper-Children's Audio, 2003.

Sidelights

Canadian author Susan Juby didn't intend to write a young adult novel when she set out to pen her first book. However, her first publisher, Canada's Thistledown Press, realized that *Alice, I Think* with its young teen heroine, was definitely a teen read. The novel,

Young Alice has been home-schooled for the majority of her life, but when she turns fifteen and decides to go to a public school, the humor and melodrama of Alice's wit ensues.

which has been followed by several sequels, reads as the diary of Alice McLeod, a fifteen-year-old home-schooled misfit who finally decides to enroll in public high school ten years after a first-grade costume incident in which she was publicly mortified. Ilene Cooper, reviewing the novel for *Booklist,* commented that while

Juby "needs to accept that 'less is more' and abandon the overused diary format, . . . her potential is clear." A *Publishers Weekly* critic expressed more enthusiasm for *Alice, I Think,* stating that "while Juby's novel stands out more for her narrator's voice than for its plot, her dark wit virtually glitters on every page."

A popular character, Alice has returned in several other novels. *Miss Smithers* once again finds the now-sixteen-year-old heroine engaging in a variety of comic situations, one of which is as a contestant in the Miss Smithers beauty pageant. While budget-conscious Alice is motivated to enter for the $400 clothing budget given to participants, her ex-hippie, feminist mother is none too happy with her daughter's latest quest. And in *Alice Macleod, Realist at Last,* she attempts to find solace through self-expression by writing screenplays after her boyfriend moves to Scotland and her mother is jailed for her radical environmentalism. Debbie Carton commented in a *Booklist* review that *Miss Smithers* "easily stands alone and will send new readers back to the first book," while in *Horn Book* Betty Carter praised Alice as a "charismatic character with strong appeal."

Juby discussed her inspiration for her "Alice" books on her Web site: "My intention was to write a book about a teenager who doesn't fit in, but doesn't allow that fact to crush her. Alice is my homage to oddballs. I wanted her to have the courage and integrity to find her own way and define herself independently of other people. I've always admired people who can do that."

Biographical and Critical Sources

PERIODICALS

Booklist, August, 2003, Ilene Cooper, review of *Alice, I Think,* p. 1971; October 1, 2003, Brian Wilson, review of *Alice, I Think,* p. 341; May 1, 2004, Debbie Carton, review of *Miss Smithers,* p. 1555.

Horn Book, July-August, 2004, Betty Carter, review of *Miss Smithers,* p. 454.

Publishers Weekly, June 9, 2003, review of *Alice, I Think,* p. 53; May 3, 2004, review of *The Latest Scoop,* p.194; May 31, 2004, review of *Alice, I Think,* p. 77.

School Library Journal, October, 2003, Lynn Evarts, review of *Alice, I Think,* p. 86.

ONLINE

Susan Juby Web site, http://www.susanjuby.com/ (January 5, 2005).*

*   *   *

KACZMAN, James

Personal

Male. *Education:* Massachusetts College of Art, B.F.A.; coursework at Rhose Island School of Design and School of Museum of Fine Arts, Boston.

Addresses

Home and office—27 Lake St., Ledyard, CT 06339. *Agent*—Gerald & Cullen Rapp, Inc., 108 East 35th St., New York, NY 10016. *E-mail*—james@jameskaczman. com.

Career

Artist, illustrator, and author. Commercial artist, with clients including Cisco, AT&T, Kodak, Microsoft, and Bloomberg.

Writings

(Illustrator) Rhonda Gowler Green, *When A Line Bends . . . a Shape Begins,* Houghton Mifflin (Boston, MA), 1997.

(Self-illustrated) *A Bird and His Worm,* Houghton Mifflin (Boston, MA), 2002.

Contributor of illustrations to periodicals, including *Newsweek, Time, Forbes, Adweek, New York Times, Fortune,* and the *Wall Street Journal.*

Sidelights

Connecticut-based artist James Kaczman is the author and illustrator of the children's story *A Bird and His Worm.* A bird who prefers walking to flying befriends a worm. When the time comes for the bird to fly south, his earthbound friend chooses to accompany him, and the duo set out on the back of a fox heading for Florida. The fox secretly plans to eat them for lunch, but is so overjoyed at the lovely conversation he has with the pair, that he lets them go instead. Later on down the road they try the same approach with a snake, but are not quite as lucky. *Booklist* reviewer GraceAnne A. De-Candido commented that "Kaczman mixes geometric and rolling shapes and splashes them with sunny, verdant color to make his winsome and offbeat story shine," while a *Kirkus Reviews* critic wrote that the author/illustrator's "sly, good humor, exuberant, original illustrations, and positive message make this a must read."

Kaczman, who is primarily a commercial artist for a number of New York City-based clients, began his secondary career as a book illustrator with *When a Line Bends . . . a Shape Begins,* by Rhonda Gowler Greene. Praising this toddler-attuned introduction to geometric shapes, a *Publishers Weekly* reviewer noted in their "clever and fun" book, "Greene and Kaczman collaborate effectively . . . through bouncy rhyme, familiar examples and clean-edged artwork."

Biographical and Critical Sources

PERIODICALS

Booklist, September 15, 2002, GraceAnne A. DeCandido, review of *A Bird and His Worm,* p. 240.

Kirkus Reviews, September 1, 2002, review of *A Bird and His Worm,* p. 1311.

A bird who doesn't fly walks South with his new companion, a worm, on a journey that provides him with lessons about self-preservation and the value of friendship. (From A Bird and His Worm, *written and illustrated by James Kaczman.)*

Publishers Weekly, September 1, 1997, review of *When a Line Bends . . . a Shape Begins,* p. 104; August 26, 2002, review of *A Bird and His Worm,* p. 67.
School Library Journal, September, 2002, Shawn Brommer, review of *A Bird and His Worm,* p. 195.

ONLINE

James Kaczman Web site, http://www.jameskaczman.com/ (March 29, 2005).

*   *   *

KATZ, Susan 1945-

Personal

Born January 17, 1945, in Reading, PA; daughter of Frank (an insurance company employee) and Clara (a homemaker; maiden name, Frankhouser) Rea; married David Katz (a teacher); children: Demian. *Education:* Drexel University, B.S. (English), 1966; University of Michigan, M.A. (English language and literature), 1967; Goddard College, M.F.A. (poetry), 1978. *Hobbies and other interests:* Powwows, walking, botanizing, animals.

Addresses

Home—PA. *Agent*—c/o Author Mail, Greenwillow Books, 13500 Avenue of the Americas, New York, NY 10019. *E-mail*—katz@netaxs.com.

Career

Drexel University, Philadelphia, PA, adjunct instructor, c. 1970s; Community College of Philadelphia, instructor and writing specialist; teacher at poetry workshops. Member, Philadelphia Children's Reading Roundtable; volunteer at Lenni Lenape Historical Society.

Susan Katz

Member

Society of Children's Book Writers and Illustrators, National Museum of the American Indian, Rainforest Alliance, Defenders of Wildlife.

Awards, Honors

Woodrow Wilson fellow, 1967; Pennsylvania Council on the Arts fellow in poetry, 1982, 1985, 1990. Paterson Prize for Books for Young Readers, 1999; Mark Twain Award nomination, 2000; named to West Virginia Children's Book Award master list, 2001.

Writings

Snowdrops for Cousin Ruth, Simon & Schuster (New York, NY), 1998.
Mrs. Brown on Exhibit, and Other Museum Poems, illustrated by R. W. Alley, Simon & Schuster (New York, NY), 2002.
The Revolutionary Mrs. Brown, and Other Poems of Colonial America, illustrated by R. W. Alley, Simon & Schuster (New York, NY), 2004.
Looking for Jaguar, and Other Rain Forest Poems, illustrated by Lee Christiansen, Greenwillow Books (New York, NY), 2005.

Contributor of poetry and articles to periodicals, including *American Scholar, Intro, Alaska Quarterly Review, Pennsylvania Review, Shenandoah, Ladies' Home Journal, American Baby, Woman's World, Family Circle,* and *Bird Watcher's Digest.*

Sidelights

In addition to seeing her poetry published in a wide range of periodicals, Susan Katz is the author of several books of verse for young readers. In *Mrs. Brown on Exhibit, and Other Museum Poems* she introduces the intrepid mastermind of amazing field trips, Mrs. Brown, who shuttles her fortunate class to museums ranging from the traditional to the whimsical to the downright crazy. Comprised of twenty poems, the book has been followed by *The Revolutionary Mrs. Brown, and Other Poems of Colonial America,* in which the energetic educator leads her class in a host of activities designed to introduce them to life during the mid-1700s. Both books are narrated in the voices of Mrs. Brown's class participants, and poems range from blank verse to rhyme, and humorous to thoughtful. "Whether lyrically crystallizing an observation or reporting on the antics of the class cut-ups, the poems convey the excitement of kids on an adventure," noted a *Publishers Weekly* contributor in reviewing *Mrs. Brown on Exhibit.* Noting that Katz's 2005 collection, *Looking for Jaguar, and Other Rain Forest Poems,* is "as useful in the science classroom as in language arts units," *Booklist* reviewer Jennifer Mattson added that the poet's evocative text contains "child-friendly metaphor, affable humor, and plenty of mind-boggling facts."

Katz was raised in Shillington, in the heart of Pennsylvania Dutch country, and shares her hometown with noted writer John Updike. As a child she worked on the school newspaper, played clarinet in the school band, explored the woods near her home, and read every book she could get her hands on. As Katz explained to *Something about the Author* (SATA), she feels fortunate that, in college, she studied poetry with Pulitzer Prize-winning poets Lisel Mueller and Louise Glück. While writing adult poetry for several years, Katz shifted to writing for children when her son, Demian, at age two, started poems but lost interest after line three and asked his mother to finish them. Katz feels confident about her qualifications as a children's author because, in addition to being a child once herself, she also has spent considerable time with younger people through her work as a "camp counselor, a 4-H club leader, a YMCA volunteer, a summer school teacher, a visiting poet, and a mother with a certain tolerance for snakes, noise, wet sneakers, and assistant cooks who drop the eggs on the floor."

Katz's first book, the prose work *Snowdrops for Cousin Ruth,* was inspired by a real person in the author's life. As the author readily admitted to *SATA,* Cousin Ruth "is the only character [I have] . . . ever lifted from life and put directly into a story exactly as she was, right down to her favorite expression, 'Sufferin' mackerals!'" In the book, a family saddened by the loss of a seven-year-old son and brother are heartened by the arrival of eighty-two-year-old Cousin Ruth, who helps each family member deal with their grief and move on. In *Horn Book* Susan P. Bloom praised the voice of the story's narrator, nine-year-old Joanna, as "believably sensitive and poetic" and dubbed Cousin Ruth as "a contempo-

Through the poems that form her text, ostensibly written by Mrs. Brown's class of inquisitive students, Katz introduces young readers to the joys to be discovered in museums. (From Mrs. Brown on Exhibit and Other Museum Poems, *illustrated by R. W. Alley.)*

rary Mary Poppins." Citing Katz for her "extraordinary sensitivity," a *Publishers Weekly* critic added that the author "deftly weaves a story of love and rejuvenation" around the lives of her realistically drawn characters, while in *Booklist* Shelle Rosenfeld described *Snowdrops for Cousin Ruth* as "beautifully written, thoughtful, and touching."

Regarding her favored technique for writing, Katz explained to *SATA* that, on days when she has the time at home, she stays at her desk "from early morning until mid-afternoon, squinting out a second-story window at a row of lilac bushes, hoping worlds will rush into [my] . . . head."

Biographical and Critical Sources

PERIODICALS

Booklist, July, 1998, Shelle Rosenfeld, review of *Snowdrops for Cousin Ruth,* p. 1878; February 15, 2005, Jennifer Mattson, review of *Looking for Jaguar, and Other Rain Forest Poems.*

Horn Book, May-June, 1998, Susan P. Bloom, review of *Snowdrops for Cousin Ruth,* p. 345.

Kirkus Reviews, May 15, 2004, review of *The Revolutionary Mrs. Brown: Poems of Colonial America,* p. 493; February 1, 2005, review of *Looking for Jaguar, and Other Rain Forest Poems.*

Publishers Weekly, June 1, 1998, review of *Snowdrops for Cousin Ruth,* p. 48; June 3, 2002, review of *Mrs. Brown on Exhibit, and Other Museum Poems,* p. 88.

School Library Journal, August, 2002, Susan Scheps, review of *Mrs. Brown on Exhibit,* p. 177.

*   *   *

KIMMELMAN, Leslie (Grodinsky) 1958-

Personal

Born April 19, 1958, in Philadelphia, PA; married Ray Kimmelman, 1984; children: Natalie, Gregory. *Educa-*

tion: Middlebury College, B.A. (magna cum laude), 1980. *Religion:* Jewish.

Addresses

Home—Ardsley, NY. *Agent*—c/o Author Mail, Harper-Collins Children's, 1350 Avenue of the Americas, New York, NY 10019.

Career

William Morrow Publishers, New York, NY, editorial assistant for children's books, 1980-82; Taft Corp., Washington, DC, marketing associate, 1982-83; Harper & Row Publishers, New York, NY, children's book editor, 1983-89; writer and freelance editor, 1989–.

Awards, Honors

Pick of the List citation, American Booksellers Association, and Notable Book in the Field of Social Studies designation, American Library Association, both 1989, both for *Frannie's Fruits.*

Writings

PICTURE BOOKS

Frannie's Fruits, illustrated by Petra Mathers, Harper (New York, NY), 1989.

Me and Nana, illustrated by Marilee Robin Burton, Harper (New York, NY), 1990.

Hanukkah Lights, Hanukkah Nights, illustrated by John Himmelman, HarperCollins (New York, NY), 1992.

Hooray! It's Passover!, illustrated by John Himmelman, HarperCollins (New York, NY), 1996.

Sound the Shofar! A Story of Rosh Hashanah and Yom Kippur, illustrated by John Himmelman, HarperCollins (New York, NY), 1998.

Dance, Sing, Remember: A Celebration of Jewish Holidays, illustrated by Ora Eitan, HarperCollins (New York, NY), 2000.

The Runaway Latkes, illustrated by Paul Yalowitz, Albert Whitman & Co. (Morton Grove, IL), 2000.

In rhyming couplets, Leslie Kimmelman presents a Middle America town preparing for an Independence Day celebration as seen through the eyes of enthusiastic young Jenny. (From Happy Fourth of July, Jenny Sweeney!, *illustrated by Nancy Cote.*)

Round the Turkey: A Grateful Thanksgiving, illustrated by Nancy Cote, Albert Whitman & Co. (Morton Grove, IL), 2002.

Happy Fourth of July, Jenny Sweeney!, illustrated by Nancy Cote, Albert Whitman & Co. (Morton Grove, IL), 2003.

Emily and Bo, Best Friends, illustrated by True Kelley, Holiday House (New York, NY), 2005.

How Do I Love You?, illustrated by Lisa McCue, Harper-Collins (New York, NY), in press.

Sidelights

In her children's books author Leslie Kimmelman focuses on strong family relationships. Whether working together, enjoying special outings, or sharing the special joy of a holiday season, Kimmelman's books portray loving families wherein young children are nurtured and allowed to participate. In *Frannie's Fruits,* her first picture book, parents and children work side by side at the bustling, seasonal fruit-and-vegetable stand named for the family dog. There is much to be done, as the fresh produce must be washed, polished, and piled high, the flowers trimmed and freshened, and merchandise shelved and priced. Told through the eyes of the family's youngest daughter, the book chronicles the day's events and each customer's purchases and eccentricities, including, as Hanna B. Zeiger noted in *Horn Book,* everyone from "the sour woman who wants a dozen lemons to the romantic couple buying the biggest bouquet of flowers." The critic praised *Frannie's Fruits* as "a welcome addition to stories about people working and enjoying their work."

Me and Nana, revolves around the special bond between young Natalie and her sprightly, slightly unusual grandmother, a woman with whom the girl enjoys spending time. Writing in *Booklist,* Ellen Mandel remarked that Kimmelman and illustrator Marilee Robin Burton "invite readers to be part of the warm and loving twosome's perfect relationship."

Happy Fourth of July, Jenny Sweeney! finds a young girl caught up in the excitement of her town's Independence Day celebration. Jenny decides to take part in the bustle by washing her family dog, and the book recounts the preparations of the girl's family and neighbors in getting ready for the parade. Kimmelman describes the festivities in rhyming couplets enhanced by illustrations that *School Library Journal* reviewer Linda M. Kenton noted "honor America's melting pot" through the inclusion of an ethnically diverse neighborhood. Reflecting pride in the heritage the holiday represents, Kimmelman closes her book with a page detailing information regarding the flag, the Liberty Bell, and the signers of the Declaration of Independence.

Many of Kimmelman's books focus on the traditions of the Jewish faith. In *Hanukkah Lights, Hanukkah Nights* the "warmth of family love and joy of holiday celebration light up" what a *School Library Journal* reviewer called a "simple narrative." Each of the eight nights of

Hanukkah is described by Kimmelman in two sentences on a double-page spread. The rituals and activities associated with the holiday are illustrated by various family members as they engage in lighting candles, flipping latkes, and giving holiday blessings. Eleven Jewish holidays are given broader coverage in Kimmelman's *Dance, Sing, Remember: A Celebration of Jewish Holidays,* which covers not only the well-known Rosh Hashanah and Hannukkah but also includes Shavot, Shabbat, and Yom Hashoah. In *School Library Journal,* Teri Markson noted that Kimmelman's text is "wonderfully written, simple yet informative," while Stephanie Zvirin added in *Booklist* that the author introduces the holidays "in a lively, dramatic way, limiting details so as not to overwhelm [the] very young." Praising the book as "valuable for its inclusion of several holidays rarely (if ever) mentioned in secular children's literature," *Horn Book* reviewer Lauren Adams added that *Dance, Sing, Remember,* with illustrations by Ora Eitan, "is truly an invitation to celebrate."

Biographical and Critical Sources

PERIODICALS

Booklist, October 15, 1990, Ellen Mandel, review of *Me and Nana,* p. 447; September 1, 1992, p. 63; March 15, 1996, Ellen Mandel, review of *Hooray! It's Passover,* p. 1266; October 1, 2000, Stephanie Zvirin, review of *Dance, Sing, Remember: A Celebration of Jewish Holidays,* p. 356; May 15, 2003, Karen Hutt, review of *Happy Fourth of July, Jenny Sweeney!,* p.1672.

Horn Book, May-June, 1989, Hanna B. Zeiger, review of *Frannie's Fruits,* pp. 359-360; July, 1990, p. 39; November, 2000, Lauren Adams, review of *Dance, Sing, Remember,* p. 769.

Kirkus Reviews, February 1, 1989, p. 210; March 15, 2003, review of *Happy Fourth of July, Jenny Sweeney!,* p.470.

New York Times Book Review, September 10, 1989, p. 32; November 11, 1990, p. 57.

Publishers Weekly, February 24, 1989, p. 230; September 7, 1992, review of *Hanukkah Lights, Hanukkah Nights,* p. 62; February 12, 1996, review of *Hooray! It's Passover,* p. 72; July 27, 1998, review of *Sound the Shofar,* p. 70; September 15, 2000, review of *The Runaway Latkes,* p. 66.

School Library Journal, June, 1989, p. 90; November, 1990, p. 94; October, 1992, review of *Hanukkah Lights, Hanukkah Nights,* p. 42; October, 2000, review of *The Runaway Latkes,* p. 65, and Teri Markson, review of *Dance, Sing, Remember,* p. 148; September, 2002, Genevieve Gallagher, review of *Round the Turkey: A Grateful Thanksgiving,* p. 195; July, 2003, Linda M. Kenton, review of *Happy Fourth of July, Jenny Sweeney!,* p. 100.*

KOESTLER-GRACK, Rachel A. 1973-

Personal

Born August 4, 1973, in Milwaukee, WI; daughter of Arlen (an English professor) and Karen (a gift shop clerk) Koestler; married Merel Grack (an office manager), 2001; children: Victoria. *Education:* Minnesota State University, B.A., 1999. *Politics:* Republican. *Religion:* Lutheran.

Addresses

Home and office—7787 140th St., Glencoe, MN 55336. *E-mail*—rgrack@hotmail.com.

Career

Editor and author. Capstone Press, Mankato, MN, editor, 1999-2001; freelance writer.

Writings

Going to School during the Civil Rights Movement, Blue Earth Books (Mankato, MN), 2002.
Daily Life in a Southwestern Settlement: San Antonio, Lake Street Publishers (Minneapolis, MN), 2003.
Eddie Rickenbacker, Chelsea House Publishers (Philadelphia, PA), 2003.
The Iroquois: Longhouse Builders, Blue Earth Books (Mankato, MN), 2003.
The Seminole: Patchworkers of the Everglades, Blue Earth Books (Mankato, MN), 2003.
The Sioux: Nomadic Buffalo Hunters, Blue Earth Books (Mankato, MN), 2003.
Osceola, 1804-1838, Blue Earth Books (Mankato, MN), 2003.
Tecumseh, 1768-1813, Blue Earth Books (Mankato, MN), 2003.
Chief John Ross, Heinemann Library (Chicago, IL), 2004.
Chief Joseph, Heinemann Library (Chicago, IL), 2004.
The Choctaw: Stickball Players of the South, Blue Earth Books (Mankato, MN), 2004.
The Story of Mother Jones, Chelsea Clubhouse (Philadelphia, PA), 2004.
The Story of Helen Keller, Chelsea Clubhouse (Philadelphia, PA), 2004.
The Story of Harriet Tubman, Chelsea Clubhouse (Philadelphia, PA), 2004.
The Inuit: Ivory Carvers of the Far North, Blue Earth Books (Mankato, MN), 2004.
The Story of Eleanor Roosevelt, Chelsea Clubhouse (Philadelphia, PA), 2004.
Kim Il Sung and Kim Jong Il, Chelsea House (Philadelphia, PA), 2004.
Mary Baker Eddy, Chelsea House Publishers (Philadelphia, PA), 2004.
The Story of Clara Barton, Chelsea Clubhouse (Philadelphia, PA), 2004.
Sacagawea, Heinemann Library (Chicago, IL), 2004.
The Story of Anne Frank, Chelsea Clubhouse (Philadelphia, PA), 2004.
The Space Shuttle Columbia Disaster, ABDO Daughters (Edina, MN), 2004.

Work in Progress

More nonfiction titles; a novel; a children's fiction book.

Sidelights

Rachel A. Koestler-Grack has had a passion for writing ever since she was a little girl. While working as an editor of a publishing house for several years, she had the opportunity to see her work published in book form, and as a freelance writer she has authored such nonfiction titles as *The Story of Clara Barton,* a biography of the U.S. Civil War heroine; *Osceola: 1804-1838,* an account of the life of the Seminole warrior who fought and led his people against the American army; and *Tecumseh, 1768-1813,* which recounts the attempts of a Shawnee leader to protect his people's way of life and heritage. These books provide children with a detailed biography, while filling in key bits of information that adds to the reader's understanding of the history of the period. Hazel Rochman wrote in a *Booklist* review that

In her biography for young readers, Rachel A. Koestler-Grack tells the life story of the dedicated nurse who followed her work on the battlefields of the Civil War with the ambitious task of founding the American Red Cross. (From The Story of Clara Barton.*)*

works such as Koestler-Grack's *The Story of Clara Barton* and *The Story of Eleanor Roosevelt* "will stimulate readers to find out more about the women and their times." Linda Greengrass noted in her *School Library Journal* review of *Osceola* that the author provides readers with "events in a sympathetic, yet neutral, tone," and added that, "in general, the stories are told in a straightforward and descriptive manner with a minimum of fictionalization."

Koestler-Grack told *Something about the Author:* "Writing has been a huge part of my life for many years. When I was in grade school, I occupied my time writing short poems, stories, and plays. My best friend and I spent long hours planning and performing the many dramas we created together. We'd even create scripts for all of the characters in our productions. My creativity followed me into high school. With my loyal co-writer at my side, I'd create skits for class and school functions. Many skits had a humorous twist and entertained audiences of classmates, parents, and school patrons.

"After graduation, I attended Minnesota State University, Mankato, then called Mankato State University. From 1991 to 1994, I majored in English. To help support myself, I worked at the campus tutorial center, tutoring English composition and math, and algebra. In April of 1994, I gave birth to my daughter, Victoria. The stresses and demands of single parenthood took me out of school and into the work force. Three years later, however, I found myself back in school, this time prepared to finish. I graduated in 1999 with a major in English, concentration in creative writing, and a minor in sociology. Before commencement even took place, I accepted a position as an editor with Capstone Press Publishers in Mankato. I passed up the formal graduation for a job in the field I loved most: writing.

"Two years of editing landed me an opportunity to author a book. Even though my true passion was in fiction, this chance was a key stepping stone to the published author I had always dreamed of becoming. The following season, I accepted two more titles. I felt I was running on the road of my wildest aspirations. About this time, my managing editor took a job with another publisher. I expressed to her an interest in becoming an independent freelance writer. She told me if I was willing to make that leap, she'd set me up with a series of books to write. So in the spring of 2001, I resigned my position as editor in lieu of a career as a full-time writer.

"A career change wasn't the only plunge I took that spring. I married the true love of my life: Merel Grack. It was a slightly unorthodox hitch, not one you hear of much anymore—love at first sight, and married six months to the day after we met. A devoted husband and father, he later tickled my daughter with the greatest gift of all: a real dad. In January, 2004, Victoria Kathryn Koestler officially became Victoria Kathryn Grack.

"Since the beginning of my freelance career in 2001, I have authored over twenty books, wrote a revision to one previously published book, and edited another. But my dreams are far from quenched. I am currently working on a children's fiction book as well as a novel. I am confident these stories will one day find a happy home on some bookworm's bedside table."

Biographical and Critical Sources

PERIODICALS

Booklist, March 1, 2004, Hazel Rochman, review of *The Story of Clara Barton,* p. 1203.

School Library Journal, April, 2003, Linda Greengrass, review of *Osceola: 1804-1838,* p. 150; June, 2004, Marilyn Fairbanks, review of *Kim Il Sung and Kim Jong Il,* p. 154.

L

LAFAYE, A(lexandria R. T.) 1970-

Personal

Born March 9, 1970, in Hudson, WI; daughter of Patrick (an airline mechanic) and Rita (an insurance staff agent) LaFaye. *Education:* University of Minnesota-Twin Cities, B.A. (summa cum laude); Mankato State University, M.A. (creative writing and multicultural literature); University of Memphis, M.F.A.; Hollins College, M.A. (children's literature). *Politics:* "Democratic Socialist." *Religion:* "Non-denominational Christian." *Hobbies and other interests:* Movies, storytelling, fine arts.

Addresses

Home—CA. *Agent*—Marcia Wernick, Sheldon Fogelman Agency, 10 East 40th St., New York, NY 10016. *E-mail*—ALaFayeBooks@aol.com.

Career

Writer and educator. Roanoke College, Salem, VA, instructor in English, 1997-98; visiting professor, Plattsburgh State University, NY, beginning 1998.

Member

Society of Children's Book Writers and Illustrators.

Awards, Honors

Books in the Middle: Outstanding Titles of 1998, *Voice of Youth Advocates,* 1999, for *The Year of the Sawdust Man.*

Writings

The Year of the Sawdust Man, Simon & Schuster (New York, NY), 1998.

A. LaFaye

Edith Shay, Viking Penguin (New York, NY), 1998.
Strawberry Hill, Simon & Schuster (New York, NY), 1999.
Nissa's Place, Simon & Schuster (New York, NY), 1999.
Dad, in Spirit, Simon & Schuster (New York, NY), 2001.
The Strength of Saints, Simon & Schuster (New York, NY), 2002.
Worth, Simon & Schuster (New York, NY), 2004.

Sidelights

A. LaFaye is the author of a number of highly praised works of historical fiction that focus on young people's efforts to navigate inter-familial relationships and the desire to gain their independence. She often casts these issues in a new light by setting them in the past. In a trilogy of novels that include *The Year of the Sawdust Man*, *Nissa's Place*, and *The Strength of Saints*, she follows several young women as they attempt to make it on their own during the difficult days of the Great Depression. In *Edith Shay* readers are carried back in time to the Chicago of the mid-1800s, as a country girl attempts to make her way in the fast-paced city. Moving forward to the 1970s, *Strawberry Hill* finds a young teen longing for the simpler life of half a century earlier, an age that the memories of an elderly friend vividly bring to life for her. Praising *The Year of the Sawdust Man* in a *Publishers Weekly* review, a contributor called LaFaye's debut "beautifully written" and added that the novel "reveals a writer capable of plumbing the depths of a painful situation to surface triumphantly with compassion and humor."

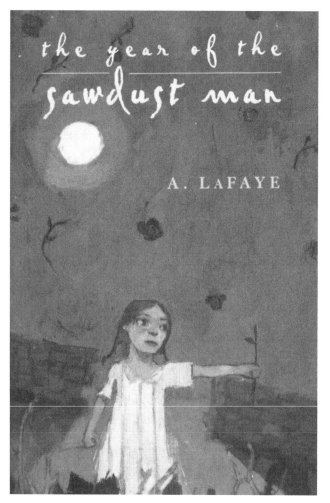

In the 1930s, as rumors spread around small-town Harper, Louisiana, after eleven-year-old Nissa's mother runs off, the young girls feels rejected and fears that talk of an affair with The Sawdust Man are probably true. (Cover illustration by Natalie Ascensios.)

LaFaye first began to contemplate writing as a channel for her natural curiosity because, as she once recalled to *Something about the Author* (SATA) she was "obsessed with learning from a young age, often hunting down odd little historical facts, like what exactly is a 'coffin corner'?," and "forever inventing stories in my head." Her talent for writing down those stories was encouraged by LaFaye's sixth-grade teacher, "who said I had the talent to become a writer." While she continued creative writing into high school, she ended up majoring in history in college because it seemed more practical; however, "my love for writing won out before I graduated from the University of Minnesota." Pursuing literature in graduate school, she studied literature from the writer's perspective. "An avid fan of writers like Gabriel García Márquez, Toni Morrison, Robert Cormier, and Patricia MacLachlan, I aspired to create realistic stories about everyday life in the past," LaFaye added. "Frustrated by pejorative attitudes toward the literary quality of books for child readers, I strive to create tales with literary and psychological depth." LaFaye's well-received debut novel, *The Year of the Sawdust Man,* was inspired by a television documentary about the Great Depression. "I wondered what would happen if a parent told a child that they had to leave home and could only take one suitcase," LaFaye told Cindi Di Marzo in a *Publishers Weekly* interview. "And then I wondered how a child might feel if her mother left home with one suitcase." Set in Louisiana during the 1930s, LaFaye's story explores the plight of young Nissa Bergen, who comes home from school one afternoon to find that her free-spirited mother, Heirah Rae, has departed, leaving the distraught eleven-year-old narrator in the care of her father. "The author creates a believable set of characters and a realistic environment, and sustains them well with a lyrical and leisurely use of language," maintained *School Library Journal* contributor Darcy Schild. Calling *The Year of the Sawdust Man* a "searching, character-driven debut," a *Kirkus Reviews* critic asserted: "LaFaye depicts complex, profoundly disturbed characters with a sure hand." A *Publishers Weekly* commentator noted that LaFaye's novel "is filled with poignant insights into a hurt child's fragile psyche and resilient spirit."

In *Nissa's Place* LaFaye's protagonist gains the same self-awareness and independence that Heirah Rae acquires in *The Sawdust Man*. Now thirteen years old, Nissa needs to learn to live for herself and not her mother, and also has to make room in her life for her father's new wife, Lara. Visiting her mother in Chicago, she gains a new perspective on not only Heirah Rae and the bohemian life she has chosen, but also on her family back in Harper and the divisions that racism have created within her home town. Calling *Nissa's Place* a "fine, upstanding sequel to *The Year of the Sawdust Man*," *Booklist* contributor GraceAnne A. De-Candido praised LaFaye's treatment of her characters as "full-hearted." Equally enthusiastic, a *Publishers Weekly* contributor added that in *Nissa's Place* the author "surpasses the lyricism and emotional depth of her sparkling debut."

In her sequel to The Year of the Sawdust Man, *LaFaye follows now thirteen-year-old Nissa as she struggles with loyalty to her absent mother and resentment toward changes her new stepmother makes in their home life. (Cover illustration by Jeff Chapman-Crane.)*

Nissa's story continues in *The Strength of Saints.* It is now 1936, and the treatment of blacks has begun to violently divide the population of Harper, Louisiana. With leverage gained as the daughter of the editor of the town's main newspaper, Nissa decides to help balance the racial equation by founding two equal libraries, one for blacks and one for whites, but both with the same book collection. She is supported in her endeavor by her mother, who returns for a visit and to offer moral support for Nissa's venture, which ultimately sparks a violent denouement due to the passions of people on both sides of the race issue. LaFaye's novel *Edith Shay* is a character study set in post-Civil War America that blends travel and adventure with the coming-of-age of young Katherine Lunden. Assuming the name she has found on an abandoned suitcase, sixteen-year-old Katherine leaves her home in a small Wisconsin town and travels by train to Chicago, where she takes a job as a seamstress. Katherine later determines to find the real Edith Shay and return her suitcase, a mission that takes her to Richmond, Virginia, by way of Philadelphia and Washington, D.C. "While Katherine does travel

far and have many adventures, there is more introspection than action," maintained *School Library Journal* contributor Bruce Anne Shook, who added: "The book's main appeal will be to readers who can identify with her independent spirit." A *Publishers Weekly* critic asserted that in *Edith Shay* "LaFaye offers a multidimensional portrait of a young woman in transition, one capable of seeing her flaws and rising above them, revealed in poetic and poignant language." *Strawberry Hill* focuses on Raleia Pendle, who is spending the summer in Tidal, Maine—the ideal antidote to the turbulent, free-spirited 1970s lifestyle she has been raised in by her hippy parents. Tidal looks almost exactly as it did in 1911, when a tidal wave crushed the town and killed more than one hundred people. It is the ideal place for Raleia to live out her daydreams about life at the turn of the twentieth century and to avoid her cranky pregnant mother and her self-absorbed father. In Tidal,

In the second half of the nineteenth century, sixteen-year-old Katherine leaves her rural community and, under the name of Edith Shay, attempts to find an identity for herself, enduring unexpected misfortune along the way. (Cover illustration by Jeff Chapman-Crane.)

Level-headed Ebon, in a family of creative, inventive individuals, surprises himself when he finds a way to connect with his father, who has slipped into a coma after a life-threatening accident. (Cover illustration by Chris Sheban.)

Raleia believes she has found her living link to the past in Ian Rutherford, the reclusive old man on the hill who has hardly left home since the tidal wave hit. As their friendship grows, Raleia discovers that the past was not the golden time she imagined. Of the book, LaFaye said that she was inspired by the age-old question, "What if?" During the Vietnam War, her father served in the navy as a mechanic on an aircraft carrier, and her mother worked as a clerk in a county auditor's office. As a child, LaFaye wondered what it would be like to be raised by hippies, and *Strawberry Hill* is one possible answer to that question.

Dad, in Spirit is a departure for LaFaye in that it takes place during the present and includes elements of the otherworldly. Described by a *Publishers Weekly* reviewer as "far-fetched yet engaging," the novel finds nine-year-old Ebon Jones feeling like an outcast in his family; everyone else is highly creative, while Ebon provides them an audience. Only after tragedy strikes in the form of an accident that puts his father in a coma does Ebon's talent come to the fore: he alone is able to make contact with his unconscious father and help in

his father's eventual recovery. Miriam Lang Budin noted in a *School Library Journal* review that *Dad, in Spirit* requires some leeway on the part of rational-minded readers, the novel is "original, provocative, and ultimately joyous." *Booklist* reviewer Kay Weisman dubbed the novel an "introspective fantasy" and added that its greatest strength is in LaFaye's "believable depiction of strong family bonds."

Biographical and Critical Sources

PERIODICALS

Booklist, October 15, 1999, GraceAnne A. DeCandido, review of *Nissa's Place,* p. 444; July, 2001, Kay Weisman, review of *Dad, in Spirit,* p. 2006.
Bulletin of the Center for Children's Books, December, 1998, p. 137.
Kirkus Reviews, May 15, 1998, review of *The Year of the Sawdust Man,* p. 740; October 1, 1998, pp. 1460-1461.
Publishers Weekly, June 1, 1998, review of *The Year of the Sawdust Man,* p. 63; June 29, 1998, Cindi Di Marzo, interview with LaFaye, p. 28; October 12, 1998, review of *Edith Shay,* p. 78; October 18, 1999, review of *Nissa's Place,* p. 83; June 4, 2001, review of *Dad, in Spirit,* p. 81.
School Library Journal, July, 1998, Darcy Schild, review of *The Year of the Sawdust Man,* p. 97; October, 1998, Bruce Anne Shook, review of *Edith Shay,* p. 138; June, 2001, Miriam Lang Budin, review of *Dad, in Spirit,* p. 152; June, 2002, Susan Cooley, review of *The Strength of Saints,* p. 140.

ONLINE

Alexandra LaFaye Web site, http://www.alafaye.com/ (December 2, 2004).*

*   *   *

LAWSON, Amy
See GORDON, Amy

*   *   *

LOW, Alice 1926-

Personal

Born June 5, 1926, in New York, NY; daughter of Harold (in textiles) and Anna (a children's book author under pseudonym Ann Todd; maiden name, Epstein) Bernstein; married Martin Low (a film studio owner), March 25, 1949; children: Andrew, Katherine, David (died, 1978). *Education:* Smith College, B.A., 1947; attended Columbia University, 1956-58. *Hobbies and other interests:* "Painting and ceramics were my first interests. I still sing in a local chorus. Travel stimulates, and many a line has come to me on a tennis court."

Addresses

Home—441 Sleepy Hollow Rd., Briarcliff Manor, NY 10510. *Agent*—Scott Tremel, 434 Lafayette St., New York, NY 10003.

Career

Warren Schloat Productions, Tarrytown, NY, writer and producer of educational filmstrips, 1968-72; Birch Wathen School, New York, NY, teacher of creative writing, 1972-73; freelance reading program editor for Random House and Harcourt Brace, New York, NY, beginning 1975; Scholastic Book Services, New York, NY, editorial consultant to Children's Choice Book Club, 1978-85, co-editor, then editor. Volunteer at Metropolitan Museum of Art.

Member

Authors Guild, Authors League of America, American Society of Composers, Authors, and Publishers (AS-CAP), PEN, Society of Children's Book Writers and Illustrators.

Awards, Honors

Notable Children's Trade Book in the Field of Social Studies selection, Children's Book Council, 1985, and Washington Irving Children's Book Choice Award, Westchester Library Association, 1988, both for *The Macmillan Book of Greek Gods and Heroes.*

Writings

Open up My Suitcase, illustrated by Corinne Malvern, Simon & Schuster (New York, NY), 1954.

Grandmas and Grandpas, Random House (New York, NY), 1962.

Out of My Window, Random House (New York, NY), 1962.

Summer, illustrated by Roy McKie, Random House (New York, NY), 1963.

Taro and the Bamboo Shoot (adaptation of a folk tale), Pantheon (New York, NY), 1964.

A Day of Your Own: Your Birthday, illustrated by Roy McKie, Random House (New York, NY), 1965, girl's edition illustrated by Lisl Weil, 1964.

What's in Mommy's Pocketbook?, Golden Press (New York, NY), 1965.

Kallie's Corner, illustrated by David Stone Martin, Pantheon (New York, NY), 1966.

At Jasper's House, and Other Stories, Pantheon (New York, NY), 1968.

Herbert's Treasure, illustrated by Victoria de Larrea, Putnam (New York, NY), 1971.

Witches' Holiday, illustrated by Tony Walton, Pantheon (New York, NY), 1971.

David's Windows, illustrated by Tomie de Paola, Putnam (New York, NY), 1974.

The Witch Who Was Afraid of Witches (also see below), illustrated by Karen Gundersheimer, Pantheon (New York, NY), 1978, illustrated by Jane Manning, HarperCollins (New York, NY), 1999.

(With Bernard Stone) *The Charge of the Mouse Brigade,* illustrated by Tony Ross, Pantheon (New York, NY), 1980.

(Adaptor of verses) Colin McNaughton, *If Dinosaurs Were Cats and Dogs,* illustrated by McNaughton, Four Winds Press (New York, NY), 1981.

Genie and the Witch's Spells, illustrated by Lady McCrady, Knopf (New York, NY), 1982.

All around the Farm, illustrated by Maggie Swanson, Random House (New York, NY), 1984.

All through the Town, illustrated by Denise Fleming, Random House (New York, NY), 1984.

The Macmillan Book of Greek Gods and Heroes, illustrated by Arvis Stewart, Macmillan (New York, NY), 1985, published as *The Simon & Schuster Book of Greek Gods and Heroes,* Simon & Schuster (New York, NY), 2002.

Who Lives in the Sea?, illustrated by Rowan Barnes-Murphy, Fisher-Price, 1987.

(Selector) *The Family Read-aloud Christmas Treasury,* illustrated by Marc Brown, Little, Brown (Boston, MA), 1989.

Zena and the Witch Circus, illustrated by Laura Cornell, Dial (New York, NY), 1990.

(Selector) *The Family Read-Aloud Holiday Treasury,* illustrated by Marc Brown, Little, Brown (Boston, MA), 1991.

The Quilted Elephant and the Green Velvet Dragon, illustrated by Christopher Santoro, Simon & Schuster (New York, NY), 1991.

(With Zheng Zhensun) *A Young Painter: The Life and Paintings of Wang Yani—China's Extraordinary Young Artist,* photographs by Zheng, Scholastic (New York, NY), 1991.

The Popcorn Shop, illustrated by Patricia Hammel, Scholastic (New York, NY), 1993.

(Author of script and lyrics) *The Witch Who Was Afraid of Witches* (play; based on Low's book of same title), music by Jacob Stern, first produced in New York, NY, 1993.

(Editor) *Spooky Stories for a Dark and Stormy Night,* illustrated by Gahan Wilson, Hyperion (New York, NY), 1994.

Mommy's Briefcase, illustrated by Aliki Brandenberg, Scholastic (New York, NY), 1995.

Stories to Tell a Five Year Old, illustrated by Heather Harms Mailone, Little, Brown (Boston, MA), 1996.

Stories to Tell a Six Year Old, illustrated by Heather Harms Mailone, Little, Brown (Boston, MA), 1997.

Aunt Lucy Went to Buy a Hat, illustrated by Laura Huliska-Beith, HarperCollins (New York, NY), 2004.

Blueberry Mouse, illustrated by David Michael Friend, Mondo (New York, NY), 2004.

Also contributor to anthologies, including *Captain Kangaroo's Read Aloud Book,* Random House, 1962, and *Captain Kangaroo's Sleepytime Book,* Random House, 1963. Author of scripts for filmstrips, including *Folk Songs and the American Flag, Folk Songs and the Declaration of Independence, Folk Songs and Abraham Lincoln,* and *Folk Songs and Frederick Douglas,* all for Warren Schloat Productions, 1968-70; "First Things, Social Reasoning" (series of eight filmstrips), Guidance Associates, 1973-74; *You Can Be Anything,* Teaching Resource Films, 1975; and *Bringing Home the Beach,* Guidance Associates, 1975. Author of filmstrip scripts and producer of *Folk Songs and the Railroad, Cowboys,* and *Whaling,* all for Warren Schloat Productions, 1970-72; and *History of the City,* Warren Schloat Productions, 1972. Author of operetta for elementary school children, and of material for UNICEF. Contributor of stories to magazines, including *Ingenue* and *Seventeen,* and of book reviews to *New York Times.*

Several of Low's works have been translated into French and Japanese.

Adaptations

The Witch Who Was Afraid of Witches was made into an animated film, Learning Corporation of America.

Sidelights

In addition to her work as a writing teacher and an editor of several book clubs for New York City-based publishing houses, Alice Low has authored a wide selection of fiction, nonfiction, and poetry books for children and young adults. Her writings, especially those geared for younger readers, are known for their humorous plots and fanciful characters. In addition, Low has compiled several selections of short stories and verse for some highly regarded anthologies, and has produced a well-received volume compiling the traditional myths of the ancient Greeks. Born in New York City in 1926, Low earned her bachelor's degree at Smith College, and in 1949 married Martin Low, a film studio owner, with whom she had three children. She published her first children's book, *Open up My Suitcase,* in 1954, then took a break from writing to undertake further college study at Columbia University between 1956 and 1958. She began her career as a children's book author in the early 1960s, supplementing that with work as a teacher at the Birch Wathen School during the 1972-73 school year before moving into a series of editorial positions within the publishing industry. One of Low's earliest successes as a writer came with her 1966 book *Kallie's Corner,* the story of a new girl at a private school who does not fit in with the popular group. When Jane, one of the girls in the group, tentatively befriends Kallie, they discover they do not need the group's arbitrary approval. The book garnered praise for its lively prose, engaging setting and characters, and its satisfying conclusion.

Low scored another success with *At Jasper's House,* a collection of short stories for young adults. "Candy for Oriana" tells the story of a young black girl at camp who encounters racism but ultimately gets her needs met by a camp counselor. The title story was commended for its tender depiction of a thirteen-year-old girl's transition from child to young adult. Max Steele, reviewing Low's short-fiction collection for the *New York Times Book Review,* stated that "the reader wishes some of these stories, such as 'A Real Country Christmas,' had been the first chapters of novels. Others, such as 'The Naked Spot,' are complete in themselves—and completely amusing."

Frequently turning her attention to younger readers, Low has produced a number of picture books and easy readers. *Herbert's Treasure* is the story of a boy who collects junk, much to his mother's dismay. One day he finds a key that fits a lock and builds himself a shack out of all the "useless" things he had been collecting. While some reviewers wrote that the story lacks the exaggeration necessary for a truly tall tale, Susanne Gilles remarked in her review for *School Library Journal* that as "a fantasy without a moral," *Herbert's Treasure* "will be especially enjoyed by other young treasure collectors." In *The Quilted Elephant and the Green Velvet Dragon* she examines jealousy and sibling rivalry between two stuffed animals brought along on a sleepover. Her 1995 picture book, *Mommy's Briefcase,* is an interactive book in which children can explore pockets within the story's pages, pulling Mommy's address book, glasses, and even a cardboard sandwich from their hiding places. Through Mommy's tasks at the Stuft Bear Company, as explained by Low in simple, rhyming couplets, youngsters gain a "playful introduction to the working world," according to a *Publishers Weekly* contributor who dubbed *Mommy's Briefcase* a "candidate for repeated readings."

The adventures—and misadventures—of witches have been featured in several of Low's works. *Witches' Holiday* is a rhyming tale for young children that depicts a group of witches who pop out of a closet on Halloween night to fingerpaint on the ceiling, roller-skate throughout the house, and eat up all the Halloween candy before flying away. A picture book that Low also adapted as a play produced in New York City in 1993, *The Witch Who Was Afraid of Witches* tells the story of Wendy, whose older, more powerful sisters make her stay at home on Halloween. When a young boy comes trick-or-treating and invites Wendy along, the young witch gains self-confidence and finds her own witch power during their adventures. A *Publishers Weekly* reviewer called this parable of sibling rivalry "an irresistible way to add joy to the scarey fall holiday."

In *Genie and the Witch's Spells* two little girls having trouble in school strike a bargain to help each other out, only to find the improvement in their grades was due to their own efforts rather than magical spells. A *Booklist* critic remarked that while "the pat ending is telegraphed far too early, . . . Genie and her magical counterpart are engaging enough to lure some into the mixture of magic and reality." *Zena and the Witch Circus* is the humorous tale of a young witch who is prevented from participating in the witch circus because she can't perform magic. Zena gains self-confidence and self-esteem when she saves the witch circus from disaster with the help of a friendly cat she rescues in the woods. While some reviewers found the plot a bit confusing, Julie Corsaro, writing in *Booklist*, called the work "an entertaining and challenging romp."

Low explores the myths and legends of ancient Greece in *The Macmillan Book of Greek Gods and Heroes*, a highly praised introduction to this topic for young readers. While some reviewers found that these shortened, simplified versions lack animation, many have agreed that this attractive collection is ideal for presenting complex ancient myths to a young audience. Reviewing *The Macmillan Book of Greek Gods and Heroes*, a *Booklist* critic complimented the volume's "broad scope" and "useful index," noting as well that the tales are "clearly told" by Low. The volume was re-released in 2002 as *The Simon & Schuster Book of Greek Gods and Heroes.*

Together with writer and photographer Zheng Zhensun, Low presents another work of nonfiction in *A Young Painter: The Life and Paintings of Wang Yani—China's Extraordinary Young Artist*. A prodigy who uses traditional Chinese rice papers and ink, Wang began painting monkeys at age three, and by the time she was ten years old solo exhibitions of her works had been staged in galleries throughout the world. In addition to describing her talent, *A Young Painter* also provides readers with a profile of Wang as a somewhat reclusive but pleasant person, and opens a window into the famous young artist's simple day-to-day life. "Budding artists will find a wealth of inspiration" in Low and Zhensun's biography, noted a *Publishers Weekly* reviewer who added that the text "leads readers to admire [Wang] from a respectful distance."

In addition to her writing, Low has selected works by others for two well-received anthologies, *The Family Read-aloud Christmas Treasury* and *The Family Read-aloud Holiday Treasury*. These anthologies mix well-known with lesser-known pieces and have been commended for their inclusion of tales and poems from other cultures. A reviewer in *Publishers Weekly* praised the selection of stories by such writers as Langston

Rhyming couplets and pocket pages reveal the contents of a mother's briefcase as she wends her way through a working day at the Stuft Bear Company. (From Mommy's Briefcase, *written by Alice Low and illustrated by Aliki Brandenberg.)*

Hughes, Beverly Cleary, Russell Hoban, and Eleanor Farjeon, calling *The Family Read-aloud Holiday Treasury* "richly diverse" and "exuberant;" while another contributor to the same periodical applauded the "well-chosen collection" of "cheery stories, songs, and poems" found in *The Family Read-aloud Christmas Treasury.*

Tales of a different nature are collected in Low's *Spooky Stories for a Dark and Stormy Night.* Featuring illustrations by Gahan Wilson, the volume presents nineteen tales drawn from a variety of cultures and countries. Folk tales retold by Alison Lurie and Isaac Bashevis Singer, classic stories by Washington Irving and Charles Dickens, as well as contemporary tales by Penelope Lively, Bruce Coville, and Laurence Yep round out a volume in which, according to a *Publishers Weekly* contributor, "the quality of the storytelling is consistently high." Noting the book's appealing design, *Booklist* reviewer Carolyn Phelan praised Low's choice of "eclectic and occasionally macabre" tales, and noted that Wilson's quirkily characteristic pen-and-ink drawings "effectively" highlight each selection.

Other anthologies edited by Low include *Stories to Tell a Five Year Old,* which presents over twenty tales "with surefire appeal for youngsters," according to *Booklist* reviewer Susan Dove Lempke. Classic characters such as Mary Poppins and Dr. Doolittle make a brief appearance in selections from longer works, and a parade of folk characters also are introduced in tales that focus on humor. Low's follow-up volume, *Stories to Tell a Six Year Old,* continues the formula, including folk tales, short stories, picture-book excerpts, and chapters from popular novels. Noting the inclusion of works by such popular writers as Margery Williams, Astrid Lindgren, Nicolasa Mohr, and Beverly Cleary, *Booklist* critic John

Peters predicted that Low's "compact" compendium "should be a hit for travel and bedtime reading both."

Biographical and Critical Sources

PERIODICALS

Booklist, April 1, 1982, review of *Genie and the Witch's Spells,* p. 1019; November 15, 1985, review of *The Macmillan Book of Greek Gods and Heroes,* p. 497; September 15, 1990, Julie Corsaro, review of *Zena and the Witch Circus,* p. 177; October 1, 1994, Carolyn Phelan, review of *Spooky Stories for a Dark and Stormy Night,* p. 321. *Bulletin of the Center for Children's Books,* February, 1967, p. 94; May, 1971, p. 140; October, 1974, p. 32; June 1, 1996, Susan Dove Lempke, review of *Stories to Tell a Five Year Old,* p. 1735; March 1, 1998, John Peters, review of *Stories to Tell a Six Year Old,* p. 1144.
Kirkus Reviews, November 1, 1968, p. 1226; May 1, 1974, p. 475.
Library Journal, May 15, 1971, Susanne Gilles, review of *Herbert's Treasure,* p. 1798; January 15, 1972, p. 275.
New York Times Book Review, November 3, 1968, p. 10.
Publishers Weekly, September 4, 1978, review of *The Witch Who Was Afraid of Witches,* p. 114; December 8, 1989, review of *The Family Read-aloud Christmas Treasury,* p. 53; September 20, 1991, review of *A Young Painter,* p. 132; October 18, 1991, review of *The Family Read-aloud Holiday Treasury,* p. 60; September 19, 1994, review of *Spooky Stories for a Dark and Stormy Night,* p. 26; August 28, 1995, review of *Mommy's Briefcase,* p. 112.
Saturday Review, November 12, 1966, p. 51.
School Library Journal, December, 1978, p. 45; November, 1981, p. 80; May, 1991, p. 81; December, 1991, p. 96; January, 1992, p. 92.

M

MacDONALD, Amy 1951-
(Del Tremens)

Personal

Born June 14, 1951, in Beverly, Massachusetts; daughter of Alexander S. (a doctor) and Mary (a psychotherapist; maiden name, Wright) MacDonald; married Thomas A. Urquhart (an environmental consultant), June 26, 1976; children: Emily (stepdaughter), Alexander, Jeremy. *Education:* Pingree School, 1965-69; University of Pennsylvania, B.A., 1973; Centre de Formation des Journalistes, 1982-83, fellow. *Politics:* Democrat. *Religion:* Unitarian.

Addresses

Home—10 Winslow Rd., Falmouth, ME 04105. *E-mail*—amymac@maine.rr.com.

Career

Proposition Theatre, Cambridge, MA, publicity directory, 1975-76; *Harvard Post,* Harvard, MA, editor, 1976-82; *Highwire* magazine, Lowell, MA, senior editor, 1983-84; Cambridge University Press, Cambridge, England, copy editor, 1984-88; full-time freelance journalist, editor, and children's book author, 1988—. Harvard University, summer writing instructor, 1988; Stonecoast Writers' Conference, instructor, 1991-93; University of Maine, Farmington, ME, adjunct professor, 1995; John F. Kennedy Center for Performing Arts, Washington, DC, teaching artist, 2003—. Coproducer (and contributor of story idea) of "On This Island" (documentary film), Public Broadcasting Service, 2002.

Member

Society of Children's Book Writers and Illustrators, Maine Writers and Publishers Alliance (board member, 1993—; president 1995-98, 2004), numerous environmental groups.

Amy MacDonald

Awards, Honors

Columnist of the Year Award, New England Women's Press Association, 1980; Silver Stylus Award for best children's book, Collectieve Propaganda van her Nederlandse Boek (Dutch Book Association), 1990, for *Little Beaver and the Echo; Little Beaver and the Echo* was named one of the ten children's books of the year by the *New York Times* and *Parents Magazine,* and was shortlisted for the Kate Greenaway Award and Children's Book Award, England; *Horn Book* Fanfare Selection citation for *Rachel Fister's Blister;* Oppenheim Toy Portfolio Platinum Award for *Please, Malese!;* Parent's Choice Silver Honor Award for *No More Nice;*

No More Nasty was shortlisted for Children's Choice Awards in eleven states.

Writings

(Compiler) *The Whale Show* (play), first produced at Proposition Theatre, Cambridge, MA, 1975, produced in New York, NY, 1977.

(Under pseudonym Del Tremens) *A Very Young Housewife* (parody of children's books), Harvard Common Press (Boston, MA), 1979.

Little Beaver and the Echo, illustrated by Sarah Fox-Davies, Putnam (New York, NY), 1990.

Rachel Fister's Blister, illustrated by Marjorie Priceman, Houghton (Boston, MA), 1990.

Let's Do It (part of "Let's Explore" series), illustrated by Maureen Roffey, Candlewick Press (Cambridge, MA), 1992.

Let's Make a Noise (part of "Let's Explore" series), illustrated by Maureen Roffey, Candlewick Press (Cambridge, MA), 1992.

Let's Play (part of "Let's Explore" series), illustrated by Maureen Roffey, Candlewick Press (Cambridge, MA), 1992.

Let's Try (part of "Let's Explore" series), illustrated by Maureen Roffey, Candlewick Press (Cambridge, MA), 1992.

Let's Pretend (part of "Let's Explore" series), illustrated by Maureen Roffey, Candlewick Press (Cambridge, MA), 1993.

Let's Go (part of "Let's Explore" series), illustrated by Maureen Roffey, Candlewick Press (Cambridge, MA), 1993.

Stop That Noise! (children's musical), music by Katharine Ohno, Shawnee Press, 1995.

The Spider Who Created the World, illustrated by G. Brian Karas, Orchard Books (New York, NY), 1996.

Cousin Ruth's Tooth, illustrated by Marjorie Priceman, Houghton (Boston, MA), 1996.

No More Nice, illustrated by Cat Bowman Smith, Orchard Books (New York, NY), 1996, published as *No More Nice/No More Nasty,* illustrated by Cat Bowman Smith, Farrar, Straus & Giroux (New York, NY), 2005.

No More Nasty, illustrated by Cat Bowman Smith, Farrar, Straus & Giroux (New York, NY), 2001, published as *No More Nice/No More Nasty,* illustrated by Cat Bowman Smith, Farrar, Straus & Giroux (New York, NY), 2005.

Please, Malese!: A Trickster Tale from Haiti, illustrated by Emily Lisker, Farrar, Straus & Giroux (New York, NY), 2002.

Quentin Fenton Herter III, illustrated by Giselle Potter, Farrar, Straus & Giroux (New York, NY), 2002.

Contributor to anthologies by Walker Books Ltd., including *Bedtime: First Words, Rhymes and Action* and *Stories and Fun for the Very Young.* Contributor to national and international magazines, including *Child, Parents, Parenting, Guardian, Times,* and *New Yorker. Little Beaver and the Echo* has been published in twenty-five languages.

Sidelights

Amy MacDonald's first picture book, *Little Beaver and the Echo,* tells the story of a lonely beaver who calls out his need for a friend and hears the exact same plea echoing from across the pond. He goes in search of this voice to befriend it and comes across a duck, an otter, and a turtle, also in need of friends. When the group reaches the other side of the pond, the mystery of the echo is explained by a wise old beaver. At the book's end, the pond echoes with the gleeful noises made by the four new friends. While one reviewer found the story somewhat predictable, many considered it a gentle and satisfying parable for young children. Carolyn Phelan, writing in *Booklist,* described *Little Beaver and the Echo* as "a simple, satisfying picture book. . .. There's a bit of Little Beaver in every kid."

MacDonald once related to *SATA* the genesis of *Little Beaver and the Echo:* "I have always loved children's books, but I never intended to write one. [*Little Beaver and the Echo*] came about entirely by accident. I was staying at a beautiful lake and playing with the echo there when my one-year-old son asked me what an echo was. Instead of answering, I wrote a story. The setting, of course, was the lake where I had spent so many happy summers as a child. And the main character was a beaver—like the ones who lived on the lake. The resulting book combines my love of a simple story with my love of the outdoors."

After completing her first book, MacDonald decided to continue to write for children. *Rachel Fister's Blister* is the humorous, rhyming story of Rachel, who has a blister on her toe, and all the people in her town, from the fireman to the priest and rabbi, who offer silly solutions to her problem. A reviewer for *Publishers Weekly* commented, "MacDonald's sparkling tale has the exceptional virtue of making her verse seem effortless," while Kathy Piehl remarked in *School Library Journal:* "This book's infectious rhythm and rhyme demand that it be read aloud."

The antics of the Fister clan make another appearance in *Cousin Ruth's Tooth,* "a great read-aloud story," according to *School Library Journal* writer Anne Parker, that "will also be enjoyed by beginning readers." After the youngster tells her aunt that she has lost her first tooth, Mrs. Fister sends the whole house into an uproar trying to locate it. Instead of treating this event as a normal part of growing up, the Fisters scramble about their home, searching for Ruth's missing tooth. As Cousin Keith suggests buying a new one at the department store, Uncle Drew insists that gluing in a new tooth would fix the problem. Chaos ensues as the family members struggle to find the missing part and eventually decide to ask the Queen for help in deciding what to do. As the Fisters anxiously await the Queen's solution, little Ruth makes a surprise announcement. A replacement tooth is growing where the old one was, a fact she knew about the whole time, but kept to herself, enjoying the panic she created. Reviewers praised

MacDonald's text. A *Kirkus Reviews* contributor wrote that "a sophisticated vocabulary and carefully composed cadence make it a perfect piece to read aloud or perform." "It's a perfect romp," remarked a *Publishers Weekly* critic, "and readers can only hope for more collaborations between" MacDonald and illustrator Marjorie Priceman.

In her next work, the author turned to an original creation story, *The Spider Who Created the World.* Explaining the development of the Earth, MacDonald devised a tale about a young spider called Nobb who is looking for a home to lay her first egg. Suffering rejections from Sun, Moon, and Cloud, Nobb decides to create a place of her own, stealing pieces from the three rude elements. Mixing these parts together, the spider designs a home of her own, the Earth. Here she lays her egg, and when it hatches all of the creatures of the world are released to inhabit the new world. *Booklist*'s Hazel Rochman observed that *The Spider Who Created the World* "has an easy rhythm for reading aloud, with satisfying reversals in the echoing text," while a *Publishers Weekly* critic claimed that "MacDonald finds poetry in concise, repetitive language, and explores a metaphor that young naturalists will easily grasp." Speaking of the difficulty in creating original *pourquoi* tales, *Bulletin of the Center for Children's Books* reviewer Deborah Stevenson found the work "an elegant and well-structured one that spins its story thread with a gentle formality, careful progression, and pleasing rhythm."

Eleven-year-old Simon and his eccentric Aunt Mattie and Uncle Philbert are featured in *No More Nice,* a book about the young boy on a week-long stay with the pair. Imagining that the two will be old, feeble, and impatient with young children, Simon dreads the trip. To his surprise, however, the two are exactly the opposite of what he expected, with his aunt telling him he needs to ask more questions and his uncle explaining to him the art of cussing creatively. Unlike his neat and orderly home life, Simon's aunt and uncle's house is in disarray and he has to sleep with their ornery cat. But Simon slowly begins to appreciate Mattie and Philbert's nonconformity, and by the end of the week, he heads off for home with his newfound knowledge and a greater appreciation for the role of manners in civilized society. According to *Booklist* critic Susan DeRonne, "This book . . . tells a humorous story with a warm message."

Simon's zany relatives return in *No More Nasty.* After his fifth-grade teacher leaves the school in mid-year, Simon learns that his Aunt Mattie has been hired to fill in for the absent teacher. Loving his aunt's unusual ways but at the same time embarrassed by her crazy antics, Simon keeps his relationship with the new teacher a secret from the other kids in the class. While initially dismissive of Aunt Mattie, who seems unfazed at all of the pranks the children attempt, the students eventually begin to enjoy her unorthodox teaching methods and become the highest-achieving class in the school. "The

delightful black-and-white illustrations highlight moments of the humorous plot, which readers will enjoy as a read-aloud or read-alone," remarked *School Library Journal* critic Betsy Fraser, and Martha V. Parravano of *Horn Book* said "MacDonald keeps the pace lively and her prose crisp."

In the picture book *Please, Malese!: A Trickster Tale from Haiti,* MacDonald adapts a legend of a lazy, sneaky man who hoodwinks several friends into providing him with free shoes, rum, and donkey rides. When his companions finally become wise to his conniving ways, they stick him in jail. But he continues to pester them until they agree to set him free, whereby he wastes no time in convincing them to fix his house while he lounges in a hammock. MacDonald got the idea for the story from the 1929 book *The Magic Island* by W. B. Seabrook, which described the manipulative ways of a supposedly real-life Haitian peasant, Theot Brun. The picture book features "spiky and fresh" language, according to a Nell D. Beram of *Horn Book,* who called it "a trickster tale of the highest order." A reviewer for *Publishers Weekly* likened Malese to Tom Sawyer and said that MacDonald "spins a narrative with authenticity and verve."

MacDonald has also written the text for several board books in the "Let's Explore" series from Candlewick Press. The books combine simple ideas and bright, colorful drawings that together introduce the youngest children to activities and objects around them. Phelan remarked of the series in *Booklist,* "Simple, bright, and appealing, this set of board books offers a pleasant introduction to the world of reading."

Biographical and Critical Sources

PERIODICALS

Booklist, January 1, 1991, Carolyn Phelan, review of *Little Beaver and the Echo,* p. 938; March 15, 1992, Carolyn Phelan, review of *Let's Do It* and *Let's Make a Noise,* p. 1385; April 1, 1996, Carolyn Phelan, review of *Cousin Ruth's Tooth,* p. 1372; April 15, 1996, Hazel Rochman, review of *The Spider Who Created the World,* p. 1446; September 1, 1996, Susan DeRonne, review of *No More Nice,* p. 130; September 1, 2001, Chris Sherman, review of *No More Nasty,* p. 106; May 15, 2002, Michael Cart, review of *Quentin Fenton Herter III,* p. 1602; August, 2002, Linda Perkins, review of *Please Malese!: A Trickster Tale from Haiti,* p. 1968.
Bulletin of the Center for Children's Books, May, 1996, Deborah Stevenson, review of *The Spider Who Created the World,* p. 307.
Horn Book, November-December, 1990, Ellen Fader, review of *Rachel Fister's Blister,* p. 731; July-August, 1992, p. 457; September-October, 1996, Ellen Fader, review of *The Spider Who Created the World,* p. 582;

November-December, 2001, Martha V. Parravano, review of *No More Nasty*, p. 754; May-June, 2002, Susan P. Bloom, review of *Quentin Fenton Herter III*, p.318; September-October, 2002, Nell D. Beram, review of *Please, Malese!: A Trickster Tale from Haiti*, p. 590.

Kirkus Reviews, February 1, 1996, review of *Cousin Ruth's Tooth*, p. 230; October 1, 1996, review of *No More Nice*, p. 1471; March 15, 2002, review of *Quentin Fenton Herter III*,. 418; August 1, 2002, review of *Please Malese!: A Trickster Tale from Haiti*, p. 1136.

Publishers Weekly, June 29, 1990, review of *Little Beaver and the Echo*, p. 100; August 31, 1990, review of *Rachel Fister's Blister*, p. 63; February 12, 1996, review of *The Spider Who Created the World*, p. 76; February 19, 1996, review of *Cousin Ruth's Tooth*, p.215; August 27, 2001, review of *No More Nasty*, p. 86; January 14, 2002, review of *Quentin Fenton Herter III*, p. 58; May 27, 2002, review of *Please, Malese!: A Trickster Tale from Haiti*, p. 59.

School Library Journal, November, 1990, Kathy Piehl, review of *Rachel Fister's Blister*, p. 96; March, 1991, Margaret Bush, review of *Little Beaver and the Echo*, p. 175; June, 1992, Steven Engelfried, review of *Let's Do It* and *Let's Try*, p. 99; August, 1992, Gale W. Sherman, review of *Let's Make a Noise* and *Let's Play*, p. 143; May, 1994, Linda Wicher, review of *Let's Go*, p. 100; March, 1996, Patricia (Dooley) Lothrop Green, review of *The Spider Who Created the World*, p. 178; May, 1996, Anne Parker, review of *Cousin Ruth's Tooth*, p. 94; September, 1996, John Sigwald, review of *No More Nice*, p. 204; September, 2001, Betsy Fraser, review of *No More Nasty*, p. 230.

OTHER

Amy MacDonald Web site, http://www.amymacdonald. com/ (January 28, 2005).

Autobiography Feature

Amy MacDonald

Amy MacDonald contributed the following autobiographical essay to *SATA:*

MY LIFE SO FAR

When I look back at my school years I have only one regret: that I wasn't naughty enough. In fact, I think I only did one naughty thing in my entire life at school. And I can't even remember what that was.

All I know is, I got kicked out of kindergarten. It was a nice little kindergarten run by our nice little church, and for some reason they decided to give me the old heave-ho. But it's so long ago, and I was so little at the time, that I've forgotten what I did to make them kick me out.

This is where fiction comes in. With fiction you can make it all up. Who cares what *really* happened? In my mind, I got kicked out because I put a frog in the coffee of the lady who ran the kindergarten, the minister's wife. Or I asked her to explain, if God made everything, then who made God, huh? Something funny or rude like that.

Because the rest of my school career I was one big goody goody. Teacher's pet. That was me. The Student Council leader. The kid who always had her hand up. Who always knew the answer and never got in trouble. Whose report cards were as regular as clockwork: "Keep up the good work" was all the teachers could think of to say about me.

How dull.

You'd think most parents would be happy to have a child like me. And I'm sure they were very proud of all those straight-A report cards. But one day when I was grown up my mother confessed to me that she had always wanted to write a story about a child who was *so* good that he bored his parents to tears. My mother had always wanted to be a writer, so then and there we created a story together about a boy who was "too good-for-his-own-good." It started:

Quentin Fenton Carter Third
Was seldom seen and never heard.
He always did what he should ought,
And never did what he should not.

Many years later—after my mother had died—I found those words written down in a sort of diary. It wasn't until then that I realized I had used them, with only a slight change, as the beginning of a children's picture book called *Quentin Fenton Herter III*. It's the story of a little boy who is completely perfect in every way. Sooo good. But he has a shadow who is just the opposite of him—sort of his "evil twin":

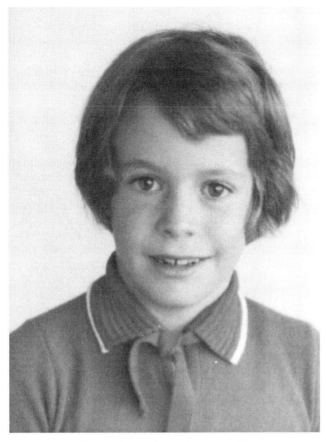

Young Amy, about six years old.

Quentin Fenton had a Shadow:
Never good and always bad! Oh—
He was bad as bad can be,
Was Quentin Fenton Herter *Three*.

This was the way I wanted to be: naughty. I just never dared to.

Except at home. At home, I was a little hellion. I think sometimes my mother wondered whose report cards I was bringing home, because it certainly couldn't have been the child she knew. As a little girl I had a fierce temper and was in the habit of beating up my older brother—at least until he got bigger than me. One day when my mother had sent me to my room for some offense, I emptied the entire contents of my room out the second floor window onto her head while she was gardening beneath me. I was also fiercely independent. One of my earliest memories is telling my parents that I would hold my *own* hand while crossing the street, thank you very much. Although I probably didn't say, Thank you very much.

I had three siblings—a brother and two sisters. I was number two—my brother came first—and the four of us fought lustily for most of our childhood. My brother and I were particularly competitive. I remember the day I decided I should stop beating him up. I was much too old for that nonsense, I told myself. I think it was the day he beaned me with a metal wastebasket and I learned what the word "goose egg" meant. Or

maybe it was the day he threw a pencil at me, leaving a permanent, lead-colored scar just below my left eye.

We lived in a big old rambly house with about eighteen rooms, right on the ocean in Beverly, Massachusetts. My parents bought it when it was a ruin. My mother, who was pregnant with me, worked so hard fixing it up that she went into labor and I was born several weeks too soon. That event—my birth—is the only time in my entire life I have ever been early for anything. Most often, I'm late—especially when writing something on a deadline. (Just ask my editors.)

This was a magical house to grow up in. It was one hundred years old, with high ceilings and sunny windows that looked out to sea. The toilets had wooden seats with overhead tanks and pull chains for flushing. A primitive telephone system connected the upper floors to the kitchen, so you could order the servants to bring you tea or whatever. The only problem: we didn't have servants.

But our house did have a "servants' wing." In the old days (when people did have servants) these servants lived in a closed-off section of the house that was dark and mysterious. It even had a third floor with lots of cramped little attic rooms. The door that separated our half of the house from the empty servants' wing was like the door in *The Lion, the Witch and the Wardrobe* that opens to Narnia. When my sisters and I passed through that door, we felt free to create our own fantasy land in what seemed to us the world's biggest playhouse.

The house had its sinister side: an unlit, dirt-floored cellar, where I never dared venture alone, even as a teenager. My parents' bedroom, with a saggy ceiling that rose and fell like an ocean swell. (I was sure it would cave in on them one night, leaving four orphans who would have to go live in a Lemony Snicket book.) Windows so old the glass in them had melted, making everything outdoors look wavy. (Glass does melt, you know—but very very very very very slowly.) Lying on my right side in bed I could look out these windows to the wavy ocean. (I couldn't lie on my left side, because then I could see into the mirror on the opposite wall, and after reading *The Haunted Looking Glass* there was no way I would ever fall asleep looking into a mirror.)

But I loved my windows. I insisted on sleeping with them open, even in the winter, and especially when it rained. There is no sound in the world I love better than rain beating on a roof. Open windows used to drive my father crazy. He couldn't stand the thought of wasting anything—especially heat. He'd come in after he thought I was asleep and close the windows. As soon as he left I'd get up and open them again. The heat would go out and the rain would get in and ruin the wallpaper. And that's how I liked it.

(All my life I have needed to have the sound of rain around me. I still sleep with the window open— and in Maine it gets below zero in the winter. When I went off to college in a big city and lived in a skyscraper-sized dorm, I missed the sounds of nature so much that I stuck a plank of wood out my window in order to hear the rain when it fell. This irritated all my roommates.)

My bedroom at home was right above the kitchen. A heating grate in the floor led by some sort of duct to the furnace in the sinister cellar. The kitchen below me shared the same duct. This meant I could lie on my floor with my ear to the grate and hear every word that was said in the kitchen. It was a good way, as a writer, to gather material. I gathered a lot of material, because I got sent to my room every time I was naughty. And I was naughty a lot.

Being so naughty might also be the reason I became such a good reader. All that boring time spent in my room passed much more quickly with a book. I can't remember when I first learned to read. It seems I was always able to. I read when I ate. I read when I brushed my teeth. I read and read and read. I think I read every single book for children before I was ten. I even read when I was in math class. My fifth-grade yearbook notes that, "During the year Amy read the entire [school] library by the simple method of keeping the books on her lap through all her classes."

What did I read? The Landmark history books about Paul Revere and John Paul Jones. All the Beverly Cleary books. Mysteries like the Hardy Boys. Animal tales: the Lassie and Black Stallion books, the *Ring of Bright Water* otter books, *Black Beauty*. Adventure stories like *The Swallows and Amazons*. Most of all I loved books with magic: the *Wizard of Oz* and *Doctor Dolittle* books, all of E. Nesbit (*The Five Children and It*), and *Mrs. Piggle Wiggle's Magic*. I devoured entire series.

I also loved any book with a feisty tomboy heroine. Scout in *To Kill a Mockingbird*. Nancy Drew and her "chums." Pippi Longstocking. I hated prissy girls and never forgave Louisa May Alcott for naming the prissy girl in *Little Women* Amy. All the Laura Ingalls Wilder "Little House on the Prairie" books I read lying on the floor of my room, including *On the Shores of Silver Lake*, which I finished the same day my mother bought it. It was supposed to be a present for my best friend Sally's tenth birthday, which was that afternoon. I read the whole book that morning, trying hard not to open it too far and crack the spine, so it wouldn't look like I was giving her a used book.

The floor, by the way, is still my favorite place to read.

My mother also read to us. I'm sure she did it to keep peace at the dinner table. She read us the classics: *The Wheel on the School, Hurry Home Candy, The Peterkin Papers.*

It was my mother who got me into reading the newspapers, a lifelong addiction that started one day when I was ten. "You should read about this," said my usually cheerful mother one morning, putting the *Boston Herald* down on the breakfast table. "This is about

as close as we might ever come to nuclear war." It was the week of the Cuban Missile Crisis, a time when the United States and the Soviet Union came within a whisker of launching their nuclear missiles at each other. That's when we—and many families—began building "bomb shelters" in the basement. It's also when I began reading the newspaper cover to cover each day.

Why did I love reading so much? There was always a sense in our house of a connection to writing and books, especially through my mother's family in St. Paul, Minnesota. One of the most famous writers in America, F. Scott Fitzgerald, played in my grandparents' backyard as a boy and wrote about them in his stories. *The Peterkin Papers* was written by an old friend of my grandparents. The introduction to it says that the wise "Lady from Philadelphia," who solves all the Peterkin family's silly problems, is based on a "Mrs. Susan Lesley," who turns out to be my great-great-grandmother. (I am sure, by the way, that the "Lady from Philadelphia" was the inspiration for the Queen in *Rachel Fister's Blister* and *Cousin Ruth's Tooth*—a similarity that I didn't notice until my son Jeremy pointed it out as I was reading *The Peterkin Papers* to him.)

I read as a way of escaping the world around me. Open the page and I was gone from my boring old room in Beverly. Gone from dull Cove School. Gone from painful middle school. With one breath I was getting my wish granted to have wings and learning to fly high over an English cathedral. Or I was sailing in the Lake District of England. I was battling flying monkeys in the *Wizard of Oz*. I was training and befriending a wild horse on a desert island.

For a while my mother would bring me back stacks of books each week from the Beverly Public Library. Then I began going there myself, on foot. I did the journey so often that I took to counting how long it took to walk back and forth. I can tell you this confidently: between my house and the Beverly Library, there are exactly 2,856 steps.

I still carry my Beverly Public Library card in my wallet, along with all my other public library cards from everywhere I've ever lived. I loved the old-fashioned cards, the kind that had a silver metal slug with numbers stamped into it. I loved the way that funny machine went "ka-*chug*" when they stuck the card in to date stamp the lined paper that went into the pocket in the back of the book. I loved looking at that piece of paper with all its date stamps and thinking about the other people who had held the book in their hands like me, voyaging to the same spot in their imaginary world during those two weeks they had had it out. I loved that you could walk into any library anywhere, get out a card, and keep it forever in your purse to use whenever you wanted. I loved those 2,856 steps home, with the weight of all my new books in my book bag, waiting for the moment I could open and devour them.

*

The other journey I knew by heart was the walk to Cove Elementary School. We all set off each morning, the three girls forced to walk a few steps behind our brother. We'd pass the swamp where, if only I hadn't been wearing a dress, I'd much rather have gone to hunt for tadpoles. One of my favorite games was to balance a long piece of grass on my finger or my nose for as long as I could. Then we'd cross the road with the fifth-grade school crossing guard in his natty orange vest, and there we were: at school.

At Cove School, I put behind me my disgrace in kindergarten and began my illustrious career as the perfect student. In the four years I was there I got in trouble only once. That was for falling in a mud puddle on the way to school (while balancing something on my nose no doubt) and arriving with a dirty dress. My first-grade teacher, Mrs. Ward, sent me to the principal's office, for the first and last time in my life. My mother had to come and get me. Oh the shame of it all.

The one thing I was really bad at was . . . writing. Which, in first grade, meant "penmanship." Mrs. Ward tried her hardest to get me to grip my pencil the right way—the end of the pencil pointing at my shoulder, those fat letters sitting neatly on the widely spaced lines, with their graceful swoops above and below the dotted line. But no matter how hard I tried, my letters fell off the rails. They weren't nice and plump but squashed and crooked. In fifth grade, my handwriting was pronounced to be so bad I got yanked out of class and sent to a special "remedial handwriting" teacher. It didn't work. Finally everyone gave up on me. When people commented on my horrid scrawl, I began to tell them I had inherited it from my father. He is a doctor and it is well known that all doctors have Egyptian hieroglyphs for handwriting.

(By the way, you might think that now that I have a computer, I wouldn't bother with handwriting anymore. Not true. Today I still write most of my first drafts by hand. Then I put them on a computer to edit and revise.)

The great sadness of my early years was that I left Cove School before fifth grade. So I never got to be a crossing guard.

You see what I mean by dull.

But outside school was lots of excitement. On both sides of our house was water: the ocean on one side, a small swamp on the other. In the swamp I spent hours and hours with my friend, Carl from next door, collecting tadpoles and frogs and looking for birds' nests. Once—or maybe I dreamed this—we even found a snake's nest. In winter we skated on the swampy pond. In spring when the ice melted we made rafts of the ice floes and poled around on them.

I spent every summer day with my siblings on the beach, swimming, climbing around the rocks, making sand castles, catching crabs, creating little dams in the streams that flowed into the sea. A favorite game was for each of us to find a periwinkle—a kind of tiny black snail that lives on rocks—and "race" them against each other to see which was fastest. We searched for sand dollars at low tide. We made what we called "pizza boards"—round boards cut from plywood—which we skimmed along the shallow water of low tide, and then ran and jumped onto, skittering for yards on top of them like little surf boards.

But as nice as it was to play in the sun, perhaps my favorite time to go to the beach was during a storm. Any kind of storm: blizzards were spectacular, with grey waves full of snow and wind blasting the tops off them. Best of all were the hurricanes. My father describes finding me sitting at the edge of the lawn, as a little girl, at the height of Hurricane Carol, watching the waves crash over the top of the sea wall and the wind whip the spray inland. The third important place in my life also involved water. When I was about five my parents bought a piece of land on a pond at the end of a long dirt road. They built a single-room house with one bedroom. There were no neighbors. There was no running water—just a hand pump and a well. There was no electricity. There was no telephone. There was no heat but the fireplace.

What were we to do for entertainment? We had a canoe, a Sailfish, a leaky rowboat, and four homemade, mini one-man boats we could paddle. We spent every minute in or on Bear Camp Pond.

And then there was the wildlife. There were chickadees and chipmunks that we trained to eat from our hands—and even our lips. There were turtles we could catch in homemade turtle traps. We fished for sunfish and perch and scary hornpout and fierce-toothed pickerel. We canoed to the end of the pond to watch osprey and great blue herons fishing, and (at dusk) beavers building dams. We watched deer and moose swim across the pond and even managed to spot a few bears in the woods.

Where were we—my brothers and sisters and I—to sleep? Simple. My parents built a wooden platform and erected a big canvas tent on it. It was an Army surplus tent from my father's days in the Navy during WWII. We had crude bunk beds, where we would lie watching daddy longlegs walk along the top of the tent and listening to the sound of dozens of mosquitoes buzzing in our ears (they always got in, no matter what we did). I remember the rain dripping through the places in the canvas that were worn or where the seams met. If you touched your finger to the roof, you could get the rain to come through where you had touched it. I remember the smell of the worn WWII sleeping bags, with the lumpy stuffing that barely kept out the chill of a summer night.

I especially remember lying there one night and listening to a faint cheeping sound that seemed to be coming from somewhere very close by.

"Can you hear that?" I asked my siblings.

"Go to sleep!" my brother growled at me.

"You're imagining things," hissed my sisters.

Suddenly something ran across my sleeping bag. Something small, but determined. I gave a little scream and pulled the bag over my head.

"I'm not imagining things!" I yelled. "There's something in here."

But no one would believe me. I went inside the main house and woke my parents.

"You're just having a dream," they insisted sleepily. I found a flashlight and went back to the tent. There, at the bottom of my sleeping bag, was a little nest made out of the stuffing of the bag. In it were three very pink baby mice, squeaking faintly for their mother. She, alas, was nowhere to be found. Perhaps she found it just too alarming that the comfy mountain where she had chosen to make her nest suddenly came alive and started shrieking and shaking.

I insisted on being allowed to raise the baby mice. We found an eye-dropper and warmed some milk. For the next few days I fed those mice regularly, trying hard to save them. I failed. Babies, I learned the hard way, need their mother.

This was not to be the last time I tried to rescue an animal. My second attempt was more successful. My mother heard a noise in the driveway one morning and came out to find me shouting at a garter snake that was trying to eat a frog it had caught. The frog looked very unhappy, with its hind legs already halfway down the snake's throat. The snake looked mad at having its meal interrupted, but it was too weighed down by the frog to make a getaway.

It was a plain old garter snake, but it had got its mouth open so wide it was actually swallowing the young frog whole. The snake ignored my shouts, and my mother clearly had no intention of getting involved. So I grabbed the snake with one hand and the frog with the other. I pulled. The frog popped free, then hopped off happily. The snake slithered away in disgust. I like to think that frog lived to tell its grandchildren about the beautiful princess who saved it from the evil snake.

And there were others: baby rabbits, baby birds, even spiders that had fallen into bathtubs. I don't know why I did it. Maybe I had just read too many tales of lions who rescued mice and then were saved by the mice. Maybe I thought one day a frog would save my life. Or maybe I knew that one day one of the spiders I rescued would help me write a book. Who knows—maybe it *was* the spirit of one of those spiders who helped me write *The Spider Who Created the World!*

Certainly the spirit of other animals at our camp helped me with all my writing—both as a child and as

With youngest sister, Gene, 1958: "Putting a worm on a hook for my sister at Bear Camp Pond. Worms, spiders, snakes—nothing fazed me!"

a grown-up. I remember four stories—homework assignments—that were written in the car on the way home from our camp. All were clearly inspired by animals—in some pretty odd ways. The first, which I wrote in fifth grade, is called "What the Black Powder Did." My mother, who was convinced that I was going to be a Famous Writer someday, despite having very little evidence to go by (if you judge by the quality of these compositions) saved everything I ever wrote, including the Black Powder story.

It starts off: "Once there was a boy and a girl. Their father had died of hay fever." The children find a magic powder that allows them to become any animal they want. They wish to be ducks but then discover that two evil men had tricked them so that they were stuck being ducks for the rest of their life. They outwit the men, and then (this is my second-favorite part, after the fatal hay fever) once they get turned back into children they "told the King and he hung one man and turned the other into an owl and put him in a cage in the park." So there!

The school magazine for some reason reprinted this story a year after I left middle school, and added this note at the bottom of the story: *"Editor's note: Amy MacDonald won the English prize after graduating from eighth grade last year. Courage, all you fifth graders!"* It seems to me that this is something of an insult to my fifth-grade writing ability!

*

Another fifth-grade epic—this one inspired by my battle with the garter snake—was called "Adventures in the Woods," and it featured a boy who went into the woods as part of a science project and got bitten by a poisonous snake.

The next year, also on the way home from Bear Camp, I wrote a story called "The Chicken Who Saved the Day." It too is inspired by an animal—a dead chicken. It tells the true tale of how our house at Bear Camp nearly caught on fire one day when we were out skiing. If my mother hadn't been hurrying us home to get a chicken in the oven, we might have arrived back to find our camp a smoking ruin. As it was, we arrived back just in time to find it smoldering. A close call.

The last composition that my mother saved I wrote in seventh grade. It is clearly influenced by two things: *The Yearling,* a novel by Marjorie Rawlings that I had just read, about a boy who raises a wild fawn as a pet; and the fact that it was hunting season in New England, which meant that when we were at Bear Camp, we all had to wear red to keep the hunters from mistaking us for deer. The story was about a girl—a tomboy named Georgiana who answers only to the name of George. She and her twin brother find an orphaned fawn and raise it as a pet. When it is full grown, they have to let it go back to the wild, but they are worried sick that it will be killed by hunters. Their solution? Tie a red scarf

around its antlers during hunting season. When the poor hunter who almost shoots it realizes he's been tricked, he "didn't know whether to laugh or cry."

I never actually learned to write in any real sense, at least not at school. I never had to brainstorm or do a story map or a second draft of anything I wrote. I was given a writing topic—or, worse, just told to write "something"—every weekend and had to produce it Monday morning. Most of the time I wrote it in the car coming home from Bear Camp.

I was not one of those kids who wrote and wrote from the time they could hold a pen. The only time I wrote for my own pleasure, as a child, was lying in bed at night. I would lull myself to sleep each night by "writing" (in my head) a scene to add to a favorite book. Or I would create a new episode of a favorite TV show. After reading *Gone with the Wind,* for example, I felt so angry at the author for making it end badly that I simply refused to accept her ending and made up my own, much more satisfying one.

All this might seem like copying, but it's the way I learned to write. I got a huge amount of pleasure out of mimicking my favorite authors. In high school, my best friend and I wrote a spoof of Nancy Drew books. We noticed, for example, that Nancy and her "chums" spent a great deal of time eating during her "sleuthing" adventures. So we had our heroine stop every few pages to eat a meal that always featured frozen peas. I was also a big fan of the James Bond spy books when I was in high school. So I wrote a spoof of those, with a female spy called Jane Bomb. In eighth grade, after going to see *West Side Story,* a movie about street gangs in New York City, I went home and wrote a story about boys and girls in a gang. In college I wrote a parody of a story by Edgar Allan Poe (the author of horror stories like "The Telltale Heart").

My fifth-grade teacher, whom I had again in seventh grade, was wonderful. His name was Mr. Wise (really!). He encouraged me to write, wrote interesting comments on all my papers, and made me believe I actually was good at this thing called writing.

He also edited the school's literary magazine. I remember something I wrote for him—the best thing I wrote in middle school—which he advised me not to publish in the magazine. It was a very short piece—one paragraph—called "The Third Paper Cup." As you might guess from the title, it didn't have a lot of drama in it. But unlike the *West Side Story* imitation, I was finally writing about something I *knew* about: misery. A girl—an awkward, shy, wallflower of a girl—feels miserable at her first girl/boy party. She watches the pretty, Popular Girl flirting with boys and dancing gaily. As she sits alone in a corner, staring into the fireplace, someone tosses some cups into the fire. One lands right in the flames and burns up instantly, making a brilliant flame. A second cup lands near the flames, finally catches fire, and then burns slowly but steadily. Long after the first cup has burned to ash, the second one is

"The four of us at the beach: (from left) brother Alex, me, Susan, Gene," 1963.

still glowing away. The girl is comparing herself to that second paper cup—and the Popular Girl to the first paper cup—when she notices a third cup. It has landed in a corner of the fireplace, away from the flames. It never catches fire, and clearly never will. The last line: "She got up and joined the party."

Mr. Wise had the sense to realize I was writing about myself and might not want to publish this little personal insight. It had never occurred to me that anyone reading it might guess it was about *me*. But it was. That was me in middle school: shy, awkward, wallflower. I had friends, and was even popular enough to be on the student council. I just wasn't popular enough to have a boyfriend. I was usually too tongue-tied to say anything to anyone in a group, like the classroom, or the party I described in that story. But I discovered one day that I could still make an impression without opening my mouth: I could write it instead of speak it. The teacher read aloud a story I had written, and it made the class laugh. This was a very powerful moment: hey, I *made* them do that! Then I got bold enough to make a joke that made the Popular Boy (whom I had a huge crush on) laugh. (I still remember the joke: I had written something on my hand in ink.

He asked me what it was. I said, "Hand writing." Get it? *Hand writing!* Very witty! Okay, well *he* liked it.) I definitely enjoyed the feeling of power that came with being able to get a group of people to respond to something I created. I think that year, fifth grade, was when I decided I wanted to be a writer when I grew up.

Although I'll always be grateful to Mr. Wise for starting me on this course, not all teachers were as talented or as kind as he was. In sixth grade and again in eighth grade I had the bad luck to have the kind of teachers who seem to enjoy humiliating kids. Usually it wasn't me, because I was so well behaved. But I'll never forget watching those two teachers reading one story I had written. It was the story inspired by the street gang movie. I'm the first to admit that story would have struck any grown-up as comical, coming from a girl who had only lived in the nice comfy suburbs. But what I remember is the sixth-grade teacher saying, with a sneer, that it "reminded him of a cross between *A Tale of Two Cities* and *West Side Story*." The eighth-grade teacher snickered. I had no idea what they meant by this, but their jeering tone was unmistakable. In my mind, they had singled me out for humiliation, cackling hideously over my pathetic writing. In reality, they probably had just made some wry comment with a little smile. The important thing is—I wanted to die. Thirteen-year-olds are *very* sensitive to any kind of ridicule.

Many years later, by the way, I got my revenge, as many writers do. Writing my chapter books, *No More Nice* and *No More Nasty,* I needed to make a teacher be the bad guy. I took those two teachers from my childhood who had made my classmates so miserable and used them as models for "Mrs. Biggs"—the "nasty" teacher in the two books. Anyone who had been their student many years ago would recognize them. I didn't do it for revenge, just for realism. But I can't deny there was a certain satisfaction in it.

However, there was even more satisfaction in getting to return to my old school recently as a guest, invited to address the whole school about being a writer. This was my chance to thank Mr. Wise publicly for being so supportive of me in those days, and I did it with great pleasure. To my even greater pleasure, when he heard I was coming to the school, though he was ill and had a very hard time getting around, he came to hear me and had lunch with me afterwards in the old cafeteria. It was lovely.

My greatest literary feat in high school was a movie I made at the end of senior year. There was a wildly popular TV show called "Rowan and Martin's Laugh-In" which was pretty much just a series of people telling bad jokes and puns, and doing sight gags. I decided, along with my best friend, Kathy Bell (the one who wrote Nancy Drew parodies with me) that for our "senior class present" to the school, the seniors should make our own version of this show. My friend Sally rented a movie camera (it was a silent camera; we had to tape the sound separately). Kathy and I wrote all the jokes and called it the "Bell and Howl Laugh-In." (Bell and Howell is a company that made movie cameras.) This pathetic pun on our names gives you an idea of the level of humor in the movie. Example:

Amy (interviewing our Japanese exchange student): Tell me, Chie, how did you find America?

Chie: I turned left at Hawaii.

We also somehow managed to convince the usually straight-laced school administrators to participate in this project:

Assistant Headmaster (running into the Headmaster's office in panic): Sir! Sir! The students are revolting!

Headmaster: You said it. They sure are.

(Admittedly that joke would be funnier if you knew that this was made in 1969, a time when students actually *were* revolting and taking over college campuses all over the country.)

When I tell you that the most hilarious moment in the film was when we convinced the Assistant Headmaster to ride a tricycle into a tree and fall over . . . well, you can tell what a "howl" our "Bell and Howl Laugh-In" was.

(On second thought, the funniest moment was when, after days of filming this epic, the "camera man" [Sally] came to Kathy and me and admitted that she had filmed the whole movie without taking the lens cap off the movie camera . . . That was really a howl! We had to do it all over again. We laughed until we cried.)

These days it is not unusual for a high school to make a "video" yearbook. But back then, in the days before camcorders, nobody else had done it and it felt pretty special.

*

Was I destined for a career writing for TV or for stand-up comics? I had no idea as I set off for college in the Big City. At the University of Pennsylvania I felt I had left behind everything that I cared about, from frogs and snakes to my idyllic childhood and the sound of rain on the roof. Everything, that is, except for books and reading. I decided if I became an English major, that meant I got to read lots of books and write about them. So that's what I did.

I also discovered a way to keep alive my love of all my favorite childhood books. The 1960s were heady days on college campuses: any student could teach a course in something called the "Free University." So as a freshman I put together a course on . . . children's literature. Basically I just got a group of people together and we discussed our favorite children's books. I gave everyone A's.

I took some creative writing courses in college, and I recently pulled those stories out and looked at them. With a few exceptions (like the Edgar Allen Poe parody) they were all so bad I decided it would be embarrassing if they fell into the hands of my enemies. I burned everything. It's a shame I didn't write anything worth saving, since I had some terrific, and very well known, teachers. And I really wanted to be a writer. I wanted it so badly that I even sneaked into a class with one of the most famous authors in America, Philip Roth. (You were supposed to get advance permission to take his class, but I had missed the semester of school when you needed to turn in that permission slip. Undaunted, I—who never did anything naughty—forged my permission slip. One day Mr. Roth looked at me and said, "Who are you? How'd you get in here?" I just shrugged and smiled and he let me stay. It was worth it. He was a fascinating teacher.)

The trouble with my writing was I had nothing interesting to say, because nothing interesting had ever happened to me. It was like me trying to write that story in eighth grade about gang wars, when all I had ever known was sunny rooms and happy families. Writers have to write about what they know, or they risk sounding very silly. I figured I didn't know enough about anything to be a writer. Yet.

I decided that while I waited for something interesting to happen to me, I would become a journalist. I had done a little writing for the college newspaper, I loved newspapers, and journalists get to see some interesting stuff.

I was never a big believer in learning to write by taking courses in it. Like Mark Twain, I believed your schooling should not interfere with your education. So instead of more "schooling"—that is, graduate school—I decided that after college I would learn journalism by simply doing it.

I got a job working as an "intern" for a local newspaper. Intern is basically a fancy word for unpaid slave labor. It means you work for free and in exchange they train you to do something. My boss, Mr. Wasserman, took me on because he was a friend of my mother's. Mr. Wasserman scared me. He had a wooden leg and a biting wit. He owned a chain of newspapers north of Boston, and he put me straight to work writing the kind of story nobody else on the newspaper wanted to write. I had to interview the little businesses who advertised in the papers and find something interesting to say about them. This was done simply to keep the advertisers happy and the money rolling in to the newspaper—not because the people or businesses had anything interesting to say. Quite the opposite. Imagine having to write a story about "Joe's Function Room" or "Suzi's Gifte Shoppe." What exactly can you say about a "function room"—except why on earth is it called a "*function*" room? And I challenge anybody to write something fascinating about a shop that sells glass trinkets to tourists. Somehow I managed to. I think it was good training as a writer: You learn that, underneath, everyone has a story to tell, no matter how dull they might seem on the surface. And you learn to dig for those interesting bits. Having learned how to make something interesting out of something so ordinary, it was a snap, later on, when I got to write about truly fascinating things.

After a while, however, I had learned about as much as I could. I quit my intern job on the day that Mr. Wasserman decided I should write about the disgusting state of the bathrooms on the state highway rest stops. This would have involved my investigating every rest stop bathroom north of Boston and looking into the toilets. Even interns have their limits.

Besides, I had a much more fascinating job possibility—a job that would actually pay money. While at Penn I had worked in the college's theater, which I loved. A friend who worked there with me called one day to tell me he was leaving his job as the publicity director at a small theater company near Boston. So I applied for his job. I figured writing publicity was similar to writing newspaper stories. It combined journalism with my love of the theater. Why not give it a try?

It was a fateful day when I went to that interview. I had just bought myself my first car—a very old and very used Volkswagen Beetle. The car cost me all of $250. It was a perfect little Bug with only one small problem: the previous owner had removed a wheel,

"Standing in front of my childhood home, with husband-to-be, Thomas," 1975.

probably to change a tire, and had screwed the wheel back on wrong. As I drove down the three-lane highway into Boston for my job interview (late as always, and so speeding along in the passing lane), I felt a sudden jolt. Looking in my rear view mirror, I saw a wheel (the entire wheel, not just the tire!) rolling down the highway behind me. Hmmm, I said to myself, this is not right. I was able to stop on the median strip and check: sure enough, my little car was missing a back wheel. I hunted and hunted but never did find that wheel.

I had to call the theater company boss and tell him I would be . . . a little late. I was more than a little late. But I got that job and two years later I married my boss. I always tell him that he knew from Day One that being on time was not something I was going to be good at.

His name was Thomas. He was British. And he had a cute six-year-old daughter named Emily. The three of us bought a house in a small town in rural Massachusetts, and we all moved into it the day after the wedding.

The problem with marrying your boss is that you can't go on working for him. One day I saw an ad in the local newspaper, the *Harvard Post,* for an investigative reporter to write for the paper. I sent them a letter saying I was interested in the job—as long as they didn't want me to investigate rest rooms. The editors, a husband-and-wife team named Ed Miller and Kathleen Cushman, thought my letter was funny and came over to interview me at my house. They arrived in a Volkswagen Bug, with their own cute six-year-old daughter Montana in the back seat. The two girls took one look at each other and became instant best friends. The editors looked at my rusty VW bug in the driveway . . . and decided to hire me on the spot.

Why? Because the main requirement for the job was to own a car that could make it up the long, steep, dirt driveway that led to the newspaper office, a road too twisty to plow in the winter. In their experience, the only car that could handle that road was a VW. So they basically hired me because of a funny letter, a six-year-old daughter, and a nine-year-old VW.

That's how I really learned to be a journalist. And boy did I learn. The *Harvard Post* was a weekly newspaper that was read by every single citizen of the small town of Harvard. Ed and Kathleen had created it from scratch, working from an office in the basement of their house. My first job was as a "cub reporter," which meant I covered the town meetings: the Planning Board, the School Committee, the Annual Town Meeting. This was pretty dull, but, hey, I could do dull.

As I got better, I was allowed to write feature stories, which meant interviewing all the interesting people in town. For a teeny, tiny town, Harvard had quite a few. Like a man named Gary Wolfe who was writing a book called *Who Framed Roger Rabbit?* I remember thinking at the time, What a silly idea. (Five years later it was made into a hit movie.) I also interviewed the woman who twenty years later would write a wacky, funny novel called *The Divine Secrets of the Ya Ya Sisterhood* (also made into a hit movie). I can't claim that I recognized her future talent, either.

Soon I got promoted to Associate Editor. This meant a pay raise ($75 a month!). Now every Wednesday Emily and I would drive up that Xtreme driveway to the newspaper office where she played with Montana while I helped "put the newspaper to bed." That's a newspaper term that, loosely translated, meant that we didn't go to bed but instead stayed up all night creating the newspaper. It was enormous fun.

In those days before everything was done with computers, we took the long strips of typeset copy that Ed produced at the typesetting machine and cut them into short strips, laid them out in stories, and pasted them onto the thirty-two blank newspaper pages. These strips contained everything that goes into a newspaper from the front-page news to the classified ads. Lastly we proofread each page carefully. Then, at around four in the morning, I stumbled home to sleep all the next day while Ed drove the finished pages to the printer. The printer made the pages into the newspaper that arrived twenty-four hours later in everyone's mailbox in the little town of Harvard.

Ed and Kathleen between them did all the jobs of newspaper editors and publishers: Kathleen sold ads, edited stories and press releases, assigned reporters and photographers. She was a fantastic editor and a wonderful writer herself, and she taught me everything I needed to know about writing—far more than I ever learned in college.

Ed wrote a funny weekly column and set the type for the paper each week at a typesetting machine that he nicknamed "Typo," right there in his living room.

"Typo" looked like a little upright piano but was really a kind of giant word processor. Ed never finished these two jobs until two or three in the morning the next day. Often, to amuse himself and us late at night, he would insert slyly funny made-up classified ads or other invented news items into the copy he was typing. Usually we caught these jokes and deleted them. But sometimes they slipped past all the editors and got into the paper. Many years later Ed told me that the ad I had answered for an "investigative reporter" had been one of these, inserted by him into the paper for fun. He'd heard a rumor that a world-famous investigative reporter was spending the summer in Harvard, so he put the ad in as a joke. Nothing worth investigating ever happened in the sleepy little apple-farming town of Harvard. But I didn't know that.

*

By the end of five years, I had learned just about everything there was to know about writing for and publishing a small town newspaper. About this time I saw an ad for a journalism program based in Paris, France, that offered young journalists from all over the world a chance to learn about Europe. Even better, they paid all your expenses for a whole year while you got to live in Paris. I had always dreamed of going to Paris, so I applied. But they could only pick one or two people from the whole United States, and I never believed that such a grand sounding program would want me—an editor of a mom-and-pop newspaper, with no journalism degree, whose experience had been limited pretty much to writing about a small town in the middle of nowhere. I was competing against staff writers for the *New York Times* and the *Boston Globe*. What chance did a nobody like me have?

To this day I don't know why they picked me—but they did. I was ecstatic. Thomas agreed to take a year off from his job. Emily sobbed her eyes out at having to leave her middle school friends to go to some loathsome country she knew she'd hate. But one day in August we all packed our belongings into a few suitcases and flew to Paris to start this huge adventure.

I turned out to be the only one of the twenty-nine journalists who arrived in Paris with not only a husband but a child as well. As we went around the room and introduced ourselves that first day I realized that everyone else was a hot-shot journalist for one of the major papers or TV networks in the world: there was Wen from the *Peoples Daily* in Beijing, China. Lucio from *Il Mondo* in Rome, Italy. Roma of the London *Times* in England. Louise from CBS TV in Paris. Joy from *Newsday* in New York . . . and then there was me, Amy from the *Harvard Post,* Harvard, Massachussets. Everyone else had been writing stories about national elections. I had been writing about school board elections. They'd written about big scandals. I'd written about big apple crops. They'd interviewed presidents and queens. I'd interviewed Flower Club presidents and homecoming queens. I didn't even know how to use the machines in the room where we were supposed to "file" our stories. I was terrified they would find out I was a complete fraud.

It was Emily who saved the day for me. The first week of the program we all went on a field trip into the French countryside to learn something about making wine in France. Emily was allowed to come along. A fetching, bespectacled twelve-year-old in waist-long braids, she charmed the entire group by passing the long bus ride teaching them all American camp songs. I will never forget the sight of Emily leading those hard-ened international journalists in singing "The Other Day I Saw a Bear." Somehow they all seemed less ter-rifying after that.

As for me, I discovered something about myself that year. I might have been a fake. I might not have known a single thing about "real" journalism at the start of that year. But I learned. It was like being thrown into a deep pond. You sink. Or you swim. I never admitted I couldn't swim. But I watched the others. I followed my instincts. I made friends and asked careful questions. And you know what? I did pretty darn well. I figured out how to use the machines. I wrote stories about na-tional elections and wars and presidents. No one ever guessed I couldn't swim.

At the end of the year we went back to Harvard for a few months, but suddenly my husband was offered a

The author with daughter, Emily, in Paris, "trying to look very French," 1982.

job in England. Being English, he longed to go back to his country for a few years. I had grown up reading children's books about England. I was dying to see the land of *Swallows and Amazons,* of *The Five Children and It,* of *Winnie the Pooh,* of Harry Potter. Oops—except that Harry Potter hadn't been born yet. It was 1984.

The first thing was to find a place to live. We hunted and hunted and couldn't find anything we liked. We were about to buy a cottage—just to have somewhere to live—when someone told us about a house that was for rent. I went to look at it.

I didn't even have to go inside to know that this was the house for us. I called my husband at work. "You won't believe this house," I said, unable to hide my excitement. "It's *Tom's Midnight Garden!*"

My husband knew exactly what I meant. *Tom's Mid-night Garden* had been, without question, my favorite book as a child. Written by Phillipa Pearce, it was about a large old house by a river in England. Visiting there one summer, Tom awakes at night to hear the grandfa-ther clock striking thirteen. He gets up to investigate and finds the house is transformed. Instead of being di-vided up into many modern, cramped apartments, it is now one big old house. He opens the back door, which leads to an alley, and finds it also transformed, into a sunny garden with high walls around it and a river flow-ing beyond it. A young girl in old-fashioned clothes is playing there. Tom befriends the girl, and each night at thirteen o'clock they have wonderful adventures.

For me, this had been the most magical of all the magic books I read, perhaps because it reminded me of my childhood home in Beverly. Standing in the garden of the house in Great Shelford, England, on that day in 1984, I felt I had been transported into *Tom's Midnight Garden.* Of course we rented it. It was such an old house it was hard for me—an American—to understand how old it was. To an American, "old" usually means 100, or maybe 200, years old. This house was *600* years old. When it was built, America hadn't even been dis-covered by Columbus yet.

It was called the Rectory Farmhouse and belonged to Farmer Funston, who lived next door. It had a big circular driveway in front, and a large, perfectly trimmed green lawn (which the British call a "garden") that surrounded it. On two sides, the "garden" was hemmed in by a twelve-foot-tall wall, exactly like the wall I had imagined in Tom's garden. Behind the house the "garden" ended in a stream—the Cam River, which wound through cow pastures all the way from Great Shelford to Cambridge, and from Cambridge on to Ely. If you went the other way on the stream, you quickly came to a mill house with a great mill wheel and a mill pond.

One day, after we had lived there several months, I mentioned to someone in the village that I had fallen in love with the Rectory Farmhouse because it reminded me so strongly of *Tom's Midnight Garden.* The person

"Sitting on the fallen trunk of our quince tree in the magical garden of our home in England. Just as in **Tom's Midnight Garden,** *when our favorite tree came down in a storm, we knew it was time to move on, and a month later we moved to America": (from left) Amy, Emily (holding Jeremy), Thomas, and Alex, 1987.*

looked at me with a funny expression. "Do you know," he asked me, "that the author of that book lives almost next door to you?"

You could have knocked me down with a feather. First of all, I had no idea where *Tom's Midnight Garden* was really set. I just knew it was on some river in England. I really couldn't believe that such an enormous coincidence could have brought my husband and me across the Atlantic Ocean to the exact, tiny village in all of England where Phillipa Pearce lived. To, in fact, the same *street* where she lived. Almost to the same *house*. And that a book I had read twenty-five years ago had made such a huge impression on me that I actually recognized the village and stream it was written about. I began to feel like I was in a magic book of my own. I *had* to meet Ms. Pearce. But how? More magic. By another coincidence, when a friend of my husband's heard this story, she announced that her mother was Philippa Pearce's editor. She could get us an introduction!

And so it came to pass that I actually walked down the street one day, to the house next to the mill where Philippa Pearce now lived. I knocked on the door and

was shown inside. I had tea with her and a chance to tell the wonderful author of that book how much this little American girl had loved her story, written so long ago. She was gracious and kind to me and gave me a copy of *Tom's Midnight Garden* that she autographed for me. Then she told me that the setting had actually been, not my house, but the great mill house opposite her, where she (and her father, the miller) both grew up. It was heaven. It was magic.

So now when people ask me how I came to write books for children, I think back to that meeting. I know in some strange way I was just always *meant* to write children's books.

*

Living in England renewed my passion for children's books—after all, the best of them are English. But oddly enough, it was coming to America that inspired my first children's book. Or maybe it was just my old friend—being close to water—that did the trick.

And I needed to have small children as well. There is something about being around babies that encourages people to write stories for them. By now Emily was fourteen, and she had been bugging me for years to give her a brother or a sister. So I did. Alex was born about a year after we moved to England.

Ever since my year in Paris, I had been working as a freelance writer. That meant, when I had an idea for an interesting story, I would ask a magazine or newspaper if they would like me to write the story for them. This allowed me to work from home, which is important when you have kids. It also often gave me a great way to get back to America to visit my family and friends.

One day, when Alex was about eighteen months old, I asked a British newspaper if they would like me to write an article for them about a famous hiking trail in America near my parents' house. They agreed, and this assignment allowed me, and Alex, to come back to my parents' house for a short visit. While we were home, I decided to take Alex to Bear Camp, which my family still owned. My friend Kathleen, the editor of the *Harvard Post,* would meet me there, with her children.

The first thing Kathleen and I did at Bear Camp, of course, was to take our children down to the water's edge. I suddenly remembered one of the secrets about Bear Camp Pond.

"Listen to this, Alex," I said. "There's an echo on this pond." Then I cupped my hands and yelled, "Hello!" Faintly, on the other side of the pond, you could hear the echo say, "Hello!" I did it a few times. Then Alex took a turn doing it. I was feeling proud that I had taught him all about echoes. But just as we got back to the cabin, I could see he was feeling confused.

"Mama," he said, shaking his head, "what's an *echo?*"

Kathleen and I looked at each other and laughed. Alex was way too young to understand the idea of an echo being your own voice bouncing back at you. He was just one-and-a-half.

"Listen," I said. "Why don't I write you a story that helps explain what an echo is?" He nodded. I looked at Kathleen. "Why don't we each write a story about an echo?" It was just the kind of challenge Kathleen loved. I hunted around and found a few scraps of paper. (By now Bear Camp had electricity and plumbing, but not much else!) Then we sat down and started writing.

Why did I make the main character a beaver? I've often wondered this. Kathleen, working on her own story, made her main character a boy. But I've always loved baby animals. So which animal? It would have made sense to use a bear—for Bear Camp Pond. Lots of children's books have bears for characters. But I knew that the animal most likely to live on the edge of a pond—where you can hear the echo—was a beaver. The other characters I chose also were ones I had seen on the pond: a duck, a turtle, and an otter. Forty-five minutes later, I had written the story of *Little Beaver*

"Emily brought us back these wonderful clothes after a stint in the Peace Corps in West Africa," Christmas, 1994: (clockwise, from top left) Emily, Thomas, the author, Alex, and Jeremy.

and the Echo. It was an unusual experience for me. I had often tried to write fiction for adults. But when I did, I never finished the story. Usually I struggle to write and do so very slowly. This time it was completely different. I felt as if the story already existed out there and that I was simply writing it down, pulling it out of the air. It came into my head almost fully written. This feeling of just "taking dictation" is one many writers have described. For me, the feeling was so strong, I wondered if the story I was writing was one I'd somehow heard before. I was also sure that Kathleen was writing the exact same story because it seemed to me that in the whole world there was only this *one* possible story about an echo.

After I got back to England, I decided I liked the story enough to make it into a little book for Alex. Since I can't draw at all, I asked an artist friend to do some illustrations. I took the story to a typesetter (I didn't own a word processor in those days) and paid to have it turned into type. Then I put the story and pictures together into a little book and gave it to Alex for Christmas.

One day the friend whose mother had been Philippa Pearce's editor was visiting me. She saw the book sitting on my table and said the story was excellent and I should try to publish it. I began to wonder if it was publishable. A few weeks later, another friend of mine mentioned that she was having dinner that night with a man named Sebastian Walker. Mr. Walker had recently started his own children's publishing company. I saw my chance. Rashly I thrust my book into my friend's hands. "Would you do me a little favor and give this to him?" I asked. She agreed to do it.

As soon as she left I realized how rude and pushy this was—and that I was actually asking my friend to do a *huge* favor. You don't just give a publisher a manuscript to read over dinner at a fancy restaurant! And my friend admitted later that she *really* hadn't wanted to do it—until she read the story. But she liked it so much that she kept her word and passed it on to Mr. Walker that evening.

Two weeks later the phone rang. It was Mr. Walker himself. "I've just read your story," he said. "I think it's the best children's story I've ever read. I want to publish it."

Well, as they say, the rest is history. *Little Beaver and the Echo* went on to become an international best seller, thanks in large part to the extraordinarily beautiful illustrations by Sarah Fox-Davies. (It was her first picture book, too!) It has now been published in more than twenty-five languages all over the world. And though I've gone on to publish more children's books, I will always remember the moment that Mr. Walker called to tell me that I was going to be a real author—that I had finally achieved my childhood dream.

Just before the book came out, our family (which now included a new baby boy, Jeremy), moved to Maine. I had loved England, but I was happy to be back by the ocean again—where I could watch the waves and listen to the foghorn, and sit as I am while I write these words, watching a fantastic blizzard swirl outside my window. It may not be the land of Harry Potter, but it is for sure the land of Little Beaver.

MACKLER, Carolyn 1973-

Personal
Born 1973, in New York, NY; married Jonas Rideout, June, 2003. *Education:* Vassar College, graduated, 1995.

Addresses
Home—New York, NY. *Agent*—c/o Author Mail, Candlewick Press, 2067 Massachusetts Ave., Cambridge, MA 02140.

Career
Writer.

Member
Authors League.

Awards, Honors
Love and Other Four-Letter Words was an American Library Association Quick Pick for Reluctant Readers and an International Reading Association Young Adults Choice.

Writings

Love and Other Four-Letter Words, Delacorte (New York, NY), 2000.
The Earth, My Butt, and Other Big Round Things, Candlewick Press (Cambridge, MA), 2003.
Vegan Virgin Valentine, Candlewick Press (Cambridge, MA), 2004.

Carolyn Mackler

Also author of e-book *The Class of 2000.* Contributor to the anthologies *250 Ways to Make America Better,* 1999, and *Body Outlaws.* Contributor of short stories

After her parents' divorce, sixteen-year-old Sammie Davis must deal with many changes in her life, including a move to New York City which brings with it new discoveries and growth.

and articles to *American Girl, Girl's Life, Glamour, Teen People, Jump, Self, Los Angeles Times, Seventeen,* and *Shape.* Contributing editor, *Ms.*

Sidelights

Carolyn Mackler writes young-adult novels about ordinary girls who feel awkward about themselves and are trying to find a place in their world. In addition to writing popular novels with eye-catching, quirky titles that include *Love and Other Four-Letter Words, The Earth, My Butt, and Other Big Round Things,* and *Vegan Virgin Valentine,* she has also published short stories and articles in a variety of magazines, including *Seventeen, Girl's Life,* and *American Girl.*

Mackler grew up in western New York state in a house of storytellers. Her mother read to her constantly, while her father told stories about his life. When she

was four or five years old, Mackler used a tape recorder to record herself reciting her own stories, and later, in high school, she moved to writing in daily journals, mostly about the boys she had crushes on. While a student at Vassar College, she began to formally write stories and poems, and after graduating in 1995, she started writing the manuscript that became her first novel, *Love and Other Four-Letter Words.*

Love and Other Four-Letter Words is a coming-of-age story about sixteen-year-old Sammie Davis, whose parents are going through a trial separation. Her college-professor father decides to go to California, while her mother, overwhelmed by the situation, has become withdrawn and refuses to get out of bed, leaving Sammie to deal with making the best of things in their newly downsized home in a small New York City apartment. Meanwhile, Sammie's self-absorbed best friend Kitty has become sexually active and too involved with a new boyfriend to have much time for Sammie. Sammie herself struggles with her self-image, concerned over her heavy-set figure and her inexperience with boys. Vicki Reutter, reviewing the novel for *School Library Journal,* wrote that, "despite the stressful situation, there is a lighthearted element to the novel that keeps the mood balanced." "Many teens will read this for the facts about sex and growing up as well as the story," Hazel Rochman added in *Booklist,* calling *Love and Other Four-Letter Words* a "funny first novel."

In *The Earth, My Butt, and Other Big Round Things* Mackler again features a character with a self-image problem. Virginia Shreves belongs to the "perfect family." Her older sister Anaïs is in Africa with the Peace Corps; her brother Byron is a rugby star attending college; and her mother is a psychologist. Meanwhile, overweight Virginia is being pressured by her mother to go on a diet, and with best friend Shanna out of state for the school term, Virginia feels lonely and alone. Besides, the big question looms as to whether boyfriend Froggy really cares about her. When Byron is accused of date rape and kicked out of school, Virginia begins to realize that maybe her "perfect family" is not so perfect after all. Michele Winship, reviewing the novel in *Kliatt,* called *The Earth, My Butt, and Other Big Round Things* "funny, touching, and very real," while a critic for *Kirkus Reviews* wrote that "Virginia's emotions progress from despondence to anger, joy, and strong independence, all portrayed with clarity." A critic for *Publishers Weekly* maintained that "the heroine's transformation into someone who finds her own style and speaks her own mind is believable—and worthy of applause."

A type-A teen is the focus of *Vegan Virgin Valentine,* which finds high school senior Mara Valentine vying with an ex-boyfriend for the valedictorian spot while trying to counteract the disappointment her parents feel over the foibles of an older sister, now in her mid-thirties. When her sister's daughter, Mara's slightly younger niece, V, comes to live with the family, Mara's life—and assumptions—are thrown into a tailspin: V smokes pot, cuts class, wears skimpy clothes, and breaks all the rules Mara lives her life by. With V's help, when a new romance blooms with a less-than-"perfect" young man, Mara is able to reassess her situation and be open to new possibilities, in a "fast, often humorous" book that touches on "the universal theme of growing up and figuring out what's important," according to *School Library Journal* reviewer Karyn N. Silverman. While V also makes a turn-around and finds herself through acting, her character serves more as a "catalyst" for Mara, noted *Booklist* contributor Ilene Cooper. Citing Mara's decision to let go of feeling responsible for her parents' feelings and the teen's willingness to be less strident in her opinions, Cooper added that Mackler's protagonist undergoes a "transformation . . . [that is] entirely credible and, for readers, . . . thoroughly enjoyable."

As Mackler explained in an interview posted on her Web site: "I'm a professional snoop. As I ride in the subway or walk in Central Park, I eavesdrop on any teenager who comes within earshot." "None of the events in my novels have happened to me," she added. "But at the same time, when I'm writing a story, I often draw on my feelings (about my parents' divorce or my first relationship or a challenging friendship) and that helps me create more realistic characters."

Biographical and Critical Sources

PERIODICALS

American Libraries, December, 2001, Beverly Goldberg, "Principal Bans Love," p. 25.
Booklist, August, 2000, Hazel Rochman, review of *Love and Other Four-Letter Words,* p. 2131; June 1, 2004, Ilene Cooper, review of *Vegan Virgin Valentine,* p. 256
Bookseller, November 9, 2001, review of *Love and Other Four-Letter Words,* p. 36.
Journal of Adolescent and Adult Literacy, November, 2002, review of *Love and Other Four-Letter Words,* p. 216.
Kirkus Reviews, June 15, 2003, review of *The Earth, My Butt, and Other Big Round Things,* p. 861.
Kliatt, July, 2003, Michele Winship, review of *The Earth, My Butt, and Other Big Round Things,* p. 14.
Observer (London, England), February 17, 2002, review of *Love and Other Four-Letter Words.*
Publishers Weekly, September 25, 2000, review of *Love and Other Four-Letter Words,* p. 118; July 21, 2003, review of *The Earth, My Butt, and Other Big Round Things,* p. 197.
School Library Journal, December, 1999, Becky Ferrall, review of *250 Ways to Make America Better,* p. 166; September, 2000, Vicki Reutter, review of *Love and Other Four-Letter Words,* p. 233; August, 2004, Karyn N. Silverman, review of *Vegan Virgin Valentine,* p. 228.

ONLINE

Carolyn Mackler Web site, http://www.carolynmackler. com/ (January 23, 2005).*

MARSTON, Elsa 1933-

Personal

Born March 18, 1933, in Newton, MA; daughter of Everett Carter (a professor of English) and Harriet (Peirce) Marston; married Iliya Harik (a professor of political science), July 25, 1959; children: Ramsay, Amahl, Raif. *Ethnicity:* "Anglo-Saxon." *Education:* Attended Vassar College, 1950-52; University of Iowa, B.A., 1954; Radcliffe College, M.A., 1957; attended American University of Beirut, 1957-59; Indiana University, M.S. (art education), 1980. *Hobbies and other interests:* Tennis.

Addresses

Home—1926 Dexter St., Bloomington, IN 47401. *E-mail*—harik@indiana.edu.

Career

American University of Beirut, Beirut, Lebanon, instructor in English, 1959; Pig Industry Development Authority, London, England, secretary, 1959-60; American Society for Public Administration, Chicago, IL, editor and liaison, 1960-63; freelance writer, 1983—; instructor, Institute of Children's Literature, 1985-89. Artist, with exhibitions in Tunisia, 1975, and New York, 1979. President of cooperative nursery school, 1976-77; coordinator of local jail improvement committee and director of local art gallery, both 1980-81.

Member

National Society of Arts and Letters, Authors Guild, Authors League, Society of Children's Book Writers and Illustrators, Nature Conservancy.

Awards, Honors

Illinois Wesleyan Writers' Conference, short story award, 1983; Society of Children's Book Writers, Oklahoma chapter, young-adult short story contest winner, 1989; *Highlights for Children* historical article award, 1991; *Highlights for Children* fiction contest winner, 1992, and International Reading Association Paul A. Witty Short Story Award, 1994, both for "The Olive Tree"; New York Public Library Books for the Teen Age designation, and Friends of American Writers runner-up award for juvenile fiction, both 1997, and Bank Street College Best Book of the Year, 1998, all for *The Fox Maiden.*

Writings

FICTION

The Cliffs of Cairo (juvenile novel), Beaufort Book Co. (New York, NY), 1981, new edition, Hoopoe Books (Cairo, Egypt), 1998.

Elsa Marston

How to Be a Helper (juvenile short stories), Doubleday (Garden City, NJ), 1982.

Cynthia and the Runaway Gazebo, illustrated by Fristo Henstra, Tambourine/Morrow (New York, NY), 1992.

A Griffin in the Garden, Tambourine/Morrow (New York, NY), 1993.

Free as the Desert Wind, Hoopoe Books (Cairo, Egypt), 1996.

The Fox Maiden, illustrated by Tatsuro Kiuchi, Simon & Schuster (New York, NY), 1996.

The Ugly Goddess, Cricket Books (Chicago, IL), 2002.

Figs and Fate: Stories about Growing up in the Arab World, Braziller (New York, NY), 2005.

NONFICTION

Some Artists: Their Lives, Loves, and Luck, Cambridge Book Co. (New York, NY), 1983.

Art in Your Own Home Town, Cambridge Book Co. (New York, NY), 1984.

The Politics of Education in Colonial Algeria, Ohio University Press (Athens, OH), 1984.

Mysteries in American Archaeology, Walker (New York, NY), 1986.

The Lebanese in America, Lerner Publications (Minneapolis, MN), 1987.

Lebanon: New Light in an Ancient Land, Dillon/Macmillan (New York, NY), 1994.

The Ancient Egyptians, Marshall Cavendish (Freeport, NY), 1995.

(With son, Ramsay M. Harik) *Women in the Middle East: Tradition and Change,* Franklin Watts (New York, NY), 1996, revised and expanded edition, 2003.

Muhammad of Mecca, Prophet of Islam, Franklin Watts (New York, NY), 1999.

The Phoenicians, Benchmark Books (New York, NY), 2001.

The Byzantine Empire, Benchmark Books (New York, NY), 2002.

OTHER

(Adaptor) *The Phoenix and the Carpet* (juvenile play; based on the novel by E. Nesbit), first produced in Bloomington, IN, 1984.

Stories anthologized in *Join In: Multiethnic Stories for Young Adults,* edited by Donald Gallo, Delacorte (New York, NY), 1993; *Short Circuits: Thirteen Shocking Stories by Outstanding Writers for Young Adults,* edited by Gallo, Dell (New York, NY), 1992; *Soul Searching: Thirteen Stories about Faith and Belief,* edited by Lisa Rowe Fraustino, Simon & Schuster (New York, NY), 2002; *First Crossing, and Other Stories of Immigrant Teens,* edited by Gallo, Candlewick Press (New York, NY), 2004; and *Memories of Sun: Stories of Africa and America,* edited by Jane Kurtz, Greenwillow Press (New York, NY), 2004. Also contributor of essays, reviews, and other articles to numerous other books. Contributor of stories, articles, and reviews to periodicals, including *ASK, Calliope, Cricket, Faces, Highlights for Children, Multicultural Review, Hopscotch, Modern Journal of Ancient Egypt, Odyssey, Single Parent, Looking Glass Online,* and *Writer.*

Sidelights

Elsa Marston incorporates her lifelong interest in Middle-Eastern history and culture into both nonfiction and fiction for younger readers. "Having lived in several countries of the Middle East and North Africa, with family ties through marriage, I am still very much a New England Yankee at heart but drawn to the history and peoples of the Arab world," she once explained. In her fiction works, which include *A Griffin in the Garden, The Fox Maiden,* and *The Ugly Goddess,* she often combines everyday events with an element of the fantastic. In *The Fox Maiden* a mountain fox draws on magic powers to transform itself into a beautiful young woman so that it can become part of the human society in the valley below, and a young Egyptian princess who is destined to become the wife of the Sun king Amun is released from kidnappers and reunited with her true love, a Greek prince, through the aid of the Ugly Goddess Taweret. In *School Library Journal* Angela J. Reynolds praised *The Ugly Goddess* for its "fast-paced story and interesting characters," while in *Booklist* Hazel

Rochman dubbed the book a "quirky novel of ancient Egypt [that] blends well-researched history, fiction, and fantasy." Much of Marston's work is nonfiction, which she has produced in the hopes that it will help "young Americans acquire a better understanding of the Middle East, present and past." *Women in the Middle East: Tradition and Change,* which Marston coauthored with her eldest son, Ramsay M. Harik, was praised by *School Library Journal* reviewer Jane Halsall for offering young readers "a remarkable look at the diversity and changes in the lives of contemporary Middle Eastern women" within a culture that is undergoing revolutionary changes. In a 2003 update of the 1996 edition, Marston and Harik expand their discussion to include recent information on women's advances in the areas of health, politics, religion, and veiling, and expand their focus to include Afghanistan. In *Booklist,* Hazel Rochman noted the book's balanced perspective, and cited the authors' "extensive personal experience in the region" as contributing to the book's value. Other nonfiction works include three volumes in Marshall Cavendish's "Cultures of the Past" series: *The Ancient Egyptians, The Phoenicians,* and *The Byzantine Empire.* Featuring a wealth of illustrations, the volumes explore some of the unique characteristics of these now-vanished cultures,

and open a window into the day-to-day lives of those whose lives were a part of them. In a review of *The Byzantine Empire* for *School Library Journal,* Cynthia M. Sturgis praised the book as a "clearly written and well organized" overview of the sophisticated Greek-based culture that, from its base at Constantinople (now Istanbul), withstood numerous attacks by Ottoman and other forces for over a thousand years.

In her work Marston employs a time-honored writer's technique: using the library. "Library research is half the fun," she explained; "I don't think the Internet will ever keep me out of the stacks. After a rough outline of a new story or article—I need some idea where I'm going—I compose on the word processor. Though hardly a stylist, I take pains to write well: I really do like grammar. The revision process—trying to work through the problems that pop up and incorporate new insights—brings me much greater pleasure than pain." Why does Marston write for younger readers? "For more reasons than I can mention: . . . There are inevitable limitations, and very little fabulous wealth; but the opportunity I find to explore almost anything in the world that interests me—and, above all, to leave some lasting good in the lives of young people—are at the top of my list."

Marston delves into the culture of the wealthy city-states of the Mediterranean region at the height of the Phoenician's power from roughly 1000 BC to 600 BC. (From The Phoenicians.*)*

From the majestic city of Constantinople, the Byzantines ruled the eastern Mediterranean region from the fourth to the fifteenth century as explained by Marston in her comprehensive history of the empire. (Cover illustrated by Robert Frerck.)

Biographical and Critical Sources

PERIODICALS

Booklist, January 1, 2003, Jean Franklin, review of *The Ugly Goddess,* p. 891; April 15, 2003, Hazel Rochman, review of *Women in the Middle East: Tradition and Change,* p. 1460.
School Library Journal, December, 2002, Angela J. Reynolds, review of *The Ugly Goddess,* p. 144; February, 2003, Cynthia M. Sturgis, review of *The Byzantine Empire,* p. 165; May, 2003, Jane Halsall, review of *Women in the Middle East,* p. 170.

ONLINE

Elsa Marston Web site, http://www.elsamarston.com/ (December 2, 2004).*

*   *   *

MCBRIER, Michael
See OLDER, Jules

McDERMOTT, Eleni

Personal
Female.

Addresses
Home—Queensland, Australia. *Agent*—c/o Author Mail, Ages to Ages Publications, P.O. Box 436, Mount Gravatt, Queensland, Australia 4122. *E-mail*—eleni@fdcqld.org.

Career
Family Day Care Association Queensland, Inc. (family day care and in-home care service), Balmoral, Queensland, Australia, resource and advisory officer. Formerly director of child care center and teacher.

Writings

Tears in a Treasure Box, illustrated by Suzy Brown, Ages to Ages Publication, 2002.
Cranky Granny, illustrated by Suzy Brown, Ages to Ages Publication, 2003.

Contributor of articles to periodicals.

Work in Progress
A sequel to *Cranky Granny* titled *Cranky Granny Shops Till She Drops.*

Sidelights
A family day care specialist by profession, Australian native Eleni McDermott is the author of the picture books *Tears in a Treasure Box* and her more recent effort, *Cranky Granny.* McDermott's purpose in writing *Cranky Granny* was to provide children with a humorous look at the human aging process and to hopefully enhance the relationship between today's youth and the elderly. In an article posted on the *Ages to Ages Web site,* Linda Muller quoted McDermott as commenting: "Childen who get to know or learn more about older people develop more positive attitudes towards aging and learn that growing old is not something to be feared. I want to explore that third-generation connection in a funny yet intimate way." McDermott plans to follow her book with a sequel entitled *Cranky Granny Shops Till She Drops.*

Biographical and Critical Sources

ONLINE

Ages to Ages Web site, http://www.ages2agespublications.com/ (September 6, 2004), Lisa Muller, "Cranky Grannies."

Aussiereviews.com, http://www.aussiereviews.com/ (January 5, 2005), Sally Murphy, review of *Cranky Granny.**

*   *   *

McFADDEN, Kevin Christopher 1961-
(Christopher Pike)

Personal

Born 1961. *Education:* Attended college. *Hobbies and other interests:* Astronomy, meditating, long walks, and reading.

Addresses

Home—CA. *Agent*—c/o Author Mail, Tor Books, St. Martin's Press, 175 Fifth Ave., New York, NY 10010.

Career

Writer. Worked as a house painter, factory worker, and computer programmer.

Writings

HORROR FICTION; FOR YOUNG ADULTS

Slumber Party, Scholastic (New York, NY), 1985.
Chain Letter, Avon (New York, NY), 1986.
Weekend, Scholastic (New York, NY), 1986.
Thrills, Chills, and Nightmares (short stories), Scholastic (New York, NY), 1987.
Spellbound, Archway (New York, NY), 1988.
Last Act, Archway (New York, NY), 1989.
Scavenger Hunt, Archway (New York, NY), 1989.
Gimme a Kiss, Archway (New York, NY), 1989.
Witch, Archway (New York, NY), 1990.
Fall into Darkness, Archway (New York, NY), 1990.
See You Later, Simon & Schuster (New York, NY), 1990.
Bury Me Deep, Pocket Books (New York, NY), 1991.
Whisper of Death, Pocket Books (New York, NY), 1991.
Die Softly, Pocket Books (New York, NY), 1991.
Monster, Pocket Books (New York, NY), 1992.
Master of Murder, Pocket Books (New York, NY), 1992.
Chain Letter 2: The Ancient Evil, Pocket Books (New York, NY), 1992.
The Eternal Enemy, Pocket Books (New York, NY), 1993.
The Immortal, Pocket Books (New York, NY), 1993.
Road to Nowhere, Pocket Books (New York, NY), 1993.
The Wicked Heart, Pocket Books (New York, NY), 1993.
Chained Together, Pocket Books (New York, NY), 1994.
The Midnight Club, Pocket Books (New York, NY), 1994.
The Return, Pocket Books (New York, NY), 1994.
The Visitor, Pocket Books (New York, NY), 1995.
The Last Story, Pocket Books (New York, NY), 1995.
The Lost Mind, Pocket Books (New York, NY), 1995.
The Starlight Crystal, Archway (New York, NY), 1996.

Christopher Pike's Tales of Terror, Archway (New York, NY), 1996.
Alien Invasion, Pocket (New York, NY), 1997.
Time Terror, Pocket (New York, NY), 1997.
Execution of Innocence, Pocket Books (New York, NY), 1997.
The Blind Mirror, Pocket Books (New York, NY), 1997.
The Star Group, Archway (New York, NY), 1997.
The Hollow Skull, Archway (New York, NY), 1997.
See You Later, Archway (New York, NY), 1998.
Christopher Pike's Tales of Terror, Volume 2, Pocket Books (New York, NY), 1998.
(With Jerry Olton) *Where Sea Meets Sky: The Captain's Table,* Pocket Books (New York, NY), 1998.
Magic Fire, Archway (New York, NY), 1999.
The Grave, Archway (New York, NY), 1999.

Also author of *Getting Even* in Scholastic's "Cheerleaders" series.

"FINAL FRIENDS" SERIES; FOR YOUNG ADULTS

The Party, Archway (New York, NY), 1989.
The Dance, Archway (New York, NY), 1989.
The Graduation, Archway (New York, NY), 1989.

"THE LAST VAMPIRE" SERIES; FOR YOUNG ADULTS

The Last Vampire, Pocket Books (New York, NY), 1994.
Black Blood, Pocket Books (New York, NY), 1994.
Red Dice, Pocket Books (New York, NY), 1995.
The Phantom: The Last Vampire, Pocket Books (New York, NY), 1996.
Evil Thirst, Pocket Books (New York, NY), 1996.
Creatures of Forever, Pocket Books (New York, NY), 1996.

"REMEMBER ME" SERIES; FOR YOUNG ADULTS

Remember Me, Archway (New York, NY), 1989.
Remember Me 2: The Return, Pocket Books (New York, NY), 1994.
Remember Me 3: The Last Story, Pocket Books (New York, NY), 1995.

"SPOOKSVILLE" SERIES; FOR CHILDREN

The Haunted Cave, Pocket Books (New York, NY), 1995.
Aliens in the Sky, Pocket Books (New York, NY), 1995.
The Howling Ghost, Pocket Books (New York, NY), 1995.
The Secret Path, Pocket Books (New York, NY), 1995.
The Deadly Past, Pocket Books (New York, NY), 1996.
The Hidden Beast, Pocket Books (New York, NY), 1996.
The Wicked Cat, Pocket Books (New York, NY), 1996.
The Wishing Stone, Pocket Books (New York, NY), 1996.
Cold People, Pocket Books (New York, NY), 1996.
Invasion of the No-Ones, Pocket Books (New York, NY), 1996.

The Witch's Revenge, Pocket Books (New York, NY), 1996.

The Dark Corner, Pocket Books (New York, NY), 1996.

Spooksville, Pocket Books (New York, NY), 1997.

The Thing in the Closet, Pocket Books (New York, NY), 1997.

Night of the Vampire, Pocket Books (New York, NY), 1997.

Attack of the Killer Crabs, Pocket Books (New York, NY), 1997.

The Dangerous Quest, Pocket Books (New York, NY), 1997.

The Living Dead, Minstrel Books (New York, NY), 1998.

Creepy Creatures, Pocket Books (New York, NY), 1998.

Phone Fear, Minstrel Books (New York, NY), 1998.

The Witch's Gift, Pocket Books (New York, NY), 1999.

OTHER

The Tachyon Web (adult science fiction), Bantam (New York, NY), 1987.

Sati (adult fiction), St. Martin's (New York, NY), 1990.

The Season of Passage (adult science fiction), Tor (New York, NY), 1992.

The Cold One (adult fiction), Tor (New York, NY), 1995.

The Listeners (adult fiction), Tor (New York, NY), 1995.

The Blind Mirror (adult fantasy), Tor (New York, NY), 2003.

Alosha (young-adult fantasy), Tor (New York, NY), 2004.

Adaptations

Several of McFadden's novels have been adapted as audiobooks.

Work in Progress

A sequel to *Alosha.*

Sidelights

With over half a million books in print, Kevin Christopher McFadden—who took his pseudonym Christopher Pike from a character in the long-running *Star Trek* television series—has made a name for himself as a master of the teen horror novel. Since his first novel, *Slumber Party* was published, McFadden produced fiction at a remarkable rate, and novels such as *Monster, The Hollow Skull,* and *The Grave* have given thrills and chills to young readers, much to the dismay of conservative parents, who recoil from the graphic violence and references to teen sexuality that are sometimes found in Pike's books. Praising McFadden as "probably one of the most original and exciting authors of teenage fiction this decade," Jonathan Weir noted in *Books for Keeps* that "His writing is flawless, his ideas breathtaking, and there's a mystique about him that's hard to pinpoint. He knows what his readers want and never fails to deliver."

Born in 1961, and starting his writing career after leaving college, McFadden did not set out to pen horror novels; he originally wanted to write adult mystery and

science fiction, but had little luck getting his book proposals accepted. By chance, an editor at Avon Books read some of McFadden's writing and saw enough potential to suggest that the young writer try his hand at a teen thriller. The result was the 1985 novel *Slumber Party.* McFadden wrote two follow-ups to *Slumber Party*—*Weekend* and *Chain Letter.* By the time *Chain Letter* appeared, word-of-mouth had made all three books bestsellers and "Christopher Pike" was fast on the way to becoming a publishing phenomenon. While after 2000 McFadden moved increasingly into adult novels and fantasy fiction such as the 2004 novel *Alosha,* his many teen novels continue to attract new fans.

Teenagers play a big role in most of McFadden's novels. His early books are especially noted for the presence of young female narrators whose observations about people and events are key to the novel's plotline. McFadden explained his use of female narrators to Kit Alderdice of *Publishers Weekly:* "I romanticize a lot about females because they seem more complex, and because

Teenager Ali Warner can save the Earth if she can uncover a powerful talisman at the top of a forbidden mountain, but to do so, she must pass a series of grueling challenges that demand physical power and metaphysical insight. (Cover illustration by Larry Rostant.)

in horror novels, it's easier for the girl to seem scared." Scaring the reader is a major goal of McFadden's; he spins plots that often involve such disparate elements as murder, ghosts, aliens, and the occult. Above all, he is savvy about what interests his teen readers, and includes references to current youth culture and concerns in his stories. "McFadden doesn't talk down to kids; he treats them as individuals," noted Pat MacDonald in *Publishers Weekly,* adding: "He writes commercial stories that teens really want to read." Even with an emphasis on murder and other ghastly deeds, McFadden has been praised for inventing well-defined characters whose motivations, good and bad, are examined in detail. Most of his characters, usually high school students, have lives that mirror those of average teens: they go to dances, throw parties, fall in and out of love, and sometimes have difficulty talking to parents and teachers. The difference between McFadden's protagonists and most real teens lies in how some of the fictional characters solve their more difficult problems. In *Gimme A Kiss,* for example, Jane tries to recover her stolen diary through a complicated plan of revenge that ultimately involves her in a killing. Melanie wins the lead role in a school play only to find herself playing detective after real bullets are placed in a prop gun in *Last Act.* And in McFadden's "Final Friends" series, the merging of two high schools results in new friendships, rivalries, and the violent death of a shy girl.

Sometimes McFadden's protagonists encounter problems that require particularly drastic measures. In *Monster,* "a brilliant horror story," according to Weir, Mary shoots three teens at a party, claiming they were actually monsters. Mary's best friend Angela doesn't believe her until the evidence becomes overwhelming. Then Angela decides to take over where Mary left off. Sometimes circumstances are less horrific but still drastic: In the fantasy novel *Alosha,* when thirteen-year-old environmentalist Alison Warner learns, telepathically, that she is actually queen of the Fairies, she has to save the world from a mass immigration of trolls, dwarves, and other mythical creatures who threaten to disrupt Earth's human dimension.

One of the reasons for McFadden's popularity among teen readers is that the violence in his books is graphically detailed. For some critics, such brutality does more harm than good. Amy Gamerman, writing in the *Wall Street Journal,* described McFadden's mysteries as "gorier than most," noting that they are guaranteed to make "Nancy Drew's pageboy flip stand on end." In *Harper's,* Tom Engelhardt stated that McFadden's books "might be described as novelizations of horror films that haven't yet been made. In these books of muted torture, adults exist only as distant figures of desertion . . . and junior high psychos reign supreme. . .. No mutilation is too terrible for the human face." McFadden has also been criticized for his treatment of teen sexuality and the afterlife. In his defense, he offers books such as *Remember Me,* in which a young murder victim tries to prove her death was not a suicide with

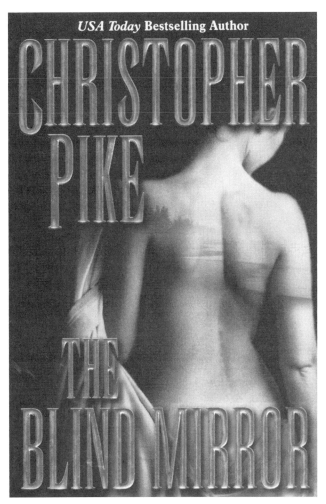

When he is told his ex-girlfriend has been killed in a savage, ritualistic murder, artist David searches for some answers despite the risk of what the truth may reveal. (Cover photos by Maria Taglienti and Chip Forelli.)

the help of another teen "ghost." As the author told Gamerman: "Teenagers are very fascinated by the subject of life after death. I got very beautiful letters from kids who said they were going to kill themselves before they read that book." James Hirsch wrote in the *New York Times* that the popularity of young-adult mysteries with increasingly action-filled plots reflects a teen readership that has "revealed more sophisticated—some say coarse—reading tastes." "Topics that were once ignored in . . . mystery books, like adolescent suicide and mental illness, are now fair game," Hirsch added. Michael O. Tunnell made a similar point in *Horn Book,* noting that "as readers mature, they graduate to a more sophisticated mystery" that follows "the 'rules' of mysteries more subtly. Readers must take a far more active part in unraveling plot and understanding characters."

While the bulk of his books have been geared for teen readers, McFadden has also penned several adult novels, including *The Cold One* and *The Blind Mirror.* Called a "briskly paced new sci-fi/fantasy/horror endeavor" by a *Kirkus Reviews* critic, *The Cold One* focuses on a university graduate student specializing in near-death experiences who comes into contact with an ancient being that sucks the souls out of its victims. Although initially faced with what looks to be a brutal serial killer, Julie and reporter Peter find themselves battling the Cold One, who is able to disguise itself as a human. Incorporating elements of Eastern philosophy, the work is "visceral and intellectually stimulating at the same time," Tim Sullivan noted in the *Los Angeles Times Book Review*. Praising such efforts, Sullivan went on to reference a well-known New England writer of the early twentieth century by describing McFadden as "a modern [H. P.] Lovecraft, a master of creeping dread relentless disturbing the reader."

In *The Blind Mirror* a California-based artist who has recently been deserted by his girlfriend, Sienna, returns from a trip to New York to find the corpse of an unidentifiable woman on the beach near his home. Soon David Lennon hears a familiar voice leaving messages on his answering machine and he wonders whether, in fact, he has murdered his lover in a ritualized fashion and her spirit is now tormenting him. Soon vampirism, encounters with a series of old friends that bring up nagging questions from his past, time in jail on murder charges, and unethical medical experiments come into play, leading to what a *Kirkus Reviews* critic called a "bizarre denouement" to a "rattling good read." In *Publishers Weekly*, a reviewer praised McFadden for his "tight, clean writing and engaging secondary characters," dubbing *The Blind Mirror* "an entertaining . . . dark fantasy." Noting that David's "slightly surreal odyssey" compels readers to keep turning pages, *Booklist* reviewer David Pitt wrote that readers who "crave that hypnotic effect will find everything they need," while in *Library Journal* Jackie Cassada praised the fact that *The Blind Mirror* "relies more on atmosphere than gore for its emotional impact."

Ultimately, McFadden writes mysteries because he enjoys the work. His attraction to the young-adult genre is partially due to the fact that he finds teenage characters "extreme," more prone to exaggerated actions and reactions. While he appreciates the celebrity status his readers have given "Christopher Pike," McFadden also admits there is a down side to literary fame. "A bunch of kids found out where I lived and I had to move," he told Gamerman. "It spread like a rumor where I was. . . .. It got weird. I have very intense fans."

Biographical and Critical Sources

PERIODICALS

Booklist, December 15, 1993, Candace Smith, review of *Fall into Darkness* (audio book), p. 772; December 15, 1994, p. 736; November 15, 1995, Mary Romano Marks, review of *The Lost Mind*, p. 548; May 1, 2003, David Pitt, review of *The Blind Mirror*, p. 1552.

Books for Keeps, November, 1994, Jonathan Weir, "Christopher Pike: Master of Murder," pp. 8-9.

Harper's, June, 1991, Tom Engelhardt, "Reading May Be Harmful to Your Kids," pp. 55-62.

Horn Book, March-April, 1990, Michael O. Tunnell, "Books in the Classroom: Mysteries," pp. 242-244.

Kirkus Reviews, November 1, 1994, review of *The Cold One*, pp. 1439-1440; April 1, 2003, review of *The Blind Mirror,* p. 502.

Kliatt, July, 2004, Michele Winship, review of *Alosha*, p. 12.

Library Journal, April 15, 2003, Jackie Cassada, review of *The Blind Mirror*, p. 130; July, 2004, Jackie Cassada, review of *Alosha*, p. 76.

Los Angeles Times Book Review, April 30, 1995, Tim Sullivan, review of *The Cold One*, p. 8.

New York Times, October 9, 1988, James Hirsch, "Nancy Drew Gets Real."

Publishers Weekly, April 29, 1988, Kit Alderdice, "Archway Launches Christopher Pike Novels in Multi-Book Contract," p. 49; January 12, 1990, review of *Fall into Darkness*, p. 62; June 29, 1990, review of *See You Later,* p. 104; August 17, 1990, review of *Sati,* p. 53; November 23, 1990, review of *Witch,* p. 66; February 15, 1993, review of *Road to Nowhere,* p. 240; June 14, 1993, review of *The Immortal,* p. 72; January 24, 1994, review of *The Midnight Club,* p. 57; November 21, 1994, p. 69; March 24, 2003, review of *The Blind Mirror,* p. 62; June 28, 2004, review of *Alosha,* p. 36.

School Library Journal, July, 1995, p. 96; November, 1995, p. 120; October, 2004, Donna Marie Wagner, review of *Alosha,* p. 176.

Voice of Youth Advocates, December, 1993, p. 312; June, 1994, p. 100.

Wall Street Journal, May 28, 1991, Amy Gamerman, "Gnarlatious Novels: Lurid Thrillers for the Teen Set," p. A16.*

*   *   *

McMENEMY, Sarah 1965-

Personal

Born August 2, 1965, in Welwyn Garden, England; daughter of James McMenemy (an advertising executive) and Gilia (Leather) Florentin-Lee (a homemaker and artist); married Malcolm Dixon; children: Georgia, Theo. *Education:* Attended Chelsea School of Art, 1983-84; Brighton University, B.A. (illustration), 1987. *Hobbies and other interests:* Dancing, theatre, cinema, live music, singing.

Addresses

Home—Crouch End, London, England. *Office*—Unit C105, The Chocolate Factory, Clarendon Rd., London N22 6XJ, England. *Agent*—Arworks, 70 Rosaline Rd., London SW6 7QT, England. *E-mail*—sarah@sarah mcmenemy.com.

In Sarah McMenemy's frolicking picture book, illustrated with her paper collage and gouache artwork, young Rosie acquires a new puppy, who promptly earns the name of Waggle because of his continually moving tail. (From Waggle.)

Career

Illustrator, beginning 1987. Commercial artist, with clients including periodicals, design groups, publishers, and businesses such as Toyota, Kodak, British Airways, Mastercard, Hertz, and Royal Mail. Visiting lecturer at Chelsea School of Art, Central St. Martin's School of Art, Liverpool School of Art, and Bath School of Art. *Exhibitions:* Work exhibited at group shows at Royal Festival Hall, Smiths Gallery, Hardware Gallery, Artworks Gallery, and Tallberg Taylor Gallery.

Member

Association of Illustrators.

Writings

SELF-ILLUSTRATED

Waggle, Candlewick Press (Cambridge, MA), 2003.
Jack's New Boat, Candlewick Press (Cambridge, MA), 2005.

McMenemy's work has been translated into Japanese.

Work in Progress

More books for children.

Sidelights

London-based illustrator and author Sarah McMenemy brings to life the close relationship between a young girl and her high-spirited puppy with her debut children's book, *Waggle.* When Rosie's father brings home a new pup for the family, the two new best friends find all manner of ways to keep busy. It is Rosie's task to choose a name for her new friend, which she does when she realizes that Waggle's tail never stops moving. Praising McMenemy's simple text and "bright, uncluttered collage illustrations," *Booklist* reviewer Helen Rosenberg described *Waggle* as "a truly satisfying read-aloud," while in *Publishers Weekly* a reviewer noted that the author/illustrator's "playful page design and enthusiastic narration" make her "a new talent to watch." "Young readers . . . will instantly adore this doggy dynamo," concluded a *Kirkus Reviews* critic.

McMenemy, who has also authored and illustrated the picture book *Jack's New Boat* in her characteristic loosely drawn ink-over-collage style, told *Something about the Author:* "I have worked as an illustrator for years, for a largely adult audience, on a broad range of projects from regular magazine columns to packaging, brochures for cars, schools, and hospitals. I've drawn on location in New York and Paris, and made eighteen images to go on large enamel panels in Shadwell Station for the London Underground. So it was a wonderful voyage of discovery and a steep learning curve to write and illustrate a children's book. My agent had shown some pictures and little books that I had done for my own children to Walker Books at the Bologna Book Fair. I met them back in London and we decided to create a picture book together.

"In creating my first book, *Waggle,* it was very satisfying to be able to tell a story that combined the experiences of playing with my children and my own memories of having a puppy as a child. I really wanted to convey the sense of fun and joy that a child and puppy find wherever they are. In creating the artwork for *Waggle* I wanted a sense of freshness and enjoyment, a simplicity of color, line, and movement. Using pure, bold colors was a daily uplifting experience. It was also a challenge to condense all lines and shapes to an essential minimum. I relished working as part of a small team with an editor and designer as illustration can be quite a solitary occupation.

"My original inspiration for drawing came from watching my mother drawing plants and pets in the garden. As a child I was fascinated by the ease and fluidity with which her line flowed onto the page. Drawing started to become a stronger theme in my life when, as a teenager and also through college, I generated income drawing facades of elegant Victorian terraced houses where my family lived in North London and also in Philadelphia, Pennsylvania, whilst on an exchange trip there.

"In school I was more drawn to painters than illustrators for inspiration. I loved the graphic work of Toulouse L'Autrec, Bonnard, Picasso, Dufy, and Matisse. I know now that the work of Edward Ardizzone, Eric Ravillious, and David McKee were important influences in my childhood reading. After having my daughter, I became very interested in children's books, and quickly found I had a strong opinion about what I liked. I admire illustrators such as Emma Chichester-Clark, Charlotte Voake, Lucy Cousins, Melanie Walsh, and Patrick Benson. I think the field of children's book illustration is one of the most exciting and vibrant areas of the business at the moment. It is also refreshing that it is not dominated by computer-generated imagery.

"I have a studio in an old converted chocolate factory where we hold annual open-studio exhibitions. I love going to art exhibitions and having fun with my children. I also love the city of Paris, and have visited it many times. I stayed there once for a few months, in the Bastille area, drawing every day. Inspiration was everywhere I looked!"

Biographical and Critical Sources

PERIODICALS

Booklist, May 15, 2003, Helen Rosenberg, review of *Waggle,* p. 1672.
Chicago Tribune, July 6, 2003, review of *Waggle.*
Kirkus Reviews, May 15, 2003, review of *Waggle,* p. 754.
Publishers Weekly, April 23, 2003, review of *Waggle,* p. 60.
School Library Journal, August, 2003, Carol Schene, review of *Waggle,* p. 138.

ONLINE

Sarah McMenemy Web site, http://www.sarahmcmenemy.com/ (January 17, 2005).*

*   *   *

MOORE, Liz
See MOORE, M. Elizabeth

*   *   *

MOORE, M. Elizabeth 1959-
(Liz Moore)

Personal

Born May 20, 1959, in Zwiebruken, Germany; daughter of Ronald Alexander and Mary Jennet (MacKinnon) Hunt; married Jim Moore; children: Jesse, Emily, Sam. *Education:* Wilfrid Laurier University, B.A., 1980; attended Saint Mary's University (Halifax, Nova Scotia, Canada), 1995-97, and University of Western Ontario, 2003-04; Althouse Faculty of Education, University of Western Ontario, B.Ed., 2004.

Addresses

Agent—c/o Author Mail, Orca Book Publishers Ltd., P.O. Box 5626, Sta. B, Victoria, British Columbia, Canada V8R 6S4. *E-mail*—lizmoore@rogers.com.

Career

Public school teacher in Ontario, Canada; presenter at writer's workshops and at public schools. Member, Althouse Faculty of Education choir, 2003-04.

Member

Writers Federation of Nova Scotia.

Awards, Honors

Centre for Communicative and Cognitive Disabilities Award for Academic Achievement and Practicum Skill, 2004; two-time winner of Atlantic Writing competition.

Writings

(Under name Liz Moore) *Zizi and Tish,* Orca Book Publishers (Custer, WA), 2003.

Sidelights

Liz Moore told *Something about the Author:* "I began writing when we lived in Halifax, Nova Scotia. Two of my stories, a children's story and a work of adult short fiction, won the Atlantic Writing competition. I wrote a popular column in the local paper of the village where we lived, and later in the town we moved to in Ontario.

"My love of writing for children has led me to becoming a teacher. While I hope and plan to continue writing, I look forward to sharing the joy of discovery of works with future students."

Biographical and Critical Sources

PERIODICALS

Booklist, May 1, 2003, Hazel Rochman, review of *Zizi and Tish,* p. 1605.
Resource Links, June, 2003, Isobel Lang, review of *Zizi and Tish,* p. 6.*

*   *   *

MORTON, Joseph C. 1932-

Personal

Born December 13, 1932, in Minneapolis, MN; married Deanne E. Morton (a homemaker), June 19, 1954. *Education:* University of Maryland, B.A., 1959, M.A., 1961, Ph.D., 1964. *Politics:* "Liberal Democrat." *Religion:* Presbyterian.

Addresses

Home—316 West Fremont St., Arlington Heights, IL 60004-5404. *E-mail*—DEMJCM@comcast.net.

Career

Waynesburg College, Waynesburg, PA, associate professor of history, 1964-67; Northeastern Illinois University, Chicago, professor of history, 1967-2001. Foreign expert at Nanjing University, Nanjing, China, 1990. *Military service:* U.S. Air Force, 1953-57.

Writings

The American Revolution, Greenwood Press (Westport, CT), 2003.

Work in Progress

Biographical sketches of the fifty-five delegates to the Constitutional Convention of 1787.

Biographical and Critical Sources

PERIODICALS

School Library Journal, July, 2004, G. Alyssa Parkinson, review of *The American Revolution,* p. 126.*

O

OLDER, Jules 1940-
(Lorraine Avery, a joint pseudonym, Michael McBrier, a joint pseudonym)

Personal

Born May 1, 1940, in Baltimore, MD; son of Morris (a certified public accountant) and Ruth (a social worker) Older; married Effin (a writer), 1965; children: Amber, Willow. *Education:* University of Vermont, B.A., 1962; New York University, Ph.D., 1970. *Hobbies and other interests:* Skiing, mountain biking, gardening.

Addresses

Home and office—P.O. Box 163, Albany, VT 05820. *Agent*—Sally Brady, Hartland Four Corners, VT 05049. *E-mail*—jules@julesolder.com.

Career

Writer and editor-in-chief of *Ski Press* and *Adventure Press.* Worked variously as a ski instructor, medical educator, college counselor, psychology professor, and writing instructor. Regular commentator on Vermont Public Radio.

Member

PEN, National Writers Union, North American Snowsports Journalists, League of Vermont Writers.

Awards, Honors

Books of the Year, National Book Guild of Great Britain, 1985, for *Jane and the Pirates;* runner-up, Other Award, 1986, for *Hank Prank in Love;* Best resort and travel production, and grand prize (co-recipient), both from International Ski Film Festival, and Vermont Travel and Tourism Recognition of Excellence, all 1995, all for *Tales from the Mountain: Mount Snow's First Forty Years;* Pick of the Lists, American Booksellers Association, 1997, and Best Books of 1997, Rathbone Children's Book Service, both for *Cow;* Kroepsch-Maurice Award for Excellence in Teaching, University of Vermont, 1997; four-time winner of Harold Hirsch Award for Excellence in Snowsports Writing; numerous awards and grants for work in the field of psychology, including New York University Department of Psychology's Philip J. Zlatchin Award, and New Zealand Psychological Society Award.

Writings

The Pakeha Papers, McIndoe (Dunedin, New Zealand), 1978.

Touching Is Healing, Scarborough House, 1982.

Hank Prank and Hot Henrietta, illustrated by Lisa Kopper, Heinemann (London, England), 1984.

Jane and the Pirates, illustrated by Michael Bragg, Heinemann (London, England), 1984.

Hank Prank in Love, illustrated by Lisa Kopper, Heinemann (London, England), 1985, Scholastic, 1991.

Don't Panic!, illustrated by J. Ellen Dolce, Golden Books (New York, NY), 1986.

Who Hates Harold?, illustrated by Bruce Lemerise, Golden Books (New York, NY), 1986.

Don't Start!, illustrated by Carolyn Bracken, Golden Books (New York, NY), 1986.

(With wife, Effin Older) *Hot Henrietta and Nailbiters United,* illustrated by Lisa Kopper, Heinemann (London, England), 1987.

(With Effin Older) *Little Smugglers,* Smugglers' Notch Ski Resort, 1987.

(With Effin Older, under joint pseudonym Michael McBrier) *Oliver's Barnyard Blues,* illustrated by Blanche Sims, Troll (Mahwah, NJ), 1987.

(With Effin Older, under joint pseudonym Lorraine Avery) *The Runaway Winner,* illustrated by Linda Thomas, Troll (Mahwah, NJ), 1990.

(With Effin Older, under joint pseudonym Lorraine Avery) *The Creepy Carousel,* illustrated by Linda Thomas, Troll (Mahwah, NJ), 1990.

(With Effin Older) *Hank and Henrietta Take Off,* illustrated by Lisa Kopper, Heinemann (London, England), 1991.

Shipwreck!, Octopus (New Zealand), 1991.

Ski Vermont!, Chelsea Green Press, 1991.

Ben & Jerry—The Real Scoop!, illustrated by Lyn Severance, Chapters Publishing, 1993.

Cow, illustrated by Lyn Severance, Charlesbridge (Watertown, MA), 1997.

Anita! The Woman behind the Body Shop, illustrated by Lisa Kopper, Charlesbridge (Watertown, MA), 1998.

Cross-Country Skiing for Everyone, photography by Effin Older, Stackpole Books (Mechanicsburg, PA), 1998.

Telling Time: How to Tell Time on Digital and Analog Clocks!, illustrated by Megan Halsey, Charlesbridge (Watertown, MA), 2000.

Backroad and Offroad Biking, Stackpole Books (Mechanicsburg, PA), 2000.

Ice Cream, illustrated by Lyn Severance, Charlesbridge (Watertown, MA), 2002.

Pig, illustrated by Lyn Severance, Charlesbridge (Watertown, MA), 2004.

Also co-author, with Effin Older, of screenplay *Tales from the Mountain: Mount Snow's First Forty Years.* Contributor of articles to newspapers and magazines, including London *Times, New York Times, Los Angeles Times, Washington Times, Guardian, GEO, Hemispheres, New Choices, Skiing, USAir, Powder,* and *Cross Country Skier.* Columnist for *Vermont Business.*

Sidelights

Something of a celebrity in his home state of Vermont due to his public profile as a radio commentator and newspaper columnist, as well as the editor-in-chief of two of the region's major magazines focusing on winter sports, Jules Older has also found time to write both fiction and nonfiction for younger readers. Published in England and New Zealand as well as in the United States, his books range from the fictional adventures of young boys and girls in *Jane and the Pirates, Hank Prank in Love,* and *Who Hates Harold?* to nonfiction picture books about cows, ice cream, and famous entrepreneurs. Several of his books, including *Hot Hen-*

The history of ice cream and various facts about the dairy treat can be found in Older's lighthearted picture book on the subject. (Cover illustration by Lyn Severance.)

rietta and Nailbiters United, Little Smugglers, and *Hank and Henrietta Take Off,* have been collaborations between Older and Older's wife, author and photographer Effin Older.

Older grew up in Baltimore, Maryland, and attended the University of Vermont because, as he once told *Something about the Author,* "I wanted to see if I could survive in the Frozen North; and . . . they (then) accepted under-achievers." While at University of Vermont he learned the sport he would frequently write about—and sometimes teach—as an adult: skiing. "As an undergraduate I participated in the historic picketing of Woolworths [Department Store], one of the first attempts at ending racial segregation in the United States. I also helped lead one of the first of the sixties campus protests, in our case, against unwarranted intrusion into the private lives of students. The protest was peaceful, humorous, serious, and successful." Other accomplishments included editing the campus newspaper, the *Vermont Cynic,* and meeting the woman who would later become his wife.

Older's academic future gained its path from a most unpromising source: a summer job spent working as a ditch-digger. "At first I was a success," he told *SATA,* "but that success created problems. The company hired another college boy, the owner's nephew, and we spent more time talking than we did digging. By week's end, we were both fired. Now unemployed, and with more than half a summer to go, I signed on as a child care worker at a hospital for disturbed kids. Despite bruised shins, a sore jaw, and some amazing new word combinations in my vocabulary, I got hooked on the helping racket and spent the next few months as a nurse's aide in the locked ward of a psychiatric hospital and as a trainee with disturbed preschoolers. By now I was thoroughly addicted and went on to study clinical psychology at New York University, which eventually gave me a Ph.D."

Time spent in New York City as a student also proved eventful for Older: "I was: a.) arrested for allegedly assaulting the biggest policeman in New York while I was leading a civil rights picket line (I weighed 145 pounds at the time, the cop weighed at least 200, and I've never been *that* crazy!); b.) given the Philip J. Zlatchen Award for Courage in Serving Humanity; and c.) congratulated by all the local cops and most of my neighbors for hitting an armed junkie with a brick as he was robbing my neighbor's apartment." Not long after his altercation with the armed drug abuser, Older and his wife decided that New Zealand might make a nice change from the bustle of New York.

In New Zealand Older worked for Otago Medical School, coordinating the school's behavioral science course. Not surprisingly, he also pursued several other outside interests. "For three years I hosted *American Pie,* a weekly radio show on a rock-and-roll station. A critic described it as 'one of the most original and indi-

vidualistic programmes to be heard in New Zealand.' And, largely through having the right accent at the right time, I played the lead in a TV documentary about the last man to be hanged in New Zealand. I am one of the happy few who have been hung and are still walking. While in New Zealand I was [also] an organizer of a successful day of learning about Maori land rights and was a frequent visitor to the New Zealand Women's Prison. It was a proud moment when the inmates gave me the Good Guy of the Month Award."

Returning to the United States in 1986, Older and his wife moved to Vermont, deciding to make a career shift to freelance writing. In addition to writing children's books and writing on skiing, he has published articles about travel, food, gardening, and working from home. Older has also taught a writing class at his alma mater, and won the University of Vermont teaching award in 1997.Older's first children's book, *Hank Prank and Hot Henrietta* chronicles the everyday adventures of young Hank and his sister Henrietta. A *Junior Bookshelf* critic considered the stories of "excellent length for bedtime reading" and complimented their "agreeable authenticity." Similarly, a *Books for Keeps* reviewer recommended the book for its "super dialogue" and "fresh and tangy" jokes.

In 1997's *Cow,* Older and illustrator Lyn Severance team up for an entertaining and educational look at dairy cows. Deborah Stevenson, reviewing the book for the *Bulletin of the Center for Children's Books* commended the collaborators for the book's "cheerful simplified graphics and ebullient text," while a *Publishers Weekly* contributor described *Cow* as a "trivial but amusing offering" that would pair well with a pint of ice cream. Older has since followed *Cow* with the equally concisely titled *Pig,* which contains enough pig-related facts to satisfy even the most curious pig enthusiast.

Perhaps because Vermont has a strong dairy industry, Older has published several books that, like *Cow,* focus on dairy products; specifically one dairy product: ice cream. His first collaboration with Severance, *Ben & Jerry—The Real Scoop!,* profiles the Vermont-based company that in the 1990s became well-known for their hip-folksy attitude and creation of such flavors as "Cherry Garcia" after Grateful Dead lead guitarist Jerry Garcia. The book also benefited from the fact that Severance is the designer of Ben & Jerry ice cream containers, and she brings that same style to her illustrations. *Ice Cream,* which the duo released in 2002, broadens the presentation of the ice-cream business to cover the history and manufacture of the frozen dessert, as well as all manner of ice-cream lore and trivia. Describing *Ice Cream* as "lighthearted and informative," *School Library Journal* contributor Marlene Gawron added that Older's "text is chock-full of facts along with wisecracks," while Ilene Cooper remarked upon the author's "sassy comments" and "irreverent look" at his subject in her positive *Booklist* review. Praising the

Older's signature wit is brought to play in his informative picture book about various breeds of pigs, with interesting facts and statistics. (Cover illustration by Lyn Severance.)

book in the *New York Times Book Review,* Kathleen Krull noted that *Ice Cream* hits its target audience due to its "bold, brassy, cartoony, wisecracky" style.

Biographical and Critical Sources

PERIODICALS

Booklist, March 1, 2000, Kathy Broderick, review of *Telling Time: How to Tell Time on Digital and Analog Clocks,* p. 1246; February 15, 2002, Ilene Cooper, review of *Ice Cream,* p. 1011.

Books for Keeps, November, 1987, review of *Hank Prank and Hot Henrietta.*

Bulletin of the Center for Children's Books, February, 1998, Deborah Stevenson, review of *Cow,* p. 215.

Junior Bookshelf, April, 1985, review of *Hank Prank and Hot Henrietta,* pp. 83-84.

New York Times Book Review, May 19, 2002, Kathleen Krull, review of *Ice Cream.*

Publishers Weekly, August 11, 1997, review of *Cow,* p. 400.

School Library Journal, March, 2000, Anne Chapman Callaghan, review of *Telling Time,* p. 230; May, 2002, Marlene Gawron, review of *Ice Cream,* p. 142.

Teaching Children Mathematics, May, 2001, Joanne L. Parent, review of *Telling Time,* p. 549.

ONLINE

Jules Older Web site, http://www.julesolder.com/ (December 2, 2004).*

P

PECK, Robert Newton 1928-

Personal
Born February 17, 1928, in Vermont; son of Haven (a farmer) and Lucile (maiden name, Dornburgh) Peck; married Dorothy Anne Houston, 1958; married Sharon Ann Michael (SAM), 1995; children: (first marriage) Christopher Haven, Anne Houston. *Education:* Rollins College, A.B., 1953; Cornell University, graduate coursework in law. *Religion:* Protestant. *Hobbies and other interests:* Playing ragtime piano, sports.

Addresses
Home—500 Sweetwater Club Circle, Longwood, FL 32779.

Career
Writer and farmer. Worked variously as a lumberjack, in a paper mill, as a hog butcher, and as a New York City advertising executive. Director of Rollins College Writers Conference, 1978-82; owner of publishing company, Peck Press; teacher and speaker at conferences. *Military service:* U.S. Army Infantry, 1945-47; served with 88th Division in Italy, Germany, and France during World War II; received commendation.

Awards, Honors
Best Books for Young Adults, American Library Association, and Spring Book Festival Award older honor, *Book World,* both 1973, *Media & Methods* Maxi Award (paperback), 1975, and Colorado Children's Book Award, 1977, all for *A Day No Pigs Would Die; New York Times* Outstanding Book designation, 1973, for *Millie's Boy;* children's book of the year designation, Child Study Association of America, 1973, for *Millie's Boy,* 1975, for *Bee Tree and Other Stuff,* 1976, for *Hamilton,* and 1987, for *Soup on Ice;* Books for the Teen Age, New York Public Library, 1980 and 1981, for *A Day No Pigs Would Die,* 1980, 1981, and 1982,

Robert Newton Peck

for *Hang for Treason,* and 1980 and 1982, for *Clunie;* Mark Twain Award, Missouri Association of School Librarians, 1981, for *Soup for President;* Notable Children's Trade Book in the Field of Social Studies, National Council for Social Studies/Children's Book Council, 1982, for *Justice Lion,* and 1986, for *Spanish Hoof;* Michigan Young Reader's Award, Michigan Council of Teachers, 1984, for *Soup;* Bologna International Children's Book Fair includee, 1985, for *Spanish Hoof.*

Writings

FICTION; FOR YOUNG ADULTS

A Day No Pigs Would Die, Knopf (New York, NY), 1972.
Millie's Boy, Knopf (New York, NY), 1973.
Soup, illustrated by Charles Gehm, Knopf (New York, NY), 1974.
Bee Tree and Other Stuff (poems), illustrated by Laura Lydecker, Walker & Co. (New York, NY), 1975.
Fawn, Little, Brown (Boston, MA), 1975.
Wild Cat, illustrated by Hal Frenck, Holiday House (New York, NY), 1975.
Soup and Me, illustrated by Charles Lilly, Knopf (New York, NY), 1975.
Hamilton, illustrated by Laura Lydecker, Little, Brown (Boston, MA), 1976.
Hang for Treason, Doubleday (New York, NY), 1976.
King of Kazoo (musical), illustrated by William Bryan Park, Knopf (New York, NY), 1976.
Rabbits and Redcoats, illustrated by Laura Lydecker, Walker & Co. (New York, NY), 1976.
Trig, illustrated by Pamela Johnson, Little, Brown (Boston, MA), 1977.
Last Sunday, illustrated by Ben Stahl, Doubleday (New York, NY), 1977.
The King's Iron, Little, Brown (Boston, MA), 1977.
Patooie, illustrated by Ted Lewin, Knopf (New York, NY), 1977.
Soup for President, illustrated by Ted Lewin, Knopf (New York, NY), 1978.
Eagle Fur, Knopf (New York, NY), 1978.
Trig Sees Red, illustrated by Pamela Johnson, Little, Brown (Boston, MA), 1978.
Mr. Little, illustrated by Ben Stahl, Doubleday (New York, NY), 1979.
Basket Case, Doubleday (New York, NY), 1979.
Hub, illustrated by Ted Lewin, Knopf (New York, NY), 1979.
Clunie, Knopf (New York, NY), 1979.
Trig Goes Ape, illustrated by Pamela Johnson, Little, Brown (Boston, MA), 1980.
Soup's Drum, illustrated by Charles Robinson, Knopf (New York, NY), 1980.
Soup on Wheels, illustrated by Charles Robinson, Knopf (New York, NY), 1981.
Justice Lion, Little, Brown (Boston, MA), 1981.
Kirk's Law, Doubleday (New York, NY), 1981.
Trig or Treat, illustrated by Pamela Johnson, Little, Brown (Boston, MA), 1982.
Banjo, illustrated by Andrew Glass, Knopf (New York, NY), 1982.
The Seminole Seed, Pineapple Press, 1983.
Soup in the Saddle, illustrated by Charles Robinson, Knopf (New York, NY), 1983.
Soup's Goat, illustrated by Charles Robinson, Knopf (New York, NY), 1984.
Dukes, Pineapple Press, 1984.
Jo Silver, Pineapple Press, 1985.
Spanish Hoof, Knopf (New York, NY), 1985.
Soup on Ice, illustrated by Charles Robinson, Knopf (New York, NY), 1985.

Soup on Fire, illustrated by Charles Robinson, Delacorte (New York, NY), 1987.
Soup's Uncle, illustrated by Charles Robinson, Delacorte (New York, NY), 1988.
Hallapoosa, Walker & Co. (New York, NY), 1988.
The Horse Hunters, Random House (New York, NY), 1988.
Arly, Walker & Co. (New York, NY), 1989.
Soup's Hoop, illustrated by Charles Robinson, Delacorte (New York, NY), 1990.
Higbee's Halloween, Walker & Co. (New York, NY), 1991.
Little Soup's Hayride, Dell (New York, NY), 1991.
Little Soup's Birthday, Dell (New York, NY), 1991.
Arly's Run, Walker & Co. (New York, NY), 1991.
Soup in Love, Delacorte (New York, NY), 1992.
FortDog July, Walker & Co. (New York, NY), 1992.
Little Soup's Turkey, Dell (New York, NY), 1992.
Little Soup's Bunny, Dell (New York, NY), 1993.
A Part of the Sky, Knopf (New York, NY), 1994.
Soup Ahoy, illustrated by Charles Robinson, Knopf (New York, NY), 1995.
Soup 1776, illustrated by Charles Robinson, Knopf (New York, NY), 1995.
Nine Man Tree, Random House (New York, NY), 1998.
Cowboy Ghost, Random House (New York, NY), 1999.
Extra Innings, HarperCollins (New York, NY), 2001.
Horse Thief, HarperCollins (New York, NY), 2002.
Bro, HarperCollins (New York, NY), 2004.

FICTION; FOR ADULTS

The Happy Sadist, Doubleday (New York, NY), 1962.

NONFICTION

Path of Hunters: Animal Struggle in a Meadow, illustrated by Betty Fraser, Knopf (New York, NY), 1973.
Secrets of Successful Fiction, Writer's Digest Books, 1980.
Fiction Is Folks: How to Create Unforgettable Characters, Writer's Digest Books, 1983.
My Vermont, Peck Press, 1985.
My Vermont II, Peck Press, 1988.
Weeds in Bloom: The Autobiography of an Ordinary Man, Random House (New York, NY), 2005.

Also author of songs, television commercials, and jingles. Adapter of novels *Soup and Me, Soup for President,* and *Mr. Little* for television's *Afterschool Specials,* American Broadcasting Companies, Inc. (ABC-TV).

Adaptations

Soup was adapted for television and broadcast by ABC-TV, 1978. *A Day No Pigs Would Die* was adapted for cassette and released by Listening Library; several of Peck's other novels have been adapted as audiobooks.

Sidelights

Beginning with his first title in 1972, *A Day No Pigs Would Die,* Robert Newton Peck has carved out a territory in YA fiction for himself. Dissecting the past, Peck takes readers back to a rural America which honors the old-fashioned virtues of hard work, self-sufficiency, and the importance of education. Often set in Vermont, Peck's stories reflect the influence of Mark Twain's *Tom Sawyer,* especially so in Peck's humorous set of books based on the character Soup. But Peck's works also engage serious themes, portraying adolescents in their struggles on the cusp of adulthood in such titles as *A Day No Pigs Would Die* and its 1994 sequel, *A Part of the Sky,* and the novels *Millie's Boy, Justice Lion, Spanish Hoof, Arly,* and *Arly's Run.* Teachers often appear in Peck's fiction where they serve as supporting and life-affirming role models, and he details their importance to his development as both an adult and a writer in his autobiography *Weeds in Bloom: The Autobiography of an Ordinary Man.* Born in 1928, the seventh child of rural Vermont farmers, Peck was the first member of his family to attend school. There he fell under the influence of an inspiring teacher, Miss Kelly, who he has often memorialized in his fiction in one guise or another. He also formed a childhood friendship with a young boy named Luther, nicknamed Soup, who has also become a fixture in Peck fiction. Peck's father slaughtered hogs during the difficult Depression years, and memories of this also feature in Peck's writing. Academically inclined, Peck went on to attend college, earning an A.B. from Rollins College in 1953 and then studying law at Cornell University. Married in 1958, he and his wife had two children while Peck pursued a successful career as an advertising executive in New York City. By his mid-forties, however, Peck was ready to try something different, and his love of books drew him to writing.

Peck's first novel, *A Day No Pigs Would Die,* is a semi-autobiographical account of his memories of growing up on his family's Vermont farm. Written in only three weeks, the tale portrays a young boy's coming-of-age when faced with the task of killing his pet pig, thereby becoming a man in the eyes of his Shaker family. Dubbed "charming and simple" by Christopher Lehmann-Haupt in the *New York Times Book Review,* the novel became an instant favorite, especially with reluctant readers, and also won numerous awards. Lehmann-Haupt went on to note that the novel is "a stunning little dramatization of the brutality of life on a Vermont farm, of the necessary cruelty of nature, and of one family's attempt to transcend the hardness of life by accepting it." This theme of the objective cruelty of nature and man's need to fit into its pattern has been replayed in much of Peck's subsequent fiction and nonfiction alike. Jonathan Yardley, also writing in the *New York Times Book Review,* remarked that *A Day No Pigs Would Die* "is sentiment without sentimentality . . . an honest, unpretentious book." Since its publication, the novel has found a place on most best-of-YA lists and has also been included in the curriculum of some college young-adult literature courses.

Peck reprised the protagonist of *A Day No Pigs Would Die* over two decades later in *A Part of the Sky.* With

Robert begins to understand his strict Shaker father and suffers through sacrificing his pet pig in Peck's nostalgic coming-of-age novel set in rural Vermont. (Cover illustration by Richard Hess.)

his father now dead, young Rob Peck is forced to work at a store in order to keep up with payments on the family farm. Most critics felt, however, that the sequel is not as strong as the initial title, which depicted the strong bond between boy and father and presented a compelling evocation of Shaker ideals.

Peck has revisited the coming-of-age theme in several other novels. In *Millie's Boy,* which takes place in Vermont at the turn of the twentieth century, he tells the story of another boy on the edge of adulthood. Left an orphan after his prostitute mother is killed, sixteen-year-old Tit Smith is chased by wild dogs when he runs away from the county work farm, and is ultimately taken in by a kindly doctor. A reviewer for *Booklist* noted that the novel contains "well-done characterizations, dialog and . . . background," and is "laced with adventure and humor."

In *Arly* and it's sequel, *Arly's Run,* Peck portrays teachers as positive and supportive. Miss Binnie Hoe serves up education as a way to freedom for the children of workers in the factory town of Jailtown, Florida. Young Arly is forced into labor too, as his father falls ill and bills need to be paid. Miss Hoe arranges for Arly's escape from the virtual prison of Jailtown. Jennifer Brown, writing in *Children's Book Review Service,* declared that this "is a powerful book which any caring adult should read," while Katharine Bruner concluded in *School Library Journal* that "Arly's adventures at school, his encounters with evil, his moments of grief and despair, remain vivid long after the last page has been turned." In the sequel, *Arly's Run,* the young boy discovers that freedom is something that must be won everywhere, and he ultimately finds a new home for himself. Kathy Elmore noted in *Voice of Youth Advocates* that his "historical adventure grabs the reader from the first chapter" and would serve as an "eye-opening" introduction to "the plight of migrant workers."

Both *Clunie* and *Spanish Hoof* mark a change of pace for Peck in that they feature female protagonists. His novel *Extra Innings* also features a strong female central character, this time an older woman named Vidalia, who inspires a young man with her stories of touring with an all-black, all-woman baseball team during the lean Depression years. *Clunie,* based on Peck's research at an institution, focuses on a young girl named Clunie Finn who is mentally disabled; she is relentlessly teased and called "simple" by her fellow students at school. The novel was praised as a "moving story, though not altogether free of sentimentality," according to a critic in *Kirkus Reviews.* Reviewing *Clunie* in the *New York Times Book Review,* Patricia Lee Gauch commented that "Peck has never been more the consummate storyteller than in this book about . . . a retarded farm girl caught in a web of adolescent cruelty."

In *Spanish Hoof,* Peck tells "an utterly predictable yet endearingly sweet-'n'-earthy tale of cattle-ranching in Depression-era Florida," according to a critic for *Kirkus Reviews.* Narrated by eleven-year-old tomboy Harriet "Harry" Beecher, the novel follows one family's attempt to stay above water financially, an effort that is aided by Harry's sacrifice: selling her horse to help save the ranch. *Booklist* contributor Karen Stang Hanley concluded that Peck's "rewarding story about a girl's departure from childhood and a loving extended family is . . . a natural for independent reading."

Spanish Hoof also introduced a new setting for Peck's novels when it was published in 1985. Whereas most of his early books are set in Vermont, after relocating to Florida in the 1980s, he began using that location more and more in his fiction. In *Hallapoosa* and *The Horse Hunters,* as well as in *Arly, Nine Man Tree, Cowboy Ghost,* and *Bro,* Peck spins his coming-of-age tales about young boys against a Florida backdrop. In *Hallapoosa* he presents an orphan brother and sister who are sent to live with a relative, a justice of the peace in the small southern Florida town of Hallapoosa, during the Depression years of the 1930s. Peck weaves a tale involving "murder, a kidnapping, and . . . return from the dead," according to a *Kirkus Reviews* contributor, who concluded that the author's "language is a pungent, evocative pleasure." In *Bro,* which also takes place in the 1930s, Tug Dockery, an orphaned boy is haunted by a horrific incident he witnessed at his grandfather's ranch six years before. Now orphaned by a train wreck that killed his parents and forced to live with his moody grandfather, Tug awaits the release from jail of an older brother who Tug hopes will rescue him from his ghosts; however, fate has other plans in store in a "compelling tale" that *School Library Journal* contributor Gerry Larson praised for its "wit, insight, compassion, and hope." *The Horse Hunters* once again evokes Depression-era Florida in its tale of a young boy who moves into manhood while on a wild mustang roundup. Reviewing *The Horse Hunters* for *Voice of Youth Advocates,* Allan A. Cuseo felt that this "coming-of-age epic" is "more lethargic" than Peck's other works, but that the author's "usual themes of endurance, freedom of choice, and humankind's basic goodness are affirmed."

In addition to mining the social history and customs of his own lifetime, Peck sometimes reaches into the more distant past when setting his novels. Taking readers back to the colonial and Revolutionary War periods, he has crafted the coming-of-age stories *Eagle Fur, Fawn, Hang for Treason, The King's Iron,* and *Rabbits and Redcoats.* Throughout these tales, Peck shares his love of history as well as his belief in the importance of the father-son bond. Additionally, he continues to employ a graphic style of writing well suited to descriptions of often violent circumstances.

During the mid-1990s Peck left writing and undertook a personal battle with cancer. Winning the fight, the author returned with more fiction in 1998. *Nine Man Tree* is set in 1931 in the backwoods of Florida where "an illiterate dirt-poor family suffers under the rule of an abusive father," according to a *Publishers Weekly* commentator. Eleven-year-old Yoolee Tharp protects his little sister Havilah, as well as his mother, from his father's drunken rages, but soon an even bigger enemy looms: a giant wild boar that is attacking and eating humans. Few tears are shed when Yoolee's father is killed on an expedition to kill the animal, but the boy suffers a loss at the death of Henry Old Panther, an elderly Calusa native who is ultimately killed by the beast, a long-time enemy that the Indian refuses to kill. Helen Rosenberg, writing in *Booklist,* remarked that in *Nine Man Tree* Peck "tells a haunting story in which the wild boar and the abusive father meet similar fates, but it is also an adventure and a . . . tale that will have reluctant readers glued to their chairs."

In *Cowboy Ghost,* Peck tells another growing-up story against the backdrop of a Florida cattle drive in the early years of the twentieth century. Young Titus battles

Seminole Indians and bad weather in the 500-mile drive, rising from cook's helper to leader of the drive. William C. Schadt noted in *School Library Journal* that readers will be "entertained by the way Peck portrays the cowboy lifestyle, including his liberal use of folksy, country jargon," and concluded that *Cowboy Ghost* spins "a good story."

Ranch life is also the backdrop of *Horse Thief,* which finds seventeen-year-old rodeo rider Tullis Yoder desperate to save the lives of thirteen rodeo horses after the Big Bubb Stampede Rodeo show that owns them goes bankrupt and plans are made to send the horses to slaughter. Joining with several unlikely partners—including a horse-thieving gambler and his daughter, a doctor—Tullis steals the horses, and soon finds that the crime stirs up more trouble than he could possibly imagine in a novel that *School Library Journal* reviewer Carol Schene called "witty, unpredictable, and a . . . story that refuses to take itself too seriously." Noting that the author's love of horses is apparent throughout the novel, *Kliatt* contributor Paula Rohrlick added that *Horse Thief* is a "fun, folksy read" that reflects Peck's "understanding of boys' longing to prove themselves." "Western fans are in for a treat," added *Booklist* reviewer Debbie Carton, dubbing the novel a "convoluted and surprisingly funny odyssey, chock-full of engaging characters."

While many of his books have involved hardships of one sort or another, Peck has penned several other books that, like *Horse Thief,* contain more-lighthearted fare. He turns to less-serious themes with his "Soup" series of books about young Rob and his friend, Soup. Soup is a boy who can talk Rob into almost any mischief, from smoking cornsilk to rolling downhill in a barrel. Episodic and filled with humor, the first novel in the series, *Soup,* chronicles life among poor, rural Vermonters during the 1930s. Critics compared the book to Mark Twain's *The Adventures of Tom Sawyer,* and a reviewer for *Booklist* called the first "Soup" title "a series of entertaining, autobiographical recollections." Peck has continued the "Soup" series in over ten installments, which have been praised for helping to bring reluctant readers into the literacy fold. Though Zena Sutherland reflected the feelings of some reviewers by noting in a review of *Soup for President* for the *Bulletin of the Center for Children's Books* that Peck's "corn-fed nostalgia" comes off as "just a bit too jolly," other critics have been more enthusiastic. Mary M. Burns wrote in *Horn Book* that the adventures of Soup and Rob succeed "primarily as a humorous reminiscence of small-town attitudes and customs in the pre-World War II era." Other titles in the series include *Soup on Ice,* "a story that portends the real Christmas spirit in subtle style," according to Peggy Forehand in *School Library Journal,* and *Soup 1776,* which *School Library Journal* contributor Connie Pierce called "a blast."

Biographical and Critical Sources

BOOKS

Children's Literature Review, Volume 45, Gale (Detroit, MI), 1997, pp. 93-126.

Fifth Book of Junior Authors and Illustrators, edited by Sally Holmes Holtze, H. W. Wilson (Bronx, NY), 1983, pp. 240-241.

Peck, Robert Newton, *Fiction Is Folks,* Writer's Digest Books, 1983.

St. James Guide to Young Adult Writers, edited by Tom Pendergast and Sara Pendergast, St. James Press (Detroit, MI), 1999, pp. 683-685.

Something about the Author Autobiography Series, Volume 1, Gale (Detroit, MI), 1986, pp. 235-247.

PERIODICALS

Booklist, April 1, 1974, review of *Soup,* p. 878; December 1, 1975, review of *Millie's Boy,* pp. 382-383; April 15, 1985, Karen Stang Hanley, review of *Spanish Hoof,* p.1198; June 1, 1994, p. 1799; January 15, 1995, p. 946; February 15, 1996, p. 1036; August, 1997, p. 1920; August, 1998, Helen Rosenberg, review of *Nine Man Tree,* p. 2008; February 1, 2001, Kelly Milner Halls, review of *Extra Innings,* p. 1046; May 15, 2002, Debbie Carton, review of *Horse Thief,* p. 1605; March 15, 2004, Carolyn Phelan, review of *Bro,* p. 1299.

Bulletin of the Center for Children's Books, June, 1978, Zena Sutherland, review of *Soup for President,* p. 165.

Children's Book Review Service, June, 1989, Jennifer Brown, review of *Arly,* p. 126.

Horn Book, May-June, 1978, Mary M. Burns, review of *Soup for President,* pp. 279-280; November-December, 1995, p. 776.

Kirkus Reviews, February 1, 1980, review of *Clunie,* p. 125; March 1, 1985, review of *Spanish Hoof,* p. J13; April 15, 1988, review of *Hallapoosa,* p. 567; September 1, 1998, p. 1291; May 15, 2004, review of *Bro,* p. 496.

Kliatt, July, 2003, Paula Rohrlick, review of *Horse Thief,* and Stacey Conrad, review of *Extra Innings,* p. 26; July, 2004, Paula Rohrlick, review of *Bro,* p. 11.

New York Times, January 4, 1973.

New York Times Book Review, January 4, 1973, Christopher Lehmann-Haupt, review of *A Day No Pigs Would Die,* p. 35; May 13, 1973, Jonathan Yardley, review of *A Day No Pigs Would Die,* p. 37; February 24, 1983, Patricia Lee Gauch, review of *Clunie,* p. 33; November 13, 1994, p. 27.

Publishers Weekly, July 21, 1997, p. 203; August 17, 1998, review of *Nine Man Tree,* p. 73; January 11, 1999, review of *Cowboy Ghost,* p. 73; January 15, 2001, review of *Extra Innings,* p. 77; June 10, 2002, review of *Horse Thief,* p. 61.

School Library Journal, October, 1985, Peggy Forehand, review of *Soup on Ice,* p. 192; June, 1989, Katharine Bruner, review of *Arly,* p. 108; March, 1994, p. 183;

August, 1994, p. 70; October, 1995, Connie Pierce, review of *Soup 1776,* p. 139; November, 1998, p. 126; March, 1999, William C. Schadt, review of *Cowboy Ghost,* p. 213; March, 2001, Todd Morning, review of *Extra Innings,* p. 255; July, 2002, Carol Schene, review of *Horse Thief,* p. 124; August, 2004, Gerry Larson, review of *Bro,* p. 128.

Voice of Youth Advocates, June, 1989, Allan A. Cuseo, review of *The Horse Hunters,* p. 105; April, 1992, Kathy Elmore, review of *Arly's Run,* p. 34.

ONLINE

Robert Newton Peck Web site, http://www.athenet.net/~blahnik/rnpeck/ (December 2, 2004).*

*   *   *

PIKE, Christopher
    See MCFADDEN, Kevin Christopher

R-S

RAND, Gloria 1925-

Personal

Born November 8, 1925, in San Francisco, CA; daughter of Roy E. (an electrical engineer) and Minnie Arthur (a homemaker) Kistler; married Ted Rand (an illustrator), May 1, 1948; children: Theresa Rand Schaller, Martin Lee Rand. *Education:* Attended University of Washington; attended writing course at King County (WA) night school.

Addresses

Home—7621 Southeast 22nd St., Mercer Island, WA 98040. *Agent*—c/o Author Mail, Henry Holt & Co., 115 West 18th St., New York, NY 10011.

Career

Writer.

Writings

Salty Dog, illustrated by husband, Ted Rand, Henry Holt (New York, NY), 1989.

Salty Sails North, illustrated by Ted Rand, Henry Holt (New York, NY), 1990.

Salty Takes Off, illustrated by Ted Rand, Henry Holt (New York, NY), 1991.

Prince William, illustrated by Ted Rand, Henry Holt (New York, NY), 1992.

The Cabin Key, illustrated by Ted Rand, Harcourt (New York, NY), 1994.

Aloha, Salty!, illustrated by Ted Rand, Henry Holt (New York, NY), 1995.

Willie Takes a Hike, illustrated by Ted Rand, Harcourt (New York, NY), 1996.

Baby in a Basket, illustrated by Ted Rand, Dutton/Cobblehill (New York, NY), 1997.

A Home for Spooky, illustrated by Ted Rand, Henry Holt (New York, NY), 1997.

Fighting for the Forest, illustrated by Ted Rand, Henry Holt (New York, NY), 1999.

Sailing Home: A Story of a Childhood at Sea, illustrated by Ted Rand, Henry Holt (New York, NY), 2001.

Little Flower, illustrated by R. W. Alley, Henry Holt (New York, NY), 2002.

Mary Was a Little Lamb, illustrated by Ted Rand, Henry Holt (New York, NY), 2004.

A Pen Pal for Max, illustrated by Ted Rand, Henry Holt (New York, NY), 2005.

Sidelights

Working in collaboration with her husband, illustrator Ted Rand, Gloria Rand has authored a variety of picture books, from adventure stories based on real-life occurrences to thoughtful works of fiction. Like her book series about a young dog and his master, Rand often focuses on the out of doors, whether it be sea or forest, and frequently casts animal characters, as in *Willie Takes a Hike,* about a runaway mouse, and *Little Flower,* which features a pot-bellied pig as its main protagonist. "My stories are usually based on a true happening," Rand once explained to *Something about the Author* (*SATA*), adding: "I research carefully with each new manuscript, no matter what the subject. Research usually means meeting interesting people, and that is a plus in life. It also frees me from worrying that I'm going to pass on misinformation to my readers, something I never want to do. I try to keep my writing simple and clear. If I find myself getting wordy, or over-writing, I read some Beatrix Potter, and that usually gets me back on track."

In her picture-book debut, *Salty Dog,* Rand introduces a young puppy and his human caretaker, Zack. Zack builds sailboats, and at first he brings his new housemate to work with him each day. In *Salty Dog* the young pup shows his ingenuity by figuring out how to get by ferry to Zack's boat shop after Zack begins leaving Salty at home because of the dog's increasing size. As the story progresses, so does work on Zack's new sailboat, and at story's end both dog and master sail off for

Little Flower, Miss Pearl's pet pig, uses her wiles to bring assistance when the elderly lady is injured in a fall in Gloria Rand's lively picture book based on a true story. (From Little Flower, *illustrated by R. W. Alley.)*

a trip around the world. *Salty Dog* "offers a pleasing nautical twist on the theme of boy-dog companionship," noted Ellen Mandel in a review for *Booklist. Salty Sails North* finds a now-fully grown Salty accompanying Zack on a sailing trip to Alaska. Along the way the pair encounter a rough storm, some Tlingit Indian artifacts, unfriendly wildlife, and treacherous icebergs. More high adventure marks the third entry in this series, *Salty Takes Off,* which takes place in Alaska. On one of his regular airborne jaunts alongside pilot Jarman, Salty falls out of the airplane during a turbulent part of the flight. "The drama and tension are scaled just right for the readaloud audience, who will of course also appreciate the canine protagonist," remarked Roger Sutton in the *Bulletin of the Center for Children's Books.* Likewise, *Booklist* reviewer Carolyn Phelan called *Aloha, Salty!,* in which Zack and Salty are swept overboard during a terrible storm off the coast of Hawaii, "a satisfying adventure for fans of *Salty Dog.*"

Rand's picture books *Prince William* describes the plight of the animal victims of the 1989 oil tanker spill in Prince William Sound, and centers her story on one seal pup that is rescued by a little girl. The book was praised for engaging children's sympathies without sentimentality and teaching them about ecological damage and human attempts to repair it without sermonizing.

Like *Prince William, Baby in a Basket* is also based on a real-life adventure. A small group traveling in the Alaskan winter of 1917 encounters disaster when a spooked horse overturns the party's sleigh, including a four-month-old infant sleeping in a basket. All narrowly escape to safety except the baby, whose basket is carried away downriver, where it is rescued by fur trappers. "The pacing is steady for scene-setting and swift for the crisis, and the details are well-chosen," commended a reviewer for *Publishers Weekly.* Sometimes the tables turn in life, and animals do the rescuing, as Rand shows in her 2002 picture book, which has its source in an actual event. In *Little Flower* a house-pig saves the day when her elderly owner, Miss Pearl, has an accident. Trained to roll over and play dead, just like a dog, is something Little Flower usually does at her affectionate owner's command. However, when Miss Pearl falls in her home, the wise and resourceful pot-bellied pig finds her way out of the house and into the street, where she rolls over and plays dead until a car stops and her owner is rescued. Rand's only book to be illustrated by someone other than her husband—in this case R. W. Alley—*Little Flower* has "flashes of both humor and drama," according to a *Publishers Weekly* reviewer who dubbed the work an "upbeat and poignant tale."

Rand's *A Home for Spooky* is also based on a real-life rescue, in this case the rescue of a scared and underfed dog. In the story, young Annie finds a stray dog and begins to secretly feed it, for she knows her parents will not allow any further pets in their home. Unfortunately, Annie's scraps are not enough to properly nourish the dog, whom she names Spooky, and he almost dies before Annie can enlist her parents' help to save him. "Worthwhile lessons" about compassion for animals and trusting parents "are bound together in this compelling book," Ellen Mandel concluded of *A Home for Spooky* in *Booklist.*

With *Willie Takes a Hike* Rand weaves what some critics found an exciting drama with a solemn message about the necessity of being properly prepared when hiking. Willie, a small mouse, disobeys his parents and hikes off into the junkyard, the family's new home, and quickly lands himself in trouble. "The message is . . . well integrated into the story," remarked Virginia Golodetz, adding in her *School Library Journal* review that "readers will stay involved in the drama." Rand's 1999 picture book *Fighting for the Forest* also has hikers as central characters, although this time they are a father and son, who discover that their favorite hiking trail is about to be deforested by loggers. In contrast to *Willie Takes a Hike* and *Fighting for the Forest, The Cabin Key* trades drama for atmosphere: in the book's simple plot, a young girl opens the door on her family's log cabin in the mountains, a place that, while lacking such modern amenities as heat and running water, is rich with her family's history. "Although there is virtually no plot here, what will hold kids are all the fantasy-building details of a cozy hideaway," contended Sutton in his *Bulletin of the Center for Children's Books* review.

Soft-hearted Annie feeds a stray dog she sees at a dump and tries to hide him until he falls ill and she must find help to save his life. (From A Home for Spooky, *written by Rand and illustrated by Ted Rand.)*

Rand once told *SATA:* "I began writing children's picture books . . . at the suggestion of my husband, book illustrator Ted Rand. Four elements in my background were a decided help. I had worked as a copywriter, saying a lot in small spaces, a requirement for picture books. I had taken one writing class, an extremely good ten-week course at night school. This gave me a sound basis for writing anything. I like to write and I'm a natural exaggerator, which doesn't hurt.

"My advice to aspiring writers: . . . Have fun writing. Write about what interests you, and if you don't know the subject well, research. Don't talk about writing, write."

Biographical and Critical Sources

PERIODICALS

Booklist, March 1, 1989, Ellen Mandel, review of *Salty Dog,* p. 1195; March 1, 1990, p. 1348; November 1, 1994, p. 509; April 1, 1996, Carolyn Phelan, review of *Aloha, Salty!,* and Shelley Townsend-Hudson, review of *Willie Takes a Hike,* p. 1373; April 1, 1998, Ellen Mandel, review of *A Home for Spooky,* p. 1333.

Bulletin of the Center for Children's Books, March, 1991, Roger Sutton, review of *Salty Takes Off,* p. 175; March, 1992, p. 191; October, 1994, Roger Sutton, review of *The Cabin Key,* p. 63.

Kirkus Reviews, March 1, 2002, review of *Little Flower,* p. 344.

Publishers Weekly, December 9, 1988, p. 64; April 13, 1992, p. 58; July 25, 1994, p. 54; October 27, 1997, review of *Baby in a Basket,* p. 75; February 18, 2002, review of *Little Flower,* p. 95.

School Library Journal, March, 1990, pp. 199-200; April, 1991, p. 101; November, 1994, p. 89; June, 1996, Virginia Golodetz, review of *Willie Takes a Hike,* p. 108; August, 2002, Jody McCoy, review of *Little Flower,* p. 165.

*   *   *

SHOUP, Barbara 1947-

Personal

Born May 4, 1947, in Hammond, IN; daughter of Richard (a payroll clerk) and Gladys (a department store clerk; maiden name, Farmer) White; married Steven V. Shoup (an attorney), January 29, 1967; children: Jennifer, Katherine. *Education:* Indiana University, B.S., 1972, M.S., 1976. *Hobbies and other interests:* Travel, art.

Addresses

Home and office—6012 Broadway, Indianapolis, IN 46220. *Agent*—Transatlantic Literary Agency, 72 Glengowan Rd., Toronto, Ontario, Canada M4N 1G4. *E-mail*—barbshoup@aol.com.

Career

Learning Unlimited, North Central High School, Indianapolis, IN, community programs coordinator, 1975-78; Indiana University, Bloomington, associate instructor in creative writing, 1979; Indianapolis Museum of Art, school programs coordinator, 1980; Broad Ripple High School Center for the Humanities and the Performing Arts, Indianapolis, writer-in-residence, 1982-2001; Prelude Academy, Indianapolis Children's Museum and Penrod Society, Indianapolis, coordinator, 1985-87, 2000; Butler University School of Education, adjunct instructor, 1998—; Writers' Center of Indianapolis, writer-in-residence and program coordinator, 2002. Member, Indiana Arts Commission grants panels, 1983-86; fiction judge, Society of Midland Authors and National Society for Arts and Letters, 1988; Butler University Writers' Studio literary fellow, 1999-2000; member, board of directors, Writers' Center of Indiana, 2002—.

Member

Authors Guild, Authors League, Indiana Teachers of Writing, Indiana Writers' Center, Midland Society of Writers.

Awards, Honors

Best Book in Field, Association for Experiential Education, 1980, for *Living and Learning for Credit;* master artists fellowship, Indiana Arts Commission (IAC)/ National Endowment for the Arts, 1990; Butler University Writers' Studio Literary fellowship, 1990-91, 1994; Pushcart Prize nomination, 1994; Notable Young Adult Book citation, *Bulletin of the Center for Children's Books,* 1994, Best Books for Young Adults designation, American Library Association (ALA), 1995, and Midland Society of Authors Children's Book Award finalist, all for *Wish You Were Here;* International Reading Association Young Adult Choice, and Great Lakes Book Award finalist, both 1998, and ALA Best Book for Young Adults designation, 1999, all for *Stranded in Harmony;* Eliot Rosewater Award nomination, 1998; Arts Council of Indianapolis Creative Renewal fellowship, 1999; IAC individual artist program grant, 2000.

Writings

NOVELS

Night Watch, Harper (New York, NY), 1982.
Wish You Were Here, Hyperion Books for Children (New York, NY), 1994.

Stranded in Harmony, Hyperion Books for Children (New York, NY), 1997.
Faithful Women, Guild Press (Carmel, IN), 1999.
Vermeer's Daughter, Guild Press/Emmis Publishing (Zionsville, IN), 2003.

OTHER

Living and Learning for Credit, Phi Delta Kappa, 1978.
(With Joan G. Schine and Diane Harrington) *New Roles for Early Adolescents in Schools and Communities,* National Commission on Resources for Youth, 1981.
(With Freddi Stevens-Jacobi) *Learning Unlimited: A Model for Options Education,* Washington Township Schools, 1981.
(With Margaret Love Denman) *Novel Ideas: Contemporary Authors Share the Creative Process,* Alpha Books (Indianapolis, IN), 2001.

Contributing editor, *Arts Insight,* 1984, and *Other Voices,* beginning 1991. Contributor to periodicals, including *Mississippi Valley Review, Crazy Quilt, Persuasions, Hurricane Alice, Other Voices, Louisville Review, Rhino, Artful Dodge, Writer, Voice of Youth Advocates, Nuvo Newsweekly,* and *New York Times.*

Sidelights

In addition to her long career as an educator, Barbara Shoup has been active as a writer, producing articles, poems, stories, and reviews as well as interviews for various periodicals and also penning longer works of fiction for children and adults. Her novels include *Night Watch, Wish You Were Here, Stranded in Harmony,* and *Vermeer's Daughter.*

Wish You Were Here, Shoup's first novel for teens, finds seventeen-year-old Jackson Watt attempting to weather the fall-out from his parents' divorce, trying to sort out his mixed feelings toward a now-absent friend, and figuring out where his responsibility for others ends— including an emotionally dependant girfriend he knows he does not love. "This ambitious debut touches on safe sex, death, self-worth, relationships, love, and the meaning of it all," noted a *Publishers Weekly* reviewer, while in *Booklist* Jeanne Triner praised *Wish You Were Here* as "beautifully written" and "a touching, thought-provoking, and very candid coming-of-age tale." "Jackson . . . is exactly the kind of teenager I love," Shoup once explained of her novel. "He's earnest and funny. He desperately tries to understand things. He's a much, much better person than he believes himself to be. What I find most compelling about him, however, is the grief he feels about his parents' divorce and how the divorce complicates the large and small problems of his adolescent life. I think that it is in the way Jackson wrestles with the ongoing effects of the divorce that he most poignantly represents so many real teenagers of his generation and offers some useful insights into their lives." Praising *Vermeer's Daughter* as a "warm, compelling story" that introduces readers to the "loving, but

BARBARA SHOUP

In her fictional account of the daughter of seventeenth-century painter Johannes Vermeer, Shoup depicts her creative longings, fuelled by her glimpses into the world of her father's artistic genius.

chaotic household" of the seventeenth-century Dutch painter Johannes Vermeer, *School Library Journal* contributor Kathy Tewell added that through Shoup's book "the luminous glory of Vermeer's masterpieces are brought vividly to life." While in *Vermeer's Daughter* Shoup creates a fictional protagonist in the person of Carelina—Vermeer did not have a daughter of that name—many of the historical details are accurate. Carelina serves as the painter's pupil and confidante, working alongside her father in his studio, and sits with him as he discusses the ideas of the day with friends. In addition, the young woman's passion for her father's work, and her continuation of her narrative two decades after her father's death, provides insight into not only Vermeer's art but also into the art's place within the culture that inspired it.

Shoup once told *Something about the Author:* "I wanted to be a writer from the time I understood what a book was. As soon as I learned how to form the alphabet, I began to write stories in a special blue notebook. I was eleven when I attempted my first novel, the story of a black slave girl journeying north by Underground Railroad. I came home every day after school and worked diligently, secretly until I got the story told. Certainly fame and fortune were imminent—or so I thought until we got to the unit on the Civil War in Social Studies and I learned that the slave railroad was not a subway train that ran from Atlanta to New York City, as I'd imagined it to be. I was so mortified by my mistake that I gave up writing for nearly twenty years. When I began again, it was because one of my high school students asked me whether teaching was what I had always meant to do with my life.

"Teaching has played an important part in my writing and my sense of myself as a writer ever since. I am infinitely fascinated by the lives of my young writers, inspired by the earnestness and courage with which the best of them approach their work. In my years as writer-in-residence at Broad Ripple High School's Center for the Humanities, I collected a wealth of insight about the lives of my students and their families. I've unearthed wonderful details that just cry out to be put into stories."

Biographical and Critical Sources

PERIODICALS

Booklist, October 15, 1994, Jeanne Triner, review of *Wish You Were Here,* p. 420; July, 1997, Randy Meyer, review of *Stranded in Harmony,* p. 1811.
Kirkus Reviews, August 1, 1982, p. 898.
Library Journal, October 1, 1982, p. 1896; October 1, 2001, Denise Sticha, review of *Novel Ideas: Contemporary Authors Share the Creative Process,* p. 116.
Publishers Weekly, July 30, 1982, p. 63; October 24, 1994, review of *Wish You Were Here,* p. 62; May 12, 1997, review of *Stranded in Harmony,* p. 77; July 28, 2003, review of *Vermeer's Daughter,* p. 96.
School Library Journal, September, 2003, Kathy Tewell, review of *Vermeer's Daughter,* p. 241.

ONLINE

Barbara Shoup Web site, http://www.barbarashoup.com/ (December 31, 2004).

*   *   *

SHREEVE, Elizabeth 1956-

Personal

Born January 17, 1956, in Riverhead, NY; daughter of Walton (a research physician) and Phyllis (Heidenreich) Shreeve; married Louis Robinson (a toy merchant), March 16, 1991; children: James, Samuel, David. *Ethnicity:* "Caucasian" *Education:* Harvard College, A.B.

Elizabeth Shreeve

(geology; cum laude), 1978; Harvard Graduate School of Design, M.A. (landscape architecture), 1983. *Politics:* Democrat. *Hobbies and other interests:* Gardening, hiking, piano, art.

Addresses

Home—15 Sky Road, Mill Valley, CA 94941. *Office*—SWA Group, 2200 Bridgeway, Sausalito, CA 94965. *Agent*—Barbara Kouts, P.O. Box 560, Bellport, CA 11713-0560. *E-mail*—elizabethshreeve@comcast.net.

Career

EDAW Inc., San Francisco, CA, resource planner, 1979-81; SWA Group, Sausalito, CA, principal planner, beginning 1984. School Environmental Education Docent (SEED), lead docent, 2000-02.

Member

Society of Children's Book Writer and Illustrators, Northern California Children's Booksellers Association.

Awards, Honors

Presidential Environmental Award, 1974, for *Carmans River Story: A Natural and Human History.*

Writings

(With Pamela Borg) *The Carmans River Story: A Natural and Human History,* privately printed, 1974.

Hector Springs Loose, illustrated by Pamela Levy, Aladdin Paperbacks (New York, NY), 2004.
Hector on Thin Ice, illustrated by Pamela Levy, Aladdin Paperbacks (New York, NY), 2004.
Hector Finds a Fortune, illustrated by Pamela Levy, Aladdin Paperbacks (New York, NY), 2004.
Hector Afloat, illustrated by Pamela Levy, Aladdin Paperbacks (New York, NY), 2004.

Work in Progress

A middle-grade fantasy novel.

Sidelights

In addition to her work as an environmental planner, California writer Elizabeth Shreeve has begun a second career as a children's book author. Her books, which focus on a six-legged wumblebug named Hector Fuller, include *Hector Afloat, Hector Finds A Fortune, Hector on Thin Ice,* and *Hector Springs Loose.* A *Kirkus Reviews* critic, remarking on Shreeve's first children's book, commented that in *Hector Springs Loose* Shreeve keeps the tone "light, though, tucking in tongue-in-cheek details." Overall the critic praised the book as "lighthearted, silly, challenging fare for easy reader graduates." Enjoying the amusing pencil sketches by illustrator Pamela Levy, *School Library Journal* reviewer Shelley B. Sutherland added that Shreeve's concise style makes her picture-book debut "well pitched to beginning chapterbook readers." Reading a more recent volume in the "Adventures of Hector Fuller" series, James K. Irwin appraised *Hector Finds a Fortune* for *School Library Journal* and concluded that "fans will look forward to more adventures starring this down-to-earth bug."

Shreeve told *Something about the Author:* "To engage children in reading, in living a wider and deeper life, and in delighting in the natural world—this is my primary motivation for writing.

"I was a great reader as a child—the classics: 'The Wizard of Oz,' 'Narnia,' and 'Mrs. Pigglewiggle' books—and I love to read to my kids. But I'd never written fiction until the bug hero, Hector Fuller, popped into my head. The name is a 'lady's swear word' invented by my grandmother, and the character became the basis for my four-book series that changed my life. Now I cannot imagine living without the double life of following a character through a plot.

"As for my writing process, my stories are inspired by my kids and by physical places, not surprising given my professional training in environmental design. I also strive to energize my writing with the humor and fast pace that kids expect these days. I love doing research; the animal characters in the 'Hector' series are all created around the clues provided by researching the real creatures. For example, Henriette the snapping turtle has a big appetite for food, singing—life in general! To make a story I hit on a basic problem, then I let little bits of the story come to me when I'm hiking or driving to work. I write every bit down, until I've got enough to weave together into a plot. I use outlines, but I stray quite a bit. My husband, a toy merchant, gets to hear all the rough drafts. He is my muse.

"Then I edit. I love it! And now I'm doing lots of school visits to talk to kids about bugs, books, and reading. The big reward is seeing children enjoy the books, and to receive their wonderful letters and drawings."

Biographical and Critical Sources

PERIODICALS

Kirkus Reviews, December 15, 2003, review of *Hector Springs Loose,* p. 454.
School Library Journal, March, 2004, Shelley B. Sutherland, review of *Hector Springs Loose,* p. 181; May, 2004, James K. Irwin, review of *Hector Finds a Fortune,* p. 124.

ONLINE

Elizabeth Shreeve Web site, http://www.elizabethshreve. com/ (January 4, 2005).

*   *   *

SMITH, Sherri L. 1971-

Personal
Born March 17, 1971, in Chicago, IL. *Education:* New York University, B.F.A. (film and journalism), 1991; San Francisco State University, M.S.B.A. (marketing), 1993; California State University, Dominguez Hills, graduate work toward M.A. (literature).

Addresses
Agent—c/o Author Mail, Delacorte Press, Dell Publishing, 1540 Broadway, New York, NY 10036. *E-mail*—letters@sherrilsmith.com.

Career
Disney TV Animation, Los Angeles, CA, development assistant, 1996-97, development associate, 1997-99; worked for a Los Angeles construction company; Bongo Comics, Santa Monica, CA, currently office manager.

Member
Society of Children's Book Writers and Illustrators.

Awards, Honors
American Library Association Best Book for Young People designation, 2003, for *Lucy the Giant.*

Teenaged Lucy joins the crew of a crabbing boat to escape her mean classmates and brutal, alcoholic father, then finds the experience brings her unhoped for camaraderie with the ship's crew. (Cover photo by Michael Frost.)

Writings

Lucy the Giant (young-adult novel), Delacorte Press (New York, NY), 2002.
Sparrow (young-adult novel), Random House (New York, NY), in press.

Contributor to *Ladybug* magazine.

Sidelights
Focusing on a young-adult readership, Sherri L. Smith is the author of the novels *Lucy the Giant* and *Sparrow.* Smith's first published novel, *Lucy the Giant* focuses on fifteen-year-old Lucy Otsego, who lives in Alaska. Lucy is over six feet tall and because of her height is constantly the brunt of jokes at school. As if that is not bad enough, Lucy's father is an alcoholic and her mother skipped town years ago. Tired of her life, Lucy travels to Kodiak when she is mistaken for an older woman

and offered a season-long job to work on a crabbing boat. While working in the numbing cold and isolation aboard the boat sailing the Bering Sea, Lucy learns a lot about what it means to be an adult. Reviewing *Lucy the Giant* for *Booklist,* Michael Cart dubbed the book an "absorbing first novel," while Francisca Goldsmith commented in her *School Library Journal* review that, "Fast paced and emotionally resonant," Smith's fiction debut "will be easy to book-talk and to get into appreciative hands."

Smith told *Something about the Author:* "I started seriously writing for young adults and children a few years ago, when I realized how much I loved the books I had read at that age. I hope that my writing touches people, and makes them feel more connected to one another. I try to write two to three pages a day, or at least work on my writing in some form every week day. It doesn't always go that way, and I'm a big procrastinator. But I'm happiest when I'm writing, so I always get back to it eventually.

"Some of my favorite writers are Virginia Woolf, E. B. White, Lewis Carroll, J. M. Barrie, Lloyd Alexander (especially his older work), China Mieville (fascinating), and Jasper Fforde. Oh, and Susan Cooper, especially the 'Dark Is Rising' series! Every single book I've read has influenced me, but these are some of the writers I go back to.

"There are so many rich, interesting stories being told today. I hope that my fellow writers continue to stretch the limits of their imaginations. The rewards are incredible and benefit us all.

"The best advice I can give anyone who wants to write is: don't say you want to be a writer, show that you ARE a writer. Write!"

Biographical and Critical Sources

PERIODICALS

Booklist, February 15, 2002, Michael Cart, review of *Lucy the Giant,* p. 1010.
Horn Book, March-April, 2002, Christine M. Heppermann, review of *Lucy the Giant,* p. 219.
Publishers Weekly, December 24, 2001, review of *Lucy the Giant,* p. 65.
School Library Journal, January, 2002, Francisca Goldsmith, review of *Lucy the Giant,* p. 140.

ONLINE

Sherri L. Smith Web site, http://www.sherilsmith.com/ (January 5, 2005).

*   *   *

STERN, Maggie 1953-

Personal

Born November 29, 1953, in New York, NY; daughter of Edwin (a stock broker) and Margaret (an artist;

maiden name, Schwarz) Stern; married Daniel Terris (director of an academic center), November 20, 1983; children: Ben, Eli, Theo, Sam. *Education:* Kirkland College, B.A., 1976; Simmons College, M.A., 1981; Lesley College, M.A. (counseling psychology), 1985. *Politics:* Democrat.

Addresses

Home and office—Concord, MA. *Agent*—Karen Klockner, Transatlantic Literary Agency, 72 Glengowan Rd., Toronto, Ontario, Canada M4N 1G4. *E-mail*—maggie@maggiestern.com.

Career

Worked as a school counselor. Writer, beginning 1997.

Member

Foundation for Children's Books.

Awards, Honors

Bank Street School Award, 1999, for *George,* and 2000, for *George and Diggety.*

Writings

The Missing Sunflowers, illustrated by Donna Ruff, Greenwillow Books (New York, NY), 1997.
Acorn Magic, illustrated by Donna Ruff, Greenwillow Books (New York, NY), 1998.
George, illustrated by Blanche Sims, Orchard Books (New York, NY), 1999.
George and Diggety, illustrated by Blanche Sims, Orchard Books (New York, NY), 2000.
Singing Diggety, illustrated by Blanche Sims, Orchard Books (New York, NY), 2001.

Work in Progress

More books for children.

Sidelights

Massachusetts-based writer Maggie Stern is the author of several children's books, including *The Missing Sunflowers,* a picture book that follows a young boy's battle for ownership of some sunflowers with a hungry squirrel, and the beginning reader *George and Diggety.* *George and Diggety,* the sequel to Stern's 1999 chapter book *George,* focuses on a likeable young boy who, with his dog Diggety, engages in typically boyish behavior. In the first of the book's three chapters, George and his siblings try to measure Diggety's dog IQ using a magazine quiz; other escapades include a celebration of Diggety's birthday and finding a way to let George's patient pup enjoy winter sledding. Connie Fletcher praised Stern's "George" books as a "fun-filled

George and his amiable dog, Diggety, are featured in Maggie Stern's frolicking stories in Singing Diggety, *illustrated by Blanche Sims.*

way to move children from picture books to chapter books" in her *Booklist* review, while a *Horn Book* reviewer commented that the author"uses repetitive sequences and sentences, a valuable redundancy important for developing fluency." Praising Stern's young protagonist in the simply titled *George,* a *Publishers Weekly* reviewer cited the book's "brief sentences, punchy dialogue, ample art [by illustrator Blanche Sims], and . . . plucky young hero."

Stern told *Something about the Author:* "Ever since I was in third grade, and author Peggy Parish was my teacher, I knew I wanted to write. But of course I also wanted to be an actress in musicals. The only problem was I couldn't sing. I was an extremely shy child (just not on stage) and writing was my outlet. I wrote all through high school and went to Kirkland College, primarily to work with Natalie Babbitt. For four glorious years, I worked independently with Natalie. She was my friend and my mentor and taught me how to write. After Kirkland I sent my first book to Susan Hirschman at Greenwillow, and though we became lifelong friends, she turned down that novel, as did countless other editors. I went to graduate school at Simmons College, and had the privilege of knowing Paul and Ethel Heins, and working with such luminaries as Jane Langton and Betty Levin. Gregory Maguire was my best friend and together we sang (him magically) and continued a lifelong friendship. After several books and more rejections

than I can count, I switched careers [and became a school guidance counselor].

"I now write just about every day, whether the muse is with me or not. I know if I'm not at my computer, that's the day the muse will come! I still get more rejections than acceptances and that is difficult. But I write because it's what I love most to do. The book that inspired me most as a child was *Harriet the Spy*—I learned from Harriet to NEVER QUIT and to write everything down, or I'd forget it. When I teach young children about writing, that's the most important message I have for them; WRITE IT DOWN. WRITE IT DOWN—otherwise some of the best ideas get forgotten. Keep a journal, read books, LIVE LIFE to its fullest."

Biographical and Critical Sources

PERIODICALS

Booklist, May 15, 1997, Lauren Peterson, review of *The Missing Sunflowers,* p. 1581; September 1, 2000, Connie Fletcher, review of *George and Diggety,* p. 119.
Horn Book, September, 2000, B.C., review of *George and Diggety,* p. 582.
Publishers Weekly, January 20, 1997, review of *The Missing Sunflowers,* p. 402; November 22, 1999, review of *George,* p. 56.

ONLINE

Maggie Stern, http:www.maggiestern.com/ (December 22, 2004).

*   *   *

STOJIC, Manya 1967-

Personal
Born 1967, in Yugoslavia. *Education:* Belgrade Faculty of Applied Arts and Design, B.A. (graphic design).

Addresses
Agent—Peters, Fraser & Dunlop, Drury House, 34-43 Russell St., London WC2B 5HA, England. *E-mail*—manya@ideasforchildren.com.

Career
Author, illustrator, and graphic designer.

Writings

SELF-ILLUSTRATED

Rain, Crown (New York, NY), 2000.

Oblici (title means "Shapes"), Kreativni Centar (Belgrade, Yugoslavia), 2002.

Wet Pebbles under Our Feet, Knopf (New York, NY), 2002.

Snow, Knopf (New York, NY), 2002.

Hello World! Greetings in Forty-two Languages around the Globe!, Scholastic (New York, NY), 2002.

Zamslite Deco, Kreativni Centar (Belgrade, Yugoslavia), 2003.

Baby Goes Too!, Chrysalis Books (New York, NY), 2003.

ILLUSTRATOR

Ken Wilson-Max, *A Book of Letters,* Scholastic (New York, NY), 2002.

Sidelights

Yugoslavian-born author and illustrator Manya Stojic creates simple texts, then enriches them with her brightly colored acrylic paintings. Her picture books *Snow* and *Rain* focus on the change in weather from an animal's perspective, while a human child's viewpoint is reflected in both *Wet Pebbles under Our Feet* and the 2002 book *Hello World! Greetings in Forty-two Languages around the Globe!,* which includes pictures of children uttering the same friendly "Hello!," each in their own native language. Described as a "fast-moving" story by *Booklist* contributor Kathy Broderick, *Snow* follows geese, rabbits, a fox, a moose, and other cold-climate animals as they prepare for their first snowfall, while *Rain* similarly focuses on African creatures who sense that the seasonal rains are fast approaching their dry savannah home. Despite its simple text, *Rain* provides more than an entertaining story, according to *Booklist* reviewer Ilene Cooper, who cited the book for providing "an easy entry into a discussion of weather patterns and how they affect habitat." *Snow* also contains an easy-to-read text, making the book's highlight Stojic's brightly colored paintings. According to Broderick, these pictures "capture the physicality of the animals in a brief, transforming moment in time": the season's first snowfall.

Wet Pebbles under Our Feet is the story of a little girl who listens to her mother and uncles talk about their memories of growing up on a coastal island, where the beach and sea was a major part of their life. Traveling with these older relatives and hearing them relate their fond memories of childhood, the girl feels more comfortable about visiting the group's ultimate destination: the island home of her grandmother, where she has never been. In *School Library Journal* Lisa Gangemi Krapp wrote that Stojic's "bold brush strokes" complement a simple text full of "warmth and detail," while a *Kirkus Reviews* critic praised the "bold text [that] splashes across the lavishly applied swirls of paint that fill each page." Citing the "elegant simplicity" of Stojic's story, a *Publishers Weekly* reviewer added that readers of *Wet Pebbles under Our Feet* will share the excitement of the young protagonist as she "takes her own first walk on the pebbly island shore and implants herself into the family's story."

In addition to writing and illustrating her own books, Stojic has created illustrations for Ken Wilson-Max's concept book *A Book of Letters.* A lift-the-flap book, *A Book of Letters* contains not only one page for every letter of the alphabet; it also contains actual letters in the form of a chain of correspondence begun by Zuzu, who sends a brief note to friend Abby, who sends a brief note to a friend with a name beginning with "B" and so on until the chain comes full-circle back to Zuzu. The final page is an envelope containing a pull-out list of all the names of the twenty-six letter-writers, listed in order from A to Z.

Biographical and Critical Sources

PERIODICALS

Booklist, December 1, 2002, Kathy Broderick, review of *Hello World! Greetings in Forty-two Languages around the Globe!,* p. 670, and *Snow,* p. 679; July, 2000, Ilene Cooper, review of *Rain,* p. 2044; February 15, 2002, Hazel Rochman, review of *Wet Pebbles under Our Feet,* p. 1021.

Kirkus Reviews, October 15, 2002, review of *Snow,* p. 1539; March 15, 2002, review of *Wet Pebbles under Our Feet,* p. 428.

Publishers Weekly, February 11, 2002, review of *Wet Pebbles under Our Feet,* p. 187; May 15, 2000, review of *Rain,* p. 115.

School Library Journal, December, 2002, Shawn Brommer, review of *Snow,* p. 110, and Carol L. MacKay, review of *Hello World!,* p. 130; March, 2002, Lisa Gangemi Krapp, review of *Wet Pebbles under Our Feet,* p. 204.

ONLINE

Ideas for Children Web site, http://www.ideasforchildren. com/ (December 2, 2004), "Manya Stojic."*

*   *   *

SWEENEY, Matthew (Gerard) 1952-

Personal

Born October 6, 1952, in Donegal, Ireland; married Rosemary Barber, 1979; children: two. *Education:* Attended Gormanston College, 1965-70, University College, Dublin, 1970-72, and University of Freiburg, 1977-78; Polytechnic of North London, B.A. (German and English; with honors), 1978.

Addresses

Agent—c/o Author Mail, Jonathan Cape, Random House, 20 Vauxhall Bridge Rd., London SW1V 2SA, England. *E-mail*—matthewsweeney@writersartists.net.

Career

Freelance writer, beginning mid-1980s. Farnham College, Surrey, England, writer-in-residence, 1984-85; West Surrey College of Art and Design, Farnham, England, external advisor in creative writing, 1986-89; Poetry Society, London, England, publicist and events assistant, 1988-90; Hereford and Worcester, poet-in-residence; South Bank Centre, London, writer-in-residence, 1994-95; University of Reading, writer-in-residence, 1998; National Library for the Blind, poet-in-residence, 2000; Ledbury Festival, poet-in-residence, 2000. Judge of poetry contests; presenter at conferences; tutor.

Member

Poetry Society, Aosdana.

Awards, Honors

National Poetry Competition winner, 1980; Hammersmith Festival Poetry Competition winner, 1980; Prudence Farmer Prize, *New Statesman,* 1984; University of East Anglia Henfield writing fellow, 1986; Cholmondeley Award, 1987; Arts Council of England Writers' Award, 1993, 1999; Arts Council of Ireland Writers' bursary, 2001.

Writings

FOR CHILDREN

The Chinese Dressing-Gown, Raven Arts Press (Dublin, Ireland), 1987.
The Snow Vulture, Faber (London, England), 1992.
The Flying Spring Onion (poems), Faber (London, England), 1992.
Fatso in the Red Suit (poems), illustrated by David Austen, Faber (London, England), 1995.
Up on the Roof: New and Selected Poems, Faber (London, England), 2001.
Fox, Bloomsbury (London, England), 2002.

Contributor to books, including the poetry anthology *We Couldn't Provide Fish Thumbs,* illustrated by Colin McNaughton, Pan Macmillan (London, England), 1998.

POETRY; FOR ADULTS

Without Shores, Omens (Leicester, England), 1978.
A Dream of Maps, Raven Arts Press (Dublin, Ireland), 1981.
A Round House, Allison and Busby (New York, NY), 1983.
The Lame Waltzer, Allison and Busby (London, England), 1985.
Blue Shoes, Secker and Warburg (London, England), 1989.
Cacti, Secker and Warburg (London, England), 1992.
The Blue Taps, Prospero Poets (London, England), 1994.

(With Helen Dunmore and Jo Shapcott) *Penguin Modern Poets 12,* Penguin (London, England), 1997.
The Bridal Suite, J. Cape (London, England), 1997.
A Smell of Fish, J. Cape (London, England), 2000.
Selected Poems, J. Cape (London, England), 2002.
Sanctuary, J. Cape (London, England), 2004.

EDITOR

One for Jimmy: An Anthology from the Hereford and Worcester Poetry Project, Hereford and Worcester County Council, 1992.
(With Jo Shapcott) *Emergency Kit: Poems for Strange Times,* Faber (London, England), 1996.
(With Ken Smith) *Beyond Bedlam: Poems Written out of Mental Distress,* Dufour Editions (Chester Springs, PA), 1997.
The New Faber Book of Children's Verse, Faber (London, England), 2001.

OTHER

(With John Hartley Williams) *Writing Poetry and Getting Published,* NTC Publishing Group (Lincolnwood, IL), 1997, 2nd edition, Hodder & Stoughton (London, England), 2003.

Contributor to periodicals, including *Cyphers, Green Lines, Honest Ulsterman, Limestone, New Poetry, Pacific Quarterly, Tablet,* and *Resurgence.*

Sweeney's works have been translated into Romanian, Spanish, Latvian, Slovakian, German, Dutch, Italian, Croatian, and Japanese.

Work in Progress

A thriller novel, with Jon Hartley Williams; a second children's novel.

Sidelights

An award-winning poet in his native Ireland and in the countries wherein his work has been published in translation, Matthew Sweeney has also written several children's books, including several poetry anthologies geared for younger readers. Sweeney's poems for children, as well as those he writes for adults, are known for telling stories. According to Medbh McGuckian writing in *Books and Bookmen,* "in a short space he can manufacture a whole complicated narrative plot." Sweeney's poems often focus on characters who are facing grim situations. While the unusual is often present in these poems, the poet also portrays the ordinary in an offbeat and even eerie manner. The sometimes horrific subjects found in Sweeney's poetry for adults are also found in his work written for children. Sweeney "does not fit easily into any category," Sheila Flanagan and Rachel O'Flanagan stated in an essay published in the *St. James Guide to Children's Writers,* adding that "His works are not in the mainstream and are characterised by a somewhat bleak vision of life and a downbeat atmosphere." While Sweeney lived and worked for many years in England, he has lived in Germany and Romania as well, but frequently returns to England where he teaches and runs poetry workshops for both children and adults.

Sweeney's poems for young readers, which are included in the collections *The Flying Spring Onion, Fatso in the Red Suit,* and *Up on the Roof: New and Selected Poems,* are "comic, sad, faintly menacing, [and] sometimes possessed of strange Magritte-like properties," Charles Causley explained in the *Times Educational Supplement.* Speaking of the collection *The Flying Spring Onion,* Flanagan and O'Flanagan found "a macabre and occasionally menacing humour" at work. In the poem "Into the Mixer," for example, a boy falls into a cement mixer and comes out stiff and silent. "Worrying Days" tells of a donkey who wrongly believes himself safe from the slaughterhouse, while "Big Sister" finds an older sister pegging the baby to the clothesline along with the rest of the laundry. Morag Styles, reviewing *Up on the Roof* for the *Times Educational Supplement,* described Sweeney as "a challenging poet whose work can be tender, funny and unsettling" and whose appeal for children lies in the fact that he possesses a "terrific sense of the ridiculous."

In addition to poetry, Sweeney has also authored several books of fiction for children, including *The Snow Vulture* and the novel *Fox,* the story of a boy who, in his travels around his urban neighborhood, meets and befriends a homeless man and the man's companion, a young, tame fox. Sweeney's picture book, *The Snow Vulture* tells the story of twin brothers, Clive and Carl. Even though twins, the brothers have opposite personalities: Clive is easygoing while Carl is mean spirited. When the two brothers play in the snow, Clive builds a snowman while Carl creates a snow vulture which comes to evil life. The creature wreaks such havoc that the two boys must join forces to save themselves. The monstrous snow vulture "is a powerfully-conceived horror," Neil Philip wrote in the *Times Educational Supplement.*

Biographical and Critical Sources

BOOKS

Contemporary Poets, 7th edition, St. James Press (Detroit, MI), 2001.

Harmon, Maurice, editor, *The Irish Writer and the City,* Barnes and Noble (Totowa, NJ), 1984.

St. James Guide to Children's Writers, 5th edition, St. James Press (Detroit, MI), 1999.

PERIODICALS

Books and Bookmen, March, 1979, Derek Stanford, review of *Without Shores,* p. 34; March, 1986, Medbh McGuckian, review of *The Lame Waltzer,* p. 24.

Books for Keeps, March, 1995, review of *The Snow Vulture,* p. 12; September, 1995, Jack Ousbey, review of *Fatso in the Red Suit,* p. 25; September, 2001, Clive Barnes, review of *The New Faber Book of Children's Verse,* p. 28.

British Book News, December, 1983, Robert Greacen, review of *A Round House,* p. 774; March, 1986, review of *The Lame Waltzer,* p. 181.

Community Care, December 18, 1997, Julia Tugendhat, review of *Beyond Bedlam,* p. 29.

Critical Survey, January, 1998, Michael Faherty, "Learning How to Fall: The Not So Secret Narratives of Matthew Sweeney," p. 93; September, 2001, Michael Murphy, review of *A Smell of Fish,* p. 120.

Junior Bookshelf, October, 1992, review of *The Flying Spring Onion,* p. 212.

New Statesman, August 24, 1984, Michael Hofmann, "The Prudence Farmer Award," pp. 21-22; January 31, 1986, John Lucas, review of *The Lame Waltzer,* p. 32; January 16, 1987, John Lucas, "The Inherited Boundaries: Younger Poets of the Republic of Ireland," p. 30.

New Statesman and Society, April 7, 1989, John Lucas, review of *Blue Shoes,* pp. 39, 40.

Observer (London, England), February 12, 1984, Peter Porter, review of *A Round House,* p. 52; January 26, 1986, Peter Porter, review of *The Lame Waltzer,* p. 50; April 23, 1989, Peter Porter, review of *Blue Shoes,* p.44; December 3, 1995, Kate Kellaway, review of *Fatso in the Red Suit,* p. 16; February 1, 1998, Kate Kellaway, review of *The Bridal Suite,* p. 17; May 28, 2000, Helen Dunmore, review of *A Smell of Fish,* p. 12.

School Librarian, August, 1992, I. Anne Rowe, review of *The Flying Spring Onion,* p. 111; February, 1996, Lucinda Fox, review of *Fatso in the Red Suit,* p. 29; autumn, 2001, Martin Axford, review of *Up on the Roof,* p. 154.

Stand, autumn, 1993, Fred Beake, review of *Cacti,* pp. 79-80.

Times Educational Supplement, February 14, 1992, Charles Causley, review of *The Flying Spring Onion,* p. 27; December 4, 1992, Neil Philip, review of *The Snow Vulture,* p. 8; April 20, 2001, Morag Styles, review of *The New Faber Book of Children's Verse,* p. 21; June 22, 2001, Morag Styles, review of *Up on the Roof,* p.22.

Times Literary Supplement, September 24, 1982, Tim Dooley, review of *A Dream of Maps,* p. 1041; May 11, 1984, Michael O'Neill, review of *A Round House,* p. 516; May 16, 1986, Mick Imlah, review of *The Lame Waltzer,* p. 540; April 7, 1989, Lawrence Norfolk, review of *Blue Shoes,* p. 365; November 6, 1992, Ian Sansom, review of *Cacti,* p. 26; March 14, 1997, Kevan Johnson, review of *Emergency Kit,* p. 23; March 6, 1998, Michael Parker, review of *The Bridal Suite,* p.25; March 2, 2001, Nick Laird, review of *A Smell of Fish,* p. 24.

ONLINE

British Council Web site, http://www.contemporarywriters. com/ (December 2, 2004), "Matthew Sweeney."

Lidia Vianu Web site, http://lidiavianu.scriptmania.com/ (July, 2002), Lidia Vianu, "Imagistic Narrative: Interview with Matthew Sweeney."

Wordfest, http://www.wordfest.com/ (October 12, 2003), "Lesson Plans: *Up on the Roof* by Matthew Sweeney."*

*   *   *

SWOPE, Sam(uel)

Personal

Born in Gettysburg, PA. *Education:* Attended Middlebury College and Oxford University.

Addresses

Agent—c/o Author Mail, Farrar, Straus & Giroux, 19 Union Square West, New York, NY 10003.

Career

Prop man for film industry in New York, NY; freelance writer; teacher of creative writing. New York Library Summer Seminar for High School English Teachers (summer program), dean; workshop presenter. Open Society, independent project fellow. Co-founder, *Chapbooks.com* (Web site). Speaker and lecturer.

Awards, Honors

Grants from Spencer Foundation, Overbrook Foundation, Johnson Family Foundation, Teachers & Writers Collaborative, National Broadcasting Corporation, and Teaching Tolerance; Books for a Better life award, and Christopher Award, both 2005, both for *I Am a Pencil;* William Randolph Hearst fellowship.

Writings

FOR CHILDREN

The Araboolies of Liberty Street, illustrated by Barry Root, Potter (New York, NY), 1989.
(With Katya Arnold) *Katya's Book of Mushrooms* (nonfiction), Henry Holt (New York, NY), 1997.
The Krazees, Farrar, Straus & Giroux (New York, NY), 1997.
Gotta Go! Gotta Go!, illustrated by Sue Riddle, Farrar, Straus & Giroux (New York. NY), 2000.
Jack and the Seven Deadly Giants, illustrated by Carll Cneut, Farrar, Straus & Giroux (New York, NY), 2004.

OTHER

(Editor with Donald Letcher Goddard) *Saving Wildlife: A Century of Conservation,* H. Abrams (New York, NY), 1995.
I Am a Pencil: A Teacher, His Kids, and Their World of Stories (nonfiction), Henry Holt (New York, NY), 2004.

I Am a Pencil

A TEACHER, HIS KIDS, AND THEIR WORLD OF STORIES

SAM SWOPE

Sam Swope recounts his three-year experience with a group of grade-school students in Queens as he teaches them to write and they teach him about themselves and their struggles and joys.

Contributor of articles and reviews to periodicals, including *Parenting, New York Times Book Review, Threepenny Review, Teacher, Voices from the Middle, Teachers & Writers Collaborative, Utne Reader, Newsweek, Entertainment Weekly,* and *Good Housekeeping.*

Adaptations

The Araboolies of Liberty Street was adapted as an opera by Constance Congdon, music by Ronald Perera, Pear Tree Press (Northampton, MA), 2002; and as a musical. *The Krazees* was optioned for a film starring Robin Williams.

Sidelights

The written world is present in all facets of author Sam Swope's career. In addition to producing fiction and nonfiction for both children and adult readers, Swope helped found a short-lived but ambitious Web site to help teachers publish student writings, and also spends much of his time promoting creative writing through writers' and teachers' workshops. His nonfiction title *I Am a Pencil: A Teacher, His Kids, and Their World of Stories* recounts Swope's experiences during the three years he taught a diverse group of elementary-school students at a Queens, New York City public school, following the students from grades three through five and watching as their talent and interests expanded. In Swope's first book for children, *The Araboolies of Liberty Street,* General Pinch and his wife maintain order and quiet on Liberty Street, because everyone nearby knows that the General will call in the army on anyone who deviates from the norm. Then the Araboolies move in, a big family whose members do not speak English and can change their skin color at will. They paint their house in bright zigzags, camp out in their yard, and draw the neighborhood children into their games and colorful lifestyle. When the General orders the army to remove the "different" house, a young girl named Joy enlists the other children to decorate all the houses except the General's with bright paint and balloons. By the time the army arrives, the General's house is the house that is different, and he himself is dragged away. A reviewer for *Publishers Weekly* noted that although

Swope's message about conformity "is wordy and repetitive . . . the messages of freedom, individualism and tolerance are strong." Praising the picture book in a *Booklist* review, Deborah Abbott dubbed *The Araboolies of Liberty Street* "thought-provoking at any age."

The nature-focused picture book *Katya's Book of Mushrooms* was co-authored with Katya Arnold, who grew up in Russia where mushrooming is popular. "Perhaps this explains the convivial tone, unusual in a science book," surmised Diana Lutz in a *Horn Book* review. The book is written for the younger reader, and is intended, according to Arnold, as an introduction that "will help families discover the special excitement of hunting and naming mushrooms." The coauthors use folk names together with scientific names and illustrations ranging from paintings and cartoons to artwork resembling woodcuts. A *Publishers Weekly* reviewer called *Katya's Book of Mushrooms* "Fungal fervor at its most contagious."

There are strict rules against frivolity on the ironically-named Liberty Street and when the fun-loving Araboolies move in, the neighboring children rally to prevent their eviction from the block. (*From* The Araboolies of Liberty Street, *written by Sam Swope and illustrated by Barry Root.*)

Noting that the book is "heavy with nonsense words," a contributor to *Kirkus Reviews* called Swope's *The Krazees* "a properly silly read-aloud." "Children of all ages will recognize the Krazees, nutty creatures that infest a too-quiet house and attack only on rainy days," wrote a *Publishers Weekly* reviewer, describing the book as "a gleeful fantasy for wet-weather shut-ins." The Krazees are checkered, striped, and polka-dotted creatures who appear to a girl named Iggie. They do their mischief in her cupboards, television, and refrigerator, disappearing when the sun reappears. *School Library Journal* reviewer Heide Piehler compared Swope's style to that of popular children's author Dr. Seuss, and noted that although his cadence is not "as smooth or successful," Swope's "nonsensical rhyming text, filled with alliteration and word play, is sure to elicit giggles." Swope follows the life of a monarch caterpillar in *Gotta Go! Gotta Go!* As the story opens, a black and yellow bug is hustling across an open meadow, determined to make the 3,000-mile trip south to Mexico. Ultimately exhausted, the bug falls asleep, and awakens as a butterfly. Easily making the journey to Mexico, the butterfly joins a mass migration of monarchs, and when she hatches a new generation of bugs Swope's tale encompasses the insect's life cycle. Noting that the book's "simple and urgent" text effectively conveys the monarch's "powerful instinct," Hazel Rochman added in her *Booklist* review of *Gotta Go! Gotta Go!* that Swope's "rhythmic storytelling bears repeated readings." "The clarity of the storytelling and artwork match the heroine's determination," added a *Publishers Weekly* reviewer, noting that illustrator Sue Riddle "complements the lucid narration with charming ink-and-watercolor miniatures."

Combining the Biblical tale of the Seven Deadly Sins with the familiar folk story about Jack and the beanstalk, Swope's short children's novel *Jack and the Seven Deadly Giants* focuses on a young miscreant foster child. After misconstruing a minister's warning that some marauding giants might be attracted to the village by evil-doers, young Jack leaves his village to wander the countryside, a cow his only companion. During his travels he encounters a strange man who presents him with the gift of a magic bean in return for Jack's kindness. This gift sends the boy on a trip during which he must overcome seven giants before receiving his wish of being reunited with his true mother. Sloth, Wild Tickler, Terrible Glutton, and four other overgrown ne'er-do-wells cross Jack's path and are vanquished in turn. Calling the book an "inventive melange" of literary sources, *Booklist* reviewer Abby Nolan praised *Jack and the Seven Deadly Sins* for its "concise, graceful language" as well as illustrator Carll Cneut's "off-kilter" artwork. Reviewing the book in *Horn Book*, Christine M. Heppermann noted that Swope's message— "that hands-on learning is more effective than being lectured at"—is clearly reflected in an entertaining story that has the "spontaneous feel of a bedtime story, spun out over a week of nights."

In Swope's fairytale story, Jack tries to prove his worth to the townsfolk by fighting seven dangerous giants, each the manifestation of the deadly sins of humankind. (From Jack and the Seven Deadly Giants, *illustrated by Carll Cneut.)*

Biographical and Critical Sources

PERIODICALS

Booklist, November 1, 1989, p. 560; February 15, 1991, p. 1214; April 1, 1997, Chris Sherman, review of *Katya's Book of Mushrooms,* p. 1326; June 1, 1997, p. 1675; November 15, 1997, review of *The Krazees,* p. 567; March 1, 2000, Hazel Rochman, review of *Gotta Go! Gotta Go!,* p. 1243; May 15, 2004, Abby Nolan, review of *Jack and the Seven Deadly Giants,* p. 1622; August, 2004, Deborah Donovan, review of *I Am a Pencil: A Teacher, His Kids, and Their World of Stories,* p. 1882.

Horn Book, July, 1989, p. 60; May-June, 1997, Diana Lutz, review of *Katya's Book of Mushrooms,* p. 336; May, 2000, Maria V. Paravanno, review of *Gotta Go! Gotta Go!,* p. 300; May-June, 2004, Christine M. Heppermann, review of *Jack and the Seven Deadly Giants,* p. 336.

Kirkus Reviews, August 15, 1997, p. 1313; June 15, 2004, review of *I Am a Pencil,* p. 572.

Library Journal, September 15, 2004, Terry Christner, review of *I Am a Pencil,* p. 67.

New York Times Book Review, November 12, 1989, p. 38.

Publishers Weekly, August 11, 1989, p. 457; April 17, 1995, p. 49; March 3, 1997, review of *Katya's Book of Mushrooms,* p. 75; June 23, 1997, review of *The Krazees,* p. 90; January 31, 2000, review of *Gotta Go! Gotta Go!,* p. 105; May 17, 2004, review of *Jack and the Seven Deadly Giants,* p. 50; May 31, 2004, review of *I Am a Pencil,* p. 58.

School Library Journal, December, 1989, p. 90; April, 1997, p. 143; December, 1997, p. 101; May, 2000, Patricia Manning, review of *Gotta Go! Gotta Go!,* p.156; May, 2004, Maria B. Salvadore, review of *Jack and the Seven Deadly Giants,* p. 125.

ONLINE

Sam Swope Web site, http://www.samswope.org/ (December 2, 2004).

T

TAHA, Karen T(erry) 1942-

Personal

Born January 10, 1942, in Mena AR; daughter of Alvin R. (a banker) and Catherine C. (an office manager) Terry; married Hamdy A. Taha (a university professor); children: Tarek, Sharif, Maisa. *Education:* Arizona State University, B.A., 1963; University of Oklahoma, M.A., 1970; University of Arkansas, M.A., 1981. *Hobbies and other interests:* Reading, hiking, music, traveling.

Addresses

Home—406 Lake Road, Springdale, AR 72764.

Career

Educator, 1963-66; library media specialist, Springdale, AR, 1981-95; critique service provider, Springdale, 1995-2002.

Member

Society of Children's Book Writers and Illustrators.

Writings

Name That Book!: Questions and Answers on Outstanding Children's Books, Scarecrow Press (Metuchen, NJ), 1986.
A Gift for Tía Rosa, Dillon Press (Minneapolis, MN), 1986.
Marshmallow Muscles, Banana Brainstorms, Harcourt Brace Jovanovich (San Diego, CA), 1988.
Hotdog on TV, Dial Books for Young Readers (New York, NY), 2005.

Work in Progress

A picture book, *America Flies,* and two middle-grade novels.

Sidelights

Karen T. Taha told *Something about the Author:* "If you love to write, WRITE! But if you want to publish what you write, study the craft, take writing classes, go to workshops and conferences, read how-to books and magazines, study writing you admire. Read jillions of whatever type of book you aspire to write. And, above all, ignore the naysayers and don't give up!"

* * *

TAKABAYASHI, Mari 1960-

Personal

Born November 20, 1960, in Tokyo, Japan; daughter of Yoshimitsu and Emiko Takabayashi; married Kam Mak (an illustrator); children: Luca, Dylan. *Education:* Attended Otsama Women's College (Japan).

Addresses

Home—369 Sackett St., Brooklyn, NY 11231. *Agent*—c/o Author Mail, Houghton Mifflin, 222 Berkeley St., Boston, MA 02116-3764. *E-mail*—mari.takabayashi@verizon.net.

Career

Author and illustrator of children's books.

Writings

Baby's Things, Chronicle Books (New York, NY), 1994.
I Live in Tokyo, Houghton Mifflin (Boston, MA), 2001.
I Live in Brooklyn, Houghton Mifflin (Boston, MA), 2004.

ILLUSTRATOR

Christine Loomis, *Rush Hour,* Houghton Mifflin (Boston, MA), 1995.

Seen through the eyes of seven-year-old Mimiko, a year of life in Tokyo is defined month-by-month through customs, holidays, food, clothing, and other amusing details. (From I Live in Tokyo, *written and illustrated by Mari Takabayashi.*)

Linda Brennan Crotta, *Flannel Kisses,* Houghton Mifflin (Boston, MA), 1997.

Jean Marzollo, *Do You Know New?,* HarperCollins (New York, NY), 1998.

Patricia Hubbell, *Sidewalk Trip,* HarperFestival (New York, NY), 1999.

Linda Brennan Crotta, *Marshmallow Kisses,* Houghton Mifflin (Boston, MA), 2000.

Also illustrator for more than twenty picture books from Japanese publishers.

Sidelights

Mari Takabayashi is a Japanese-born author and illustrator whose children's books have been published both in Japan and the United States. Her illustrations, often executed in pastel watercolors, have been praised for adding energy and depth to the simple, rhyming texts they accompany. Among the author/illustrator's books for English-language readers are *I Live in Brooklyn* and *I Live in Tokyo.*

In addition to illustrating her own books in a style that *Booklist* reviewer Ilene Cooper described as "delightfully naive" and childlike, Takabayashi has created colorful artwork for the rhyming texts of other authors, including *Flannel Kisses* and *Marshmallow Kisses* by

Linda Brennan Crotta. For *Flannel Kisses,* Takabayashi's illustrations celebrate the fun to be had on a snowy day, as children divide their time between the snowy out-of-doors and the warmth of their home, an "idyllic, plank-floored cottage . . . decorated with rag rugs, crocheted afghans and toys" in Takabayashi's renderings, observed a reviewer in *Publishers Weekly.*

"Delicate line work and lively patterns are the hallmarks of the art," commented Cooper of Takabayashi's illustrations for Crotta's follow-up work, *Marshmallow Kisses;* "each picture has a childlike simplicity and presence that match the text and will appeal to young audiences." Also enthusiastic about the collaboration between author and illustrator, Gay Lynn Van Vleck wrote in *School Library Journal* that the artist's "primitive style is brimming with details of a happy, busy, country-style home in suburbia."

In *Rush Hour,* written by Christine Loomis, Takabayashi depicts the varied activities of the masses as they commute to work via car, bus, train, or airplane. Filled with "seemingly inexhaustible, enjoyable details," according to a reviewer for *Publishers Weekly,* Takabayashi's illustrations "are a kaleidoscope of color, pattern and activity." For John Peters in *School Library Journal,* they "effectively capture the hustle and bustle of it all." Because the book ends with the joyful reunion of parents returning home from work to be with their children, the result is "a loving, comforting book for grownups to share with their children," contended Stephanie Zvirin in *Booklist.*

Takabayashi once told *Something about the Author:* "I moved to New York in 1990, and I started to work for American publishers. I like to work for American publishers because I can draw many races. Also, New York City, where I live, inspires me a lot. My two kids give me ideas. When I draw pictures for American publishers I always put Asian kids somewhere."

Biographical and Critical Sources

PERIODICALS

Booklist, October 15, 1997, Ilene Cooper, review of *Flannel Kisses,* p. 411; September 15, 1999, Kathy Broderick, review of *Skidewalk Trip,* p. 268; March 15, 2000, Ilene Cooper, review of *Marshmallow Kisses,* p. 1385.

Publishers Weekly, August 25, 1997, review of *Flannel Kisses,* p. 71.

School Library Journal, September, 1996, John Peters, review of *Rush Hour,* p. 184; July, 1999, p. 74; March, 2000, Gay Lynn Van Vleck, review of *Marshmallow Kisses,* p. 189.

ONLINE

Mari Takabayashi Web site, http://www.maritakabayashi. com/ (January 5, 2005)*.

TAYLOR, G(raham) P(eter) 1959(?)-

Personal

Born c. 1959, in Scarborough, England; son of a cobbler; married; children: Hannah, Abigail, one other daughter.

Addresses

Home—Cloughton, Yorkshire, England. *Agent*—c/o Author Mail, Penguin Putnam, 375 Hudson St., New York, NY 10014.

Career

Novelist and cleric. CBS Records, London, England, band promoter, c.1970; worked as an elder-care aide, mid-1970s; policeman, c. 1988-95; entered Anglican priesthood, parish priest of Whitby, now Vicar of St. Mary's Church, Cloughton, Yorkshire, England.

Writings

Shadowmancer (self-published, 2002), Faber & Faber (London, England), 2003, Penguin Putnam (New York, NY), 2004.
Wormwood, Penguin Putnam (New York, NY), 2004.

Adaptations

Shadowmancer has been optioned for film, and has been adapted as an audiobook by Listening Library, 2004.

Work in Progress

A third novel in the trilogy.

Sidelights

At the age of forty-two, English vicar G. P. Taylor decided that if he wanted to realize his dream of being an author, it was now or never. Drawing on his surroundings—the vicarage of Cloughton, in Yorkshire, England—as well as his former vocations, which included work as a policeman, social worker, and rock-band promoter, he produced the novel *Shadowmancer*. Working from his kitchen table, Taylor self-published and distributed his novel beginning in 2002; after receiving a copy from one of Taylor's parishioners and noting the popularity of the book, London publisher Faber & Faber reissued it nationwide a year later. By 2004 the bestselling *Shadowmancer* had made its way across the Atlantic to American readers, while its author had become something of a celebrity in his native England.

Set in the history-filled lands along England's northeast coast, *Shadowmancer* draws readers back to the 1700s. Power-hungry Obadiah Demurral, vicar of the remote parish of Thorpe, begins to secretly explore the black arts, having long since lost his faith and concern over his soul in his lust for godlike power. Demurral's efforts are aided by a powerful gold artifact called the Keruvim, which he acquired from thieves who stole it from an African temple to the gods. Together with its mate, the magic artifact will allow him to gain control over all things. When African traveler Raphah traces the Keruvim to Demurral's parish, he hopes to reacquire it for the temple. Instead, he finds himself engaged in a battle with the ruthless Demurral, as well as with dead spirits capable of such awful things as cursing humans with perpetual nightmares. Aided by two children, Kate Cogland and the homeless Thomas Barrick, Raphah fights the greedy vicar, who has no qualms about robbery and murder in attempting to gain absolute power over nature.

Reviewing *Shadowmancer* for *Library Journal,* Tamara Butler described the novel as "steeped in English folklore" and added that while the book is geared for teen readers, "it is complex enough to hold the interest of adults." While finding the story, with its religious parables, "a dark and weighty morality tale," a *Publish-*

When Vicar Obadiah Demurral, a sorcerer who can speak to the dead, wants to take over the world, three young people rise up to retrieve an ancient relic and curtail his power in Taylor's exciting adventure of the occult.

In London of 1756, the Earth is threatened by a lethal comet called Wormwood and, as a tremendous clash between good and evil forces ensues, a scientist questions whether the comet will bring new enlightenment or oblivion.

ers Weekly reviewer concluded that *Shadowmancer* contains "enough surprises to keep readers madly turning the pages." In 2004 Taylor continued what he intended as a novel trilogy, producing *Wormwood*, a sequel to *Shadowmancer.* The year is now 1756, and Dr. Sabian Blake and his young housemaid, Agetta, are as fearful as their London neighbors about news that a giant comet threatens to demolish their city. Blake has more on his mind, however: the coming of the comet, Wormwood, had been foretold to him in a mysterious book, the Nemorensis, which recently and mysteriously came into his possession. While Blake at first used the book to further his own explorations into the supernatural, it quickly becomes clear that the Nemorensis is desired by an evil force, the fallen angel Hezrin, who hopes to be made mortal by the comet's power. When Agetta becomes an unwitting pawn of Hezrin and steals the book, humans and immortals line up along traditional battle lines separating good from evil, while London society falls upon itself in its panic.

In *School Library Journal* Carolyn Lehman noted Taylor's inclusion of "exquisitely detailed scenes of vio-

lence and mayhem," all of which make *Wormwood* "unremittingly dark" While a *Kirkus Reviews* critic also found the novel "relentlessly horrific," in *Kliatt* Michele Winship praised Taylor's prose as "sensuous and spellbinding," and added that *Wormwood* will transport "readers into a place where . . . angels battle over human souls and immortality." In *Publishers Weekly* a reviewer noted that the author is "even more explicit . . . about his allegory's tether to Christianity" in his second novel, with its battle between fallen and true angels, and added that *Wormwood* "brings some cohesion and depth" to Taylor's fantasy trilogy.

Although Taylor's books have benefited from the rise in popularity of fantasy novels in the wake of J. K. Rowling's "Harry Potter" novels, it gained a large following without much of the hype that publishers normally provide to first-time authors. As Taylor noted on an online interview for the *British Broadcasting Corporation Web site, Shadowmancer* "has been spoken about by kids and it's been a success through word of mouth." Interestingly, the one thing that may give potential readers qualms is the fact that the book's author is a devout Christian. "Everybody thinks the book is a Christian book, so I have to explain it is not," Taylor added. "Just because I'm a vicar does not mean I have to write a Christian book. It has hindered me in a way, because some of the reviewers look for things which are not there. The guy who wrote 'Thomas the Tank Engine' was a vicar."

Biographical and Critical Sources

PERIODICALS

Booklist, April 15, 2004, Jennifer Mattson, review of *Shadowmancer,* p. 1451; September 1, 2004, Jennifer Mattson, review of *Wormwood,* p. 109.
Christianity Today, June, 2004, Greg Taylor, "A Christian Harry Potter?," p. 63.
Entertainment Weekly, May 28, 2004, Troy Patterson, "Has G. P. Taylor Written the Next Harry Potter?," p. 78.
Horn Book, July-August, 2004, Anita L. Burkham, review of *Shadowmancer,* p. 461.
Kirkus Reviews, March 1, 2004, review of *Shadowmancer,* p. 230; September 1, 2004, review of *Wormwood,* p. 874.
Kliatt, March, 2004, Michele Winship, review of *Shadowmancer,* p. 16; September, 2004, Michele Winship, review of *Wormwood,* p. 16.
Library Journal, April 1, 2004, Tamara Butler, review of *Shadowmancer,* p. 82.
Publishers Weekly, April 5, 2004, review of *Shadowmancer,* p. 63; April 19, 2004, James Bickers, "The Vicar and the Bestseller," p. 25; August 16, 2004, review of *Wormwood,* p. 64.
School Library Journal, October, 2004, Jane P. Fenn, review of *Shadowmancer,* p. 86, and Carolyn Lehman, review of *Wormwood,* p. 180.

ONLINE

British Broadcasting Corporation Web site, http://www.
bbb.co.uk/blast/ (December 3, 2004), transcript of interview with Taylor.*

*   *   *

TIMBERLAKE, Amy

Personal

Female. *Education:* University of Illinois at Chicago,
M.A. (creative writing).

Addresses

Home—DeKalb, IL. *Agent*—c/o Author Mail, Farrar,
Straus & Giroux, 19 Union Square W., New York, NY
10001. *E-mail*—amytimber13@aol.com.

Career

Writer. University of Illinois, Chicago, former instructor
in English composition; Hand Workshop Art Center,
Richmond, VA, writing teacher; Virginia Commission
for the Arts, public information officer; has also worked
as a children's bookseller and for the Chicago Botanic
Garden.

Member

Society of Children's Book Writers and Illustrators (Illinois chapter).

Awards, Honors

Anderson Center for Interdisciplinary Studies residency
fellow, 2002; Parent's Choice Gold Medal, and Golden
Kite Award, Society of Children's Book Writers and Il-
lustrators, both 2003, and Marion Vannett Ridgeway
Award first prize, International Reading Association
Notable Book designation, Spur Award finalist, and
Southeast Booksellers Association Book Award finalist,
all 2004, all for *The Dirty Cowboy.*

Writings

The Dirty Cowboy, illustrated by Adam Rex, Farrar Straus
& Giroux (New York, NY), 2003.

Contributor of articles, reviews, and columns to periodicals, including *New Moon, Book, Riverbank Review,
Horn Book, Hues,* and *Hip Mama.*

Work in Progress

A middle-grade novel.

Sidelights

Illinois-based children's book author and teacher Amy
Timberlake is the mastermind behind *The Dirty Cowboy,* a "simple, slapstick tale that is sure to elicit some
giggles," according to *Booklist* reviewer Todd Morning.
In Timberlake's award-winning story, a flea-ridden cowboy and his dog, who have been riding the range in
New Mexico for a year, finally head to a nearby river
for the cowboy's annual bath. Leaving his faithful dog
to guard his clothes, the cowboy bathes, and returns so
clean that his loyal pet is unable to recognize him. When
the pair finally resort to grappling while the cowboy
struggles to retrieve his clothes, the cowpoke winds up
dirty once again, this time with his clothes tattered as
well. Joy Fleishhacker enjoyed the picture book, praising Timberlake for creating "descriptive language that
rolls off the tongue" and describing *The Dirty Cowboy*
in her *School Library Journal* review as "a fun look at
life on the range." Praising the artwork by Adam Rex
that "fortuitously camouflage . . . private parts," a *Publishers Weekly* contributor dubbed Timberlake's story a
"raucous romp [that] should tickle bath-averse children
everywhere."

*A filthy cowboy runs into unforeseen problems when he
takes his annual bath in the river while his dog guards his
clothes. (From* The Dirty Cowboy, *written by Amy Timberlake and illustrated by Adam Rex.)*

Biographical and Critical Sources

PERIODICALS

Booklist, September 1, 2003, Todd Morning, review of *The Dirty Cowboy,* p. 131.

Kirkus Reviews, June 15, 2003, review of *The Dirty Cowboy,* p. 865.

Publishers Weekly, July 14, 2003, review of *The Dirty Cowboy,* p. 75.

School Library Journal, September, 2003, Joy Fleishhacker, review of *The Dirty Cowboy,* p. 192.

ONLINE

Society of Children's Book Writers and Illustrators Web site, http://www.scbwi-illinois.org/ (January 5, 2005), "Amy Timberlake."*

*   *   *

TREMENS, Del
See MACDONALD, Amy

V

Van ALLSBURG, Chris 1949-

Personal

Born June 18, 1949, in Grand Rapids, MI; son of Richard (a dairy owner) and Chris Van Allsburg; married Lisa Morrison (a self-employed consultant); children: Sophia, Anna. *Education:* University of Michigan, B.F.A., 1972; Rhode Island School of Design, M.F.A., 1975. *Religion:* Jewish. *Hobbies and other interests:* "When I'm not drawing, I enjoy taking walks and going to museums. I play tennis a few times a week, like to sail—although I have fewer opportunities to do it now (I used to have more friends with boats). I read quite a lot."

Addresses

Home—Providence, RI. *Agent*—c/o Author Mail, Houghton Mifflin, 222 Berkeley St., Boston, MA 02116-3764.

Career

Artist; author and illustrator of children's books. Rhode Island School of Design, Providence, RI, teacher of illustration, 1977—. *Exhibitions:* Whitney Museum of American Art, New York, NY; Museum of Modern Art, New York, NY; Alan Stone Gallery, New York, NY; Grand Rapids Art Museum, Grand Rapids, MI; American Institute of Graphic Arts Book Show, 1983, 1984 1985; and Port Washington Public Library, NY.

Member

Awards, Honors

Best Illustrated Children's Books citations, *New York Times,* 1979, for *The Garden of Abdul Gasazi,* 1981, for *Jumanji,* 1982, for *Ben's Dream,* 1983, for *The Wreck of the Zephyr,* 1984, for *The Mysteries of Harris Burdick,* 1985, for *The Polar Express,* and 1986, for *The Stranger;* Caldecott Honor Book citation, American Li-

Chris Van Allsburg

brary Association (ALA), and *Boston Globe-Horn Book* Award for illustration, both 1980, and International Board on Books for Young People citation for illustration, 1982, all for *The Garden of Abdul Gasazi;* Irma Simonton Black Award, Bank Street College of Education, 1980, for *The Garden of Abdul Gasazi,* and 1985, for *The Mysteries of Harris Burdick; New York Times* Outstanding Books citations, 1981, for *Jumanji,* and 1983, for *The Wreck of the Zephyr;* Caldecott Medal, ALA, 1982, for *Jumanji,* and 1986, for *The Polar Express; Boston Globe-Horn Book* Award for illustration, 1982, for *Jumanji,* 1985, for *The Mysteries of Harris Burdick,* and 1986, for *The Polar Express;* Children's Choice Award, International Reading Association, and American Book Award for illustration, Association of

American Publishers, both 1982, Kentucky Bluegrass Award, Northern Kentucky University, and Buckeye Children's Book Award, Ohio State Library, both 1983, Washington Children's Choice Picture Book Award, Washington Library Media Association, 1984, and West Virginia Children's Book Award, 1985, all for *Jumanji;* Parents' Choice Award for Illustration, Parents' Choice Foundation, 1982, for *Ben's Dream,* 1984, for *The Mysteries of Harris Burdick,* 1985, for *The Polar Express,* 1986, for *The Stranger,* 1987, for *The Z Was Zapped,* and 1992, for *The Widow's Broom;* Kentucky Bluegrass Award, 1987, for *The Polar Express;* One Hundred Titles for Reading and Sharing designation, New York Public Library, 1983, for *The Wreck of the Zephyr,* and 1985, for *The Polar Express;* Ten Best Picture Books for Kids, *Redbook,* and Children's Books of the Year, Child Study Association, and Hans Christian Andersen Award nomination, all 1985, all for *The Polar Express;* Children's Books of the Year, Child Study Association, 1987, for *The Stranger;* Colorado's Children's Book Award runner-up, 1990, Virginia Young Readers Award, and Washington Children's Choice Award, both 1991, and Georgia Children's Picture Storybook Award, 1992, all for *Two Bad Ants;* Regina Medal for lifetime achievement.

Writings

FOR CHILDREN; SELF-ILLUSTRATED

The Garden of Abdul Gasazi, Houghton Mifflin (Boston, MA), 1979.
Jumanji, Houghton Mifflin (Boston, MA), 1981.
Ben's Dream, Houghton Mifflin (Boston, MA), 1982.
The Wreck of the Zephyr, Houghton Mifflin (Boston, MA), 1983.
The Mysteries of Harris Burdick, Houghton Mifflin (Boston, MA), 1984.
The Polar Express, Houghton Mifflin (Boston, MA), 1985, tenth anniversary edition, 1995.
The Stranger, Houghton Mifflin (Boston, MA), 1986.
The Z Was Zapped: A Play in Twenty-six Acts, Houghton Mifflin (Boston, MA), 1987.
Two Bad Ants, Houghton Mifflin (Boston, MA), 1988.
Just a Dream, Houghton Mifflin (Boston, MA), 1990.
The Wretched Stone, Houghton Mifflin (Boston, MA), 1991.
The Widow's Broom, Houghton Mifflin (Boston, MA), 1992.
The Sweetest Fig, Houghton Mifflin (Boston, MA), 1993.
Bad Day at Riverbend, Houghton Mifflin (Boston, MA), 1995.
Zathura: A Space Adventure, Houghton Mifflin (Boston, MA), 2002.

ILLUSTRATOR

Mark Helprin, *Swan Lake,* Houghto Mifflin (Boston, MA), 1989.

Mark Helprin, *A City in Winter,* Viking (New York, NY), 1996.
Mark Helprin, *The Veil of Snows,* Viking (New York, NY), 1997.

A selection of Van Allsburg's work is held in the Kerlan Collection at the University of Minnesota.

Adaptations

Several of Van Allsburg's books have been adapted for audio cassette. *Jumanji* was adapted for a movie of the same title starring Robin Williams, 1995; *The Polar Express* is available on CD-ROM; inspired an orchestra score by Robert Kapilow, 1998; and was adapted by Robert Zemeckis and William Broyles, Jr., as a computer-animated movie of the same title featuring the voice of Tom Hanks, 2004.

Sidelights

Two-time Caldecott Medal-winner Chris Van Allsburg has drawn readers into a magical, even surreal, world through his illustrated picture books, which include *Jumanji* and its sequel, *Zathura,* as well as *Two Bad Ants* and *The Polar Express.* "While most children's literature remains steeped in saccharin morality tales," Linnea Lannon noted in the *Detroit Free Press Sunday Magazine,* "Van Allsburg has found critical acclaim and commercial success with children's books that embrace the mystery and randomness of life." In addition to the many awards Van Allsburg has garnered for his unique, even quirky tales, he has also made illustrating and writing children's books a distinctly profitable profession and has been hailed for revolutionizing book illustration to boot. His most popular book, *The Polar Express,* has become a Christmas classic around the world, and was made into a feature film in 2004. Van Allsburg's first Caldecott Medal book, *Jumanji,* was the first book to go Hollywood, however; it was adapted as a feature film in 1995. The major theme in Van Allsburg's books is not that either good or bad things can happen in life, but that strange, inexplicable things can occur; the author/illustrator sees his books as challenging rather than comforting. As Stephanie Loer recounted in *Children's Books and Their Creators,* "Van Allsburg's illustrations never fail to fascinate the intellect, pique the senses, and emphasize the power of imagination."

Born in Grand Rapids, Michigan, in 1949, Van Allsburg "liked to do the normal kid things like playing baseball and building model cars, trucks, and planes," as he once told *Something about the Author (SATA).* Raised in the suburbs, Van Allsburg had access to open fields and dirt roads, riding his bike to school and catching tadpoles in the nearby creeks. Early reading included the Dick, Jane, and Spot books, as well as Crockett Johnson's *Harold and the Purple Crayon,* and he was also an avid fan of comic books. Drawing provided early diversion for Van Allsburg, but as he got older, art took a back seat to sports. "I had no idea what I wanted

One magical Christmas Eve, a young boy is whisked away on the Polar Express to the North Pole where Santa rewards him for being a believer. (From The Polar Express, *written and illustrated by Van Allsburg.)*

to be when I grew up," he recalled. "I thought I'd be a lawyer, mostly because I couldn't think of anything else." However, as high-school graduation approached, he once again began to focus on art as a possible vocation, and decided to enroll at the University of Michigan School of Art and Design.

In college Van Allsburg was particularly taken with sculpture, and upon graduating from the University of Michigan he enrolled at the Rhode Island School of Design (RISD), where he earned a master's degree in fine art. For several years afterward he made his living as an artist, with well-received shows in New York, and also taught illustration at RISD. Slowly his interest in art broadened to include drawing as well as sculpture. "A friend of mine who illustrated books saw my drawings and encouraged me to consider illustration," Van Allsburg told *SATA*. His wife, then working as an elementary school teacher, also encouraged him to consider illustrating, introducing him to children's picture books. Van Allsburg began to find his own expression in both illustration and writing, opting initially for black and white, and in text, choosing prose over verse.

Published in 1979, Van Allsburg's first book, *The Garden of Abdul Gasazi*, tells the story of a young boy whose curious dog—a white bull terrier that has gone on to become something of a signature for Van Allsburg—runs away into the bizarre garden of a magician that is filled with topiary creatures. Critics immediately responded to the eerie, dreamlike quality of the book's black-and-white illustrations, *Booklist* contributor Barbara Elleman noting the illustrator's ability to "provide an underlying quality of hushed surrealism, seemingly poised at the brink of expectancy." Paul Heins, a reviewer for *Horn Book*, compared Van Allsburg's "stippled tones of gray and the precisely outlined figures" to the pointillist technique of nineteenth-century French impressionist painter Georges Seurat. Named a Caldecott Honor Book, *The Garden of Abdul Gasazi* exhibits the combination of edgy, challenging story and slightly unsettling illustration that has become Van Allsburg's trademark. The puzzle motif that informs much of his work is also introduced here: the reader is left to contemplate the possibility that the runaway dog was changed into a fowl by the magician.In addition to several awards, *The Garden of Abdul Gasazi* brought Van Allsburg "almost instantaneous recognition in the field of illustration," according to *Dictionary of Literary Biography* essayist Laura Ingram. This reception came as a surprise to the artist, who thought the book would sell a few copies, with the remaining left to give to family and friends as Christmas presents. Instead, *The Garden of Abdul Gasazi* headed its creator on a new career. He has continued to write and illustrate each of his titles, breaking from that tradition only once, to join writer Mark Helprin in a three-part fantasy series based on Tchaikovsky's famous ballet "Swan Lake." Focusing on a queen who leads a battle to preserve her country against an evil usurper, the author and illustrator spin their story in *Swan Lake, A City in Winter,* and *The Veil of Snows.* While reviewers found the text of the series somewhat muddled, a *Publishers Weekly* reviewer dubbed the "richly magical paintings" illustrating *The Veil of Snows* as "among Van Allsburg's best work."

Puzzles and magic—as well as a white bull terrier—find their way into Van Allsburg's second picture book. In *Jumanji* a decidedly uncooperative magic intrudes into the domesticity of a suburban home when bored siblings Judy and Peter suddenly get more action than they bargained for while playing a board game. The two-dimensional jungle adventures of the game become real, with lions materializing in the living room and monkeys in the kitchen. The surreal game only comes to an end when Judy finally reaches the Golden City— the goal of the game. Again illustrated in charcoal pencil, this second book won the Caldecott Medal. "Van Allsburg's pictures," commented Ingram, "which at first glance could be mistaken for photographs, are impressive not only for their realism but for the skill with which he manipulates light and shadow to create a vaguely unsettling mood, and for the odd angles which present disconcerting views of common scenes." This cinematic effect, a tip of the hat to the films of twentieth-century director and actor Orson Welles, has been noted by more than one reviewer. The final frame in *Jumani* shows the magical board game, which Judy

Peter and Judy are astonished when a harmless-looking board game suddenly comes to life, filling their home with exotic creatures and outlandish adventures. (From Jumanji, *written and illustrated by Van Allsburg.)*

Twenty-one years after the publication of **Jumanji,** *Van Allsburg takes up the story hinted at in its last images and follows Danny Budwing who shares the wild exploits of a bizarre outer-space board game with his brother. (From* Zathura, *written and illustrated by Van Allsburg.)*

and Peter have deposited across the street in an empty park, being carried off by a pair of rapscalliony brothers, Danny and Walter Budwing. Fans of the book had to wait twenty-one years for Van Allsburg to answer the tantalizing question: What happened next? In *Zathura: A Space Adventure* the Budwing brothers open the box, and find, under the Jumanji game a second game decorated with flying saucers, space ships, and planets. Although readers are not caught unawares, Danny and Walter are when they suddenly find themselves hurled into a space adventure after a single roll of the dice, and Van Allsburg's heavily textured and patterned pencil drawings "create a claustrophobic intimacy that magnifies the danger" of being lost forever in space, according to *Horn Book* contributor Betty Carter. Praising *Zathura* as "masterfully executed," Wendy Lukehart pointed to the book's underlying theme of sibling rivalry, noting in her *School Library Journal* review that "savvy readers will recognize" that Danny and Walter's "lack of camaraderie does not bode well" in Van Allsburg's "surreal story."

In *The Wreck of the Zephyr,* Van Allsburg's first full-color book, he uses pastel over paint. As he noted on his Web site, although he was not trained in painting when he first started his illustration career, "as time went by, I became more interested in picture making,

and taught myself to use different materials," such as "dry and oil pastels, craypas, crayons, colored pencils, and paint. Now I decide if a book should be black and white or color as a result of how I imagine the story while I am thinking about it." *The Wreck of the Zephyr* is a story-within-a-story: the narrator tells of a boy who was the best sailor in his town. Stranded on an island during a storm, he uses magical powers to fly his ship home. In the end, the reader is left to wonder if the aged narrator is, in fact, the boy-sailor of the tale. John Russell, reviewing the book in the *New York Times Book Review,* compared Van Allsburg's illustrations to the work of French painter René Magritte, while noting that the book's "text is as spare, as sober and telling as ever." Margery Fisher, writing in *Growing Point,* dubbed *The Wreck of the Zephyr* a "joyous celebration of change and mystery."

Van Allsburg chose black-and-white illustration with *The Mysteries of Harris Burdick,* a wordless book for which the viewer is prompted to build stories by means of suggestive captions. *The Mysteries of Harris Burdick* was followed by the book that has become the artist's most well-known work: *The Polar Express,* which presents a full-color, first-person narrative of a little boy who sets off on a mysterious train for the North Pole, where he meets Santa Claus and is presented with a reindeer bell from Santa's sleigh. "When I started *The Polar Express,*" Van Allsburg remarked in a *Horn Book* transcript of his Caldecott Medal acceptance speech for the book, "I thought I was writing about a train trip, but the story was actually about faith and the desire to believe in something." Denise M. Wilms, writing in *Booklist,* noted that the book's "Darkened colors, soft edges, and the glow of illuminated snow flurries create a dreamlike adventure that is haunting even as it entertains," and dubbed *The Polar Express* an "imaginative, engrossing tale of Christmas magic." Popular when it was first published in 1985, the book reached a new generation of readers in its tenth-anniversary edition, as well as in its movie incarnation in 2004.

Fantastic tales and subtle magic appear in Van Allsburg's other titles, including *The Stranger, Just a Dream, The Wretched Stone, The Widow's Broom, The Sweetest Fig, Bad Day at Riverbend,* and *The Z Was Zapped: A Play in Twenty-six Acts,* the last an alphabet book with attitude. In *The Stranger* Farmer Bailey injures a man on the road, takes the stranger home to recuperate, and there learns that the man is mute and without memory. The stranger becomes part of the family, and a few weeks into his stay, the weather turns as warm as summer, though when he abruptly leaves, winter sets in. Every year thereafter, winter comes late to the Bailey farm. Patricia Dooley, writing in *School Library Journal,* called *The Stranger* "a down-homey modern myth." Noting the increasingly apparent versatility of the artist, Anne Rice wrote in the *New York Times Book Review* that it is "marvelous that this master painter and storyteller has added a new dimension to his consistently original and enchanting body of work" with *The Stranger.*

"Walter will *never* throw his jelly doughnut wrapper on the street again," declared Roger Sutton in a *Bulletin of the Center for Children's Books* review of *Just a Dream.* In this book, a frightening dream takes an environmentally insensitive ten-year-old into a techno-nightmare future where smog chokes the atmosphere and the forests have been reduced to toothpicks. Most reviewers found the message a bit strident, but Van Allsburg's artwork was praised as among the illustrator's best. A better critical response greeted *The Wretched Stone,* a sea tale involving the sailors of the *Rita Ann* and their adventures and misadventures under the spell of a magic stone they discover on an uncharted island. The glowing stone turns the crew into monkeys when they stare at it, making them swing through the ship's rigging. Only the sound of the captain playing his violin or reading aloud can bring the crew back to their normal selves. Lee Lorenz, writing in the *New York Times,* remarked that throughout "his distinguished career, Chris Van Allsburg has challenged, expanded and redefined our notions of what a book for children can be. . .. He continues to break new ground with *The Wretched Stone,* which is in some ways his most ambitious work." In his *Bulletin of the Center for Children's Books* review, Sutton interpreted the book as a parable on the dumbing-down influences of television, and noted in particular the nautical setting, which provides the artist with "plenty of space for his moody pastels, which add a menacing tone to the plain spoken narrative."

The Widow's Broom relates the story of a broom abandoned after it has lost the power of flight. In this book "Van Allsburg explores the nature of good and evil," according to *Booklist* reviewer Cooper, who concluded that the artwork in the book is some of his "finest: oversize, sepia-tone drawings, with precise linework that has both visual clarity and intriguing nuance." *The Sweetest Fig* deals with a Parisian dentist named Bibot who is paid in figs for his work—a magical payment, as the fruit will make his dreams come true. A folktale in format, *The Sweetest Fig* "is a sophisticated picture book," according to Betsy Hearne in *Bulletin of the Center for Children's Books,* "but not at the expense of its audience." Readers enter the life of a coloring book bedecked with the squiggles and marks of a child's scribbles in *Bad Day at Riverbend.* When greasy strings of slime cover the town of Riverbend, Sheriff Ned Hardy gathers a posse and hunts down the villain: a young artist who is busy scribbling with crayon in the coloring book that serves as the town's universe. Reviewing the book in the *New York Times,* Robin Tzannes called *Bad Day at Riverbend* "clever and entertaining," and "a good introduction to [Van Allsburg's] . . . work for the younger readers."

Van Allsburg takes between seven and nine months to create a picture book, and he completes an outline of the text before beginning the fourteen or fifteen drawings in a conventionally laid-out book. He begins his illustrations by creating crude "thumbnail" sketches, reworking them into fine, museum-quality drawings. "I

like the idea of withholding something, both in drawings and writing," he once explained to *SATA,* alluding to the sense of something missing, or something left unfinished, that gives his work its haunting, compelling quality. While he still works as a sculptor, and also teaches, his work as a picture-book author has allowed Van Allsburg to reach a large audience. As he told Lannon in the *Detroit Free Press,* "every time the book is read, the book happens. I feel, not a sense of power, but a sense of connectedness, I guess. Just to be able to make those books and have them out there, and to know kids are going to take them out and actually have an experience, not identical with the one I had . . . but they're going to be in a way, captives of my mind and their imagination. That's a stimulation."

Biographical and Critical Sources

BOOKS

Berger, Laura Standley, editor, *Twentieth-Century Children's Writers,* St. James Press (Detroit, MI), 1995, pp. 980-981.
Children's Books and Their Creators, edited by Anita Silvey, Houghton (Boston, MA), 1995, pp. 660-662.
Children's Literature Review, Gale (Detroit, MI), Volume 5, 1983, pp. 231-242; Volume 13, 1987, pp. 201-214.
Dictionary of Literary Biography, Volume 61: *American Writers for Children since 1960: Poets, Illustrators, and Nonfiction Authors,* Gale (Detroit, MI), 1987, pp. 306-313.
Holtze, Sally Holmes, *Fifth Book of Junior Authors and Illustrators,* H. W. Wilson (Bronx, NY), 1983, pp. 316-317.

PERIODICALS

Booklist, November 15, 1979, Barbara Elleman, review of *The Garden of Abdul Gasazi;* October 1, 1985, Denise M. Wilms, review of *The Polar Express,* pp. 271-272; October 15, 1990, Ilene Cooper, review of *Just a Dream,* p. 452; October 1, 1991, p. 338; September 15, 1992, Ilene Cooper, review of *The Widow's Broom,* p. 147; October 15, 1995, p. 413; October 15, 1996, p. 421; November 15, 1997, p. 560.
Bulletin of the Center for Children's Books, November, 1990, Roger Sutton, review of *Just a Dream,* p. 72; November, 1991, Roger Sutton, review of *The Wretched Stone,* p. 78; November, 1993, Betsy Hearne, review of *The Sweetest Fig,* p. 104.
Detroit Free Press Sunday Magazine, October 22, 1995, Linnea Lannon, "The Van Allsburg Express," pp. 7-9, 12-13, 17.
Growing Point, July, 1984, Margery Fisher, review of *The Wreck of the Zephyr,* p. 4292.
Horn Book, February, 1980, Paul Heins, review of *The Garden of Abdul Gasazi;* July-August, 1986, Chris Van Allsburg, "Caldecott Medal Acceptance," pp. 420-

424; January-February, 1991, p. 61; January-February, 1992, pp. 62-64; January-February, 1997, p. 57.; Nov-Dec, 2002, Betty Carter, review of *Zathura,* p. 741.

New York Times, November 10, 1991, Lee Lorenz, review of *The Wretched Stone,* p. 36; March 24, 1996, Robin Tzannes, review of *Bad Day at Riverbend,* p. 23.

New York Times Book Review, June 5, 1983, John Russell, review of *The Wreck of the Zephyr,* p. 34; November 9, 1986, Anne Rice, "Jack Frost's Amnesia," p. 58.

Publishers Weekly, September 9, 1996, p. 84; September 29, 1997, p. 90.

School Library Journal, November, 1986, Patricia Dooley, review of *The Stranger,* p. 84; February, 1995, p. 18; October, 1995, pp. 121-122; January, 1996, p. 18; November, 1997, pp. 118-119.

ONLINE

Chris Van Allsburg Web site, http://www.chrisvanallsburg. com/ (January 15, 2005).*

W

WALLACE, Daisy
See CUYLER, Margery (Stuyvesant)

* * *

WALLNER, Alexandra 1946-

Personal

Born February 28, 1946, in Germany; came to the United States 1952, naturalized citizen, 1964; daughter of Severin (a physician) and Hildegard (an artist; maiden name, Waltch) Czesnykowski; married John C. Wallner (an illustrator), July 16, 1971. *Education:* Pratt Institute, B.F.A., 1968, M.F.A., 1970. *Hobbies and other interests:* Gardening, making pressed flower collages.

Addresses

Home—2227 Mt. Vernon St., Philadelphia, PA 19130. *Agent*—Kirchoff/Wohlberg, Inc., 866 United Nations Plaza, New York, NY 10017.

Career

Illustrator and author. *American Home,* New York, NY, assistant art director, 1972-73; *New Ingenue,* New York, NY, associate art director, 1973-75; freelance illustrator and writer, 1975—. Illustrator for Kevin Corbett Designs, 1984, Portal Publications, 1985, and Argus Communications, 1986; co-owner of Greywood Studio. Educator and lecturer at writing conferences.

Writings

The Adventures of Strawberry Shortcake and Her Friends, illustrated by Mercedes Llimona, Random House (New York, NY), 1980.
Strawberry Shortcake and the Winter That Would Not End, illustrated by Mercedes Llimona, Random House (New York, NY), 1982.

Alexandra Wallner

SELF-ILLUSTRATED:

Munch: Poems and Pictures, Crown (New York, NY), 1976.
Ghoulish Giggles and Monster Riddles, Albert Whitman (Morton Grove, IL), 1982.
Twelve Days of Christmas, Warner (New York, NY), 1989.
Jingle Bells, Warner (New York, NY), 1989.
Silent Night, Warner (New York, NY), 1989.
Deck the Halls, Warner (New York, NY), 1989.
Since 1920, Doubleday (New York, NY), 1992.
Betsy Ross, Holiday House (New York, NY), 1994.

Beatrix Potter, Holiday House (New York, NY), 1995.

The First Air Voyage in the United States: The Story of Jean-Pierre Blanchard, Holiday House (New York, NY), 1996.

An Alcott Family Christmas, Holiday House (New York, NY), 1996.

Laura Ingalls Wilder, Holiday House (New York, NY), 1997.

The Farmer in the Dell, Holiday House (New York, NY), 1998.

Sergio and the Hurricane, Henry Holt (New York, NY), 2000.

Abigail Adams, Holiday House (New York, NY), 2001.

Grandma Moses, Holiday House (New York, NY), 2004.

ILLUSTRATOR WITH HUSBAND, JOHN WALLNER:

Kerby on Safari, Avon (New York, NY), 1984.

Bonnie Larkin Nims, *Where Is the Bear?,* Albert Whitman (Morton Grove, IL), 1988.

David A. Adler, *A Picture Book of Abraham Lincoln,* Holiday House (New York, NY), 1989.

David A. Adler, *A Picture Book of George Washington,* Holiday House (New York, NY), 1989.

David A. Adler, *A Picture Book of Benjamin Franklin,* Holiday House (New York, NY), 1990.

David A. Adler, *A Picture Book of Thomas Jefferson,* Holiday House (New York, NY), 1990.

David A. Adler, *A Picture Book of Helen Keller,* Holiday House (New York, NY), 1990.

David A. Adler, *A Picture Book of Christopher Columbus,* Holiday House (New York, NY), 1991.

David A. Adler, *A Picture Book of Florence Nightingale,* Holiday House (New York, NY), 1992.

David A. Adler, *A Picture Book of Robert E. Lee,* Holiday House (New York, NY), 1994.

David A. Adler, *A Picture Book of Davy Crockett,* Holiday House (New York, NY), 1995.

David A. Adler, *A Picture Book of Patrick Henry,* Holiday House (New York, NY), 1995.

David A. Adler, *A Picture Book of Paul Revere,* Holiday House (New York, NY), 1995.

David A. Adler, *A Picture Book of Thomas Alva Edison,* Holiday House (New York, NY), 1996.

David A. Adler, *A Picture Book of Patrick Henry,* Holiday House (New York, NY), 1996.

David A. Adler, *A Picture Book of Louis Braille,* Holiday House (New York, NY), 1997.

ILLUSTRATOR :

Martha Gamerman, *Trudy's Straw Hat,* Crown (New York, NY), 1977.

Malcolm Hall, *The Friends of Charlie Ant Bear,* Coward, McCann & Geoghegan (New York, NY), 1980.

Joanne E. Bernstein and Paul Cohen, *Un-Frog-Gettable Riddles,* Albert Whitman (Morton Grove, IL), 1981.

Jean Bethell and Susan Axtell, *A Colonial Williamsburg Activities Book: Fun Things to Do for Children Four and Up,* Colonial Williamsburg Foundation, 1984.

Marcia Leonard, *King Lionheart's Castle,* Silver Press, 1992.

Teddy Slater, *Alice Meets the Aliens,* Silver Press, 1992.

Gary Hines, *The Christmas Tree in the White House,* Henry Holt (New York, NY), 1998.

Rachel Mann, *The Blue Mittens,* Scholastic (New York, NY), 2002.

Meish Goldsh, *Famous Fliers,* Scholastic (New York, NY), 2002.

Gary Hines, *Thanksgiving in the White House,* Henry Holt (New York, NY), 2003.

Also illustrator of children's textbooks; author and illustrator of stories for children's magazines.

Sidelights

Alexandra Wallner is an author and artist who has produced picture-book biographies of notable woman such as Betsy Ross, Abigail Adams, and Laura Ingalls Wilder, and has also created original fiction and illustrating adaptations of traditional tales. Sometimes working in collaboration with her husband, fellow illustrator John Wallner, she has also contributed art work to the writings of others, including David A. Adler's picture-book biography series on notable Americans. Praising Wallner's self-illustrated picture book *Sergio and the Hurricane, Booklist* reviewer John Peters noted that the author/illustrator's "neatly drawn scenes, in muted colors, convey a sense of calm urgency" before the coming storm, and its storyline effectively teaches children how to deal with other forms of severe weather.

Born in Germany, Wallner moved to the United States with her family at age six. She fell in love with drawing and writing at an early age, since she was an only child and there were few other children living nearby. Her love of reading also helped Wallner learn her new language; "I spoke no English until the first grade," she once explained to *Something about the Author (SATA),* "and learned [English] by reading comic books: Donald Duck, Uncle Scrooge, Little Lulu, Katy Keene, Archie—not a bad way for a person to learn a language; pictures and words right there together. I loved the bright colors and clever stories."

Wallner was inspired to become an artist by her mother, a painter "greatly influenced by the 'Trash Can School' of art. She painted town scenes, bar scenes, and portraits and also wrote humorous stories. . . .. I suppose, subconsciously I was imitating her." After graduating from high school, Wallner attended the Pratt Institute, where she earned her B.F.A. and M.F.A. degrees. From there she moved into the art department at the New York City-based magazine *American Home,* hoping to gain experience in the commercial art field. "It was in my position with *New Ingenue* that I really learned typography, layout, illustration, and graphic design," Wallner explained of her move to a new periodical in the early 1970s. "When my husband, who is also an illustrator, started his studio, he was having so much fun with illustration, that I decided I would do it too." Beginning in 1990, Wallner started focusing almost exclusively on writing and illustrating books for children.

As she explained to *SATA,* Wallner's biographies of notable women are inspired by her interest in history, as well as her respect for women "who did not have easy lives but overcame difficulties gracefully, women like Betsy Ross, Beatrix Potter, Laura Ingalls Wilder, and Louisa May Alcott. In the midst of a difficult life the last three women turned to writing to express themselves. I feel a close kinship with them." In her self-illustrated *Betsy Ross* she reveals that Ross may not have been the seamstress who made the first American flag. The book also describes Ross's Quaker life, her multiple marriages, and her upholstery business. According to Deborah Stevenson in the *Bulletin of the Center for Children's Books,* Wallner moves Ross "from a cameo role to a starring part . . . using her to explain early American urban life." Wallner takes "pride in detail," noted *Five Owls* reviewer Mary Bahr Fritts, while Carolyn Phelan maintained in her *Booklist* review that "bright color and many details . . . tell the story and recreate" the Revolutionary era in American history.

Regarding Wallner's biography *Beatrix Potter,* a contributor to the *New Jersey Education Association Review* noted that the author makes the life story of the British author "accessible to readers" through use of a "simple text and appealing illustrations." Potter grew up in a very restrictive household and spent most of her time in solitude, writing and filling notebooks with sketches of plants and animals. She became not only a well-known children's author but also a prominent conservationist in her native England. Wallner's illustrations reflect Potter's "many periods of loneliness," stated a reviewer in *School Library Journal,* while a *New Advocate* reviewer wrote that the book's "exquisite illustrations provide detailed glimpses into late nineteenth-century English life." Noted author Wilder wrote about growing up in pioneer country in such works as *Little House on the Prairie,* and is the subject of another of Wallner's biographies for children. Wilder's father dreamed of making a living off the land, and so the family traveled west until they came to the prairie, where they made their home. Some of the events and places Wilder encountered along this journey became material for her later writings. Pamela K. Bomboy, reviewing *Laura Ingalls Wilder* for *School Library*

Abigail Adams, wife of one president and mother of another, and a forthright advocate of the American Revolution, women's rights, and the abolishment of slavery, is captured vividly in the text of Wallner's picture-book biography and in her folk-art illustrations. (From Abigail Adams.*)*

Journal, praised the book as an "accurate, concise beginning biography" with "folk-art" illustrations that range from a rendering of "patterned fabrics of pioneer clothing to a panoramic view of a sea of prairie grass." Marilyn Bousquin, writing in *Horn Book,* described Wallner's book as a "seamless interdependence" of word and picture that "captures both the hard realities of pioneer life and the hearthlike warmth of Laura's family life."

There are other biographies in Wallner's series on notable women. *Grandma Moses* is about the New York woman, born Anna Mary Robinson, who first gained fame for her brightly colored primitive paintings at age eighty. *Abigail Adams* focuses on the independent minded woman whose wise choice in a husband—John Adams was the second president of the United States—and success as a mother—son John Quincy Adams was U.S. president number six—were the result of her intelligence, strong moral values, and energetic optimism. Noting that Wallner's text in *Abigail Adams* depicts the subject as "a woman who was ahead of her time," *School Library Journal* reviewer Ilene Abramson added that the "pictures in a folk-art style contribute greatly to the text." Also noting Wallner's "naif" style, a *Horn Book* reviewer commented that the pastel portraits "suggest a woman of many moods." In *Booklist* Phelan praised *Grandma Moses* as a "charming biographical introduction" for young readers, and described the text as "clearly written" and full of "well-chosen quotations" from the artist's own writings. Remarking on the watercolor illustrations in *Grandma Moses,* Lolly Robinson noted in *Horn Book* that "Wallner's style . . . is suited to her subject: sedate" and "carefully composed."

In addition to writing and illustrating, Wallner also works as a teacher. "Since 1995, I've been teaching writing and illustrating for children's picture books at the International Women's Writing Guild summer conference. Its important to me to share my knowledge with other women. I encourage them to write brief stories. At the end of one week, they have made a small book. Their sense of accomplishment is tremendous. I am also involved in the IWWG's Mentor Program which helps high school girls complete a writing project by the end of a school term. I encourage people to express their creativity with art and writing, because that is what I do." Reflecting on her choice of career, Wallner added of being an artist and writer: "It helps me understand the world."

Biographical and Critical Sources

PERIODICALS

Booklist, February 15, 1994, Carolyn Phelan, review of *Betsy Ross,* p. 1086; September 1, 1996, p. 138; October 1, 1997, Kay Weisman, review of *Laura Ingalls*
Wilder, p. 335; September 1, 1998, April Judge, review of *The Farmer in the Dell,* p. 123; October 1, 1998, Helen Rosenberg, review of *A Christmas Tree in the White House,* p. 335; September 15, 2000, John Peters, review of *Sergio and the Hurricane,* p. 251; March 15, 2001, Ilene Cooper, review of *Abigail Adams,* p. 1402; March 1, 2004, Carolyn Phelan, review of *Grandma Moses,* p. 1206.
Bulletin of the Center for Children's Books, March, 1994, Deborah Stevenson, review of *Betsy Ross,* p. 237; January, 1998, p. 181.
Five Owls, March, 1994, Mary Bahr Fritts, review of *Betsy Ross,* p. 87.
Horn Book, November-December, 1997, Marilyn Bousquin, review of *Laura Ingalls Wilder,* p. 647; July, 2001, review of *Abigail Adams,* p. 479; July-August, 2004, Lolly Robinson, review of *Grandma Moses,* p.470.
Kirkus Reviews, September 1, 1992, p. 1136; March 1, 2004, review of *Grandma Moses,* p. 230.
New Advocate, spring, 1996, review of *Beatrix Potter,* p.163.
New Jersey Education Association Review, March, 1996, review of *Beatrix Potter.*
Publishers Weekly, September 30, 1996, p. 91; February 26, 2001, review of *Abigail Adams,* p. 88.
School Arts, May-June, 2004, Ken Marantz, review of *Grandma Moses,* p. 64.
School Library Journal, May, 1991, p. 87; December, 1996, review of *Beatrix Potter,* p. 45; November, 1997, Pamela K. Bomboy, review of *Laura Ingalls Wilder;* November, 2000, Maryann H. Owen, review of *Sergio and the Hurricane,* p. 136; April, 2001, Ilene Abramson, review of *Abigail Adams,* p. 136; September, 2003, Laurie Edwards, review of *Thanksgiving in the White House,* p. 180; May, 2004, Wendy Lukehart, review of *Grandma Moses,* p. 138.*

*   *   *

WELLS, Rosemary 1943-

Personal

Born January 29, 1943, in New York, NY; married Thomas Moore Wells (an architect), 1963 (deceased); children: Victoria, Marguerite. *Education:* Attended Boston Museum School and a small private junior college (now defunct) in New York State. *Religion:* "Nominal Episcopalian."

Addresses

Home—732 Sleepy Hollow Rd., Briarcliff Manor, NY 10510.

Career

Allyn and Bacon, Inc., Boston, MA, art editor; Macmillan Publishing Co., Inc., New York, NY, art designer; freelance author and illustrator, 1968—. Also worked at various jobs, including buyer of women's shoes and ac-

Rosemary Wells

cessories for a clothing store. Founder, with Susan Jeffers, of book design studio, New York, NY, early 1970s. Speaker for national literacy campaign "Twenty Minutes a Day," beginning 1994; founder of "Read to Your Bunny" campaign (part of "Prescription for Reading" program), 1998. *Exhibitions:* American Institute of Graphic Arts Children's Book shows.

Awards, Honors

Honor Book citation, *Book World* Spring Children's Book Festival, 1972, for *The Fog Comes on Little Pig Feet;* Children's Book Showcase Award, Children's Book Council, 1974, for *Noisy Nora;* Citation of Merit, Society of Illustrators, 1974, and Art Book for Children citation, Brooklyn Museum/Brooklyn Public Library, 1975, 1976, 1977, all for *Benjamin and Tulip;* Irma Simonton Black Award, Bank Street College of Education, 1975, for *Morris's Disappearing Bag: A Christmas Story;* Edgar Allan Poe Award runner-up, Mystery Writers of America, 1981, for *When No One Was Looking,* and 1988, for *Through the Hidden Door;* New Jersey Institute of Technology Award, 1983, for *A Lion for Lewis* and *Peabody;* Best Illustrated Books designation, *New York Times,* 1985, for *Hazel's Amazing Mother;* Washington Irving Children's Book Choice Award, Westchester Library Association, 1986, for *Peabody,* 1988, for *Max's Christmas,* and 1992, for *Max's Choco-*

late Chicken; Golden Sower Award, 1986, for *Peabody;* New Jersey Institute of Technology Award, 1987, for *Max's Christmas;* Virginia Young Readers Award, and New York Public Library Books for the Teen Age citation, both 1987, both for *The Man in the Woods;* Golden Kite Award, Society of Children's Books Writers, 1988, for *Forest of Dreams; Boston Globe/Horn Book* Award, and Parents' Choice Foundation Award, both 1989, both for *Shy Charles;* David McCord Children's Literature Citation, 1991, for body of work; Missouri Building Blocks Picture Book Award nominations, Missouri Library Association, 1998, for *Bunny Cakes* and *McDuff Moves In;* Oppenheim Toy Portfolio Platinum Award, 1999, for *Old MacDonald* and *The Itsy-Bitsy Spider; Riverbank Review* Children's Book of Distinction Award, and Notable Children's Book in the Language Arts designation, National Council of Teachers of English/Children's Literature Assembly, both 1999, both for *Mary on Horseback: Three Mountain Stories. School Library Journal* named *Noisy Nora, Morris's Disappearing Bag, Leave Well Enough Alone, Stanley and Rhoda, Max's Toys, Max's Breakfast, Max's Bedtime, Max's Bath, When No One Was Looking, Max's Christmas, Shy Charles,* and *Max's Chocolate Chicken* among the Best Books of the Year in their respective years of publication; the American Library Association (ALA) gave Notable Book citations to *Noisy Nora, Benjamin and Tulip, Morris's Disappearing Bag, Max's Breakfast, Max's Christmas, Max's Chocolate Chicken,* and *Max's Dragon Shirt;* an ALA Best Books for Young Adults citation was given to *Through the Hidden Door; Bulletin of the Center for Children's Books* gave a Blue Ribbon to *The Little Lame Prince;* American Bookseller gave Pick-of-the-List citations to *Abdul, Stanley and Rhoda, Timothy Goes to School, A Lion for Lewis, Forest of Dreams, Max's Chocolate Chicken,* and *Good Night, Fred;* Child Study Association Children's Books of the Year citations were given to *Morris's Disappearing Bag* and *Don't Spill It Again, James; Horn Book* gave Fanfare designations to *When No One Was Looking,* which also received the West Australian Young Readers' Book Award; an International Reading Association (IRA) Teacher's Choices List designation was given to *Forest of Dreams;* an IRA Children's Choice citation was given to *Max's Chocolate Chicken;* Children's Choice citations from IRA/Children's Book Council were given to *Timothy Goes to School, A Lion for Lewis,* and *Peabody;* a Cooperative Children's Book Center citation was given to *Max's Bedtime.*

Writings

SELF-ILLUSTRATED, EXCEPT AS NOTED

John and the Rarey, Funk, 1969.
Michael and the Mitten Test, Bradbury (New York, NY), 1969.
The First Child, Hawthorn, 1970.

Martha's Birthday, Bradbury (New York, NY), 1970.

Miranda's Pilgrims, Bradbury (New York, NY), 1970.

Unfortunately Harriet, Dial (New York, NY), 1972.

Benjamin and Tulip, Dial (New York, NY), 1973.

Noisy Nora, Dial (New York, NY), 1973, revised edition, with new illustrations, 1997.

Abdul, Dial (New York, NY), 1975.

Morris's Disappearing Bag: A Christmas Story, Dial (New York, NY), 1975.

Don't Spill It Again, James, Dial (New York, NY), 1977.

Stanley and Rhoda, Dial (New York, NY), 1978.

Good Night, Fred, Dial (New York, NY), 1981.

Timothy Goes to School, Dial (New York, NY), 1981.

A Lion for Lewis, Dial (New York, NY), 1982.

Peabody, Dial (New York, NY), 1983.

Hazel's Amazing Mother, Dial (New York, NY), 1985.

Shy Charles, Dial (New York, NY), 1988.

Forest of Dreams, illustrated by Susan Jeffers, Dial (New York, NY), 1988.

Fritz and the Mess Fairy, Dial (New York, NY), 1991.

Waiting for the Evening Star, illustrated by Susan Jeffers, Dial (New York, NY), 1993.

Night Sounds, Morning Colors, illustrated by David McPhail, Dial (New York, NY), 1994.

Lucy Comes to Stay, illustrated by Mark Graham, Dial (New York, NY), 1994.

The Language of Doves, illustrated by Greg Shed, Dial (New York, NY), 1996.

Mary on Horseback: Three Mountain Stories (middle grade nonfiction), illustrated by Peter McCarty, Dial (New York, NY), 1998.

(With Maria Tallchief) *Tallchief: America's Prima Ballerina* (nonfiction), Viking (New York, NY), 1999.

Streets of Gold (nonfiction; based on Mary Antin's memoir *The Promised Land*), illustrated by Dan Andreasen, Dial (New York, NY), 1999.

(With husband, Tom Wells) *The House in the Mail,* illustrated by Dan Andreasen, Dial (New York, NY), 1999.

Emily's First 100 Days of School, Hyperion (New York, NY), 2000.

Timothy's Lost and Found Day, Viking (New York, NY), 2000.

Timothy Goes to School, Viking (New York, NY), 2000.

Lassie Come-Home, Henry Holt (New York, NY), 2000.

Felix Feels Better, Candlewick Press (Cambridge, MA), 2001.

Practice Makes Perfect, Hyperion Books for Children (New York, NY), 2002.

Timothy's Tales from Hilltop School, Viking (New York, NY), 2002.

Make New Friends, Volo (New York, NY), 2002.

Leave Well Enough Alone, Dial (New York, NY), 2002.

Wingwalker, illustrated by Brian Selznick, Hyperion Books for Children (New York, NY), 2002.

Bubble-Gum Radar, Hyperion Books for Children (New York, NY), 2002.

Adding it Up, illustrated by Michale Koelsch, Viking (New York, NY), 2002.

Ready to Read, illustrated by Michale Koelsch, Viking (New York, NY), 2002.

When I Grow Up, Hyperion Books for Children (New York, NY), 2003.

The Small World of Binky Braverman, illustrated by Richard Egielski, Viking (New York, NY), 2003.

Only You, Viking (New York, NY), 2003.

Felix and the Worrier, Candlewick Press (Cambridge, MA), 2003.

Emily's World of Wonders, Hyperion Books for Children (New York, NY), 2003.

Emmett's Pig, HarperCollins (New York, NY), 2003.

I Love You! A Bushel & a Peck, HarperCollins (New York, NY), 2004.

Contributor to books, including *So I Shall Tell You a Story: The Magic World of Beatrix Potter,* edited by Judy Taylor, Warne, 1993, and *Stories and Fun for the Very Young,* Candlewick Press, 1998.

"MAX AND RUBY" SERIES; SELF-ILLUSTRATED

Max's First Word, Dial (New York, NY), 1979.

Max's New Suit, Dial (New York, NY), 1979.

Max's Ride, Dial (New York, NY), 1979.

Max's Toys: A Counting Book, Dial (New York, NY), 1979.

Max's Bath, Dial (New York, NY), 1985.

Max's Bedtime, Dial (New York, NY), 1985.

Max's Breakfast, Dial (New York, NY), 1985.

Max's Birthday, Dial (New York, NY), 1985.

Max's Christmas, Dial (New York, NY), 1986.

Hooray for Max, Dial (New York, NY), 1986.

Max's Chocolate Chicken, Dial (New York, NY), 1989.

Max's Dragon Shirt, Dial (New York, NY), 1991.

Max and Ruby's First Greek Myth: Pandora's Box, Dial (New York, NY), 1993.

Max and Ruby's Midas: Another Greek Myth, Dial (New York, NY), 1995.

Bunny Cakes, Dial (New York, NY), 1997.

Bunny Money, Dial (New York, NY), 1997.

Max's Chocolate Chicken, Dial (New York, NY), 1999.

Max Cleans Up, Viking (New York, NY), 2000.

Goodnight Max, Viking (New York, NY), 2000.

Bunny Party, Viking (New York, NY), 2001.

Max's Snowsuit, Grosset & Dunlap (New York, NY), 2001.

Play with Max and Ruby, Grosset & Dunlap (New York, NY), 2002.

Ruby's Beauty Shop, Viking (New York, NY), 2003.

Max's Christmas Stocking, Viking (New York, NY), 2003.

Max Drives Away, Viking (New York, NY), 2003.

Ruby's Tea for Two, Viking (New York, NY), 2003.

Bunny Mail, Viking (New York, NY), 2004.

"VOYAGE TO THE BUNNY PLANET" SERIES; SELF-ILLUSTRATED

Voyage to the Bunny Planet, Dial (New York, NY), 1992.

First Tomato, Dial (New York, NY), 1992.

The Island Light, Dial (New York, NY), 1992.

Moss Pillows, Dial (New York, NY), 1992.

"EDWARD THE UNREADY" SERIES; SELF-ILLUSTRATED

Edward Unready for School, Dial (New York, NY), 1995.
Edward's Overwhelming Overnight, Dial (New York, NY), 1995.
Edward in Deep Water, Dial (New York, NY), 1995.

"MCDUFF" SERIES; ILLUSTRATED BY SUSAN JEFFERS

McDuff Moves In, Hyperion (New York, NY), 1997.
McDuff Comes Home, Hyperion (New York, NY), 1997.
McDuff and the Baby, Hyperion (New York, NY), 1997.
McDuff's New Friend, Hyperion (New York, NY), 1998.
McDuff, Hyperion (New York, NY), 1998.
McDuff's Birthday, Hyperion (New York, NY), 2000.
The McDuff Stories, Hyperion (New York, NY), 2000.
McDuff Goes to School, Hyperion (New York, NY), 2001.
McDuff Saves the Day, Hyperion (New York, NY), 2002.
McDuff Steps Out, Hyperion (New York, NY), 2004.
McDuff's Favorite Things, Hyperion (New York, NY), 2004.
McDuff's Hide-and-Seek, Hyperion (New York, NY), 2004.

"BUNNY READS BACK" SERIES; SELF-ILLUSTRATED

Read to Your Bunny, Scholastic (New York, NY), 1998.
Old MacDonald, Scholastic (New York, NY), 1998.
The Bear Went over the Mountain, Scholastic (New York, NY), 1998.
Bingo, Scholastic (New York, NY), 1998.
The Itsy-Bitsy Spider, Scholastic (New York, NY), 1998.

"YOKO AND FRIENDS SCHOOL DAYS" SERIES; SELF-ILLUSTRATED UNLESS OTHERWISE NOTED

Yoko, Hyperion (New York, NY), 1998.
Mama, Don't Go!, Hyperion (New York, NY), 2001.
The School Play, Hyperion (New York, NY), 2001.
The Halloween Parade, Hyperion (New York, NY), 2001.
Doris's Dinosaur, Hyperion (New York, NY), 2001.
Yoko's Paper Cranes, Hyperion (New York, NY), 2001.
The World around Us, illustrated by Lisa Koelsch, Hyperion (New York, NY), 2001.
Be My Valentine, illustrated by John Nez, Hyperion (New York, NY), 2001.
Read Me a Story, Hyperion Books for Children (New York, NY), 2001.
The Germ Busters, illustrated by Jody Wheeler, Hyperion Books for Children (New York, NY), 2002.

"MY VERY FIRST MOTHER GOOSE BOARD BOOKS"; EDITED BY IONA OPIE

Humpty Dumpty and Other Rhymes, Candlewick Press (Cambridge, MA), 1997.
Little Boy Blue and Other Rhymes, Candlewick Press (Cambridge, MA), 1997.
Pussycat, Pussycat and Other Rhymes, Candlewick Press (Cambridge, MA), 1997.

Wee Willie Winkie and Other Rhymes, Candlewick Press (Cambridge, MA), 1997.

FICTION; FOR YOUNG ADULTS

The Fog Comes on Little Pig Feet, Dial (New York, NY), 1972.
None of the Above, Dial (New York, NY), 1974.
Leave Well Enough Alone, Dial (New York, NY), 1977.
When No One Was Looking, Dial (New York, NY), 1980, reprinted, Puffin (New York, NY), 2000.
The Man in the Woods, Dial (New York, NY), 1984.
Through the Hidden Door, Dial (New York, NY), 1987.

RETELLER

The Little Lame Prince (based on the book by Dinash Mulock Craik), Dial (New York, NY), 1990.
Lassie Come-Home (based on the book by Eric Knight), illustrated by Susan Jeffers, Holt (New York, NY), 1995.
Alan Garner, *Jack and the Beanstalk,* Dorling Kindersley (New York, NY), 1997.
The Fisherman and His Wife: A Brand-New Version, illustrated by Eleanor Hubbard, Dial (New York, NY), 1998.
Hitty: Her First Hundred Years, with New Adventures (based on the book by Rachel Field), illustrated by Susan Jeffers, Simon & Schuster (New York, NY), 1999.
Alan Garner, *Little Red Riding Hood,* Dorling Kindersley (New York, NY), 1999.

ILLUSTRATOR

William Schwenck Gilbert and Arthur Sullivan, *A Song to Sing, O!* (from *The Yeoman of the Guard*), Macmillan (New York, NY), 1968.
Gilbert and Sullivan, *W. S. Gilbert's "The Duke of Plaza Toro"* (from *The Gondoliers*), Macmillan (New York, NY), 1969.
Paula Fox, *Hungry Fred,* Bradbury, 1969.
(With Susan Jeffers), Charlotte Pomerantz, *Why You Look like You Whereas I Tend to Look like Me,* Young Scott Books, 1969.
Robert W. Service, *The Shooting of Dan McGrew [and] The Cremation of Sam McGhee,* Young Scott Books, 1969.
Rudyard Kipling, *The Cat That Walked by Himself,* Hawthorn, 1970.
Winifred Rosen, *Marvin's Manhole,* Dial (New York, NY), 1970.
Marjorie Weinman Sharmat, *A Hot Thirsty Day,* Macmillan, 1971.
Ellen Conford, *Impossible, Possum,* Little, Brown (Boston, MA), 1971.
Beryl Epstein and Dorrit Davis, *Two Sisters and Some Hornets,* Holiday House (New York, NY), 1972.
Virginia A. Tashjian, editor, *With a Deep-Sea Smile: Story Hour Stretches for Large or Small Groups,* Little, Brown (Boston, MA), 1974.

Lore G. Segal, *Tell Me a Trudy,* Farrar, Straus (New York, NY), 1977.

Jostein Gaarder, *The Christmas Mystery,* translated by Elizabeth Rokkan, Farrar, Straus (New York, NY), 1996.

Iona Opie, editor, *My Very First Mother Goose,* Candlewick Press (Cambridge, MA), 1996.

(Watercolorist) E. B. White, *Stuart Little: Collector's Edition,* HarperCollins (New York, NY), 1999.

(Watercolorist) E. B. White, *Charlotte's Web: Collector's Edition,* HarperCollins (New York, NY), 1999.

Iona Opie, editor, *Here Comes Mother Goose,* Candlewick Press (Cambridge, MA), 1999.

(Watercolorist) Garth Williams, *Benjamin's Treasure* (excerpt from *The Adventures of Benjamin Pink*), Candlewick Press (Cambridge, MA), 2001.

Oscar Hammerstein and Richard Rogers, *Getting to Know You!: Rogers and Hammerstein Favorites,* HarperCollins (New York, NY), 2002.

OTHER

Author, with Joanna Hurley, of *Cooking for Nitwits,* photographs by Barbara Olcott, Dutton, 1989. Contributor to *Worlds of Childhood: The Art and Craft of Writing for Children,* edited by William Zinsser, Houghton Mifflin, 1990.

Some of Wells's books have been translated into Spanish.

Adaptations

Morris's *Disappearing Bag* and *Max's Christmas* were adapted as short films by Weston Woods in 1982 and 1988, respectively. *Timothy Goes to School* was released as a filmstrip by Weston Woods in 1982; *Max's Christmas* was released as a filmstrip and on video by Weston Woods in 1987. *Morris's Disappearing Bag* was read on Kino's Storytime, a television program produced by KCET (Los Angeles, CA). PBS Kids, six animated programs produced by Nelvana for public television and aimed at the under-five audience. An adaptation of *Timothy Goes to School* aired in 2000. The "Max and Ruby" characters have been used in stickerbook adaptations published by Grossett & Dunlap. Several of Wells's characters, including Max and Ruby, Edward the Unready, and McDuff, have been produced as stuffed toys.

Sidelights

Described as "a master of the delicate art of story" by *School Library Journal* reviewer Christy Norris and as "one of the most gifted picture-book illustrators in the United States today" by Jennifer Farley Smith in the *Christian Science Monitor,* author and illustrator Rosemary Wells has been praised for creating delightful picture and board books; candid, incisive young adult novels; and well-received adaptations of classic tales in picture-book form. Wells addresses such genres as realistic fiction, fantasy, and a blend of the two as well as

Although exceedingly shy, Charles valiantly rescues his babysitter in Wells's self-illustrated touching story of the brave little mouse. (From Shy Charles.*)*

historical fiction, biography, the mystery story, the school story, and the psychological novel. A prolific, popular writer and artist, Wells is acclaimed for her originality, versatility, sensitivity, wry sense of humor, artistic talent, and understanding of both children and the human condition. She is also praised for her characterizations and is well known as the creator of many popular characters, such as sibling bunnies Max and Ruby, who are featured in a series of innovative board and picture books. As an illustrator, Wells has provided the pictures for works by such authors as Paula Fox, Rudyard Kipling, Beryl Epstein, Robert W. Service, and Ellen Conford. She has also illustrated several volumes of Mother Goose rhymes and has even illustrated portions of popular librettos by noted light opera composers Gilbert and Sullivan and beloved songs from musicals by Rogers and Hammerstein.

In her picture books, Wells takes a lighthearted but heartfelt approach to universal childhood experiences. Many of her books feature engaging animal characters, such as bears, bunnies, foxes, mice, raccoons, and badgers, who are caught up in childhood dilemmas or comic predicaments such as sibling rivalry, bedtime fears, distracted parents, being embarrassed in class, and dealing with bullies or a new baby-sitter. Wells is credited with evoking the painful aspects of these experiences while providing satisfying, often surprising endings. Noted for accurately reflecting the feelings of children while emphasizing the child as an individual, her works are also acknowledged for giving young readers and listeners the chance to laugh at themselves. Other picture books include a series featuring the charming West Highland White terrier McDuff, retellings of classic children's novels, and board books based on popular children's songs. Her young adult novels deal with ethical dilemmas such as betrayal, stealing, the pressures of competition, the difficulties of relationships, and the search for truth. Refusing to provide easy answers, Wells lets her characters tap their inner strength while establishing their identities and independence in a confusing world. She frequently creates a story-within-a-story and often concludes her books—some of which are written in verse—with unconventional endings.

As an artist, Wells favors line and watercolor; she is often praised for her rich use of color and for creating deceptively simple drawings that are filled with nuance and expression. "In a few lines and pale colors," noted Jennifer Farley Smith in the *Christian Science Monitor,* "Wells can speak volumes to her young audience." In *Booklist* Hazel Rochman also praised Wells' artwork, adding that the author/illustrator "has that rare ability to tell a funny story for very young children with domestic scenes of rising excitement and heartfelt emotion, and with not one word too many."Born in New York City, Wells grew up in a home that was, as she recalled in an essay for *Something about the Author Autobiography Series (SAAS)*, "always filled with books, dogs, nineteenth-century music, and other things my parents held in great esteem." Most of her childhood was spent on the New Jersey coast, where her maternal grandmother had a home right on the ocean. "I spent so much time in her enormous stucco house with its own beach that most of my sentimental and favorite memories, good and bad, come from that place and time on the New Jersey shore." The author's parents—her father was a playwright and her mother was a ballet dancer—and her grandmother encouraged her early artistic endeavors. Wells' grandmother, to whom she was very close, was widely read and had been a great beauty in New York society. She often read to Rosemary from works by authors such as Longfellow, Kipling, and Poe. As Wells recalled on her Web site, "Both my parents flooded me with books and stories. My grandmother took me on special trips to the theater and museums in New York."

From the age of two, Wells drew constantly. As she told Jean F. Mercier in *Publishers Weekly,* "I parlayed this [talent] into the sham of a school career. I discovered very early that making a picture of anything meant people saying 'Look at that!' and how else could I get that kind of attention?" Her subject matter was not the traditional childish flowers and family members; Wells sketched policemen, cowboys, baseball players, medieval soldiers, and lots of bloody fights. Encouraged in her art in first grade, she decided early on that she wanted to be an artist when she grew up.

As Wells recalled in *SAAS,* having a career goal during adolescence became increasingly important. "Because I could say artist, I had a reprieve from what, even then, I considered to be a life-sentence of drudgery. When I became a teenager, the idea of being an artist was the only thing that stood between me and despair—I was gangly, underdeveloped, a social retard whose mother didn't like her watching 'American Bandstand.'" In addition to art, writing was also important to the young teen, and when she wasn't drawing or involved with friends and sports, she read and wrote stories. "Whatever was behind those piles of drawings, the drawings themselves were behind the writing; and now that I am over forty, I can say the writing is the better part of my skills. I try mightily to improve my illustrations but my heart is probably more in writing."

At age thirteen, Wells was sent to an upscale boarding school for girls. "I reacted badly," the author/illustrator recalled in *SAAS:* "The school was a jail to me although the other girls seemed to be having a grand time." Wells found the regimentation, scrutiny, and constant supervision to be oppressive; in addition, "There was no privacy, no time to draw." Miserable, she was finally released from this torture when her parents took her out of the school. Wells remembered, "My grandmother told me, on my return home, that I had lost my first great battle with life. She was stuck with the tuition bill for the rest of the year." Back at home, Wells entered Red Bank High School, where she became an admittedly poor student. "I'd done badly in high school due to my own laziness and inability to take things like chemistry seriously. This was abetted by my parent's inability to take things like chemistry seriously." She spent her junior year "larking around England with my mother and father," and when accepted at a small private junior college in upstate New York, she decided to shed "the high school stigma of 'not being popular.'" At junior college she became a top student and made two lifelong friends. However, she soon got sidetracked by love after meeting Tom Wells, a Dartmouth student. She left school after one year and moved to Boston.

Irrepressible Max and his practical sister Ruby set about cleaning Max's room with predictably mixed results in **Max Cleans Up** *from Wells's self-illustrated series of books about the two rabbit siblings.*

In Boston, the nineteen-year-old Wells entered the Boston Museum School, where she studied anatomy, perspective, life drawing, and printing. In 1963, she and Tom Wells married, and she left school to enter the job market. On the strength of her portfolio, Wells landed a job as art editor with the publishers Allyn and Bacon. Then, as she wrote in *SAAS,* "all the laziness and reluctance to concentrate disappeared. I was assigned an American history book for Catholic high school seniors. It was thirteen hundred pages long and I had to send away for all the prints and photos that would illustrate it. The book was wonderful. The Sisters of the Sacred Heart, who were involved in the editorial end, were splendid women. There was a party when it was published and I felt like a success at something for the first time in my life."

Two years later, when Tom Wells was accepted at the Columbia University School of Architecture, the couple moved to New York City. While working as an art designer for Macmillan, Wells presented a small illustrated dummy of a Gilbert and Sullivan song, taken from their light opera *The Yeomen of the Guard,* to the company's editor-in-chief. This became her first published book, *A Song to Sing, O!,* and it was followed by *W. S. Gilbert's "The Duke of Plaza Toro,"* a picture book based on a Gilbert and Sullivan song from *The Gondoliers.* After illustrating well-received volumes by Paula Fox and Robert W. Service, Wells created her first original work, *John and the Rarey.* Published in 1969, the picture book features a little boy who does not want to be an airplane pilot like his father. What John does want is a pet: he finds a fantastic, blue-eyed creature that takes him into the sky on its back. A reviewer in *Publishers Weekly* called Wells "a fresh new talent in children's books" and praised *John and the Rarey* as a "witty story," while *Horn Book* critic Sidney D. Long wrote that her book would "appeal to all children who have been faced with a frustrating family situation."

Throughout her career Wells has continued to illustrate the work of other authors while adding to a growing list of solo picture books. In 1979 she produced the first four books in her popular "Max and Ruby" series: *Max's First Word, Max's New Suit, Max's Ride,* and *Max's Toys: A Counting Book.* Concept books inspired by the antics of her own two children that *Children's Books and Their Creators* contributor Maeve Visser Knoth called "the first funny board books for very young children," the "Max and Ruby" books use story, information, and humor to introduce preschoolers to such concepts as prepositions, getting dressed, and the importance of individuality. Max is a white bunny; Ruby is an older sister who thinks she knows what is best for Max and tries to control him. Although Max is easygoing, he remains undaunted, innocently outsmarting his sister and always getting the last word. Featuring a minimal but lively text, the books feature pictures enlivened by vivid primary colors and featuring an uncluttered page layout. Writing in *Booklist,* Judith Gold-

In six short tales, Wells depicts kindergarten at Hilltop School, where friendships and enmities, problems and solutions are presented. (From Timothy's Tales from Hilltop School, *written and illustrated by Wells.)*

berger praised the series for "driv[ing] . . . a real wedge into the existing block of unnotable, overcute, didactic baby-toddler tomes." Wells has continued to produce board books in the "Max and Ruby" series, continuing the adventures of the brother-and-sister duo for new generations of pre-readers in books such as *Bunny Money, Max Drives Away,* and *Ruby's Beauty Shop.* Reviewing *Ruby's Beauty Shop,* in which Ruby and friend Louie make Max their guinea pig in a game of beauty parlor that goes awry, a *Kirkus Reviews* critic noted that "Wells has an unerring ability to hit just the right note to tickle small-fry funny bones." "Each story portrays a typical preschool trauma resolved with humor and understanding," wrote Trev Jones in *School Library Journal,* while in a *Bulletin of the Center for Children's Books* review Zena Sutherland dubbed each book in the series "equally delectable, and they should be as useful for very young children as they are appealing."

Max's Christmas breaks with Wells' board-book tradition by presenting the first full-length picture-book treatment of the escapades of Max and Ruby. A bunny with an inquiring mind, Max has lots of unanswered questions about Santa Claus, which Ruby answers with a simple "Because!" Unsatisfied, Max sneaks downstairs to wait for Santa, who patiently answers Max's questions until he finally has to resort to "Because!" Ruby comes down to find Max on the couch with a lap full of presents, a situation that prompts questions of her own. Calling Max "that epitome of the small child in rabbit guise," Judith Glover, wrote in *School Library Journal* that Wells "has an extraordinary talent for capturing a welter of thoughts and emotions with the placement of an eye or a turn of a smile." *Horn Book* critic Karen Jameyson concluded that, despite the book's longer format, "an uncanny perceptive simplicity, both in line and in word, is still Wells's most effective tool." More recent books about Max and Ruby adhere to the picture-book format. Wells uses the frame of the story-within-a-story to introduce young readers and listeners to Greek mythology in *Max and Ruby's First Greek Myth: Pandora's Box,* wherein Ruby finds Max investigating her jewelry box. Because the box is off limits, she tells him a bunny-centric version of the classic legend. In *Bunny Cakes* and *Bunny Money* Max and Ruby prepare for their grandmother's birthday, while *Bunny Mail* finds grandma attempting to decipher Max's Christmas-present requests after the bunny's pictograph notes to Santa are mistakenly sent her way. In *Bunny Cakes,* the siblings have separate ideas for cakes: Ruby wants to make an angel surprise cake while Max wants to present his grandmother with an earthworm cake decorated with red-hot marshmallow squirters. At the end of the story, Max—who is too young to read and write—thinks of a way to communicate his shopping list to the grocer, and Grandma is thrilled when she receives two cakes. Pat Mathews, a reviewer for the *Bulletin of the Center for Children's Books,* claimed that, "in this take on written communication kidstyle, pudgy Max is at his winsome best." *Bunny Money* finds the pair shopping to buy a birthday present for Grandma. The siblings' money goes fast—most of it is spent on Max, and Wells shows the gradual reduction of the contents of Ruby's wallet at the bottom of each page—but a compromise is reached: Grandma drives the pair home wearing musical earrings from Ruby and plastic vampire teeth from Max. A *Kirkus Reviews* critic called the book "a great adjunct to primary-grade math lessons," while in the *Bulletin of the Center for Children's Books* Pat Mathews concluded that Wells' "combination of gentle comedy, shrinking assets, and those expressive bunny eyes" will attract "old and new Max and Ruby fans."

In addition to penning stories involving the irrepressible Max and Ruby, Wells has also created several other popular series. Her "Voyage to the Bunny Planet" books feature little bunnies who have bad days and imagine themselves transported to the Bunny Planet, where good times restore their equilibrium. The "Edward the Unready" series follows a little bear who is unenthusiastic about going to school or staying overnight at a friend's house and prefers to be at home among familiar surroundings. In the "McDuff" series, a West Highland white terrier—based on Wells' own pet—escapes from a dogcatcher's truck and is adopted by a young couple. The author's "Bunny Reads Back" series features board books for youngsters and parents to share that are based on favorite children's songs. Other series feature Yoko, a little Asian kitten, and Felix, a guinea pig who in *Felix Feels Better* is nursed back to health by Mom after overindulging in his favorite chocolate candy. In *The World around Us* Wells unites several of her series characters in Mrs. Jenkins' kindergarten class, where the

A little sprite called the Worrier comes to guinea pig Felix each night to remind him of the various troublesome things the future holds until Felix faces his fears and frees himself from his fretting. (From Felix and the Worrier, *written and illustrated by Wells.)*

students learn about their place in the larger worlds of family, community, country, and world.

Stand-alone picture books by Wells include *Wingwalker* and *The House in the Mail,* the latter a collaboration with her husband, Tom Wells. *Wingwalker,* which takes place during the Great Depression of the 1930s and finds a young Oklahoma boy and his family trying to make ends meet during the sustained drought that caused the Dust Bowl, was praised by a *Kirkus Reviews* critic who noted that "Wells' prose is spare but has both richness and freshness of simile and image." *The House in the Mail* takes readers back to an even earlier decade of the twentieth century, when houses could be ordered in kits from the Sears, Roebuck catalogue. The story is narrated by twelve-year-old Emily, whose father summons friends to help assemble the modern home. Complete with a refrigerator, running water, a washing machine, and other conveniences, the new six-room bungalow is put together piece, by piece, and the story is illustrated in scrap-book style by Dan Andreasen. Noting that "Anecdotes and snatches of conversation flesh out the era," a *Publishers Weekly* contributor praised *The House in the Mail* as a story that "speaks . . . to the strong bond among the members of Emily's family." "This remarkable picture book . . . is like discovering a slice of American life in a family scrap-book," added Connie Fletcher in *Booklist.*

In addition to being a prolific author of picture books, Wells has written several well-respected novels for teen readers. The award-winning *When No One Was Looking* is a mystery novel that focuses on a highly competitive teen tennis player who is placed under suspicion when her arch rival conveniently drowns just before a face-off match. *The Fog Comes on Little Pig Feet,* which is based on Wells' boarding-school experience, takes the form of a diary written by thirteen-year-old Rachel Sakasian. A Brooklyn girl who wants to become a concert pianist, Rachel longs to attend Music and Art High, a New York City public school, but her parents enroll her at North Place, an elite boarding school. Rachel dislikes North Place, which allows her no time to practice the piano or to be alone. When she becomes friends with upper-classman Carlisle Duggett, who is rumored to be mentally unbalanced, Rachel finds herself covering for her new friend when the girl leaves school to live in Greenwich Village. When she finds that Carlisle has tried to commit suicide, Rachel is torn between protecting her friend and telling the truth. In a *School Library Journal* review, Alice Miller Bregman predicted that "teens will devour this fast-paced, adequately written entertainment," while Jane Langton stated in *Book World* that *The Fog Comes in on Little Pig Feet* "says something true about life: Evil is not diabolical and nasty, but bland and blind." A contributor to *Best Sellers,* applauded the novel's "priceless vignettes" and concluded that Wells "brilliantly demonstrates [that] her writing abilities are an easy match for her already famous artistic talents."

First published in 1974, *None of the Above* outlines five years in the life of Marcia, a teen who likes pink angora sweaters, reading movie magazines, and watching television. When her father remarries, Marcia feels out of place with her sophisticated stepmother and ambitious stepsister. In reaction, she decides to turn herself around: she switches to college prep classes and succeeds, although reluctantly, in school. However, she also becomes involved with Raymond, a good-looking though hoodish classmate. The book's ending is ambivalent: Raymond, who is impotent until he meets Marcia, asks her to marry him, forcing her to choose between an uncertain future with a boy she does not love and pursuit of a college degree she is not sure she truly desires. Calling Marcia an "unusual and oddly affecting heroine," *School Library Journal* critic Joni Brodart claimed that Wells "captures the girl's confusion in this timely, realistic, and moving novel which should reach a large audience." Writing in the *Bulletin of the Center for Children's Books,* Zena Sutherland noted that Wells' "characterization is strong and consistent, and the complexities of relationships within the family are beautifully developed. Wells is particularly adept at dialogue." Although she praised the book's "uncompromising honesty," Jean F. Mercier was less than impressed with Marcia, noting in *Publishers Weekly* that the "trouble with the story is that all its people are so unsavoury. That goes double for the 'heroine,' a dolt who is more irritating than sympathetic." Writing in the *New York Times Book Review,* Dale Carlson called *None of the Above* "well-written and the characters well-conceived."

Wells has also delved into nonfiction writing with several biographies of historical and contemporary women.

Mary on Horseback: Three Mountain Stories, a book for middle graders, profiles Mary Breckinridge, founder of the Frontier Nursing Service in the Appalachian Mountains. After losing two husbands and two children, Mary worked as a nurse in Europe during World War II, and arrived in Kentucky in 1923. Wells shows both the hardships and the triumphs experienced by the valiant nurse from the perspectives of three young people whom Mary helped. Noting the "historical accuracy and elegance" of the volume, a reviewer in *Publishers Weekly* stated that the book's "well-honed first-person narratives add up to an outstanding biography." *Booklist* reviewer Helen Rosenberg added that "these beautifully written stories will remain with the reader long after the book is closed; Wells has given much deserved honor to a true heroine," while Peggy Morgan concluded in *School Library Journal:* "This one's a gem."

In *Streets of Gold* Wells presents a picture-book biography of Mary Antin, a Jewish girl who came to the United States from tsarist Russia in the early twentieth century. A year after her arrival, Antin wrote an epic poem about George Washington that was published in a Boston newspaper. A reviewer in *Publishers Weekly* claimed that, "among a profusion of books about turn-of-the-century Russian-Jewish emigrants, Wells's . . . story about Mary Antin stands out for its exceptional economy and tenderness." Wells has also produced a well-received biography of American ballet dancer Maria Tallchief, collaborating with the noted Native American dancer on the project.

In addition to her work as an author and illustrator, Wells is a strong advocate of literacy programs. She has often spoken on behalf of the "Twenty Minutes a Day" campaign, which proposes that parents should spend twenty minutes each day reading to their children. She read her 1998 picture book *Read to Your Bunny* at the White House at the opening of the nationwide Prescription for Reading Partnership program. Looking back on her long career, Wells wrote in *SAAS,* "There are hard parts but no bad or boring parts, and that is more than can be said for any other line of work." In *Worlds of Childhood,* Wells further noted: "I believe that all stories and plays and paintings and songs and dances come from a palpable but unseen space in the cosmos. . .. According to how gifted we are, we are all given a large or small key to this treasury of wonders. I have been blessed with a small key to the world of the young."

Biographical and Critical Sources

BOOKS

Authors and Artists for Young Adults, Volume 13, Gale (Detroit, MI), 1994, pp. 227-236.
Children's Books and Their Creators, edited by Anita Silvey, Houghton Mifflin (Boston, MA), 1995, p. 374.

Children's Literature Review, Volume 16, Gale (Detroit, MI), 1989.

Contemporary Literary Criticism, Volume 12, Gale (Detroit, MI), 1980.

Fourth Book of Junior Authors and Illustrators, edited by Doris De Montreville and Elizabeth D. Crawford, H. W. Wilson (Bronx, NY), 1978, pp. 343-345.

Pendergast, Tom, and Sara Pendergast, editors, *St. James Guide to Children's Writers,* Gale (Detroit, MI), 1999.

Pendergast, Tom, and Sara Pendergast, editors, *St. James Guide to Young Adult Writers,* Gale (Detroit, MI), 1999.

Sadker, Myra Pollack, and David Miller Sadker, *Now upon a Time: A Contemporary View of Children's Literature,* Harper, 1997, pp. 66-67.

Something about the Author Autobiography Series, Volume 1, Gale (Detroit, MI), 1986, pp. 279-292.

Worlds of Childhood: The Art and Craft of Writing for Children, edited by William Zinsser, Houghton Mifflin (Boston, MA), 1990, pp. 121-143.

PERIODICALS

Best Sellers, July 15, 1972, review of *The Fog Comes on Little Pig Feet,* p. 200.

Booklist, January 1, 1997, Hazel Rochman, review of *Bunny Cakes,* p. 857; September 1, 1998, Helen Rosenberg, review of *Mary on Horseback: Three Mountain Stories,* p. 113; February 1, 2001, Kathy Broderick, review of *Max Cleans Up,* p. 1059; February 15, 2001, Shelley Townsend Hudson, review of *Benjamin's Treasure,* p. 1142; May 1, 2001, Hazel Rochman, review of *Felix Feels Better,* p. 1693; November 1, 2001, Hazel Rochman, review of *Language of Doves,* p. 475; December 15, 2001, Stephanie Zvirin, review of *Felix Feels Better,* p. 728; March 1, 2002, Connie Fletcher, review of *The House in the Mail,* p. 1137; July, 2002, Shelle Rosenfeld, review of *McDuff Saves the Day,* p.1861; August, 2002, Hazel Rochman, review of *Ruby's Beauty Shop,* p. 1977; November 1, 2003, Kay Weisman, review of *Felix and the Worrier,* p. 507.

Bulletin of the Center for Children's Books, April, 1975, Zena Sutherland, review of *None of the Above,* p. 139; April, 1985, Zena Sutherland, review of *Max's Bath,* p. 157; November, 1993, Betsy Hearne, review of *Max and Ruby's First Greek Myth: Pandora's Box,* p.106; March, 1997, Pat Mathews, review of *Bunny Cakes,* p. 261; October, 1997, Pat Mathews, review of *Bunny Money,* p. 71.

Childhood Education, winter, 2000, Susan A. Miller, review of *Goodnight Max,* p. 110.

Christian Science Monitor, March 6, 1974, Jennifer Farley Smith, "Animals Are Enduring Heroes," p. F2.

Horn Book, August, 1969, Sidney D. Long, review of *John and the Rarey,* pp. 399-400; June, 1987, Roger Sutton, "A Second Look: 'None of the Above,'" pp. 368-371; July-August, Christine M. Heppermann, review of *Wingwalker,* p. 474.

Kirkus Reviews, September 1, 1993, review of *Max and Ruby's First Greek Myth: Pandora's Box,* p 1154; July 15, 1997, review of *Bunny Money,* p. 1119; April 15, 2002, review of *Wingwalker,* p. 581; May 15, 2002, review of *McDuff Saves the Day,* p. 743; June 15, 2002, review of *Timothy's Tales from Hilltop School,* p. 890; July 15, 2002, review of *Ruby's Beauty Shop,* p. 1047; August 15, 2003, review of *The Small World of Binky Braverman,* p. 1081; August 15, 2003, review of *Felix and the Worrier,* p. 1080.

New York Times Book Review, November 24, 1974, Dale Carlson, review of *None of the Above,* p. 8.

Publishers Weekly, April 21, 1969, review of *John and the Rarey,* p. 64; November 15, 1970, review of *Miranda's Pilgrims,* p. 1245; August 5, 1974, Jean F. Mercier, review of *None of the Above,* p. 58; October 9, 1978, review of *Stanley and Rhoda,* p. 76; February 29, 1980, Jean F. Mercier, interview, pp. 72-73; September 14, 1998, review of *Mary on Horseback: Three Mountain Stories,* p. 70; October 19, 1998, review of *Yoko,* p. 78; April 19, 1999, review of *Streets of Gold,* p. 73; October 23, 2000, p. 77; November 20, 2000, p. 70; June 4, 2001, review of *Felix Feels Better,* p. 79; July 9, 2001, p. 69; July 16, 2001, p. 148; November 5, 2001, p.71; January 14, 2002, review of *The House in the Mail,* p. 60; March 25, 2002, review of *Wingwalker,* p. 65; May 27, 2002, review of *Happy Anniversary, Charlotte & Wilbur,* p. 61; October 7, 2002, p. 75; May 12, 2003, review of *Only You,* p. 65; August 18, 2003, review of *The Small World of Binky Braverman,* p. 78; September 1, 2003, review of *Felix and the Worrier,* p.91; September 8, 2003, review of *Back to School,* p. 78.

School Library Journal, May, 1972, Alice Miller Bregman, review of *The Fog Comes on Little Pig Feet,* p. 89; November, 1974, Joni Brodart, review of *None of the Above,* p. 69; March, 1985, Trev Jones, review of *Max's Bath,* pp. 159-160; October, 1986, Judith Glover, review of *Max's Christmas,* p. 112; July, 1997, Christy Norris, review of *McDuff Comes Home,* p. 78; October, 1998, Peggy Morgan, review of *Mary on Horseback,* p. 130; December, 2000, Christina F. Renaud, review of *Max Cleans Up,* p. 127; November, 2001, Rosalyn Pierini, review of *Yoko's Paper Cranes,* p. 138; December, 2001, Lisa Gangemi Krapp, review of *The World around Us,* p. 129; January, 2002, Marilyn Taniguchi, review of *Mama, Don't Go!,* p. 112; March, 2002, Rita Soltan, review of *Adding It Up,* p. 223; May, 2002, Heide Piehler, review of *Wingwalker,* p. 162; July, 2002, Janie Schomberg, review of *The Germ Busters,* p. 100; July, 2002, Shara Alpern, review of *Be My Valentine,* p. 100; August, 2002, Maryann H. Owen, review of *McDuff Saves the Day,* p. 172; October, 2002, Laurie von Mehren, review of *Timothy's Tales from Hilltop School,* p. 134; October, 2002, Shara Alpern, review of *Ruby's Beauty Shop,* p. 134; December, 2002, Anne Knickerbocker, review of *Read Me a Story,* p. 112; May, 2003, Heather E. Miller, review of *Only You,* p. 132.

ONLINE

Penguin Group USA Web site, http://www.penguinputnam.com/ (December 2, 2004).

World of Rosemary Wells, http://www.rosemarywells.com/ (December 2, 2004).

A Visit with Rosemary Wells (film), Penguin USA, 1994.*

*   *   *

WIEBE, Rudy (Henry) 1934-

Personal

Born October 4, 1934, in Fairholme, Saskatchewan, Canada; son of Abram J. (a farmer) and Tena (Knelsen) Wiebe; married Tena F. Isaak, March, 1958; children: Adrienne, Michael, Christopher. *Education:* University of Alberta, B.A., 1956, M.A., 1960; Mennonite Brethren Bible College, B.Th., 1961; additional study at University of Tübingen, 1957-58, University of Manitoba, 1961, and University of Iowa, 1964. *Religion:* Mennonite. *Hobbies and other interests:* Photography, watching people, travel.

Addresses

Home—105 10610-83 Ave., Edmonton, Alberta T6E 2E2M, Canada. *Office*—Department of English, Humanities Centre 3-5, University of Alberta, Edmonton, Alberta T6G 2E5, Canada.

Career

Glenbow Foundation, Calgary, Alberta, Canada, research writer, 1956; Government of Canada, Ottawa, Ontario, foreign service officer, 1960; high school English teacher, Selkirk, Manitoba, Canada, 1961; *Mennonite Brethren Herald,* Winnipeg, Manitoba, editor, 1962-63; Goshen College, Goshen, IN, assistant professor of English, 1963-67; University of Alberta, Edmonton, Alberta, assistant professor, 1967-70, associate professor, 1970-76, professor of English, 1976-92, professor emeritus, 1992—. President, NeWest Press, beginning 1989. University of Kiel, Kiel, Germany, chair of Canadian studies, 1984. Member of Arts Panel, Canadian Council, 1974-77; member of writers advisory committee to Alberta Ministry of Culture, 1980-82; member of federal cultural policy review committee, 1981-84, and Alberta Foundation for the Literary Arts, 1984-87.

Member

Royal Society of Canada.

Awards, Honors

Rotary International fellow, 1957-58; Canada Council bursary, 1964, and senior arts award, 1971; Governor General's Award for Fiction, 1973, for *The Temptations of Big Bear,* 1994, for *A Discovery of Strangers;* Province of Alberta and City of Edmonton Arts Achievement Awards, 1974, 1975; D.Litt., University of Winnipeg, 1986; Lorne Pierce Medal for contribution to Canadian literature, Royal Society of Canada, 1987.

Rudy Wiebe

D.Litt., Wilfred Laurier University, 1991; LL.D., Brock University, 1991; admitted to Edmonton Cultural Hall of Fame, 1995.

Writings

FOR CHILDREN

Chinook Christmas, illustrated by David More, Northern Lights/Red Deer Press, 1992, published with new illustrations, 2003.
Hidden Buffalo, illustrated by Davide Lonechild, Red Deer Press, 2003.

ADULT NOVELS

Peace Shall Destroy Many, McClelland & Stewart (Toronto, Ontario, Canada), 1962, revised edition, Eerdmans (Grand Rapids, MI), 1964.
First and Vital Candle, Eerdmans (Grand Rapids, MI), 1966.
The Blue Mountains of China, Eerdmans (Grand Rapids, MI), 1970.
The Temptations of Big Bear, McClelland & Stewart (Toronto, Ontario, Canada), 1973.
Riel and Gabriel, McClelland & Stewart (Toronto, Ontario, Canada), 1973.
The Scorched-Wood People, McClelland & Stewart (Toronto, Ontario, Canada), 1977.

The Mad Trapper, McClelland & Stewart (Toronto, Ontario, Canada), 1980, reprinted, Red Deer Press, 2002.

My Lovely Enemy, McClelland & Stewart (Toronto, Ontario, Canada), 1983.

A Discovery of Strangers, Knopf (Toronto, Ontario, Canada), 1994.

Sweeter than All the World, Knopf (Toronto, Ontario, Canada), 2001.

SHORT-STORY COLLECTIONS

Where Is the Voice Coming From?, McClelland & Stewart (Toronto, Ontario, Canada), 1974.

Alberta: A Celebration, photographs by Harry Savage, edited by Tom Radford, Hurtig (Edmonton, Alberta, Canada), 1979.

The Angel of the Tar Sands, and Other Stories, McClelland & Stewart (Toronto, Ontario, Canada), 1982.

River of Stone: Fictions and Memories, Vintage Books (Toronto, Ontario, Canada), 1995.

EDITOR

The Story-Makers: A Selection of Modern Short Stories, Macmillan (Toronto, Ontario, Canada), 1970.

Stories from Western Canada, Macmillan (Toronto, Ontario, Canada), 1972.

(With Andreas Schroeder) *Stories from Pacific and Arctic Canada,* Macmillan (Toronto, Ontario, Canada), 1974.

Double Vision, McClelland & Stewart (Toronto, Ontario, Canada), 1976.

Getting Here, NeWest Press (Edmonton, Alberta, Canada), 1977.

(With Aritha van Herk) *More Stories from Western Canada,* Macmillan (Toronto, Ontario, Canada), 1980.

(With Aritha van Herk and Leah Flater) *West of Fiction,* NeWest Press (Edmonton, Alberta, Canada), 1983.

OTHER

(With Theatre Passe Muraille) *As Far as the Eye Can See* (play), NeWest Press (Edmonton, Alberta, Canada), 1977.

(And compiler with Bob Beal) *War in the West: Voices of the 1885 Rebellion* (history), McClelland & Stewart (Toronto, Ontario, Canada), 1985.

Playing Dead: A Contemplation concerning the Arctic (essays), McClelland & Stewart (Toronto, Ontario, Canada), 1989.

Silence, the Word, and the Sacred: Essays, Wilfred Laurier (Waterloo, Ontario, Canada), 1989.

(With Yvonne Johnson) *Stolen Life: The Journey of a Cree Woman* (nonfiction), Knopf (Toronto, Ontario, Canada), 1998.

(With Geoffrey James) *Place: Lethbridge, A City on the Prairie,* Douglas & McIntyre (Vancouver, British Columbia, Canada), 2002.

Work represented in anthologies, including *Fourteen Stories High,* edited by David Helwig, Oberon Press (Ottawa, Ontario, Canada), 1971; *The Narrative Voice,* edited by John Metcalf, McGraw-Hill (New York, NY), 1972; *Modern Stories in English,* edited by W. H. New and H. J. Rosengarten, Crowell (New York, NY), 1975; *Personal Fictions,* edited by Michael Ondaatje, Oxford University Press (Toronto, Ontario, Canada), 1977; and *Wild Rose Country: Stories from Alberta,* edited by David Carpenter, Oberon Press, 1977. Contributor of articles and short stories to periodicals, including *Fiddlehead, Tamarack Review, Camrose Review, Canadian Literature, Maclean's, Saturday Night,* and *The Bote.*

Adaptations

"Someday Soon" was adapted for television by the Canadian Broadcasting Corp. (CBC), January, 1977.

Sidelights

In addition to adult fiction that explores his personal religious beliefs, modern society, and the traditional values and character of western Canada, novelist Rudy Wiebe has authored several books for children. The Canadian writer's first children's book, 1992's *Chinook Christmas,* was praised by *Canadian Children's Literature* contributor Perry Nodelman as "a sort of prairie version of Dylan Thomas's sensuously evocative *Child's Christmas in Wales.*" His 2003 picture book, *Hidden Buffalo,* focuses on Cree native Sky Running, a young hunter who helps his tribe to find buffalo during a time of famine after listening to his grandmother recite tales of the Creator and how the first buffalo came to be. Wiebe has earned two of his country's most prestigious literary awards, the Governor General's Award and the Lorne Pierce medal, for his portrayal of the people who inhabit the prairie lands of western Canada.

Wiebe grew up in Saskatchewan, north of Saskatoon, and was the youngest member of an ethnic German family of seven children whose homesteading parents had emigrated from Russia. He spoke only German until he went to elementary school, and he eventually attended a Mennonite high school and the University of Alberta in Edmonton, where he later taught. Much of Wiebe's writing focuses on the northern regions where he was raised, particularly Arctic culture. One of his novels that critics have found appropriate for teen readers is 1980's *The Mad Trapper,* which explores the growing impact of technology on northern culture and man's vital yet fragile relationship with the land. Taking place in the 1930s near the Rat River, *The Mad Trapper* is based on a true story about Albert Johnson, a man who refused to cease using trap lines reserved for Native Canadians, fled into the northern woods, and, after an extensive manhunt, was killed resisting arrest.

Biographical and Critical Sources

BOOKS

Cameron, Donald, *Conversations with Canadian Novelists,* Macmillan (Toronto, Ontario, Canada), 1973, pp. 146-160.

Contemporary Literary Criticism, Gale (Detroit, MI), Volume 6, 1976, Volume 11, 1979, Volume 14, 1980.

Contemporary Novelists, 7th edition, St. James (Detroit, MI), 2001.

Dictionary of Literary Biography, Volume 60: *Canadian Writers since 1960, Second Series,* Gale (Detroit, MI), 1987.

Moss, John, editor, *The Canadian Novel: Here and Now,* NC Press, 1978.

Twigg, Alan, *For Openers: Conversations with Twenty-four Canadian Writers,* Harbour, 1981, pp. 207-218.

PERIODICALS

Books in Canada, summer, 1994, p. 39; September, 1998, p. 6.

Canadian Book Review Annual, 1998, p. 383.

Canadian Children's Literature, fall, 1994, p. 77.

Canadian Ethnic Studies Journal, spring, 2002, Kenneth Hoeppner, review of *Sweeter than All the World,* p. 157.

Canadian Forum, January, 1968; December, 1977; December, 1980, p. 42; March, 1981, pp. 5-8, 13; May, 1983; p. 29; January, 1990, p. 30; October, 1994, p. 43; April, 1995, p. 20.

Canadian Literature, summer, 1974; winter, 1975; summer, 1978, pp. 42-63; spring, 1985, pp. 7-22; spring, 1990, p. 320; winter, 2000, pp. 10, 154.

Commonweal, December 7, 2001, p. 21.

Essays on Canadian Writing, winter, 1980-81, pp. 134-148; summer, 1983, pp. 70-73; spring, 1998, p. 113.

Globe & Mail (Toronto, Ontario, Canada), June 27, 1998, Olive Patricia Dickason, "Big Bear's Spirit Provides Healing Light; Stolen Life: The Journey of a Cree Woman"; May 22, 1999, p. D14; June 19, 1999, p. D17.

Maclean's, May 30, 1994, p. 45; July 13, 1998, "Native Connection: A Writer and Convicted Murderer Tells Her Story," p. 64.

Quill and Quire, December, 1992, p. 26; April, 1994, p. 26; July, 1998, Suzanne Methot, review of *Stolen Life: The Journey of a Cree Woman,* p. 30.

Resource Links, October, 1999, p. 20; June, 2003, Lori Lavallee, review of *The Mad Trapper,* p. 37.

Rubicon, summer, 1986, pp. 126-159.

Saturday Night, April, 1971, p. 26; February, 1974, p. 33.

World Literature Today, summer, 1999, p. 575.

ONLINE

Random House Canada Web site, http://www.randomhouse.ca/ (May 16, 2003).

Swallow Press Web site, http://www.ohiou.edu/oupress/ (May 16, 2003).*

*   *   *

WILLIAMS, Colleen Madonna Flood 1963-

Personal

Born June 1, 1963, in Buffalo, NY; daughter of Patrick E. (a chief custodial engineer) and Kathleen Hoare (a mental health therapy aide) Flood; married Paul R. Williams (an instrumentation technician); children: Dillon Joseph Meehan. *Education:* University of Alaska, Anchorage, 1999, B.Ed. *Politics:* Republican. *Religion:* "Catholic/Christian." *Hobbies and other interests:* Family, biking.

Addresses

Home and office—Dragonfly Manor Enterprises, P.O. Box 3492, Homer, AK 99603. *E-mail*—colleen.williams@acsalaska.net.

Career

Freelance writer, beginning 1999.

Writings

Chuck Yeager, Famous Flyers, Chelsea House (Philadelphia, PA), 2003.

Homes of the Native Americans, Mason Crest Publishers, 2003.

The Festivals of Mexico, Mason Crest Publishers, 2003.

The People of Mexico, Mason Crest Publishers, 2003.

The Geography of Mexico, Mason Crest Publishers, 2003.

Also contributor to periodicals, and to books, including *Writer's Handbook, 2004,* and *Chicken Soup for the Grandparent's Soul.*

Work in Progress

My Adventure to the Arctic, My Adventure to the Forest Clubhouse, My Adventure to the Harbor, My Adventure to the Playground, and *My Adventure to the Secret Cave,* volumes in the "My Adventure" reader series, for Orchard Academy Press; a series of workbooks for children on the fifty United States.

Sidelights

Colleen Madonna Flood Williams told *Something about the Author:* "I have enjoyed writing since I was a child. After a battle against Stage 2b breast cancer, I decided to do what I loved to do most, which is to write. I began writing on the Internet for small publications and Web sites. Gradually, my portfolio grew and I was able to secure several magazine articles and then several book contracts.

"I am currently working with Windstorm Creative's Orchard Academy Press on a fifty-book workbook series on the United States that is designed for children."

*   *   *

WOLF, Erica (Van Varick) 1978-

Personal

Born September 4, 1978, in Mendham, NJ; daughter of James (a doctor of internal medicine) and Kathleen (a dog groomer) Wolf; married Robert Van Varick (a product designer). *Education:* Rhode Island School of Design, B.F.A. (illustration), 2000.

Addresses

Home—203 Taylorsville Road, Yardley, PA 19067. *E-mail*—Ericalwolf@hotmail.com.

Career

Author and illustrator of children's books.

Member

Society of Children's Book Writers and Illustrators.

Writings

(And illustrator) *I Love You Just the Same,* Henry Holt (New York, NY), 2003.
Brave Little Raccoon, Henry Holt (New York, NY), 2005.

Sidelights

Illustrator and author Erica Wolf's first published picture book, *I Love You Just the Same,* documents a year in the life of a young bear cub. Focusing in on the unconditional love between the cub and his mother as Little Bear begins to master the rudiments of fishing, digging roots, and other brown-bear activities, the story is supplemented by the author's colorful acrylic paintings of the bear family and their woodland surroundings. Praising Wolf's illustrations as "lovely [and] naturalistic," Andrea Tarr added in her review for *School Library Journal* that the paintings "perfectly enhance the narrative in this springboard to nature discussions." A *Publishers Weekly* critic conveyed mixed feelings for Wolf's book, however, noting that "Little Bear is never seen wondering or asking if his mother's affection is in jeopardy, . . . and the repetition of the title turns grating." Despite such qualms, the reviewer added that in her illustrations Wolf effectively "captures the steady simplicity" of her forest-dwelling subjects.

Wolf told *Something about the Author:* "My love and respect for animals inspires my art and my stories. I hope to convey this passion for animals to the children and/or adults who read my books and look at my artwork. Artists such as Arthur Rackham and more recently Jerry Pinkney and Gregory Manchess have influenced my work."

Biographical and Critical Sources

PERIODICALS

Publishers Weekly, October 6, 2003, review of *I Love You Just the Same,* p. 82.

Edward Wortis

School Library Journal, December, 2003, Andrea Tarr, review of *I Love You Just the Same,* p. 131.

*   *   *

WORTIS, Avi
See WORTIS, Edward (Irving)

*   *   *

WORTIS, Edward (Irving) 1937-
(Avi, Avi Wortis)

Personal

Born December 23, 1937, in New York, NY; son of Joseph (a psychiatrist) and Helen (a social worker; maiden name Zunser) Wortis; married Joan Gabriner (a weaver), November 1, 1963 (divorced); married Coppelia Kahn (a professor of English); children: Shaun Wortis, Kevin Wortis; stepchildren: Gabriel Kahn. *Education:* Attended Antioch University; University of Wisconsin—Madison, B.A., 1959, M.A., 1962; Columbia University, M.S.L.S., 1964. *Hobbies and other interests:* Photography.

Addresses

Home—2205-A Grove St., Boulder, CO 80302. *Agent*—Dorothy Markinko, McIntosh & Otis, Inc., 475 Fifth Ave., New York, NY 10017.

Career

Writer, 1960—. New York Public Library, New York, NY, librarian in performing arts research center, 1962-70; Lambeth Public Library, London, England, exchange program librarian, 1968; Trenton State College, Trenton, NJ, assistant professor and humanities librarian, 1970-86. Co-founder of "Breakfast Serials" (reading program), 1996; visiting writer in schools across the United States.

Member

PEN, Authors Guild, Authors League of America.

Awards, Honors

Best Book of the Year designation, British Book Council, 1973, for *Snail Tale: The Adventures of a Rather Small Snail;* grants from New Jersey State Council on the Arts, 1974, 1976, and 1978; Mystery Writers of America Special Award, 1975, for *No More Magic,* 1979, for *Emily Upham's Revenge; or, How Deadwood Dick Saved the Banker's Niece: A Massachusetts Adventure,* and 1983, for *Shadrach's Crossing;* Christopher Award, 1980, for *Encounter at Easton;* Children's Choice Award, International Reading Association (IRA), 1980, for *Man from the Sky,* and 1988, for *Romeo and Juliet—Together (and Alive) at Last; School Library Journal* best books of the year citations, 1980, for *Night Journeys,* 1987, for *Wolf Rider: A Tale of Terror,* and 1990, for *The True Confessions of Charlotte Doyle;* New Jersey Authors Award, New Jersey Institute of Technology, for *Shadrach's Crossing,* 1983; Scott O'Dell Historical Fiction Award, *Bulletin of the Center for Children's Books,* 1984, for *The Fighting Ground;* ALA best books for young adults citations, 1984, for *The Fighting Ground,* and 1986, for *Wolf Rider,* and notable book citation for *The True Confessions of Charlotte Doyle,* 1990; Library of Congress best books of the year citations, 1989, for *Something Upstairs: A Tale of Ghosts,* and 1990, for *The Man Who Was Poe;* Virginia Young Readers' Award, 1990, for *Wolf Rider: A Tale of Terror;* best book of the year citation, Society of Children's Book Authors, 1990, and Newbery Honor Book, American Library Association (ALA), *Horn Book/Boston Globe* Award, and Golden Kite Award, Society of Children's Book Authors, all 1991, all for *The True Confessions of Charlotte Doyle;* Newbery Honor Book, ALA, 1992, for *Nothing but the Truth: A Documentary Novel; Boston Globe/Horn Book* Award for Fiction, 1996, for *Poppy;* New York Public Library Best Books of the Year citation, *Booklist* Best Books of the Year citation, and *Booklinks* Best Books of the Year citation, all 1996, and *Bulletin of the Center for Children's Books* Blue Ribbon, and National Council of Social Studies/Children's Book Council Notable Book citation, both 1997, all for *Beyond the Western Sea;* Pick of the Lists, IRA, 1997, for *Finding Providence: The Story of Roger Williams;* Newbery Award, ALA, 2003, for *Crispin: The Cross of Lead.*

Writings

UNDER PSEUDONYM AVI

Things That Sometimes Happen (picture book), illustrated by Jodi Robbin, Doubleday (New York, NY), 1970, abridged edition, illustrated by Marjorie Priceman, Atheneum Books for Young Readers (New York, NY), 2001.

Snail Tale: The Adventures of a Rather Small Snail (picture book), illustrated by Tom Kindron, Pantheon (New York, NY), 1972, revised as *The End of the Beginning: Being the Adventures of a Small Snail (and an Even Smaller Ant),* illustrated by Tricia Tusa, Harcourt (Orlando, FL), 2004.

No More Magic, Pantheon (New York, NY), 1975.

Captain Grey, Pantheon (New York, NY), 1977.

Emily Upham's Revenge; or, How Deadwood Dick Saved the Banker's Niece: A Massachusetts Adventure, Pantheon (New York, NY), 1978.

Night Journeys, Pantheon (New York, NY), 1979.

Encounter at Easton (sequel to *Night Journeys*), Pantheon (New York, NY), 1980.

Man from the Sky, Knopf (New York, NY), 1980.

The History of Helpless Harry: To Which Is Added a Variety of Amusing and Entertaining Adventures, Pantheon (New York, NY), 1980.

A Place Called Ugly, Pantheon (New York, NY), 1981.

Who Stole the Wizard of Oz?, Knopf (New York, NY), 1981.

Sometimes I Think I Hear My Name, Pantheon (New York, NY), 1982.

Shadrach's Crossing, Pantheon (New York, NY), 1983.

The Fighting Ground, Lippincott (Philadelphia, PA), 1984.

S.O.R. Losers, Bradbury (Scarsdale, NY), 1984.

Devil's Race, Lippincott (Philadelphia, PA), 1984.

Bright Shadow, Bradbury (Scarsdale, NY), 1985.

Wolf Rider: A Tale of Terror, Bradbury (Scarsdale, NY), 1986.

Devil's Race, Avon (New York, NY), 1987.

Romeo and Juliet—Together (and Alive) at Last (sequel to *S. O. R. Losers*), Avon (New York, NY), 1988.

Something Upstairs: A Tale of Ghosts, Orchard Books (New York, NY), 1988.

The Man Who Was Poe, Orchard Books (New York, NY), 1989.

The True Confessions of Charlotte Doyle, Orchard Books (New York, NY), 1990.

Windcatcher, Bradbury (Scarsdale, NY), 1991.

Nothing but the Truth: A Documentary Novel, Orchard Books (New York, NY), 1991.

"Who Was That Masked Man, Anyway?," Orchard Books (New York, NY), 1992.

Blue Heron, Bradbury (Scarsdale, NY), 1992.

Punch with Judy, Bradbury (New York, NY), 1993.

City of Light, City of Dark: A Comic Book Novel, illustrated by Brian Floca, Orchard Books (New York, NY), 1993.

The Barn, Orchard Books (New York, NY), 1994.

Shadrach's Crossing Smuggler's Island, Morrow Junior Books (New York, NY), 1994.

The Bird, the Frog, and the Light: A Fable, paintings by Matthew Henry, Orchard Books (New York, NY), 1994.

Tom, Babette, and Simon: Three Tales of Transformation, illustrated by Alexi Natchev, Macmillan Books for Young Readers (New York, NY), 1995.

Poppy (also see below), illustrated by Brian Floca, Orchard Books (New York, NY), 1995.

Beyond the Western Sea, Book One: Escape from Home, Orchard Books (New York, NY), 1995.

Beyond the Western Sea, Book Two: Lord Kirkle's Money, Orchard Books (New York, NY), 1996.

What Do Fish Have to Do with Anything?: Short Stories, Candlewick Press (Cambridge, MA), 1997.

Finding Providence: The Story of Roger Williams, Harper-Collins (New York, NY), 1997.

Poppy and Rye (also see below), illustrated by Brian Floca, Avon (New York, NY), 1998.

Perloo the Bold, Scholastic (New York, NY), 1998.

Ragweed (also see below), illustrated by Brian Floca, Avon (New York, NY), 1999.

Second Sight: Stories for a New Millennium, Philomel Books (New York, NY), 1999.

Abigail takes the Wheel, illustrated by Don Bolognese, HarperCollins (New York, NY), 1999.

Midnight Magic, Scholastic (New York, NY), 1999.

Ereth's Birthday (also see below), illustrated by Brian Floca, HarperCollins (New York, NY), 2000.

The Christmas Rat, Simon & Schuster (New York, NY), 2000.

Prairie School, pictures by Bill Farnsworth, HarperCollins (New York, NY), 2001.

The Secret School, Harcourt (San Diego, CA), 2001.

Don't You Know There's a War On?, HarperCollins (New York, NY), 2001.

The Good Dog, Atheneum Books for Young Readers (New York, NY), 2001.

Tales from Dimwood Forest (includes *Ragweed, Poppy, Poppy and Rye,* and *Ereth's Birthday*), HarperCollins (New York, NY), 2001.

Crispin: The Cross of Lead, Hyperion Books for Children (New York, NY), 2002.

Silent Movie, illustrated by C. B. Mordan, Atheneum Books for Young Readers (New York, NY), 2002.

The Mayor of Central Park, illustrated by Brian Floca, HarperCollins (New York, NY), 2003.

(With Rachel Vail) *Never Mind! A Twin Novel,* HarperCollins (New York, NY), 2004.

Also author of numerous plays. Contributor to books, including *Performing Arts Resources, 1974,* edited by Ted Perry, Drama Book Publishers, 1975. Contributor to periodicals, including *New York Public Library Bulletin, Top of the News, Children's Literature in Education, Horn Book,* and *Writer.* Book reviewer for *Library Journal, School Library Journal,* and *Previews,* 1965-73.

Translations of Avi's books have been published in Germany, Austria, Denmark, Norway, Spain, Italy, and Japan.

Adaptations

Emily Upham's Revenge, Shadrach's Crossing, Something Upstairs, The Fighting Ground, The True Confessions of Charlotte Doyle, Nothing but the Truth, and *Read to Me* were produced on radio programs *Read to Me,* Maine Public Radio, and *Books Aloud,* WWON-Rhode Island; *The True Confessions of Charlotte Doyle, City of Light/City of Dark, Sometimes I Think I Hear My Name, Something Upstairs,* and *Night Journeys* were optioned for film; *Something Upstairs* was adapted as a play performed by Louisville (KY) Children's Theater, 1997; *Nothing but the Truth* was adapted for the stage by Ronn Smith; audio recording of *The Fighting Ground* produced by Listening Library and *The Man Who Was Poe* by Audio Bookshelf; many of Avi's other books have also been recorded on audio cassette, including *The Barn, Beyond the Western Sea, Blue Heron, Bright Shadow, Man from the Sky, Night Journeys, Perloo the Bold, Poppy, Poppy and Rye, Punch with Judy, Romeo and Juliet—Together (and Alive) at Last, Something Upstairs, Smuggler's Island, The True Confessions of Charlotte Doyle, What Do Fish Have to Do with Anything?, "Who Was That Masked Man, Anyway?," Wolf Rider,* and *The Good Dog.*

Sidelights

The author of inviting, readable novels, Edward Wortis is well known to critics, teachers, parents, and particularly to young readers under his nickname "Avi." His many award-winning books, which include *The True Confessions of Charlotte Doyle, Nothing but the Truth,* and the Newbery Award-winning *Crispin: The Cross of Lead,* can be mysteries, adventure yarns, historical fiction, supernatural tales, coming-of-age novels, or comic stories, and some combine a bit of all of these categories. While captivating even reluctant readers with his fast-paced, imaginative plots and the inclusion of plenty of action, Avi's books also offer complex, thought-provoking, and sometimes disturbingly realistic reflections of American culture. The author summed up his goals in writing young-adult novels in *Twentieth-Century Children's Writers:* "I try to write about complex issues—young people in an adult world—full of irony and contradiction, in a narrative style that relies heavily on suspense with a texture rich in emotion and imagery. I take a great deal of satisfaction in using popular forms—the adventure, the mystery, the thriller—so as to hold my reader with the sheer pleasure of a good story. At the same time I try to resolve my books with an ambiguity that compels engagement. In short, I want my readers to feel, to think, sometimes to laugh. But most of all I want them to enjoy a good read."

Born in New York City in 1937 and raised in Boston, Avi grew up in an artistic environment. His great-grandparents and a grandmother were writers, two uncles were painters, and both parents wrote. His family was also politically active, its members aligning themselves with the radical movements that grew out of the Great Depression of the 1930s. Politics and art led to lively family discussion in Avi's home. The author once explained that his extended family comprised "a very strong art community and what this meant for me as a child was that there was always a kind of uproarious sense of debate. It was all a very affectionate sharing of ideas—arguing, but not arguing in anger, arguing about ideas."

This early stimulation at home may have prepared Avi for challenges to come in his education. Although he was an avid reader as a child, difficulties in writing eventually caused him to flunk out of one school. He later learned that he has a dysfunction known as dysgraphia, a marginal impairment in his writing abilities that causes him to reverse letters or misspell words. "One of my aunts said I could spell a four letter word wrong five ways," he once commented. "In a school environment, I was perceived as being sloppy and erratic, and not paying attention." Despite constant criticism at school, Avi kept writing and he credits his family's emphasis on the arts for his perseverance. When school assignments came back covered in red ink, he simply saved them, corrections and all. "I think there was so much criticism, I became immune to it," he once said. "I wasn't even paying attention to it. I liked what I wrote."

Like many teens, Avi felt like an outsider in many social circles, and his family's reactionary political views gave him early knowledge of what it meant to be in a minority. "You always assumed that your point of view was quirky or different," Avi once commented. At school, aside from writing difficulties, he also harbored typical teenage insecurities: "I've led a very ordinary life in most respects. I think my adolescence was unhappy in the way that many adolescents' lives are unhappy. It has given me great empathy for the outsider."

The first step on Avi's course to writing professionally was reading: everything from comic books and science magazines to histories, plays, and novels. Despite the skepticism of his teachers, he decided to make a career of writing while still in high school. "After my junior year in high school, my parents were informed that I was in desperate need of a tutor, for somehow I had never taken the time to learn to write or to spell," he once recalled. "That summer I met every day with a wonderful teacher who not only taught me writing basics, but also instilled in me the conviction that I wanted to be a writer myself. Perhaps it was stubbornness. It was generally agreed that was one thing I could not possibly do." Avi still has the diary entry from his senior year of high school in which he logged his decision to be a writer, adding "I can't wait! I've made up my mind."

Attending Antioch University, Avi enrolled in playwriting rather than English courses. "That's where I really started to write seriously," he once commented. "The

Nine tiny stories "for little listeners" are drawn from Avi's first book and relate playful, imaginative tales of childhood. (From Things That Sometimes Happen, *illustrated by Marjorie Priceman.)*

first playwriting instructor that I had would say, 'this is the way you do it.' You didn't have much choice in it, you had to do it in a very specific way. He even had charts for you to fill out. And I think I learned how to organize a story according to this man's precepts. It didn't even matter what [his system] was except that I absorbed it. I think, although I'm not sure of this, that is still the structure I use when I write." One of the plays Avi wrote in college won a contest and was published in a magazine. The author said that during that time he wrote "a trunkfull of plays but I would say ninety-nine percent of them weren't very good." After working at a variety of jobs, Avi took a job in the theater collection of the New York Public library, beginning his twenty-four-year career as a librarian. His determination to be a writer never flagged during this time, and he had written nearly 800 pages of his "great American novel," by the time an odd series of events turned his attention toward children's literature. It all began with telling stories to his two sons. "My oldest would tell me what the story should be about—he would invent stuff, a story about a glass of water and so forth. It became a game, and here I had a writing background so I was telling some fairly sophisticated stories."

Along with telling stories, Avi was a doodler, drawing pictures for fun. A friend who was writing a children's book, having seen his drawings, wanted Avi to provide illustrations. When the friend took the book with Avi's illustrations to a publisher, although the book was rejected, Avi was asked to illustrate other children's books. Arguing with the publisher that he was a writer and not an artist, Avi agreed to illustrate if he could also write the book. "Two weeks after this conversation, I was supposed to go to England on a library exchange thing, so I took a week off of work. Some neighbors were gone and I used their apartment. I put down all the stories that I had told my son and drew the pictures, all within one week. So this gets submitted to the publisher and of course she turned everything down. But—seven publishers down the road—Doubleday accepted it." *Things That Sometimes Happen: Very Short Stories for Very Young Readers,* was published—although without Avi's artwork—in 1970.

Avi's publisher called one day and asked what name he wanted on the book. "That's an odd question to ask," Avi once recalled. "It was never an issue, but I thought about it, and I said, 'Oh well, just put Avi down,' and that was the decision. Just like that." Using his new pen name, which had been given him by his twin sister in early childhood, Avi continued to write children's books geared to his sons' reading levels, until, as he explained, "At a certain point they kept growing and I didn't. I hit a fallow period, and then I wrote *No More Magic.* Suddenly I felt 'This is right! I'm writing novels and I love it.' From then on I was committed to writing novels."

Avi has written many different forms of the novel. Since several of his early works, including *Captain Grey, Night Journeys,* and *Encounter at Easton,* are set in colonial America, he quickly earned a reputation as a historical novelist. Avi's 1984 novel *The Fighting Ground,* winner of the Scott O'Dell Historical Fiction Award for children, presents one event-filled day in the life of Jonathan, a thirteen-year-old boy caught up in the Revolutionary War. The novel begins as Jonathan slips away from his family's New Jersey farm one morning in order to take part in a skirmish with the Hessians (German mercenary soldiers hired by the English). Jonathan sets out full of unquestioned hatred for the Hessians and for Americans who were loyal to the British—the Tories—and full of hope for a chance take part in the glory of battle. "O Lord, he said to himself, make it be a battle. With armies, big ones, and cannons and flags and drums and dress parades! Oh, he could, *would* fight. Good as his older brother. Maybe good as his pa. Better, maybe. O Lord, he said to himself, make it something *grand!*"

Avi portrays no grandeur in the war. Jonathan can barely carry his six-foot-long musket, and has a worse time trying to understand the talk among the men with whom he marches. The small group's leader is a crude individual who lies to the men and is said to be "overfond of killing." After a bloody vand confusing skirmish, Jonathan is captured by three Hessians, and briefly comes to understand them as individual human beings.

Later, when called upon to be the brave soldier he had yearned to be, Jonathan's harrowing experience reveals the delusion behind his wish. At the close of the novel the reader, along with Jonathan, is brought to an understanding of what war means in human terms. *The Fighting Ground* was widely praised by critics, many of whom expressed sentiments similar to those of a reviewer for the *Bulletin of the Center for Children's Books* who, describing *The Fighting Ground* as "a small stunner," summarized that the novel "makes the war personal and immediate: not history or event, but experience; near and within oneself, and horrible."

Avi admits to being more interested in finding a way to tell a good story and to provide a means of imagining and understanding the past than he is in presenting historical fact. "The historical novel is a curious construction," he once commented. "It represents history but it's not truly accurate. It's a style." He elaborated in an interview with Jim Roginski in *Behind the Covers:* "Somewhere along the line, I can't explain where, I developed an understanding of history not as fact but as story. That you could look at a field and, with only a slight shift of your imagination, suddenly watch the battle that took place there. . ... You have to have a willingness to look beyond *things.* . . . Take the Battle of Bunker Hill during the Revolution. The leader of the American troops was Dr. Warren, who was killed during the battle. His body had been so dismembered and disemboweled, the only way he could be identified was by the nature of his teeth. And it was Paul Revere who did it. When you tell the story of war that way, a much stronger statement about how ghastly war really is, is made."

In *Something Upstairs: A Tale of Ghosts,* Avi's combination of historical novel, ghost story, and science fiction, a young man discovers the ghost of a murdered slave in the historic house his family recently moved into in Providence, Rhode Island. He travels back in time to the days of slave trading, where he learns about the murder and, perhaps more importantly, about the manner in which American history is collectively remembered. Although Avi has been widely praised for his historical representation in this work, the author once said that "the irony is that in those Providence books there is nothing historical at all; it's a kind of fantasy of my neighborhood." Like his narrator in *Something Upstairs,* Avi moved from Los Angeles to Providence; in fact, he moved into the historic house featured in this novel. The author once commented that in his neighborhood, just walking down the street can inspire a story. The move to Providence "was truly like going back in history."

The Man Who Was Poe, Avi's fictionalized portrait of nineteenth-century writer Edgar Allan Poe, intertwines fiction and history on several levels. Historically, Poe went through a period of severe depression and poverty, aggravated by alcoholism during the two years preceding his death in 1849. Avi, whose novel focuses on this period, said he became fascinated with Poe because he was so extraordinary and yet such "a horrible man." In the novel, a young boy, Edmund, has recently immigrated to Providence from England with his aunt and twin sister in order to look for his missing mother. When both aunt and sister disappear, the penniless boy must elicit help from a stranger—who happens to be Edgar Allen Poe. Poe, noticing similarities in Edmund's story to his own life and detecting material for his writing, agrees to help the boy. Between maddening bouts of drunkenness, Poe ingeniously finds a trail of clues. Edmund, who has been taught to defer to adults, alternates between awe of the great man's perceptive powers and despair at his madness.Vividly reflecting the macabre tone of Poe's fiction, Avi portrays the old port city of Providence as a bleak and chaotic world in which compassion and moral order seem to have given way to violence and greed. The character Poe, with his morbid imagination, makes an apt detective in this realm until it becomes clear that he wants the "story" of Edmund's family to end tragically. Edmund's plight is a harsh one, relying on Poe as the only adult who can help him, while at the same time attempting to ensure that Poe's vision does not become a reality. A reviewer for the *Bulletin of the Center for Children's Books,* describing *The Man Who Was Poe* as "a complex, atmospheric thriller," remarked that "Avi recreates the gloom of [the] 1840s . . . with a storyteller's ease, blending drama, history, and mystery without a hint of pastiche or calculation. And, as in the best mystery stories, readers will be left in the end with both the comfort of puzzles solved and the unease of mysteries remaining."

In another unique twist on the convention of historical novels, *The True Confessions of Charlotte Doyle* presents the unlikely story of a very proper thirteen-year-old girl who, as the sole passenger and only female on a trans-Atlantic ship in 1832, becomes involved in a mutiny at sea. Holding her family's aristocratic views on social class and demeanor, Charlotte begins her voyage trusting only Captain Jaggery, whose fine manners and authoritative command remind her of her father. She is thus shocked to find that Jaggery is a viciously brutal and inhumane shipmaster. This discovery, along with her growing fondness for members of the ship's crew, gradually leads Charlotte to question—and discard—the values of her privileged background. As she exchanges her finishing school wardrobe for a common sailor's garb and joins the crew in its work, she reveals the strength of her character, initially masked by her restrictive upbringing.

In the adventures that follow, including a mysterious murder, a storm, and a mutiny, Charlotte's reeducation and emancipation provide a new version of the conventionally male story of rugged individualism at sea. The award-winning novel has received accolades from critics for its suspense, its evocation of life at sea, and particularly for the rich and believable narrative of its protagonist as she undergoes a tremendous change in outlook. The impact of Charlotte's liberation from so-

Set in 1832, Avi's historical novel relates the first-person narrative of a thirteen-year-old girl on a transatlantic sea voyage marked by mutiny, murder, and thrilling exploits. (Cover illustration by Douglas Smith.)

cial bonds and gender restrictions in *The True Confessions of Charlotte Doyle* has a powerful emotional effect on many of its readers. Avi once said that "many people, mostly girls, and even adults, have told me of bursting into tears" at the book's ending—tears of relief that Charlotte finds the freedom to realize herself as she chooses. In his *Boston Globe-Horn Book* Award acceptance speech, referring to the words of a critic who spoke of the "improbable but deeply satisfying conclusion" of the novel, Avi commented: "I am deeply grateful for the award you have given me today. But I hope you will understand me when I tell you that if the 'improbable' life I wrote lives in someone's heart as a life *possible,* then I have already been given the greatest gift a writer can receive: a reader who takes my story and endows it with life by the grace of their own desire." In another highly lauded historical novel, the Newbery Award-winning *Crispin: The Cross of Lead,* Avi "introduces some of his most unforgettable characters," according to *Booklist* contributor Ilene Cooper. Taking place in England during the fourteenth century, as poverty, a greedy aristocracy, and the Black Plague ravages the country's peasant population, the novel

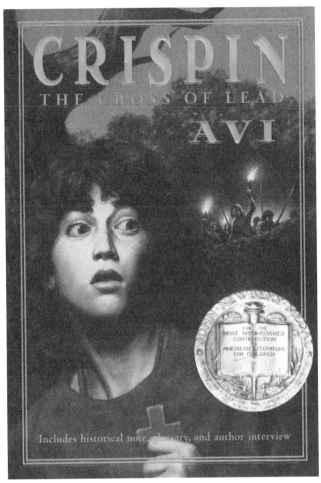

In the fourteenth century, a thirteen-year-old peasant boy is erroneously charged with a crime and must leave the village he calls home in Avi's tale of corruption and hardship in England. (Cover illustration by Tristan Elwell.)

finds a thirteen-year-old orphan framed for a murder he did not commit. He flees from the familiar surroundings where he was raised, taking with him only the clothes on his back and his mother's lead cross, with an inscription he cannot decipher. Soon, Crispin falls in with a traveling juggler who, due to his burly size, is called Bear. With Bear's help the boy learns the juggler trade, and also becomes steeped in Bear's radical political leanings, which include rebelling against a feudal system that keeps most people living lives of brutal poverty. As he gains in self-esteem, he also learns the truth about his birth and understands his place in the world. "Avi's plot is engineered for maximum thrills, with twists, turns and treachery aplenty," noted a *Publishers Weekly* contributor, adding that the "compellingly drawn" friendship between the boy and the old juggler gives *Crispin* its emotional heart.

Other historical novels by Avi include *Prairie School* and *The Secret School,* both of which stress the importance of education. *The Secret School* takes place in Elk Valley, Colorado, in 1925, as the small town's only teacher leaves unexpectedly and a fourteen-year-old girl decides to fill the learning gap. Writing about *Prairie*

School for the *School Library Journal,* reviewer Carol Schene noted, "This gentle story with a great message that is nicely woven into the daily events would make a pleasant read-aloud as well as a good addition to easy chapter-book-collections." Hazel Rochman, writing for *Booklist,* noted, "Avi's clear simple language never sounds condescending." In a review of *The Secret School* for *School Library Journal,* B. Allison Gray called it a "carefully plotted, enjoyable, old-fashioned tale" and noted, "The importance of education and dreaming of one's future are imparted in an entertaining way." An enthusiastic reader of history, Avi has continued to approach the historical novel in new ways. As he once commented: "People constantly ask 'How come you keep changing styles?' I think that's a misquestion. Put it this way, 'What makes you so fascinated with technique?' and that's the answer. You know that there are a lot of ways to tell a story. To me that's just fun."

In 1984, Avi published *S.O.R. Losers,* a humorous contemporary novel about a group of unathletic boys forced by their school (which is based on Avi's high school in New York City) to form a soccer team. Opposing the time-honored school ethic that triumph in sports is the American way, the boys form their own opinions about winning at something that means little to them. In a team meeting, they take stock of who they are and why it's so important to everyone *else* that they should win their games. The narrator, who is the team's captain, sums it up: "Every one of us is good at something. Right? Maybe more than one thing. The point is *other* things. . .. But I don't like sports. I'm not good at it. I don't enjoy it. So I say, so what? I mean if Saltz here writes a stinko poem—and he does all the time—do they yell at him? When was the last time Mr. Tillman came around and said, 'Saltz, I *believe* in your being a poet!'"

Avi uses the humor infused in *S.O.R. Losers* to make a clear statement regarding what he sees as a certain irony in the American attitude toward education. "On the one hand, our culture likes to give a lot of lip service to support for kids, but on the other hand, I don't think the culture as a whole likes kids. And kids are caught in this contradiction. I ask teachers at conferences 'How many of you have athletic trophies displayed in your schools?' You know how many raise their hands. And I ask, 'How many of you have trophy displays for the best reader or writer?' Nobody raises their hands. And I say 'What is it therefore that stands as the essential achievement in your school?' With test scores falling, we need to make kids better readers, but instead we're interested in a minority of kids, mostly males, whose primary focus is sports."

With its narrator's deadpan reporting of the fiascos involved in being consistent losers in sports, *S.O.R. Losers* does more than make a point. *Horn Book* contributor Mary M. Burns, who called the novel "one of the funniest and most original sports sagas on record," particularly praised Avi's skill with comedic form. "Short, pithy chapters highlighting key events maintain the pace necessary for successful comedy. As in a Charlie Chaplin movie, emphasis is on individual episode— each distinct, yet organically related to an overall idea." Avi has written several other comic novels, including his sequel to *S.O.R. Losers, Romeo and Juliet—Together (and Alive) at Last,* and two well-received spoofs on nineteenth-century melodrama, *Emily Upham's Revenge* and *The History of Helpless Harry.*

Avi's acclaimed contemporary coming-of-age novels include *A Place Called Ugly, Nothing but the Truth,* and *Sometimes I Think I Hear My Name.* Based on an actual incident, his 1992 Newbery honor book, *Nothing but the Truth* is the story of Philip Malloy and his battle with an English teacher, Miss Narwin. With bad grades in English keeping him off the track team, Philip repeatedly breaks school rules by humming the national anthem along with the public address system in Miss Narwin's home room. Eventually, the principal suspends Philip from school. Because the school happens to be in the midst of elections, various self-interested members of the community exploit this story of a boy being suspended for his patriotism. Much to everyone's surprise, the incident in home room snowballs into a national media event that, in its frenzied patriotic rhetoric, thoroughly overshadows the true story about a good teacher's inability to reach a student, a young man's alienation, a community's disinterest in its children's needs, and a school system's hypocrisy.

Nothing but the Truth is a book without a narrator, relating its story through school memos, diary entries, letters, dialogues, newspaper articles, and radio talk show scripts. Presented thus, without narrative bias, the story takes into account the differing points of view surrounding the incident, allowing the reader to root out the real problems leading to the incident. Avi once commented that he got the idea for the structure of this novel from a form of theater that arose in the 1930s called "Living Newspapers"—dramatizations of issues and problems confronting American society presented through a "hodge podge" of document readings and dialogues. In addition to realistic contemporary and historical novels, Avi has also successfully penned fantasy fiction and several other unique chapter books for readers in the early elementary grades. *Poppy,* which received a *Boston Globe-Horn Book* Award in 1996, tells the story of two deer mice, Ragweed and Poppy, who are about to marry when the self-proclaimed king of Dimwood Forest—an owl named Mr. Ocax—eats Ragweed, supposedly as punishment for neglecting to seek his permission to marry. Ann A. Flowers of *Horn Book* called *Poppy* "a tribute to the inquiring mind and the stout heart." *Bulletin of the Center for Children's Books* critic Roger Sutton wrote: "Sprightly but un-cute dialogue, suspenseful chapter endings, and swift shifts of perspective between Ocax and Poppy will make chapter-a-day readalouds cause for anticipation." In addition to following *Poppy* with several sequels, he has also created new animal-sized adventures in *The End of the Be-*

"The action moves along at a crackling pace."—*Publishers Weekly*

THE GOOD DOG

avi

Avi enters the world of the canine in his tale of McKinley, a malamute who feels love and loyalty for his human family, but longs for the freedom and excitement offered by running with a wolf pack. (Cover illustration by Ken McMillan.)

ginning: Being the Adventures of a Small Snail (and an Even Smaller Ant). Based on a beginning reader he authored early in his career, *The End of the Beginning* finds two friends departing on cross-country adventures, each with their own approach to travel. Praising the artwork by Tricia Tusa, a *Publishers Weekly* reviewer wrote that "bite-size chapters and the clever repartee make this a charming tale," while *School Library Journal* contributor Connie Tyrrell Burns dubbed *The End of the Beginning* "a wise little book" about friendship.

Other quirky novels for younger readers include *The Good Dog,* a tale about a malamute named McKinley who is top dog in his small town. Told from the point of view of the dog, the story takes an imaginative view of the trappings of human civilization, and brings readers into a clever canine culture. Noting the dogs' emotional connection to freedom, a reviewer for *Publishers Weekly* called *The Good Dog* "reminiscent of Jack London's *The Call of the Wild.*" Featuring striking black-and-white illustrations by C. B. Mordan, *Silent Movie* brings the drama and pathos of a silent movie of the early twentieth century to the picture-book medium.

Mimicking film subtitles with his brief text, Avi spins the story of a family of Swedish immigrants who are separated shortly after arriving in New York harbor. While young Gustave and his mother are forced to beg on the street after being robbed, they are eventually reunited with Papa after their images are captured on film by a famous silent-movie director. Sharing the same time period—the first decade of the twentieth century—*The Mayor of Central Park* finds Big Daddy Duds, head of a gang of tough-talking city rats, determined to take over Central Park, despite the objections of the park's current mayor, a long-tailed squirrel named Oscar Westerwit. When the gangster and the mayor find that they also root for opposing baseball teams, the turf battle moves to a more peaceable arena: the city ball park. In *Publishers Weekly* a contributor described *The Mayor of Central Park* as "an over-the-top romp" and added that Avi's "tough-talking prose would do an old gangster movie proud."

Although writing full time, Avi maintains regular interaction with children by traveling around the country, talking in schools about his writing. "I think it's very important for me to hold these kids in front of my eyes. They're wonderfully interesting and they hold me to the reality of who they are." Avi once commented that children are passionate and honest readers who will either "swallow a book whole" if they like it, or drop it "like a hot potato" if they don't. In *School Library Journal* he noted a telling anecdote about his approach to children: "Being dysgraphic, with the standard history of frustration and anguish, I always ask to speak to the learning-disabled kids. They come in slowly, waiting for yet another pep talk, more instructions. Eyes cast down, they won't even look at me. Their anger glows. I don't say a thing. I lay out pages of my copy-edited manuscripts, which are covered with red marks. 'Look here,' I say, 'see that spelling mistake. There, another spelling mistake. Looks like I forgot to put a capital letter there. Oops! Letter reversal.' Their eyes lift. They are listening. And I am among friends."

Avi describes himself as a committed skeptic, yet reveals an idealistic center when he discusses children and their role in American culture. He believes that children have a different outlook than most adults. "When do you become an adult?," he once remarked. "Sometimes I think the difference is that psychological shift when you start to know that tomorrow is going to be the same as today. When you're a kid, there are still options, major options. For a writer like myself, a child is a kind of metaphor for regression to idealism and passionate concern: a metaphor for the ability to change or react, to be honest about all those things that as adults we tend to slide over as we make compromises to obligations and necessities." In an article for *Horn Book* he contrasted children's literature, which generally espouses values such as "sharing, nonviolence, cooperation, and the ability to love," to the adult world where power and self-interest seem to rule. "More than anything else," Avi asserted, "children's literature is

about the place and role of the child in society. . ... If we—in the world of children's literature—can help the young stand straight for a moment longer than they have done in the past, help them maintain their ideals and values, those with which you and I identify ourselves, help them demand—and win—justice, we've added something good to the world."

As for young people who are thinking of becoming writers, Avi offers some sound advice on his Web site: "Listen and watch the world around you. Try to understand why things happen. Don't be satisfied with answers others give you. Don't assume that because everyone believes a thing it is right or wrong. Reason things out for yourself. Work to get answers on your own. Understand why you believe things. Finally, write what you honestly feel then learn from the criticism that will always come your way."

Biographical and Critical Sources

BOOKS

Authors and Artists for Young Adults, Gale (Detroit, MI), Volume 10, 1993, Volume 37, 2001.
Avi, *The Fighting Ground,* Lippincott (Philadelphia, PA), 1984.
Beacham's Guide to Literature for Young Adults, Volume 1, Beacham Publishing (Osprey, FL), 1990, Volume 10, Gale (Detroit, MI), 2000.
Roginski, Jim, *Behind the Covers: Interviews with Authors and Illustrators of Books for Children and Young Adults,* Libraries Unlimited, 1985, pp. 33-41.
St. James Guide to Young Adult Writers, St. James Press (Detroit, MI), 1999.
Twentieth-Century Children's Writers, St. Martin's Press, 1989, pp. 45-46.

PERIODICALS

Best Sellers, August, 1979, pp. 165-166; June, 1981, pp. 118-119; May, 1982, p. 76.
Booklist, January 15, 1992, Hazel Rochman, "A Conversation with Avi," p. 930; September 1, 1994, Hazel Rochman, "Focus: How to Build a Barn," p. 40; November 15, 1997, Michael Cart, review of *Poppy,* p. 731; November 15, 1997, Michael Cart, review of *What Do Fish Have to Do with Anything?: And Other Stories,* p. 560; September 1, 2000, Carolyn Phelan, review of *The Christmas Rat,* p. 127; April 15, 2001, Hazel Rochman, review of *Prairie School,* p. 1568; May 15, 2002, Ilene Cooper, review of *Crispin: The Cross of Lead,* p. 1604; October 1, 2002, Gillian Engberg, review of *Things That Sometimes Happen,* p. 332; August, 2003, GraceAnne A. DeCandido, review of *The Mayor of Central Park,* p. 1976; April 1, 2004, Hazel Rochman, review of *Never Mind!: A Twin Novel,* p.1365; September 15, 2004, Hazel Rochman, review of *The End of the Beginning: Being the Adventures of a Small Snail (and an Even Smaller Ant),* p. 242.

Bulletin of the Center for Children's Books, July, 1978, p.170; July-August, 1980, p. 206; June, 1983; June, 1984, review of *The Fighting Ground,* p. 180; December, 1986, p. 61; February, 1986, p. 102; October, 1987, p. 21; September, 1988, p. 2; October, 1989, review of *The Man Who Was Poe,* p. 27; January, 1996, Roger Sutton, review of *Poppy,* p. 154; February, 1996, Roger Sutton, review of *Beyond the Western Sea, Book One: The Escape from Home,* p. 183.

English Journal, November, 1981, p. 94.

Five Owls, January, 1991, p. 56.

Horn Book, August, 1979, p. 410; April, 1980, pp. 169-70; October, 1980, pp. 517-18; April, 1981, p. 136; June, 1981, pp. 297-98; August, 1983, p. 439; June, 1984, p. 325; January-February, 1985, Mary M. Burns, review of *S.O.R. Losers,* p. 49; November-December, 1986, Mary M. Burns, review of *Beyond the Western Sea, Book Two: Lord Kirkle's Money,* p. 731; September-October, 1987, Avi, "All That Glitters," pp. 569-576; January-February, 1989, p. 65; January-February, 1992, Avi, *Boston Globe-Horn Book* Award acceptance speech, pp. 24-27; January-February, 1996, Ann A. Flowers, review of *Poppy,* p. 70; July-August, 1996, Mary M. Burns, review of *Beyond the Western Sea, Book One: The Escape from Home,* p. 461; January-February, 2002, Peter D. Sieruta, review of *The Good Dog,* p. 75; March-April, 2003, Roger Sutton, review of *Silent Movie,* p. 197.

Journal of Adolescent and Adult Literacy, October, 2003, Vinnie Bonnit, review of *Crispin,* p. 188.

Kirkus Reviews, May 15, 2002, review of *Crispin,* p. 728; September 1, 2002, review of *Things That Sometimes Happen,* p. 1302; January, 2003, review of *Silent Movie,* p. 56.

Kliatt, November, 2002, Maureen K. Griffin, review of *Crispin,* p. 44.

Language Arts, October, 1979, p. 822; November-December, 1983, p. 1017; March, 1985, p. 283.

New York Times Book Review, September 11, 1977; March 1, 1981, p. 24.

Publishers Weekly, April 17, 1978, p. 78; December 5, 1980; January 30, 1981, p. 75; November 16, 1984, p. 65; December 26, 1986, p. 61; August 28, 1987, p. 81; September 14, 1990, p. 128; September 6, 1991, review of *Nothing but the Truth,* p. 105; July 16, 2001, review of *The Secret School,* p. 181; Nov. 5, 2001, review of *The Good Dog,* p. 68; June 3, 2002, review of *Crispin,* p. 88; September 30, 2002, review of *Things That Sometimes Happen,* p. 70; December 16, 2002, review of *Silent Movie,* p. 66; August 11, 2003, review of *The Mayor of Central Park,* p. 280; May 10, 2004, review of *Never Mind!,* p. 60; October 25, 2004, review of *The End of the Beginning,* p. 48.

School Library Journal, March, 1978, p. 124; May, 1980, p. 64; November, 1980, p. 68; September, 1984, p. 125; October, 1984, p. 164; December, 1986, pp. 111-12; January, 1987, Avi (with Betty Miles), "School Visits: The Author's Viewpoint," p. 21; October, 1987, p. 124; December, 1997, Carol A. Edwards, review of *What Do Fish Have to Do with Anything?: And Other Stories,* p. 120; September, 2000, Leda Schubert, "Breakfast Serials," p. 38, May, 2001, Carol Schene, review of *Prairie School,* p. 108; September, 2001, B. Allison Gray, review of *The Secret School,* p. 223; December, 2003, Sue Gifford, review of *The Mayor of Central Park,* p. 144; May, 2004, Eva Mitnick, review of *Never Mind!,* p. 140; October, 2004, Connie Tyrrell Burns, review of *The End of the Beginning,* p. 154.

Voice of Youth Advocates, August, 1981, pp. 23-24; August, 1982, p. 27; December, 1984, pp. 261-262; February, 1985, p. 321; February, 1989, p. 293; December 1996, Kathleen Beck, review of *Beyond the Western Sea, Book Two: Lord Kirkle's Money,* p. 267.

ONLINE

Avi's Web site, http://www.avi-writer.com/ (January 25, 2005).*

Z

ZAHN, Timothy 1951-

Personal
Born September 1, 1951, in Chicago, IL; son of Herbert William (an attorney) and Marilou (an attorney; maiden name, Webb) Zahn; married Anna L. Romo (a computer programmer), August 4, 1979; children: Corwin. *Education:* Michigan State University, B.A., 1973; University of Illinois at Urbana-Champaign, M.A., 1975, further graduate study, 1975-80. *Hobbies and other interests:* Classical music (particularly nineteenth-century Romantic era), crossword puzzles, martial arts.

Addresses
Home—OR. *Agent*—Russell Galen, Scovil, Chichak, Galen Literary Agency, 381 Park Ave. S., Suite 1020, New York, NY 10016.

Career
Writer.

Member
Science Fiction Writers of America.

Awards, Honors
Hugo Award nominations, World Science Fiction Convention, 1983, for "Pawn's Gambit," and 1985, for "Return to the Fold"; Hugo Award for best novella, 1984, for *Cascade Point.*

Writings

SCIENCE FICTION

The Blackcollar, DAW Books (New York, NY), 1983.
A Coming of Age, Bluejay (New York, NY), 1984.
Cobra (also see below), Baen (New York, NY), 1985.

Timothy Zahn

Spinneret (first published serially in *Analog Science Fiction/Science Fact,* July-October, 1985), Bluejay (New York, NY), 1985.
Blackcollar: The Backlash Mission, DAW Books (New York, NY), 1986.
Cascade Point (stories), Bluejay (New York, NY), 1986, title novella bound with *Hardfought* by Greg Bear, Tor Books (New York, NY), 1988.
Cobra Strike (also see below), Baen (New York, NY), 1986.
Triplet, Baen (New York, NY), 1987.

Cobra Bargain (also see below), Baen (New York, NY), 1988.

Deadman Switch, Baen (New York, NY), 1988.

Time Bomb and Zahndry Others (stories), Baen (New York, NY), 1988.

Warhorse, Baen (New York, NY), 1990.

Heir to the Empire ("Star Wars Thrawn Trilogy," Vol. 1), Bantam (New York, NY), 1991.

Distant Friends and Others (stories), Baen (New York, NY), 1992.

Cobras Two, Baen (New York, NY), 1992.

Dark Force Rising ("Star Wars Thrawn Trilogy," Vol. 2), Bantam (New York, NY), 1992.

The Last Command ("Star Wars Thrawn Trilogy," Vol. 3), Bantam (New York, NY), 1993.

Conquerors' Pride, Bantam (New York, NY), 1994.

Conquerors' Heritage, Bantam (New York, NY), 1995.

Conquerors' Legacy, Bantam (New York, NY), 1996.

Specter of the Past ("Star Wars: The Hand of Thrawn," Vol. 1), Bantam (New York, NY), 1997.

Vision of the Future ("Star Wars: The Hand of Thrawn," Vol. 2), Bantam (New York, NY), 1998.

(Author of introduction) Stephen J. Sansweet, *The Star Wars Encyclopedia,* Ballantine (New York, NY), 1998.

The Icarus Hunt, Bantam (New York, NY), 1999.

(With Michael A. Stackpole) *Star Wars—Mara Jade: By the Emperor's Hand* (graphic novel), illustrated by Carlos Ezquerra, Dark Horse Comics (Milwaukie, OR), 1999.

Angelmass, Tor (New York, NY), 2001.

Manta's Gift, Tor (New York, NY), 2002.

Star Song and Other Stories, Five Star (Waterville, ME), 2002.

Dragon and Thief ("Dragonback Adventure," Vol. 1), Tor (New York, NY), 2003.

Dragon and Soldier ("Dragonback Adventure," Vol. 2), Tor (New York, NY), 2004.

Cobra Trilogy (includes *Cobra, Cobra Strike,* and *Cobra Bargain*), Baen Books (Riverdale, NY), 2004.

Star Wars: Survivor's Quest, Ballantine (New York, NY), 2004.

The Green and the Gray, Tor (New York, NY), 2004.

Work included in anthologies, including *The 1983 Annual World's Best SF,* edited by Donald A. Wollheim, DAW (New York, NY), 1983, and *Alien Stars,* edited by Elizabeth Mitchell, Baen (New York, NY), 1985. Contributor of numerous stories and novelettes to magazines, including *Analog Science Fiction/Science Fact, Ares, Fantasy and Science Fiction, Fantasy Gamer, Isaac Asimov's Science Fiction Magazine, Rigel,* and *Space Gamer.*

Adaptations

Star Wars: Heir to the Empire was adapted as an audiobook, read by Denis Lawson, Bantam (New York, NY), 1991.

Sidelights

Timothy Zahn is known for penning novels of military science fiction featuring fully realized, complex characters who often face moral dilemmas that involve con-

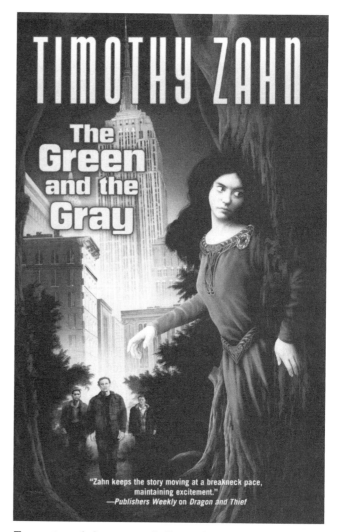

Two antagonistic groups of alien refugees live in New York City, disguised as humans and preparing for a monumental battle which can only be prevented by a group of implausible New Yorkers who find they must be the champions for peace. (Cover illustration by Jim Burns.)

flicts between human and alien cultures. He frequently focuses on seemingly impossible situations—such as dealing with uninhabitable planets or tyrannical alien rulers—and shows how ingenious, inventive, and determined individuals manage to find solutions. In addition to such popular sci-fi novels as *The Icarus Hunt* and *Angelmass,* Zahn has also moved toward the literary terrain bordering mainstream fiction, writing such books as *The Green and the Gray,* a mystery that finds a New York City cop entering a battle between two alien—and hidden—races when he comes to the aid of a married couple and an odd twelve-year-old girl. He is also well known to many readers for his contributions to the ongoing "Star Wars" book series based on the popular feature films, as well as for the wealth of short fiction he has published in magazines and which has appeared in science-fiction anthologies.

When Zahn decided to first try his hand at writing, he had no idea how successful he would become: he just knew he enjoyed making up entertaining stories.

Working towards a Ph.D. in physics at the University of Illinois, Zahn began writing science fiction as a hobby. "I was working on a mathematical project that really wasn't going anywhere," he told Chris Knight in an on-line interview for *TheForce.Net*. "It was something we hoped would be useful in plasma physics. It wasn't really working. My advisor was too stubborn to give up. And he was out of town a lot, so it gave me a fair amount of time while I was stuck waiting for him to get back into town with not much to do, so I started writing as kind of a hobby." In 1978, when he sold "Ernie," his first story, he considered taking a year off after graduation and writing fiction full time. Zahn's plans changed completely in mid-1979, when his thesis advisor died unexpectedly. The then-graduate student was faced with the prospect of beginning a new project with another professor, and decided to take time off to write instead. The nine stories he sold that year convinced him to stick with writing science fiction.

Initially, Zahn limited himself to short stories, publishing many of them in the early 1980s and becoming one of *Analog Science Fiction/Science Fact* magazine's regular contributors. In one of his early stories, "Hollow Victory," an alien ambassador has fallen seriously ill and two human biomedics must discover the cause of his sickness. To do this, they use clues about the Thrulmodi physiology and the Thrulmodi planet, where the first human-Thrulmodi conference is taking place. It was an early incidence of a common theme in Zahn's work: two cultures—generally human and alien—coming to terms with each other.

The Blackcollar, his 1983 debut novel, combines science fiction with martial arts adventure. The book centers on the conflict between the Ryqril, a conquering alien race who have vanquished Earth and its worlds, and a group of their human subjects. Among these human revolutionaries are several people who remember a time when humans had their own superwarriors: the Blackcollars, well-trained fighters whose reflexes were enhanced by drugs. Despite the fact that the Blackcollars were dissolved after the war with the Ryqril, a small band is known to still exist. Allen Caine leaves Earth to seek them out, highlighting another of Zahn's ongoing themes: the limits and strengths of human potency. *Analog Science Fiction/Science Fact* reviewer Tom Easton complimented Zahn for not allowing the predictable triumph of humans to be total. He also made special mention of *The Blackcollar*'s originality: "There is more realism here, and hence more satisfaction." Zahn returned to the same scenario in a novel sequel titled *Blackcollar: The Backlash Mission.*

Although Zahn had by now established a following in militaristic science fiction, he took a new direction in the early 1980s. Three stories the former physicist published during this period signaled his interest in the universe of the mind and the psychological difficulties that can result from working at a higher mental level: "Dark Thoughts at Noon," "The Final Report on the Lifeline

Experiment," and "The Cassandra." From that point on psychology would play an increasing role in Zahn's plots and characters.

Telekinesis and social questions form the basis of Zahn's second novel, *A Coming of Age.* Again, the author plays with the idea of a mutation whose effects bring both good and evil to humans. Because of a mutation some two hundred years before the novel begins, children on the planet Tigris develop psychic powers at five years of age. While these powers enable them to fly and move objects with their minds, among other telekinetic skills, the abilities disappear with the onset of puberty. During this eight-year interval, the children are more powerful than adults; therefore, society has developed several means by which to control the potent pre-teens and harness their powers. Once children reach puberty and lose their powers, they are allowed to go to school and are streamlined into adult society.

The characters in *A Coming of Age* include a thirteen-year-old girl who dreads the loss of her special facility, an adult detective and his preteen assistant who are looking into a kidnapping, a scientist who is researching the biology of the telekinetic phenomenon, and a criminal who plans to use this research. By using the universal experience of adolescence and the fluctuations in self-esteem experienced during that time in life, Zahn is able to address both social and psychological issues. *Analog* contributor Easton said he found *A Coming of Age* "a warm and sympathetic story very suitable for a broad range of ages," and deemed the novel "complex" enough to entertain older readers. A *Publishers Weekly* reviewer commended Zahn for writing "an entertaining science fiction police procedural that should especially appeal to teenagers."

While Zahn branched out into increasingly psychological areas, he maintained his ability to interest readers with space adventures. Despite the fact that Earth vessels can travel beyond the stars, no habitable worlds remain within reach as the author's 1985 novel *Spinneret* opens. All the potentially habitable areas have been colonized by other star-faring races. In what Hal Hoover, writing in *Voice of Youth Advocates,* described as a "first class sci-fi novel," Zahn follows Colonel Lloyd Meredith's attempt to colonize Astra, a world no one wants because it has no metals, or so everyone thinks until its dormant volcano spews a metal thread into orbit shortly after Meredith's expedition lands. One *Publishers Weekly* reviewer pronounced the book one of "Zahn's best novels," while another admired it as a "light, brisk and entertaining yarn." In reviewing *Spinneret, Booklist* contributor Roland Green remarked in particular on Zahn's "excellent narrative technique, clear prose, and intelligent characterization."

Cobra, Cobra Strike, and *Cobra Bargain* deal with the theme of the superhuman warriors Zahn began to explore in the "Blackcollar" books. The CoBRA's—Computerized Body Reflex Armament—are technologically souped-up soldiers programmed to react lethally to anything their reflexes read as an attack. They are created after one of the colony worlds of the Dominion of Man is conquered by the Troft forces, whom they manage to subdue. Because the Cobras' indiscriminate responses make them dangerous for civilian life, they are sent to protect the colonists on the far side of Troft territory. Zahn focuses on Jonny Moreau, a twenty year old from a backwater planet who is one of the first people to sign up for the Cobra program. Moreau changes from a naive, idealistic young man into a savvy politician as he becomes a leader on his new home.

In *Cobra Strike,* second in the series, Moreau's three sons must contend with another threat. On the distant planet of Quasama, a paranoid race of humans lives in a mutually beneficial and dependent relationship with predatory birds called mojos. The formerly adversarial Trofts, now trading partners with the humans, want to use the Cobras as mercenaries to destroy this race, in return for five new worlds able to support human life. The last installment of the "Cobra" series, *Cobra Bargain,* takes place after Moreau has passed away. His granddaughter, Jasmine, decides to buck the all-male tradition of the Cobras and join their ranks—she's a Moreau, after all. She successfully completes the training and proves herself to be a resourceful and independent young woman, whose diplomatic and warrior abilities mirror or surpass those of her male predecessors.

Writing in *Voice of Youth Advocates* about the ways in which Zahn manages to avert war throughout the "Cobra" series, Diane G. Yates noted that "the moral questions that [the Moreaus] struggle with are those that concern us all, and to find a character in a military SF novel who agonizes over ethical questions is a refreshing change, and a welcome one." *Analog*'s Easton lauded *Cobra Bargain* especially for its heroine, noting that Jasmine is "smart, empathetic, energetic, [and] determined" and that by the end "a number of males have had their consciousness suitably broadened or their egos ventilated." Continuing to be popular with readers, the "Cobra" series was repackaged in a single volume in 2004, almost two decades after the first novel in the series was published.

Zahn explores possible permutations of the death penalty in his 1988 work *Deadman Switch.* The galactic society the novel describes uses its convicts as pilots for space travel to the world of Solitaire, which is surrounded by a mysterious cloud that can only be navigated by corpses. Ships that seek to enter or exit the system must kill a member of their crew to create a "zombie" pilot. When Gilead Benedar, who works for the magnate Lord Kelsey-Ramos as a human lie detector, is sent on an inspection tour of Kelsey-Ramos's newly acquired Solitaire-licensed ships, he discovers that one of the ship's two intended zombies is innocent. As well, he discovers that she, like Benedar, belongs to the Watchers, a Christian sect that is one of the last remnants of organized religion left in the galaxy. Watch-

ers are trained to accurately, truly, and deeply observe the universe. Benedar's recognition and subsequent search for a replacement zombie leads to all sorts of problems with Solitaire's elite as well as with the executives whose company his boss has taken over. *Analog* reviewer Easton chided the story for its "elementary" structure and theme, adding that the "plot is too largely predictable."

In *Warhorse* the author imagines a conflict between an outwardly mobile human race and an alien species of sophisticated biological engineers. The "Tampies" have decided that all life is valuable and should be protected, a philosophy that clashes with the often-violent realities of human society. Among the Tampies' weapons are living spaceships called "warhorses," which are more powerful than anything humanity has produced and which could be used to destroy mankind if they proved a threat. Writing in *Booklist,* Roland Green deemed

While the evil Empire is fading, Grand Admiral Thrawn makes one last attempt to overthrow the New Republic by resurrecting two hundred lost Dreadnaught cruisers in Zahn's thrilling novel featuring characters from the Star Wars films. (Cover illustration by Tom Jung.)

Warhorse "Zahn at his best," and made special mention of the author's mix of "hard science and social science extrapolation."In *Conquerors' Pride* Zahn offered another military-themed work, as an aggressive nonhuman species suddenly appears and attacks several ships of the intergalactic Commonwealth Peacekeeper force. When a high-ranking Commonwealth official realizes that his son, Commander Pheylan Cavanagh, is the only human survivor and is now in alien captivity, the officer organizes a rescue mission that includes another son and a daughter. However, the rescue mission may endanger the survival of the Commonwealth, which leads to troubling questions of family, duty, and patriotism. Critics praised the novel as a readable, lively work of science fiction. Zahn returned to the story line with 1995's *Conquerors' Heritage* and 1996's *Conquerors' Legacy.*

The 1999 novel *The Icarus Hunt* tells the tale of space smuggler Jordan McKell, who agrees to deliver an unidentified cargo to Earth aboard the spaceship *Icarus.* This cargo seems to be an alien star drive, which constitutes a serious threat to the Patth, the dominant race of the galaxy. The Patth currently have the fastest star drive in existence, which lets them control all intergalactic trade, and they and their allies are in hot pursuit of the *Icarus.* They attack McKell several times and kill one of his crew members. McKell finally decides to fire up the star drive he is transporting, only to discover that it is in fact a star gate. This creates even more plot twists and excitement. Zahn does not shy away from the unpleasant but unavoidable aspects of life; in his world, wounds actually hurt and the living grieve for their dead friends. Roland Green, reviewing the novel for *Booklist,* wrote that *The Icarus Hunt* "is one of the better novels in some time for readers moving from *Star Wars* and its clones to other sf, and, as such, is highly recommended." Zahn's novel *Angelmass* takes its name from an alien force that can control human behavior through its emissions, called "Angels" and so named because they appear to encourage their users to be morally good. The Empyrean, the government of an interplanetary system, uses the Angelmass to help it govern, although Empyrean's chief opponent, the Pax Comitus, is concerned about this practice. Zahn introduces a number of heroes, including a spy, a sixteen-year-old thief, and an Empyrean senator, all of whom question official governmental and scientific opinions. Zahn pays as much attention to ethics as he does to adventure. *Booklist* reviewer Roland Green observed that the plot is the basic "good guys" against "bad guys" story that forms the classic science-fiction story mold, and that the characters are broadly drawn. Nevertheless, he wrote, "the action is abundant and vivid, and there are absorbing subplots." In *Library Journal,* Jackie Cassada called *Angelmass* "a first-rate sf space adventure."

In *Manta's Gift* Zahn combines a coming-of-age tale with a vision of alien contact. Twenty-two-year-old Matt Raimey has been made a quadriplegic following an accident, so when he is offered the chance to escape

Twenty-two-year-old Matt Raimey was paralyzed in a skiing accident, but has a chance to live again when his brain is transplanted into a sea creature-like alien, thereby linking him psychologically and emotionally to his new, threatened species. *(Cover illustration by Stephen Martiniere.)*

his body in order to communicate with an alien race he jumps at the chance. The alien Qanska have been discovered in Earth's own solar system, living in Jupiter's atmosphere. After Matt's brain is transplanted into a Qanska's womb and he is reborn as one of the manta ray-like creatures, his new life is interrupted by an impending ecological disaster and the expectations of his human sponsors. "Zahn concentrates more on the psychological processes at work than on technological advances," a *Publishers Weekly* writer observed, concluding that *Manta's Gift* is "more than the usual SF action-adventure."

Sometimes a writer decides to rework a classic—a play by William Shakespeare, for example, or a myth—but very few do what Zahn did in 1991: take a popular and celebrated film series and resume the story where the creators left off. With *Heir to the Empire* the author picked up the "Star Wars" story five years after *The Return of the Jedi,* the last of George Lucas's original three films. Zahn's "Star Wars" books reawakened the immense interest in the film series, and introduced several characters, including Mara Jade and Grand Admiral Thrawn, that now have as much legitimacy in the popular eye as the original ones who appeared in the first three movies. Zahn refuses to call himself the "savior" of *Star Wars;* he claims that he simply tapped into interest that was already present among science-fiction fans. And the interest clearly was present; the books flew off the shelves and did much to further Zahn's career.

In *Heir to the Empire* Han Solo and Princess Leia are married and expecting twins. Luke Skywalker continues to learn the secrets of the Jedi, as well as to train Leia in the Jedi arts. Darth Vader and the Evil Empire have been defeated and the Republic is at peace. All appears to be well—until Grand Admiral Thrawn, a former warlord of the empire, shows up and attacks the Republic. John Lawson noted in *School Library Journal* that while *Heir to the Empire* is "not on a par with Zahn's creative, powerful works" it is "well written." Indicative of its popularity, the book reached the top of the *New York Times* bestseller list and remained there for twenty-nine straight weeks.

Dark Force Rising, the second book in the series, joined *Heir to the Empire* on the bestseller list. The same characters are back, along with Grand Admiral Thrawn, who is preparing to crush the New Republic. To this end, he has enlisted the help of unsavory smugglers, political rivals, a well-placed snitch, and an insane Jedi Master. *Booklist* reviewer Green termed Zahn's adoption of the "Star Wars" characters "one of the more remarkable pastiches of recent years," and praised Zahn's "real flair" for incorporating elements of science fiction into the "Star Wars" saga. *Library Journal* contributor Jackie Cassada complimented Zahn's "snappy prose and cinematic style." *Dark Force Rising* reached the number-two position on the *New York Times* bestseller list.

In the final volume of Zahn's first "Star Wars" trilogy, *The Last Command,* Thrawn has been quite successful and is preparing to mount a final siege against the Republic using his new technology: clone soldiers. As Han and Leia struggle to keep up resistance—and await the arrival of their twins at any moment—it becomes clear that the Empire has too many ships and clones for the rebels to have a chance in face-to-face combat. The only solution is the infiltration of Thrawn's stronghold by a small band of fighters, led by Luke. Naturally, further dangers await them at Thrawn's headquarters. Writing in *Voice of Youth Advocates,* Lisa Prolman described *The Last Command* as "a thoroughly mesmerizing and satisfying continuation of the *Star Wars* saga," and applauded Zahn's sensitive extension of the original characters, noting that they had achieved a new depth in his trilogy. *The Last Command* "is a must read for anyone who has followed the George Lucas series from the beginning," she stated, adding that "Zahn's handling of the characters and plot create a work that readers will

enjoy and is a good read." Clearly, quite a few readers agreed with her: the book spent twelve weeks on the *New York Times* best-seller list and managed to reach third place. Zahn has continued to return to the "Star Wars" universe, penning a second set of books—*Specter of the Past* and *Vision of the Future*—that comprise the "Hand of Thrawn" series, as well as a further volume, *Survivor's Quest.* In *Specter of the Past* Luke, Han Solo, and Princess Leia fight the armies of the evil Grand Admiral Thrawn, who had been presumed dead, but seems to have been mysteriously resurrected. In *Vision of the Future* the heroic triumverate must once again keep the Empire at bay while preventing a civil war. Along the way, they engage in the intergalactic battles and intergalactic intrigue that has made the series so popular with readers. In *Survivor's Quest* Luke is now married to Mara Jade, a Jedi knight who joins him on his intergalactic travels. When the couple joins an intergalactic rescue mission, they find that the survivors of a mass migration of space travelers forced to land after being shot down fifty years before, do not want rescuing at all. Dubbing the novel "full of action and more twists than a corkscrew," a *Publishers Weekly* contributor praised *Survivor's Quest* as "another G-rated crowd pleaser" in the popular "Star Wars" series. In *Library Journal* Jackie Cassada praised Zahn's novel for retaining the "fast-paced action, clever dialogue, and intriguing characterizations of the films."

In 2003 Zahn introduced a new series of books with *Dragon and Thief,* which tells of fourteen-year-old Jack Morgan, an orphan and small-time thief who is on the run for a crime he did not commit. While Jack is hiding out in his late uncle's rocket ship on a distant, unoccupied planet, another rocket ship crashes nearby. In the wreckage is a dragon-like being named Draycos. The two unlikely partners team up to escape Draycos's enemies and to clear Jack of the criminal charge against him. "As things progress, Jack and Draycos learn to trust each other—and discover that they have enemies in common," a critic for *Kirkus Reviews* explained. A *Publishers Weekly* reviewer concluded that "Zahn keeps the story moving at a breakneck pace," while Sally Estes in *Booklist* called the novel "a romp of a space thriller." The series continues with *Dragon and Soldier,* as Jack join up with a group of soldiers-for-hire in the hopes of stopping the efforts of whoever it is that is trying to wipe out all of Draycos's race.

Zahn has become popular among readers and critics alike. Green, reviewing Zahn's writing for *Booklist,* has praised Zahn's "generally excellent military novels" as well as his "consistently acute eye for detail." And *Analog* contributor Easton has pointed out that in the vein of most traditional science fiction, Zahn deals with a vast interplanetary system in his work. However, according to Easton, like many of his contemporaries, Zahn's ideas are "smaller, of lesser sweep" than those of older writers. But in Zahn's case, he concluded, "this is a consequence of more attention to character, to individuals, to matters of soul instead of destiny."

After fourteen-year-old orphan Jack Morgan commandeers his uncle's spaceship and flies to a distant planet to escape punishment for a crime he didn't commit, he decides to team up with an alien warrior who offers to help Jack prove his innocence. (Cover illustration by Jon Foster.)

Zahn collects thirteen of his short fiction works in *Cascade Point,* among them the Hugo Award-winning title novella. *Booklist* reviewer Green praised Zahn's "consistent intelligence in both the presentation and the resolution" of his stories, going on to write that despite the traditional nature of Zahn's science fiction it is "certainly high-quality work." Gregory Frost, writing in the *Washington Post Book World,* remarked that "every story of Zahn's contains a novel idea" and that the stories center on scientific theories or possible advances in science. Frost did, however, take Zahn to task for failing to handle his ideas in an unusual way. He said that "Zahn is what is referred to as an 'idea' writer," someone whose stories "are often extrapolations from hard scientific data." In *Voice of Youth Advocates* Yates cautioned readers that both "The Energy Crisis of 2215," in which scientists try to bring about a total matter conversion from a black hole in order to meet the Earth's energy needs, and "Cascade Point," about a spaceship that ends up in an alternative universe, "provide heavy going for non-scientific types."

The other selections in *Cascade Point* include "The Giftie Gie Us," about two handicapped people who discover that love is not weakened by physical deformities, "Job Inaction," about what happens when computers do the hiring and firing, and "Teamwork," in which a man with a multiple personality disorder may have cured himself, but by doing so he destroys an alien structure. Yates noted that Zahn's stories are "decidedly upbeat" in feeling, although "the tone is wry and ironic." In *Voice of Youth Advocates,* reviewer Joni Bodart emphasized the fact that the collection is "well written, with believable situations, witty dialogue and engaging characters." Describing the collection, Zahn said in the introduction that it would give readers "five years of story development as I've slowly grown from a semi-rank amateur to at least journeyman status in this field."

Zahn himself professes no deep motives to his writing other than to tell a good tale. "I consider myself primarily a storyteller and as such have no major pulpit-thumping 'message' that I always try to insert into each story or book," he once commented. "If any theme crops up more than any other, it is my strong belief that there is no prison—whether physical, social, or emotional—that can permanently trap a person who truly wishes to break free of the bonds."

Biographical and Critical Sources

BOOKS

Contemporary Popular Writers, St. James Press (Detroit, MI), 1997.

St. James Guide to Science-Fiction Writers, fourth edition, St. James Press (Detroit, MI), 1996.

Zahn, Timothy, *Cascade Point,* Bluejay (New York, NY), 1986.

PERIODICALS

Absolute Magnitude, fall, 1996, Darrell Schweitzer, "Timothy Zahn: An Interview."

Analog Science Fiction/Science Fact, February, 1984; October, 1985; November, 1985; August, 1986; November, 1986; April, 1988; May, 1989.

Booklist, January 1, 1986; May 1, 1986; August, 1987; March 15, 1990; April 1, 1992; September 1, 1994, p. 28; September 1, 1995, p. 48; June 1, 1999, Roland Green, review of *The Icarus Hunt,* p. 1744; September 15, 2001, Roland Green, review of *Angelmass,* p. 201; November 1, 2002, Roland Green, review of *Manta's Gift,* p. 481; December 1, 2002, Roland Green, review of *Star Song and Other Stories,* p. 652; February 15, 2003, Sally Estes, review of *Dragon and Thief,* p. 1060; December 1, 2003, Roland Green, review of *Star Wars: Survivor's Quest,* p. 627.

Christian Science Monitor, January 3, 1986.

Fantasy, April, 1985; May, 1985; December, 1985; March, 1986.

Kirkus Reviews, June 15, 1999, review of *The Icarus Hunt,* p. 928; August 15, 2001, review of *Angelmass,* p. 1177; October 1, 2002, review of *Manta's Gift,* p. 1435; January 1, 2003, review of *Dragon and Thief,* p. 31.

Kliatt, November, 1992, p. 20; November, 1994, p. 25.

Library Journal, April 15, 1992; February 1, 1995, p. 112; July, 1999, Jackie Cassada, review of *The Icarus Hunt,* p. 143; October 15, 2001, Jackie Cassada, review of *Angelmass,* p. 112; December, 2002, Jackie Cassada, review of *Manta's Gift,* p. 184; February 15, 2004, Jackie Cassada, review of *Star Wars: Survivor's Quest,* p. 167; September 15, 2004, Jackie Cassada, review of *The Green and the Gray,* p. 53.

Publishers Weekly, December 14, 1984; October 25, 1985; March 21, 1986; July 3, 1987; March 23, 1992; October 1, 2001, review of *Angelmass,* p. 43; October 7, 2002, review of *Manta's Gift,* p. 57; February 3, 2003, review of *Dragon and Thief,* p. 59; December 22, 2003, review of *Star Wars: Survivor's Quest,* p. 42; August 9, 20004, review of *The Green and the Gray,* p. 235.

School Library Journal, September, 1985; February, 1992.

Science Fiction and Fantasy Book Review, December, 1983.

Science Fiction Chronicle, July, 1986.

Voice of Youth Advocates, August, 1985; June, 1986; August-October, 1986; February, 1987; February, 1989; February, 1993, p. 362; October, 1993, p. 237; April, 1994, p. 9.

Washington Post Book World, May 25, 1986.

ONLINE

TheForce.Net, http://www.theforce.net/ (February, 2000), Chris Knight, interview with Zahn.

Totse.com, http://www.totse.com/ (December 11, 2003), interview with Zahn.*

ZIMMERMAN, Naoma 1914-2004

OBITUARY NOTICE—See index for SATA sketch: Born August 2, 1914, in St. Louis, MO; died of heart failure October 21, 2004, in Chicago, IL. Social worker, therapist, and author. Zimmerman was a leading family therapist who also published several children's books. A graduate of the University of Chicago, where she earned a B.A. in 1935 and an M.A. in social service in 1940, her first job as a social worker was at the Jewish Children's Bureau in Chicago during the late 1930s. Settling down to raise a family, she helped found the Congregation Solel synagogue in Highland Park and also began publishing children's books. Her first, *Sleepy Forest* (1944) grew out of a bedtime story she told her children. It was followed by many more, including *Sleepy Village* (1945), *Little Deer* (1956), and *Farm Animals* (1966). In 1958, with her children in school, she began working at the Family Service South Lake County in Highland Park, Illinois. Here she gained great respect as a family therapist. Zimmerman was innovative in her holistic approach, looking at all aspects of a family's life—home environment, parents' jobs, education, and so on—before counseling her clients. Because of the theories she developed, she was invited to teach at the University of Chicago during the summer, which she did from 1967 to 1971. Beginning in 1969, she also worked as a freelance consultant and lecturer. Zimmerman retired in 1990.

OBITUARIES AND OTHER SOURCES:

PERIODICALS

Chicago Tribune, November 6, 2004, Section 2, p. 10.